BATMAN

ARKHAM UNHINGED

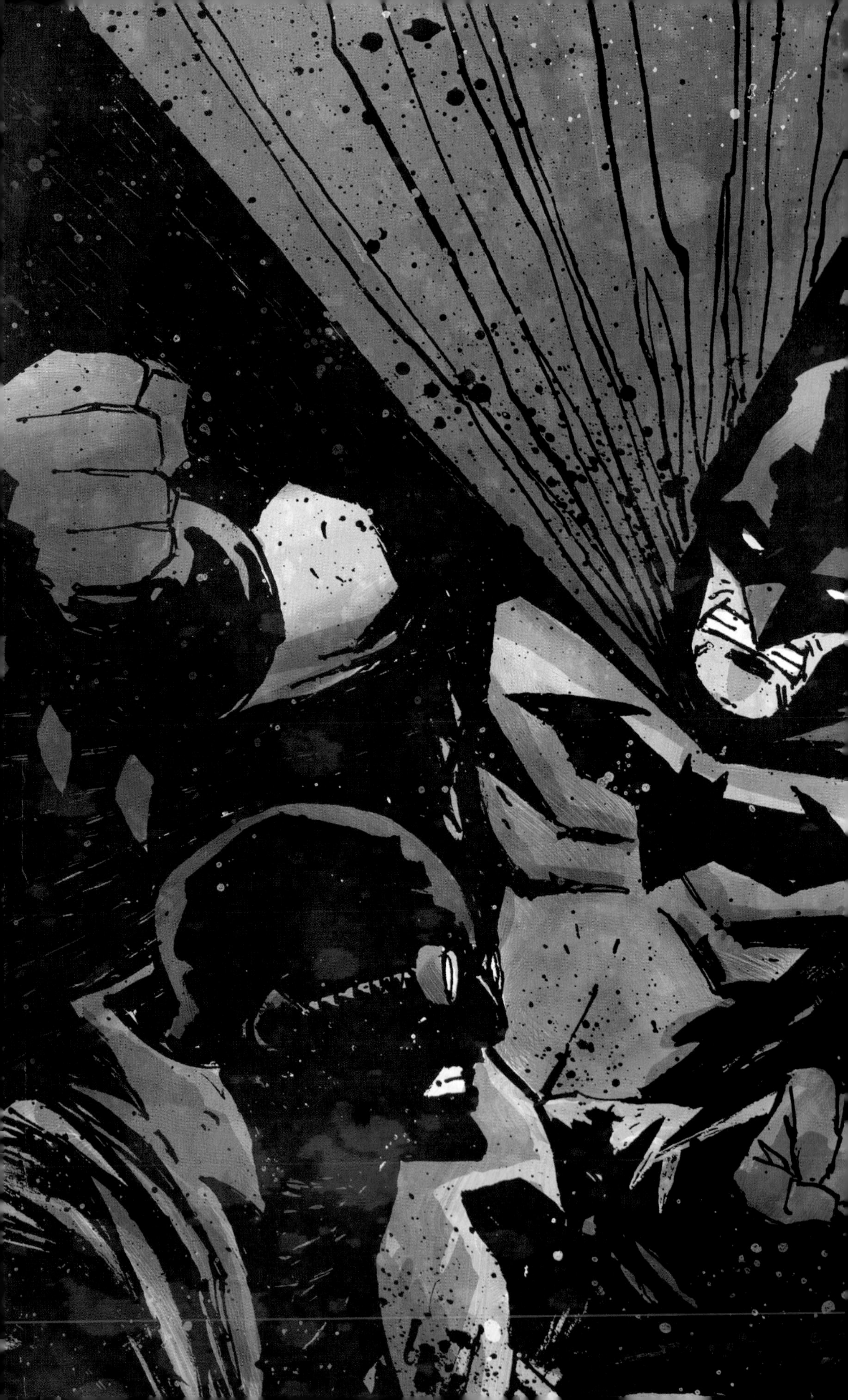

KAREN TRAVISS writer

CHRISTIAN DUCE RICCARDO BURCHIELLI
FEDERICO DALLOCCHIO TONY SHASTEEN
BEN LOBEL artists

ALEJANDRO SANCHEZ
ALLEN PASSALAQUA colorists

TRAVIS LANHAM letterer

CHRIS MITTEN collection cover artist

BATMAN CREATED BY **BOB KANE**

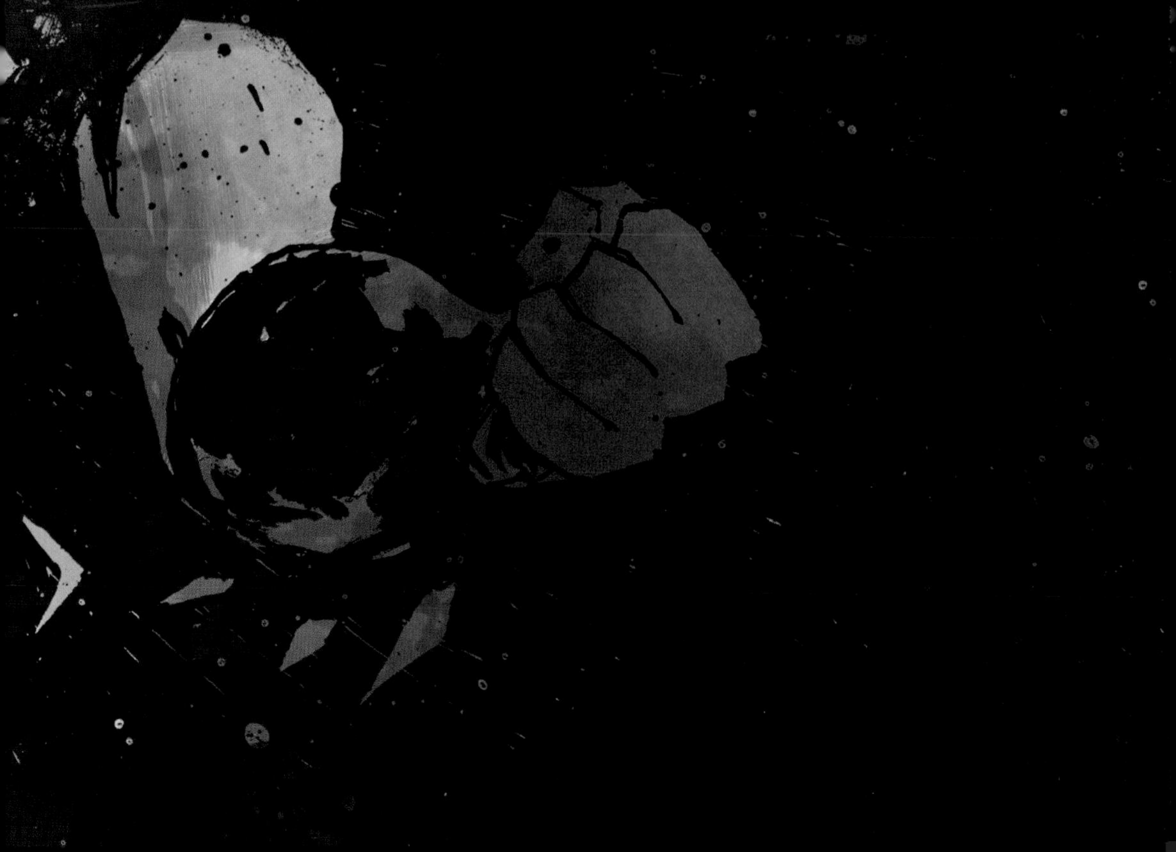

Jim Chadwick Editor – Original Series
Sarah Gaydos Assistant Editor – Original Series
Robin Wildman Editor
Robbin Brosterman Design Director – Books
Louis Prandi Publication Design

Hank Kanalz Senior VP – Vertigo & Integrated Publishing

Diane Nelson President
Dan DiDio and Jim Lee Co-Publishers
Geoff Johns Chief Creative Officer
Amit Desai Senior VP – Marketing & Franchise Management
Amy Genkins Senior VP – Business & Legal Affairs
Nairi Gardiner Senior VP – Finance
Jeff Boison VP – Publishing Planning
Mark Chiarello VP – Art Direction & Design
John Cunningham VP – Marketing
Terri Cunningham VP – Editorial Administration
Larry Ganem VP – Talent Relations & Services
Alison Gill Senior VP – Manufacturing & Operations
Jay Kogan VP – Business & Legal Affairs, Publishing
Jack Mahan VP – Business Affairs, Talent
Nick Napolitano VP – Manufacturing Administration
Sue Pohja VP – Book Sales
Fred Ruiz VP – Manufacturing Operations
Courtney Simmons Senior VP – Publicity
Bob Wayne Senior VP – Sales

BATMAN: ARKHAM UNHINGED VOLUME 4

Published by DC Comics. Copyright © 2014 DC Comics. All Rights Reserved.

Originally published as BATMAN: ARKHAM UNHINGED Chapters 44-58 © 2013, 2014 DC Comics. All
Rights Reserved. All characters, their distinctive likenesses and related elements featured in this
publication are trademarks of DC Comics. The stories, characters and incidents featured in this publication are entirely fictional. DC Comics does not read or accept unsolicited ideas, stories or artwork.

DC Comics, 1700 Broadway, New York, NY 10019
A Warner Bros. Entertainment Company.
Printed by RR Donnelley, Owensville, MO, USA. 1/2/2015. First Printing.
ISBN: 978-1-4012-5042-3

Library of Congress Cataloging-in-Publication Data

Traviss, Karen.
  Batman : Arkham Unhinged, Volume 4 / Karen Traviss,
    pages cm
  ISBN 978-1-4012-5042-3
  1. Graphic novels. I. Title.
  PN6728.B36T73 2014
  741.5'973—dc23

                    2014011628

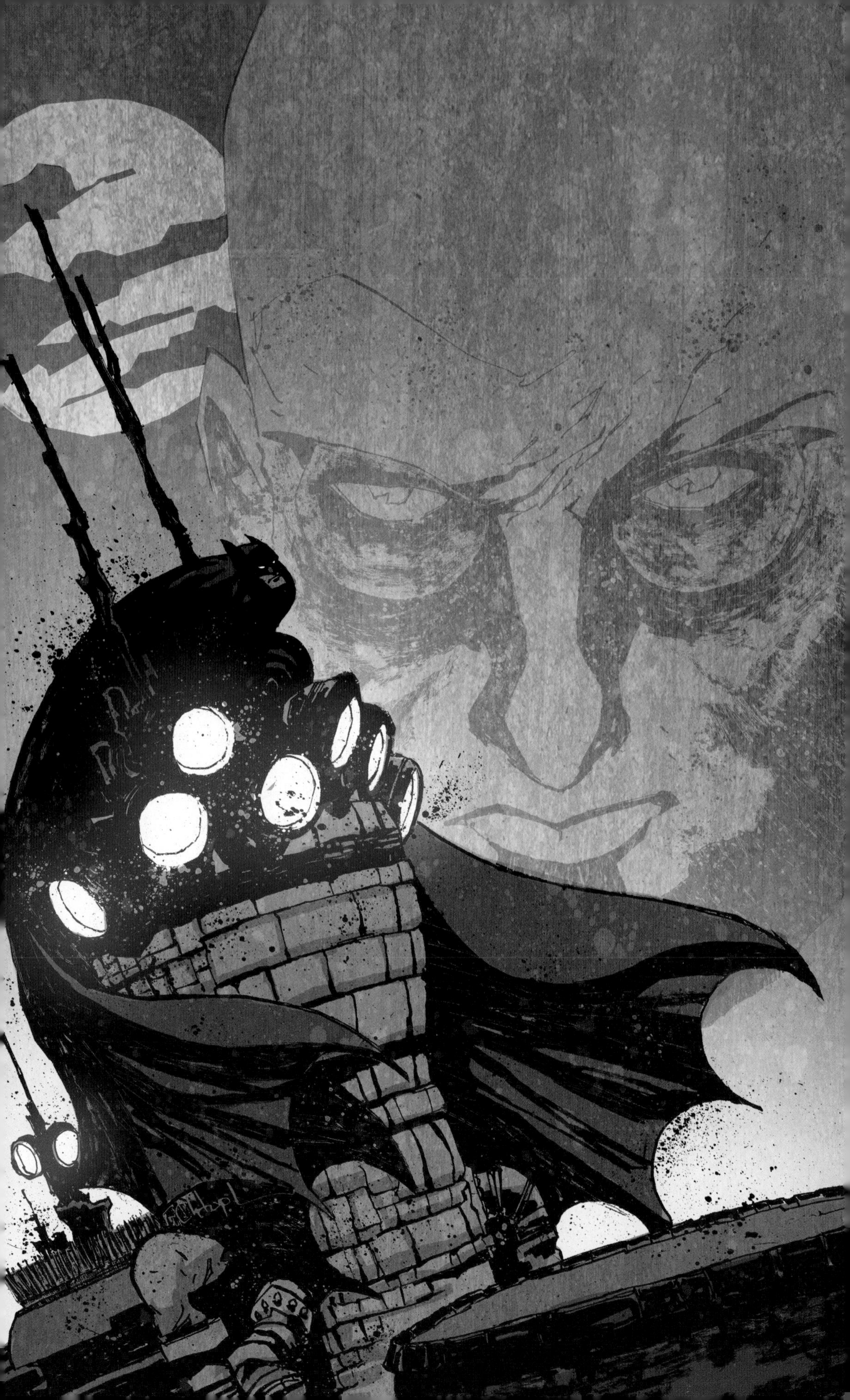

WELCOME
TO THE SLOUGH OF DESPOND
PART ONE

WRITTEN BY: KAREN TRAVISS
ART BY: RICCARDO BURCHIELLI
COLORS BY: ALEJANDRO SANCHEZ
LETTERS BY: TRAVIS LANHAM
COVER ART BY: CHRIS MITTEN

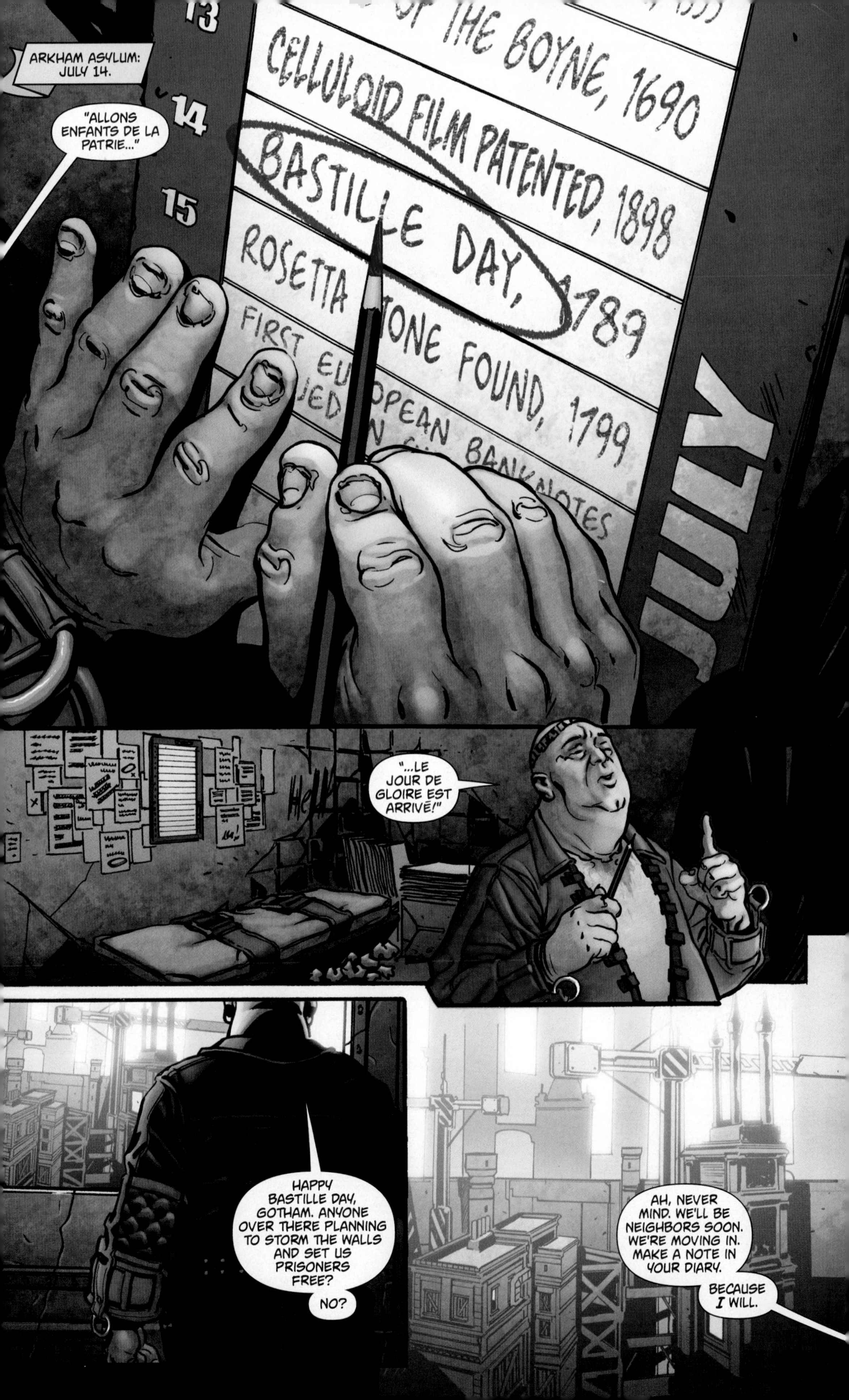

ARKHAM ASYLUM: JULY 14.
13
14
15
THE BOYNE, 1690
CELLULOID FILM PATENTED, 1898
BASTILLE DAY, 1789
ROSETTA
ONE FOUND, 1799
FIRST EU OPEAN
BAN NOTES
JULY
"ALLONS ENFANTS DE LA PATRIE..."
"...LE JOUR DE GLOIRE EST ARRIVÉ!"
HAPPY BASTILLE DAY, GOTHAM. ANYONE OVER THERE PLANNING TO STORM THE WALLS AND SET US PRISONERS FREE?
NO?
AH, NEVER MIND. WE'LL BE NEIGHBORS SOON. WE'RE MOVING IN. MAKE A NOTE IN YOUR DIARY.
BECAUSE I WILL.

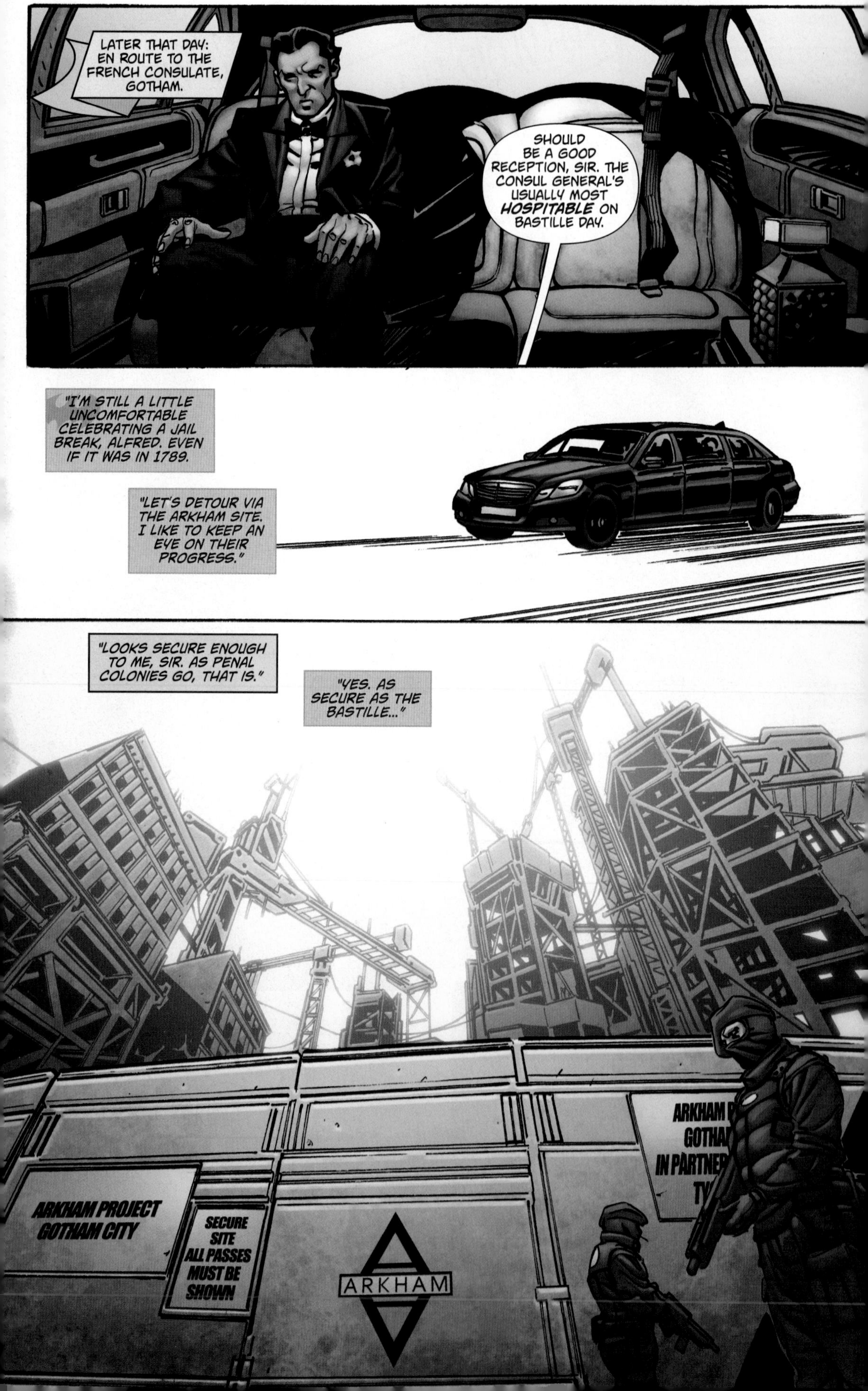
LATER THAT DAY: EN ROUTE TO THE FRENCH CONSULATE, GOTHAM.
SHOULD BE A GOOD RECEPTION, SIR. THE CONSUL GENERAL'S USUALLY MOST **HOSPITABLE** ON BASTILLE DAY.
"I'M STILL A LITTLE UNCOMFORTABLE CELEBRATING A JAIL BREAK, ALFRED. EVEN IF IT WAS IN 1789.
"LET'S DETOUR VIA THE ARKHAM SITE. I LIKE TO KEEP AN EYE ON THEIR PROGRESS."
"LOOKS SECURE ENOUGH TO ME, SIR. AS PENAL COLONIES GO, THAT IS."
"YES. AS SECURE AS THE BASTILLE..."
ARKHAM PROJECT GOTHAM CITY
SECURE SITE ALL PASSES MUST BE SHOWN
ARKHAM

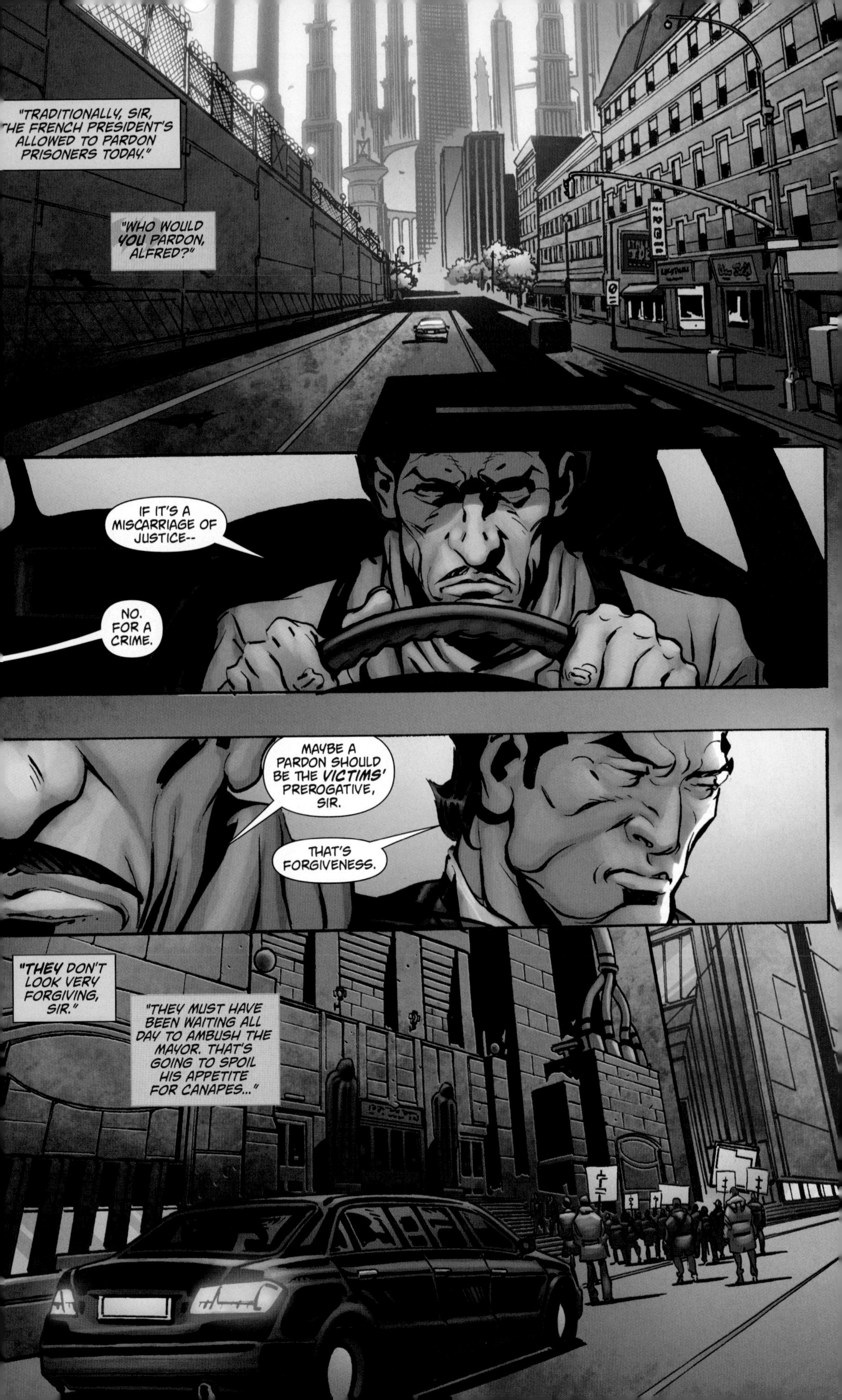
"TRADITIONALLY, SIR, THE FRENCH PRESIDENT'S ALLOWED TO PARDON PRISONERS TODAY."
"WHO WOULD YOU PARDON, ALFRED?"
IF IT'S A MISCARRIAGE OF JUSTICE--
NO. FOR A CRIME.
MAYBE A PARDON SHOULD BE THE VICTIMS' PREROGATIVE, SIR.
THAT'S FORGIVENESS.
"THEY DON'T LOOK VERY FORGIVING, SIR."
"THEY MUST HAVE BEEN WAITING ALL DAY TO AMBUSH THE MAYOR. THAT'S GOING TO SPOIL HIS APPETITE FOR CANAPES..."

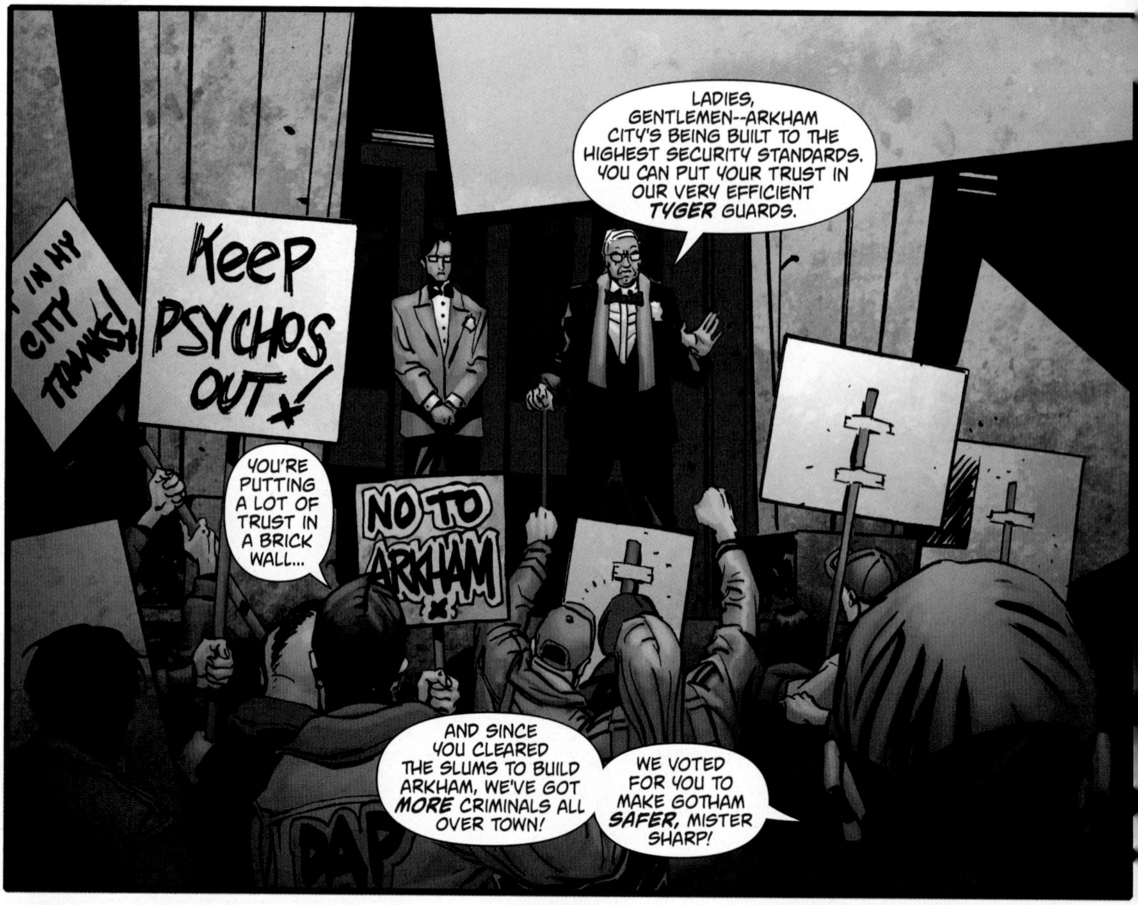
LADIES, GENTLEMEN--ARKHAM CITY'S BEING BUILT TO THE HIGHEST SECURITY STANDARDS. YOU CAN PUT YOUR TRUST IN OUR VERY EFFICIENT *TYGER* GUARDS.
IN MY CITY THANKS!
KEEP PSYCHOS OUT
YOU'RE PUTTING A LOT OF TRUST IN A BRICK WALL...
NO TO ARKHAM
AND SINCE YOU CLEARED THE SLUMS TO BUILD ARKHAM, WE'VE GOT *MORE* CRIMINALS ALL OVER TOWN!
WE VOTED FOR YOU TO MAKE GOTHAM *SAFER*, MISTER SHARP!

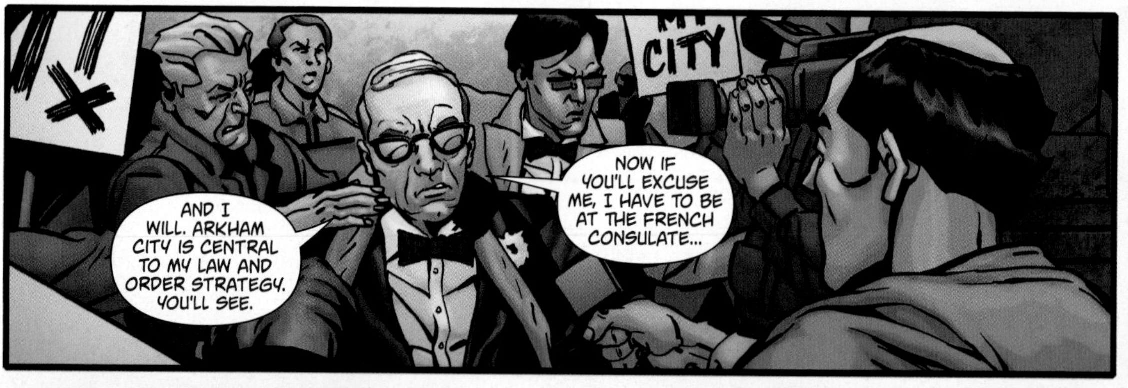
CITY
NOW IF YOU'LL EXCUSE ME, I HAVE TO BE AT THE FRENCH CONSULATE...
AND I WILL. ARKHAM CITY IS CENTRAL TO MY LAW AND ORDER STRATEGY. YOU'LL SEE.

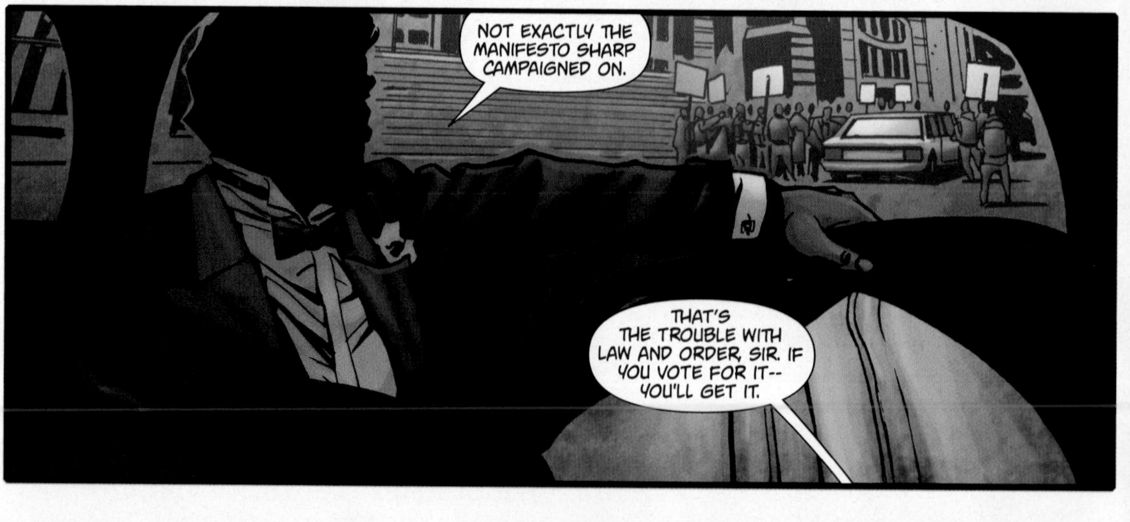
NOT EXACTLY THE MANIFESTO SHARP CAMPAIGNED ON.
THAT'S THE TROUBLE WITH LAW AND ORDER, SIR. IF YOU VOTE FOR IT-- YOU'LL GET IT.

BLOODY HELL!

WEEE-OOOO

WEEE-OOOO

"SORRY ABOUT THAT, SIR."

"LOOKS LIKE JIM GORDON'S HAVING A BUSY NIGHT."

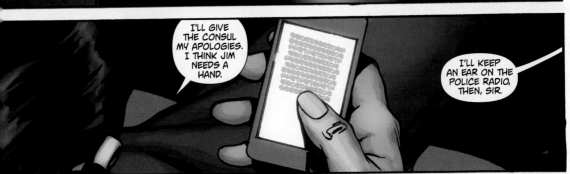

I'LL GIVE THE CONSUL MY APOLOGIES. I THINK JIM NEEDS A HAND.

I'LL KEEP AN EAR ON THE POLICE RADIO, THEN, SIR.

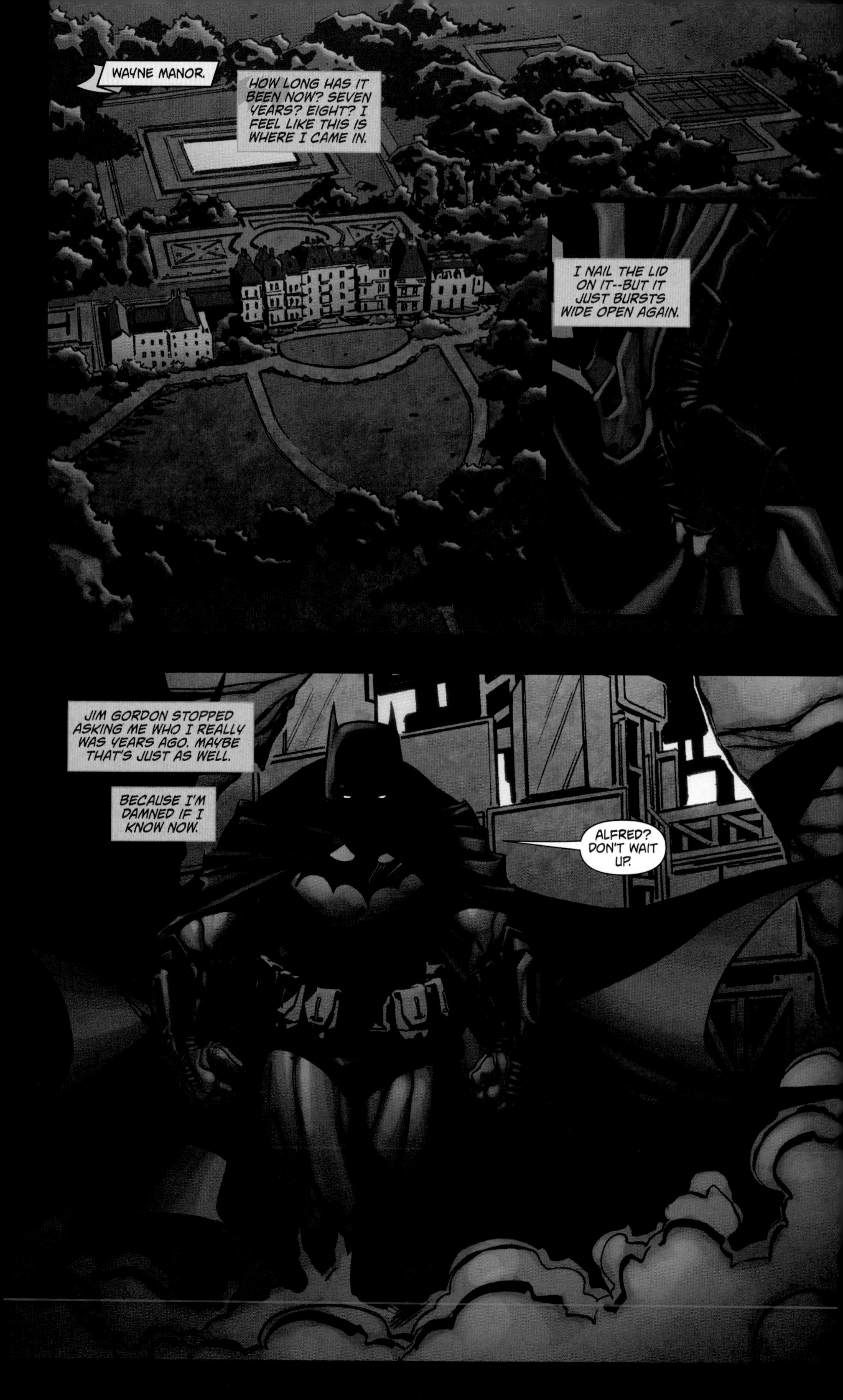
WAYNE MANOR.
HOW LONG HAS IT BEEN NOW? SEVEN YEARS? EIGHT? I FEEL LIKE THIS IS WHERE I CAME IN.
I NAIL THE LID ON IT--BUT IT JUST BURSTS WIDE OPEN AGAIN.
JIM GORDON STOPPED ASKING ME WHO I REALLY WAS YEARS AGO. MAYBE THAT'S JUST AS WELL.
BECAUSE I'M DAMNED IF I KNOW NOW.
ALFRED? DON'T WAIT UP.

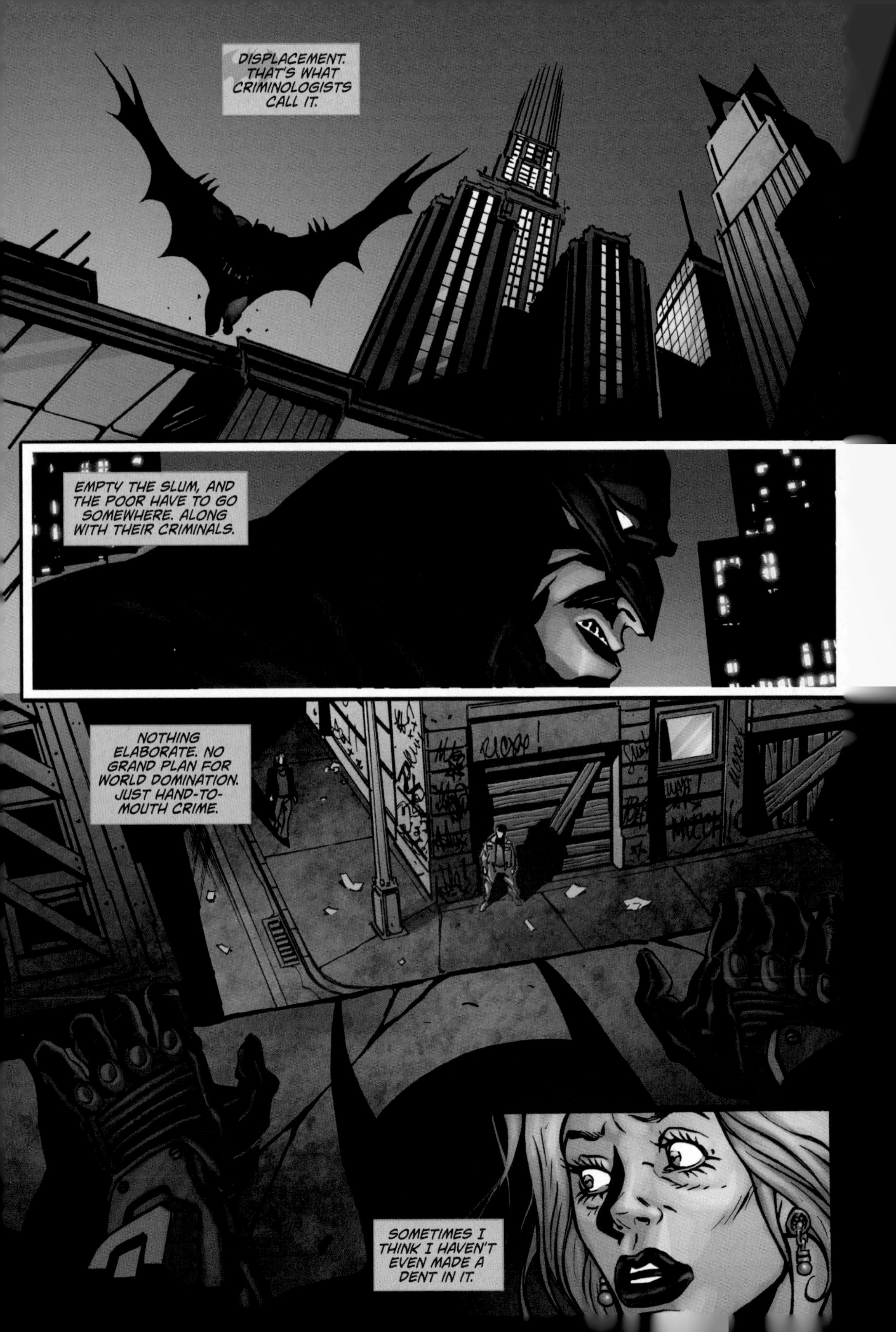
DISPLACEMENT. THAT'S WHAT CRIMINOLOGISTS CALL IT.
EMPTY THE SLUM, AND THE POOR HAVE TO GO SOMEWHERE. ALONG WITH THEIR CRIMINALS.
NOTHING ELABORATE. NO GRAND PLAN FOR WORLD DOMINATION. JUST HAND-TO-MOUTH CRIME.
SOMETIMES I THINK I HAVEN'T EVEN MADE A DENT IN IT.

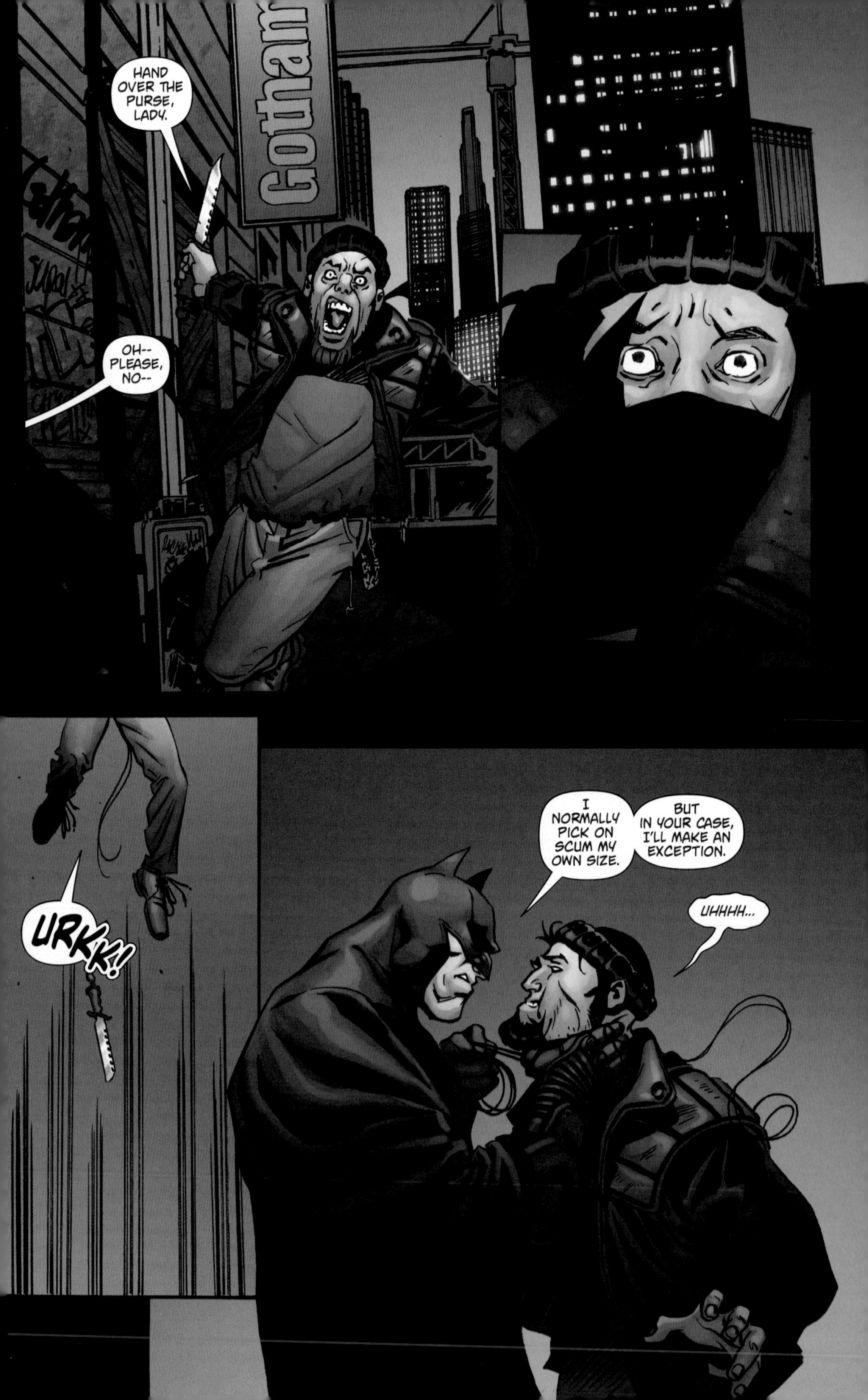
HAND OVER THE PURSE, LADY.
OH-- PLEASE, NO--
URKK!
I NORMALLY PICK ON SCUM MY OWN SIZE.
BUT IN YOUR CASE, I'LL MAKE AN EXCEPTION.
UHHHH...

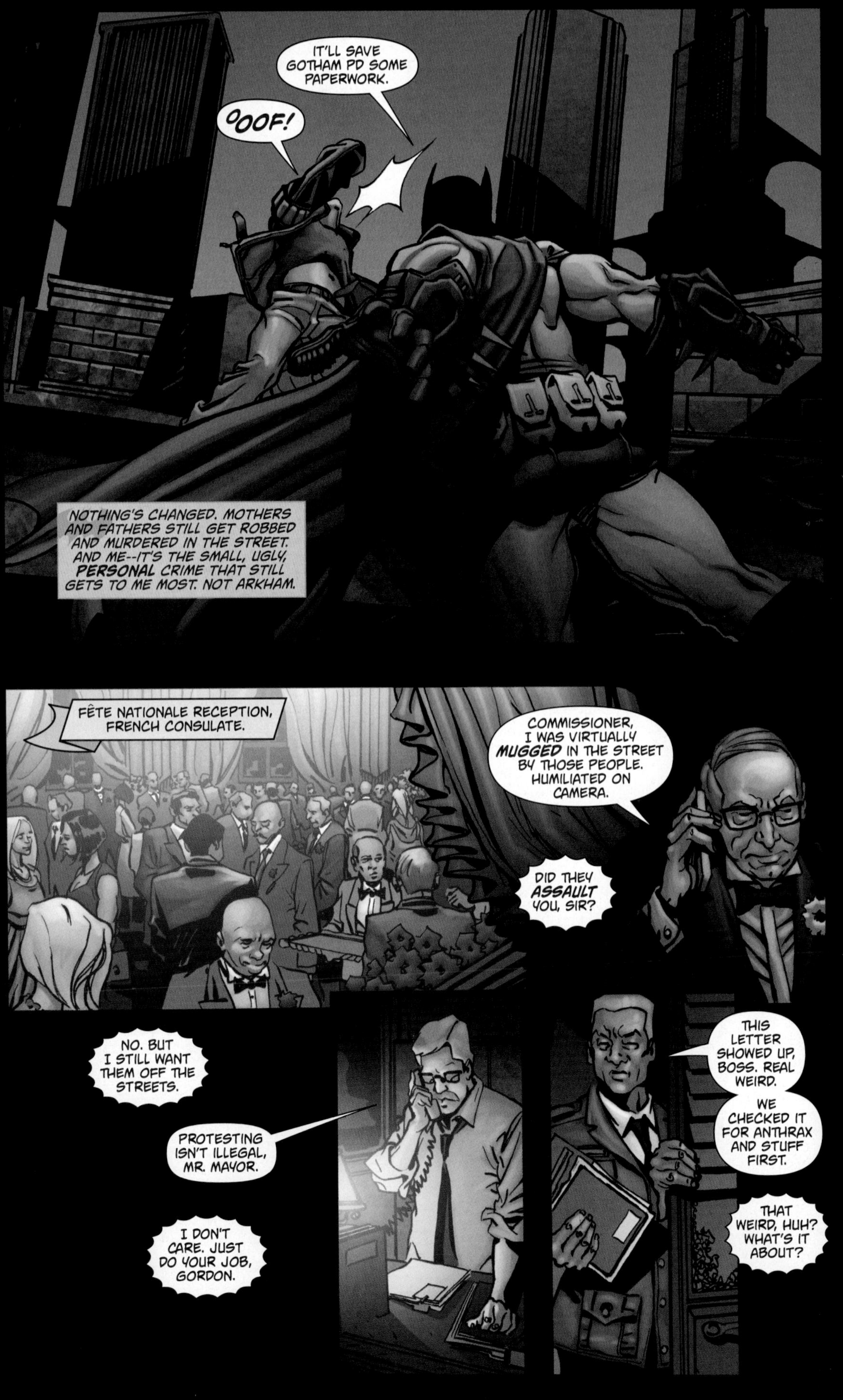
IT'LL SAVE GOTHAM PD SOME PAPERWORK.
OOOF!
NOTHING'S CHANGED. MOTHERS AND FATHERS STILL GET ROBBED AND MURDERED IN THE STREET. AND ME--IT'S THE SMALL, UGLY, PERSONAL CRIME THAT STILL GETS TO ME MOST. NOT ARKHAM.
FÊTE NATIONALE RECEPTION, FRENCH CONSULATE.
COMMISSIONER, I WAS VIRTUALLY MUGGED IN THE STREET BY THOSE PEOPLE. HUMILIATED ON CAMERA.
DID THEY ASSAULT YOU, SIR?
NO. BUT I STILL WANT THEM OFF THE STREETS.
PROTESTING ISN'T ILLEGAL, MR. MAYOR.
I DON'T CARE. JUST DO YOUR JOB, GORDON.
THIS LETTER SHOWED UP, BOSS. REAL WEIRD.
WE CHECKED IT FOR ANTHRAX AND STUFF FIRST.
THAT WEIRD, HUH? WHAT'S IT ABOUT?

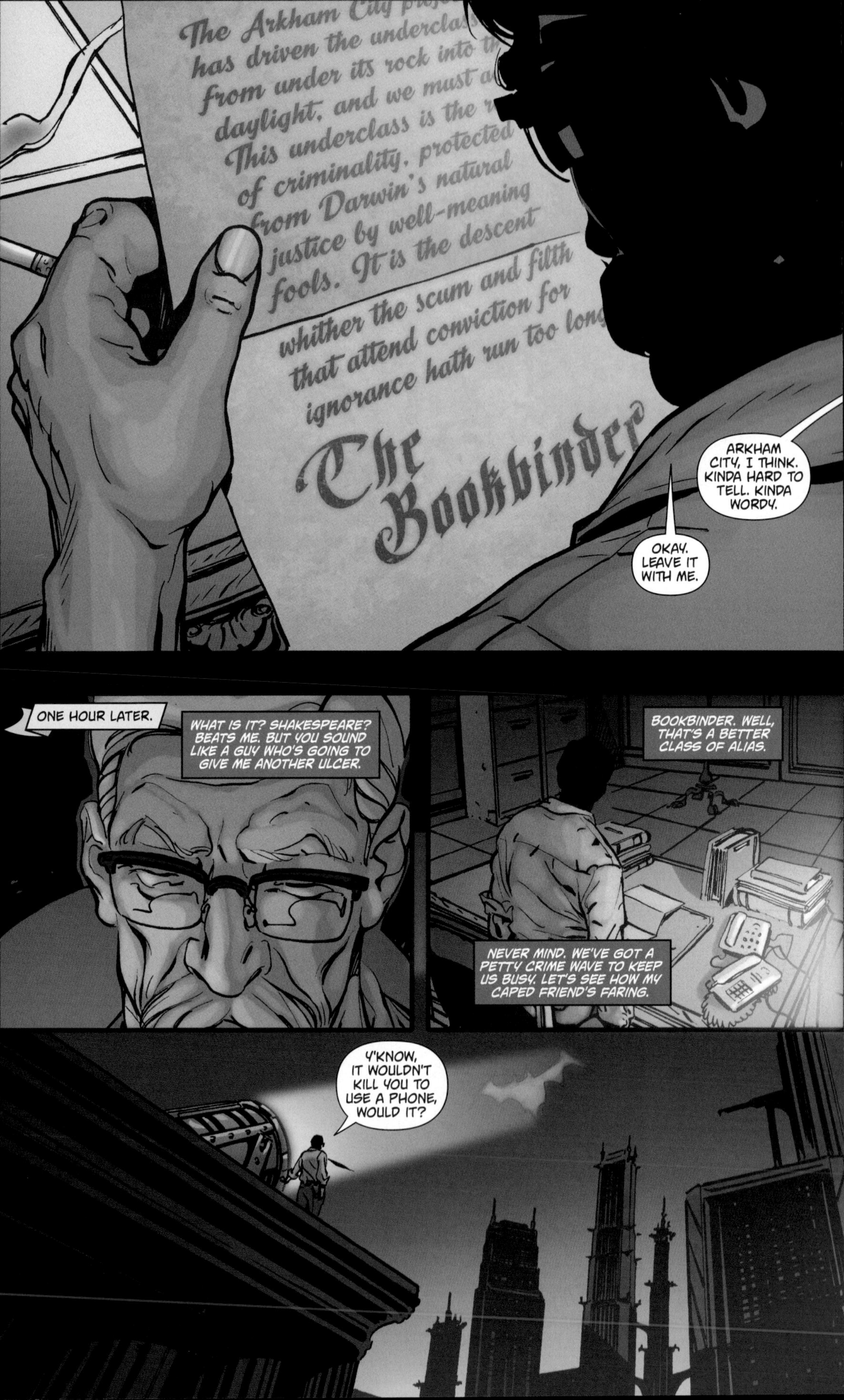
The Arkham City
has driven the underclass
from under its rock into
daylight, and we must
This underclass is the
of criminality, protected
from Darwin's natural
justice by well-meaning
fools. It is the descent
whither the scum and filth
that attend conviction for
ignorance hath run too
The Bookbinder
ARKHAM CITY, I THINK. KINDA HARD TO TELL. KINDA WORDY.
OKAY. LEAVE IT WITH ME.
ONE HOUR LATER.
WHAT IS IT? SHAKESPEARE? BEATS ME. BUT YOU SOUND LIKE A GUY WHO'S GOING TO GIVE ME ANOTHER ULCER.
BOOKBINDER. WELL, THAT'S A BETTER CLASS OF ALIAS.
NEVER MIND. WE'VE GOT A PETTY CRIME WAVE TO KEEP US BUSY. LET'S SEE HOW MY CAPED FRIEND'S FARING.
Y'KNOW, IT WOULDN'T KILL YOU TO USE A PHONE, WOULD IT?

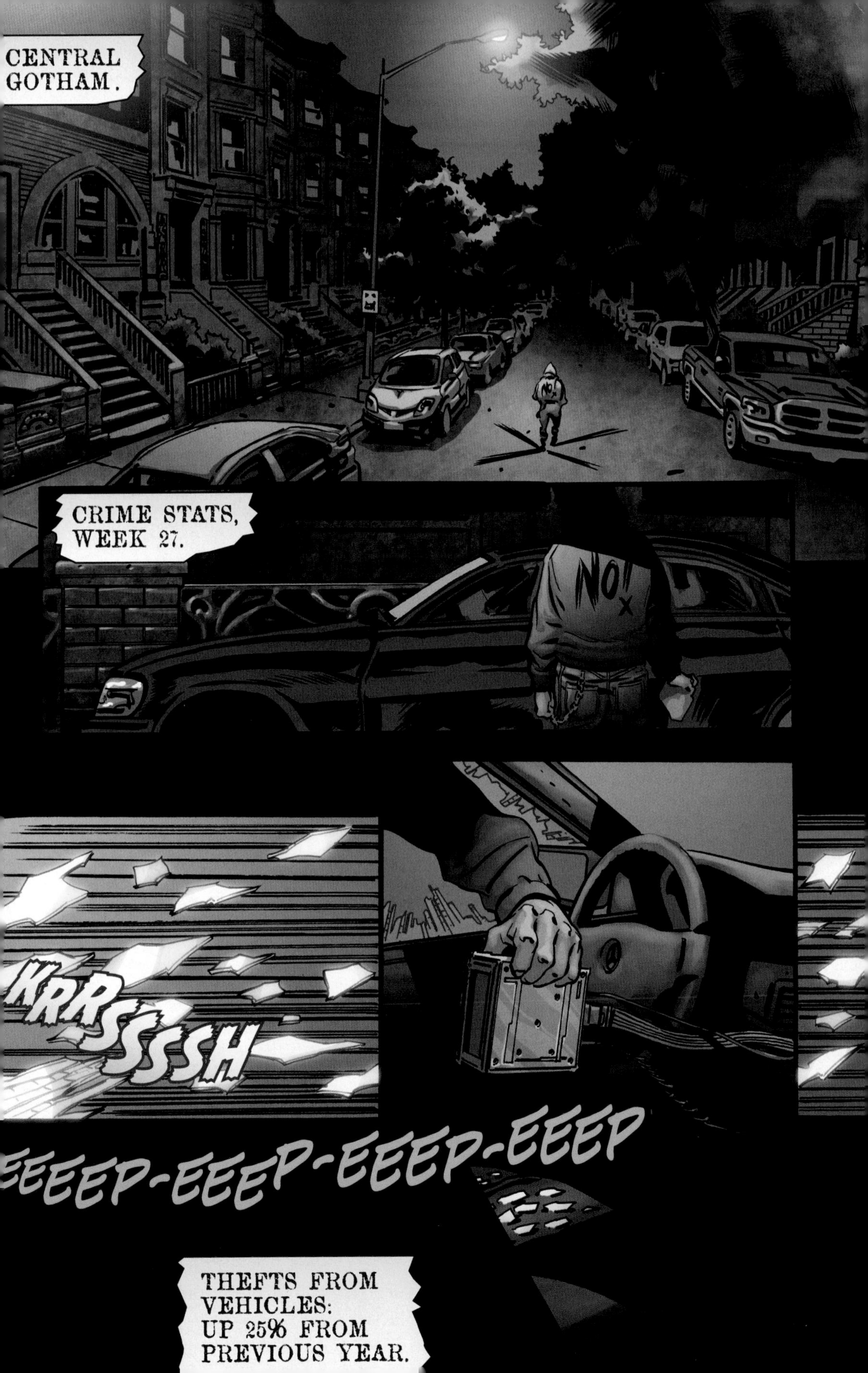
CENTRAL GOTHAM.
NO!
CRIME STATS, WEEK 27.
NO!
KRRSSSSH
EEEEP-EEEP-EEEP-EEEP
THEFTS FROM VEHICLES: UP 25% FROM PREVIOUS YEAR.

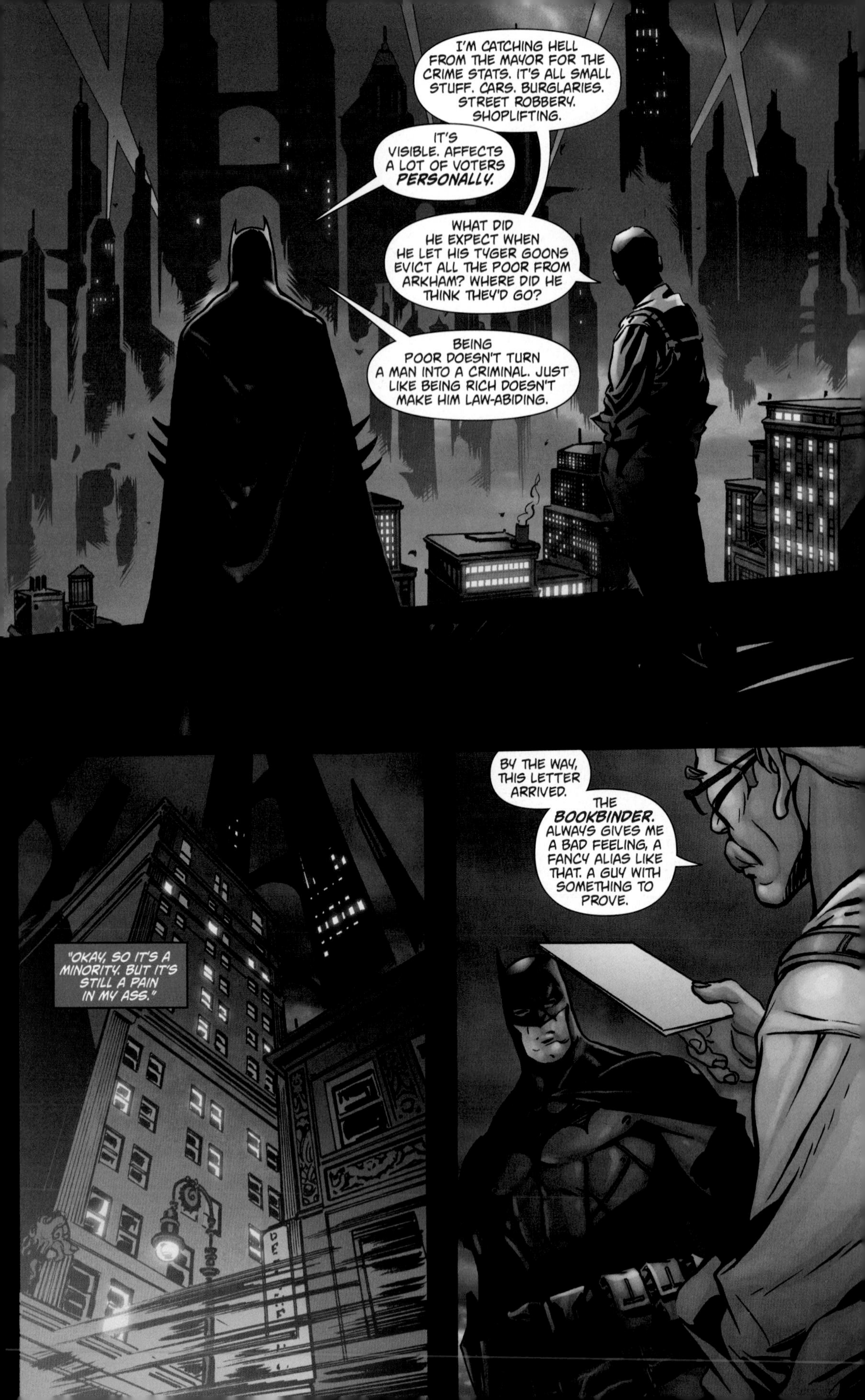
I'M CATCHING HELL FROM THE MAYOR FOR THE CRIME STATS. IT'S ALL SMALL STUFF. CARS. BURGLARIES. STREET ROBBERY. SHOPLIFTING.
IT'S VISIBLE. AFFECTS A LOT OF VOTERS PERSONALLY.
WHAT DID HE EXPECT WHEN HE LET HIS TYGER GOONS EVICT ALL THE POOR FROM ARKHAM? WHERE DID HE THINK THEY'D GO?
BEING POOR DOESN'T TURN A MAN INTO A CRIMINAL. JUST LIKE BEING RICH DOESN'T MAKE HIM LAW-ABIDING.
"OKAY, SO IT'S A MINORITY. BUT IT'S STILL A PAIN IN MY ASS."
BY THE WAY, THIS LETTER ARRIVED.
THE BOOKBINDER. ALWAYS GIVES ME A BAD FEELING, A FANCY ALIAS LIKE THAT. A GUY WITH SOMETHING TO PROVE.

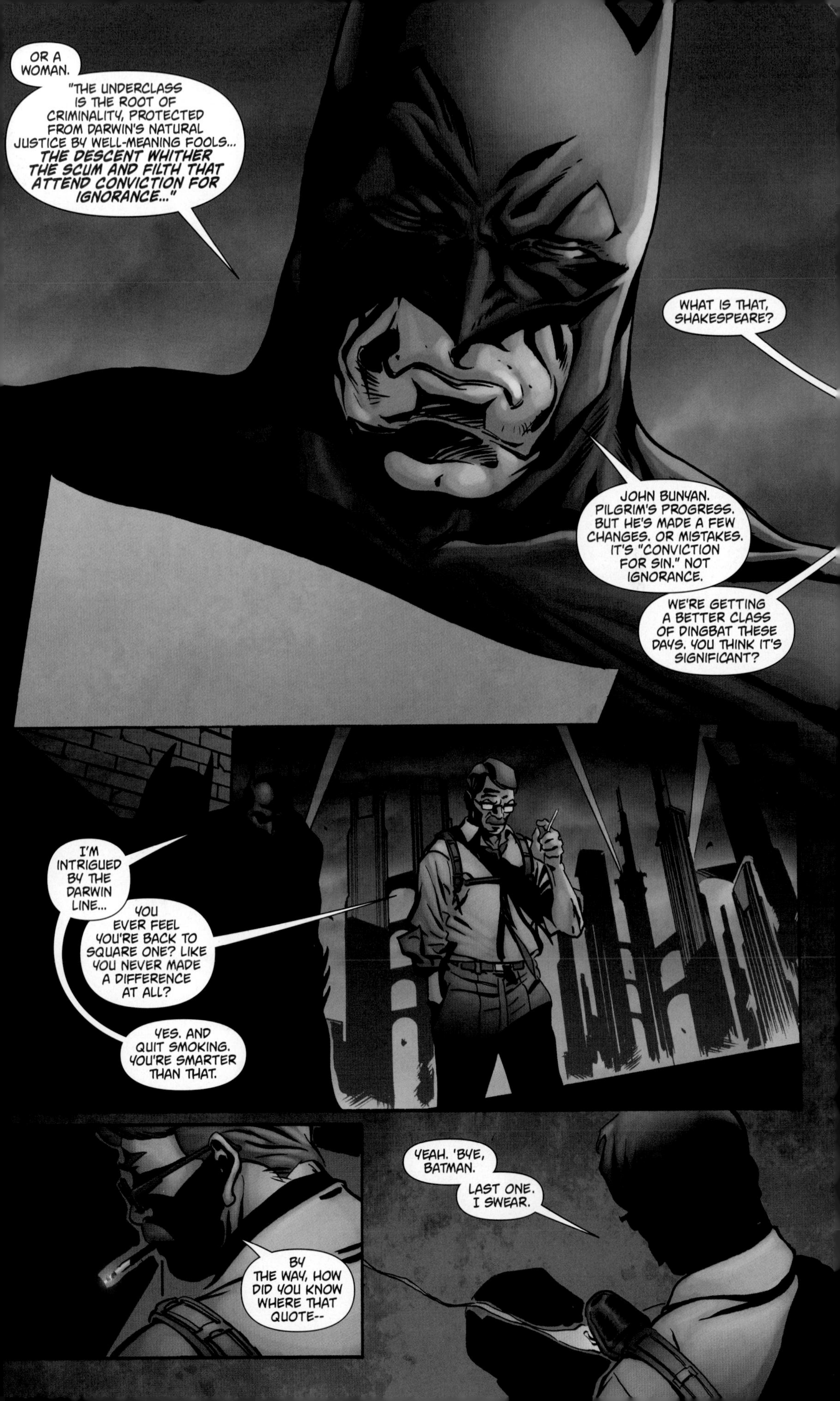

OR A WOMAN.
"THE UNDERCLASS IS THE ROOT OF CRIMINALITY, PROTECTED FROM DARWIN'S NATURAL JUSTICE BY WELL-MEANING FOOLS... *THE DESCENT WHITHER THE SCUM AND FILTH THAT ATTEND CONVICTION FOR IGNORANCE...*"
WHAT IS THAT, SHAKESPEARE?
JOHN BUNYAN. PILGRIM'S PROGRESS. BUT HE'S MADE A FEW CHANGES. OR MISTAKES. IT'S "CONVICTION FOR SIN." NOT IGNORANCE.
WE'RE GETTING A BETTER CLASS OF DINGBAT THESE DAYS. YOU THINK IT'S SIGNIFICANT?
I'M INTRIGUED BY THE DARWIN LINE...
YOU EVER FEEL YOU'RE BACK TO SQUARE ONE? LIKE YOU NEVER MADE A DIFFERENCE AT ALL?
YES. AND QUIT SMOKING. YOU'RE SMARTER THAN THAT.
YEAH. 'BYE, BATMAN.
LAST ONE. I SWEAR.
BY THE WAY, HOW DID YOU KNOW WHERE THAT QUOTE--

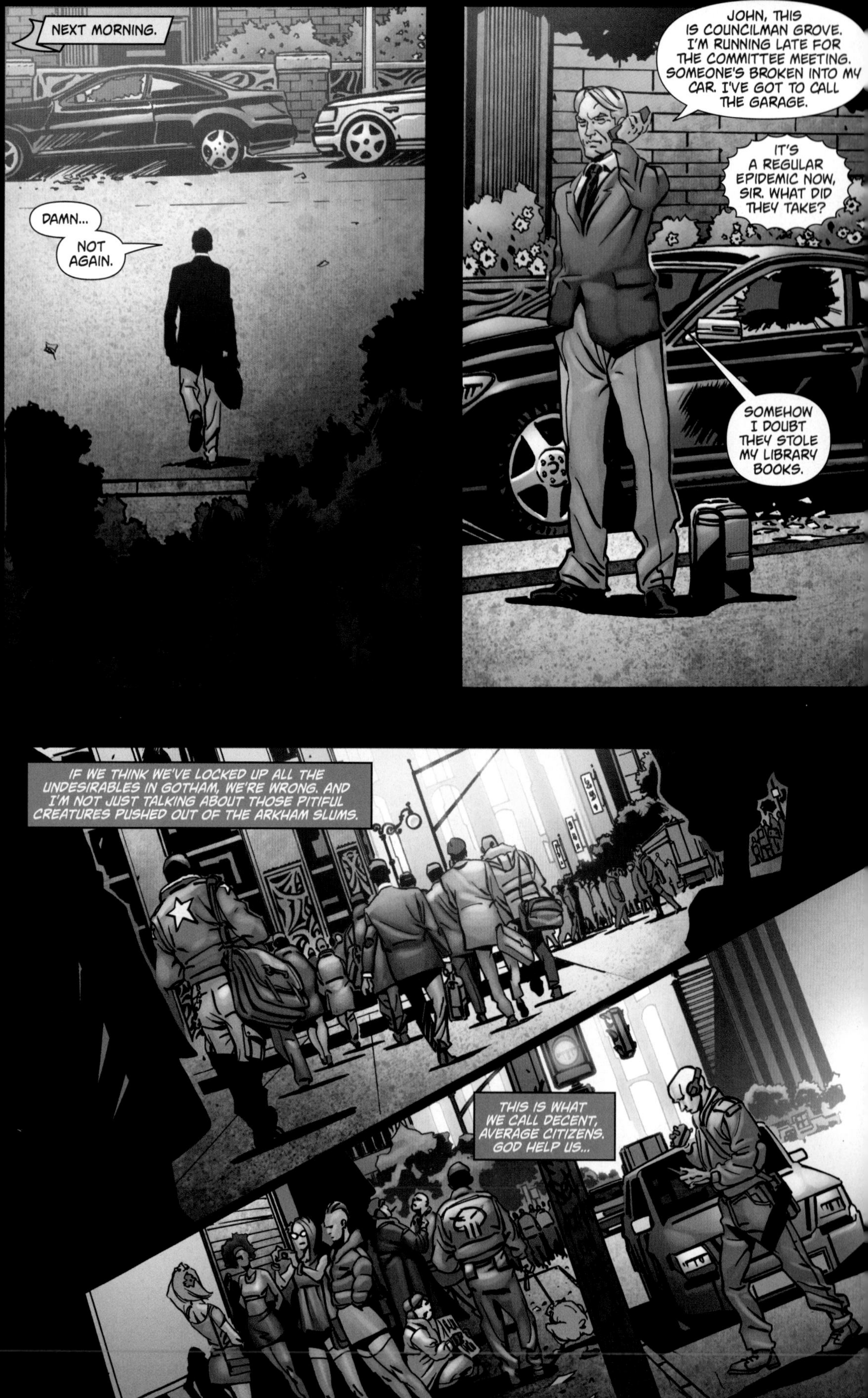
NEXT MORNING.
DAMN... NOT AGAIN.
JOHN, THIS IS COUNCILMAN GROVE. I'M RUNNING LATE FOR THE COMMITTEE MEETING. SOMEONE'S BROKEN INTO MY CAR. I'VE GOT TO CALL THE GARAGE.
IT'S A REGULAR EPIDEMIC NOW, SIR. WHAT DID THEY TAKE?
SOMEHOW I DOUBT THEY STOLE MY LIBRARY BOOKS.
IF WE THINK WE'VE LOCKED UP ALL THE UNDESIRABLES IN GOTHAM, WE'RE WRONG. AND I'M NOT JUST TALKING ABOUT THOSE PITIFUL CREATURES PUSHED OUT OF THE ARKHAM SLUMS.
THIS IS WHAT WE CALL DECENT, AVERAGE CITIZENS. GOD HELP US...

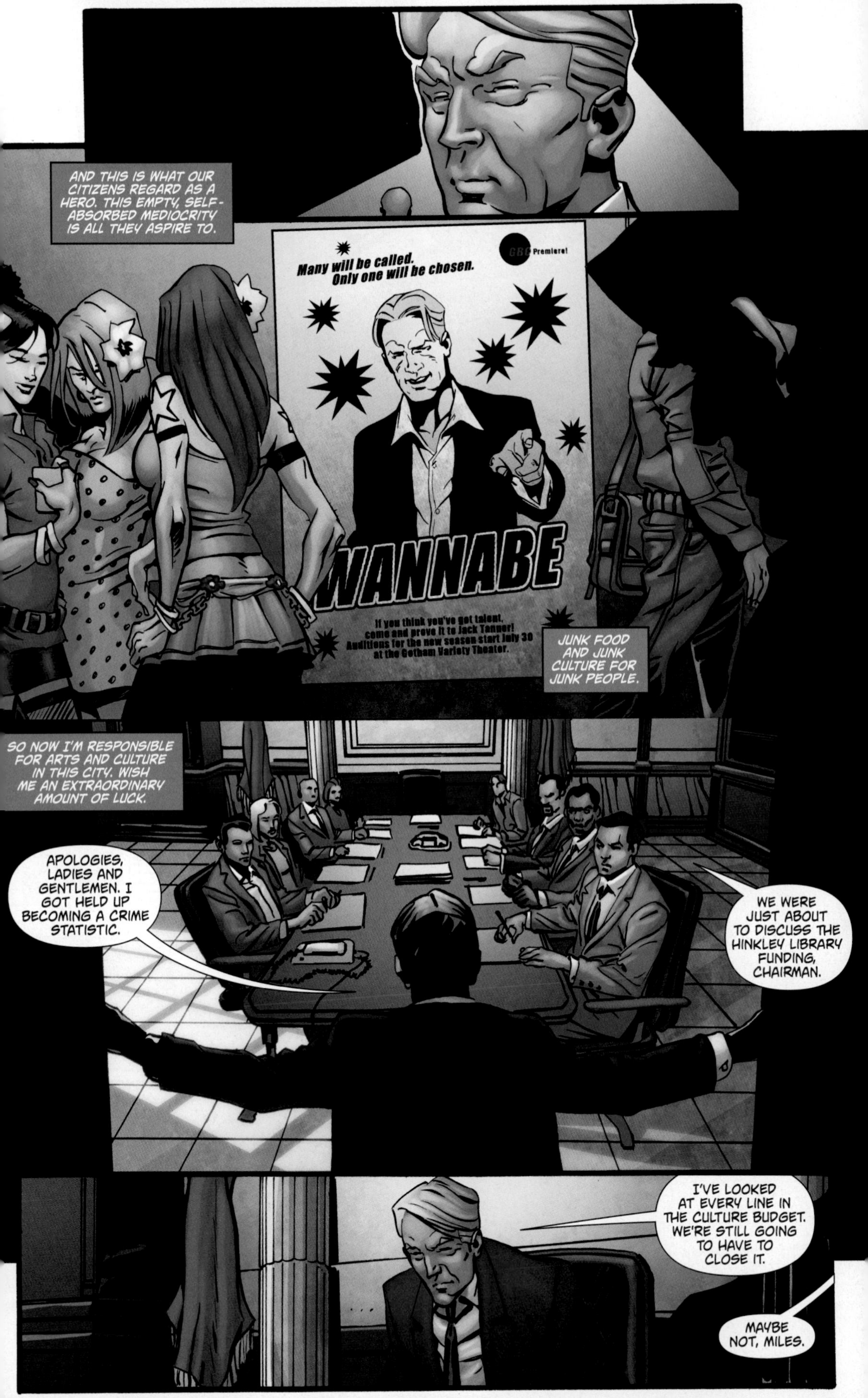
AND THIS IS WHAT OUR CITIZENS REGARD AS A HERO. THIS EMPTY, SELF-ABSORBED MEDIOCRITY IS ALL THEY ASPIRE TO.
Premiere!
Many will be called. Only one will be chosen.
WANNABE
If you think you've got talent, come and prove it to Jack Tanner! Auditions for the new season start July 30 at the Gotham Variety Theater.
JUNK FOOD AND JUNK CULTURE FOR JUNK PEOPLE.
SO NOW I'M RESPONSIBLE FOR ARTS AND CULTURE IN THIS CITY. WISH ME AN EXTRAORDINARY AMOUNT OF LUCK.
APOLOGIES, LADIES AND GENTLEMEN. I GOT HELD UP BECOMING A CRIME STATISTIC.
WE WERE JUST ABOUT TO DISCUSS THE HINKLEY LIBRARY FUNDING, CHAIRMAN.
I'VE LOOKED AT EVERY LINE IN THE CULTURE BUDGET. WE'RE STILL GOING TO HAVE TO CLOSE IT.
MAYBE NOT, MILES.

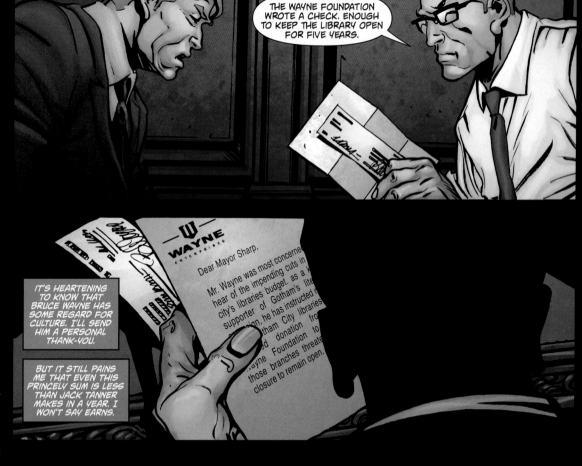

THE WAYNE FOUNDATION WROTE A CHECK. ENOUGH TO KEEP THE LIBRARY OPEN FOR FIVE YEARS.

Dear Mayor Sharp,

Mr. Wayne was most concerne... hear of the impending cuts in ... city's libraries budget. as a k... supporter of Gotham's lite... ...tion, he has instructed ... ...tham City libraries ... ...d donation fro... ...ayne Foundation to ...those branches threate... closure to remain open.

IT'S HEARTENING TO KNOW THAT BRUCE WAYNE HAS SOME REGARD FOR CULTURE. I'LL SEND HIM A PERSONAL THANK-YOU.

BUT IT STILL PAINS ME THAT EVEN THIS PRINCELY SUM IS LESS THAN JACK TANNER MAKES IN A YEAR. I WON'T SAY EARNS.

ONE WEEK LATER: BIG HEARTS TELETHON NIGHT.

ENOUGH, SWEETHEART. THAT POWDER'S JUST SETTLING IN MY LINES. GOTTA LOOK YOUNG FOR THE TELETHON.

I CAN RECOMMEND A SURGEON, IF YOU LIKE...

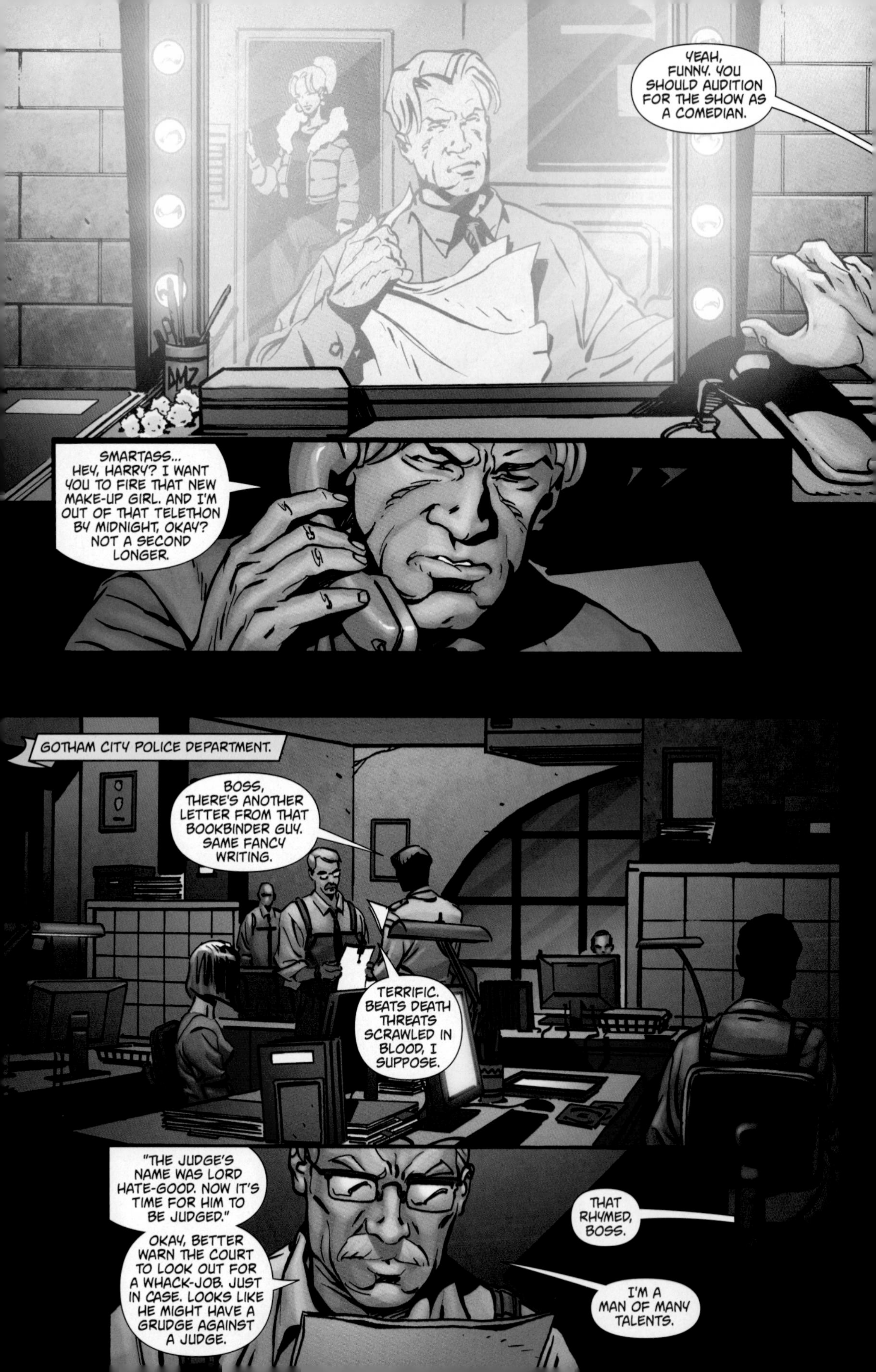
YEAH, FUNNY. YOU SHOULD AUDITION FOR THE SHOW AS A COMEDIAN.
SMARTASS... HEY, HARRY? I WANT YOU TO FIRE THAT NEW MAKE-UP GIRL. AND I'M OUT OF THAT TELETHON BY MIDNIGHT, OKAY? NOT A SECOND LONGER.
GOTHAM CITY POLICE DEPARTMENT.
BOSS, THERE'S ANOTHER LETTER FROM THAT BOOKBINDER GUY. SAME FANCY WRITING.
TERRIFIC. BEATS DEATH THREATS SCRAWLED IN BLOOD, I SUPPOSE.
"THE JUDGE'S NAME WAS LORD HATE-GOOD. NOW IT'S TIME FOR HIM TO BE JUDGED."
OKAY, BETTER WARN THE COURT TO LOOK OUT FOR A WHACK-JOB. JUST IN CASE. LOOKS LIKE HE MIGHT HAVE A GRUDGE AGAINST A JUDGE.
THAT RHYMED, BOSS.
I'M A MAN OF MANY TALENTS.

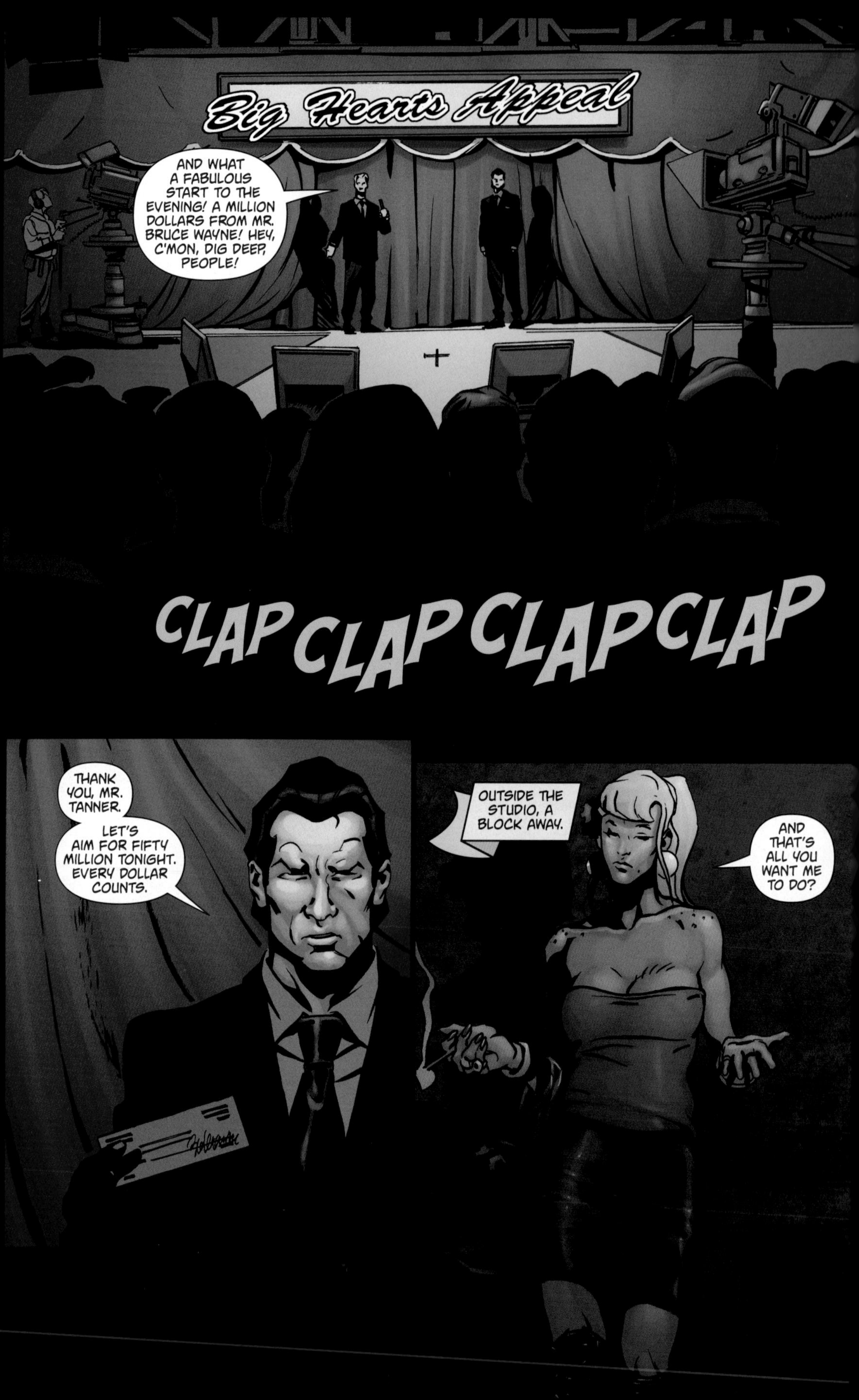
Big Hearts Appeal
AND WHAT A FABULOUS START TO THE EVENING! A MILLION DOLLARS FROM MR. BRUCE WAYNE! HEY, C'MON, DIG DEEP, PEOPLE!
CLAP CLAP CLAP CLAP
THANK YOU, MR. TANNER.
LET'S AIM FOR FIFTY MILLION TONIGHT. EVERY DOLLAR COUNTS.
OUTSIDE THE STUDIO, A BLOCK AWAY.
AND THAT'S ALL YOU WANT ME TO DO?

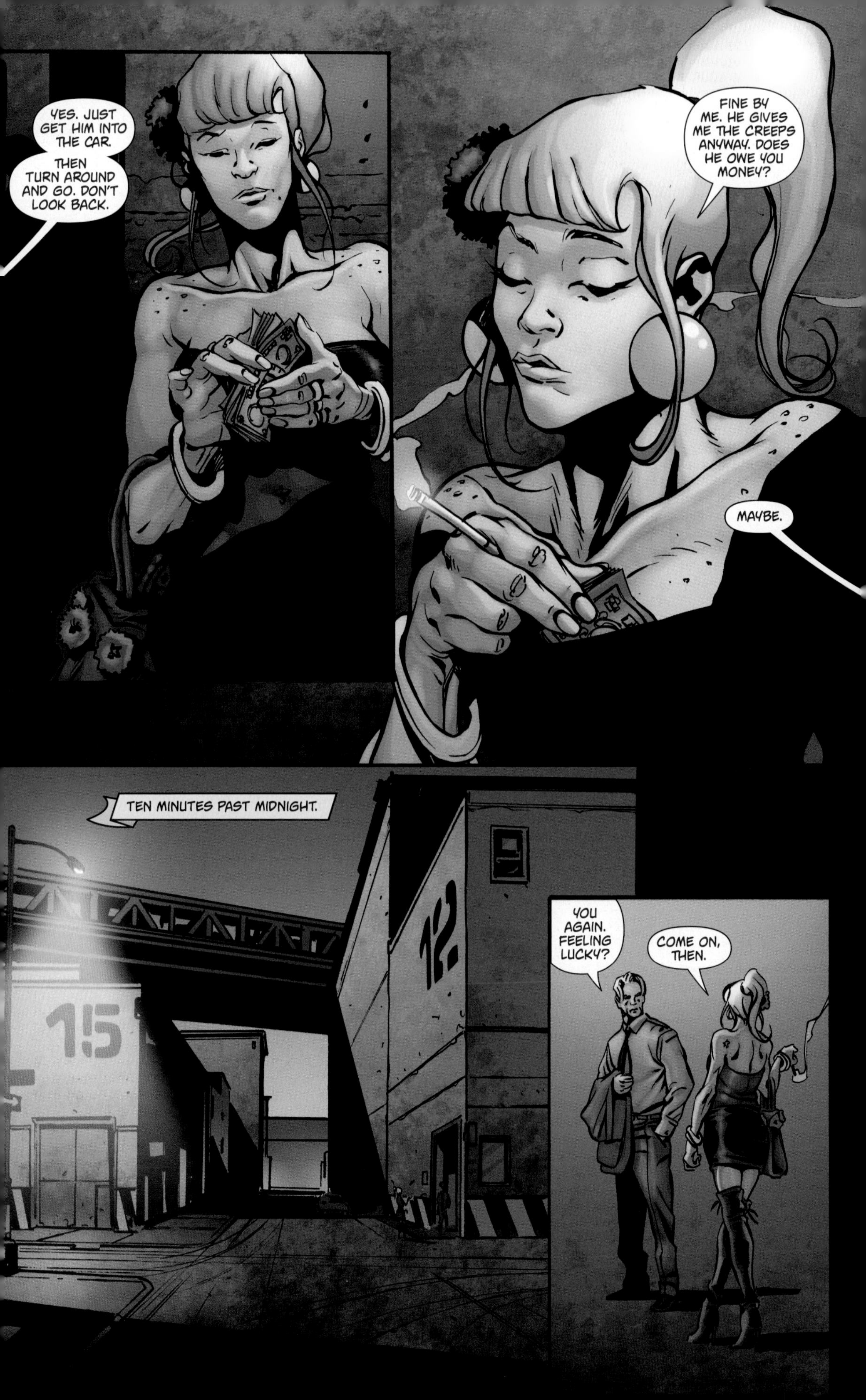
YES. JUST GET HIM INTO THE CAR.
THEN TURN AROUND AND GO. DON'T LOOK BACK.
FINE BY ME. HE GIVES ME THE CREEPS ANYWAY. DOES HE OWE YOU MONEY?
MAYBE.
TEN MINUTES PAST MIDNIGHT.
15
12
YOU AGAIN. FEELING LUCKY?
COME ON, THEN.

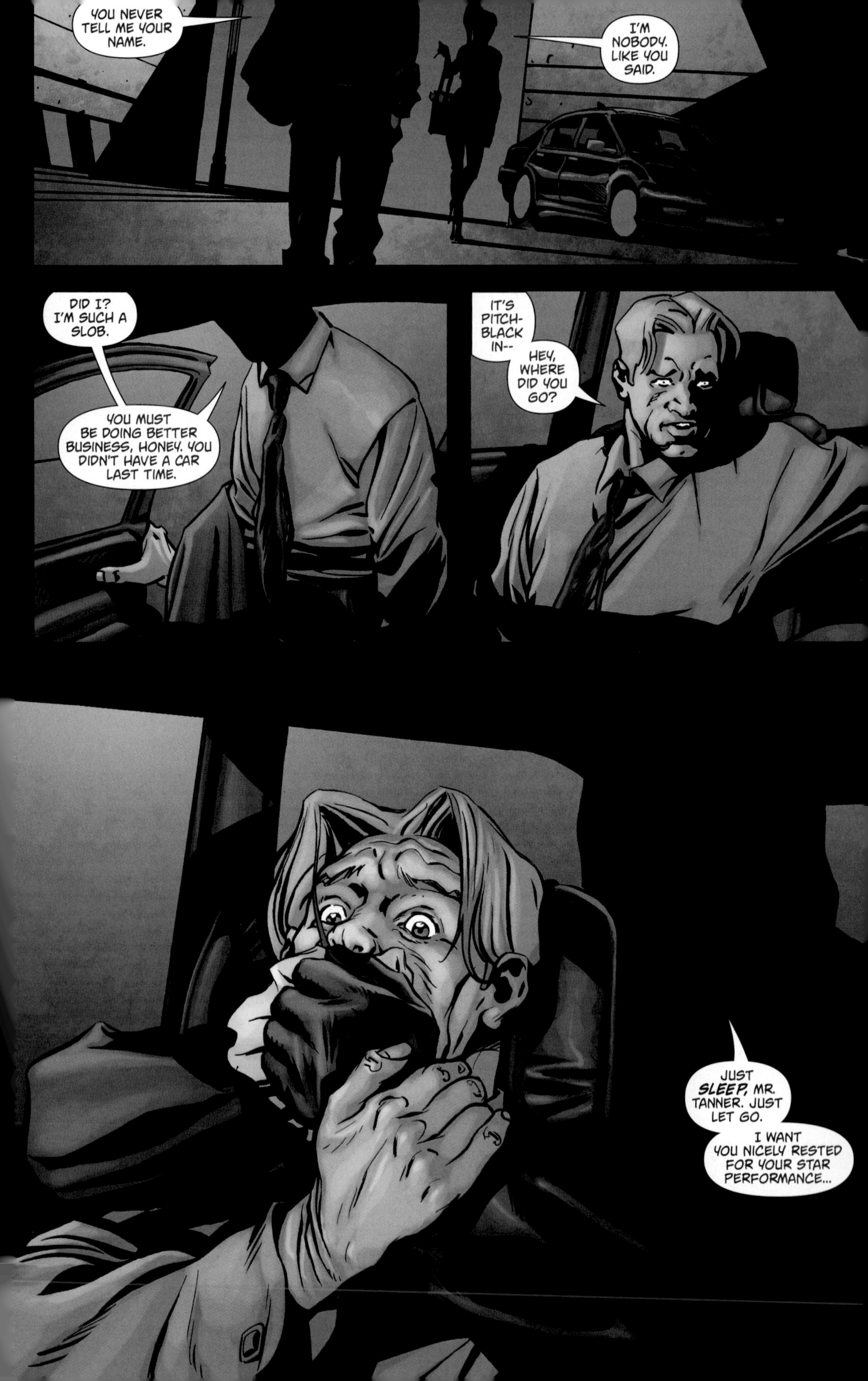
YOU NEVER TELL ME YOUR NAME.
I'M NOBODY. LIKE YOU SAID.
DID I? I'M SUCH A SLOB.
YOU MUST BE DOING BETTER BUSINESS, HONEY. YOU DIDN'T HAVE A CAR LAST TIME.
IT'S PITCH-BLACK IN--
HEY, WHERE DID YOU GO?
JUST SLEEP, MR. TANNER. JUST LET GO.
I WANT YOU NICELY RESTED FOR YOUR STAR PERFORMANCE...

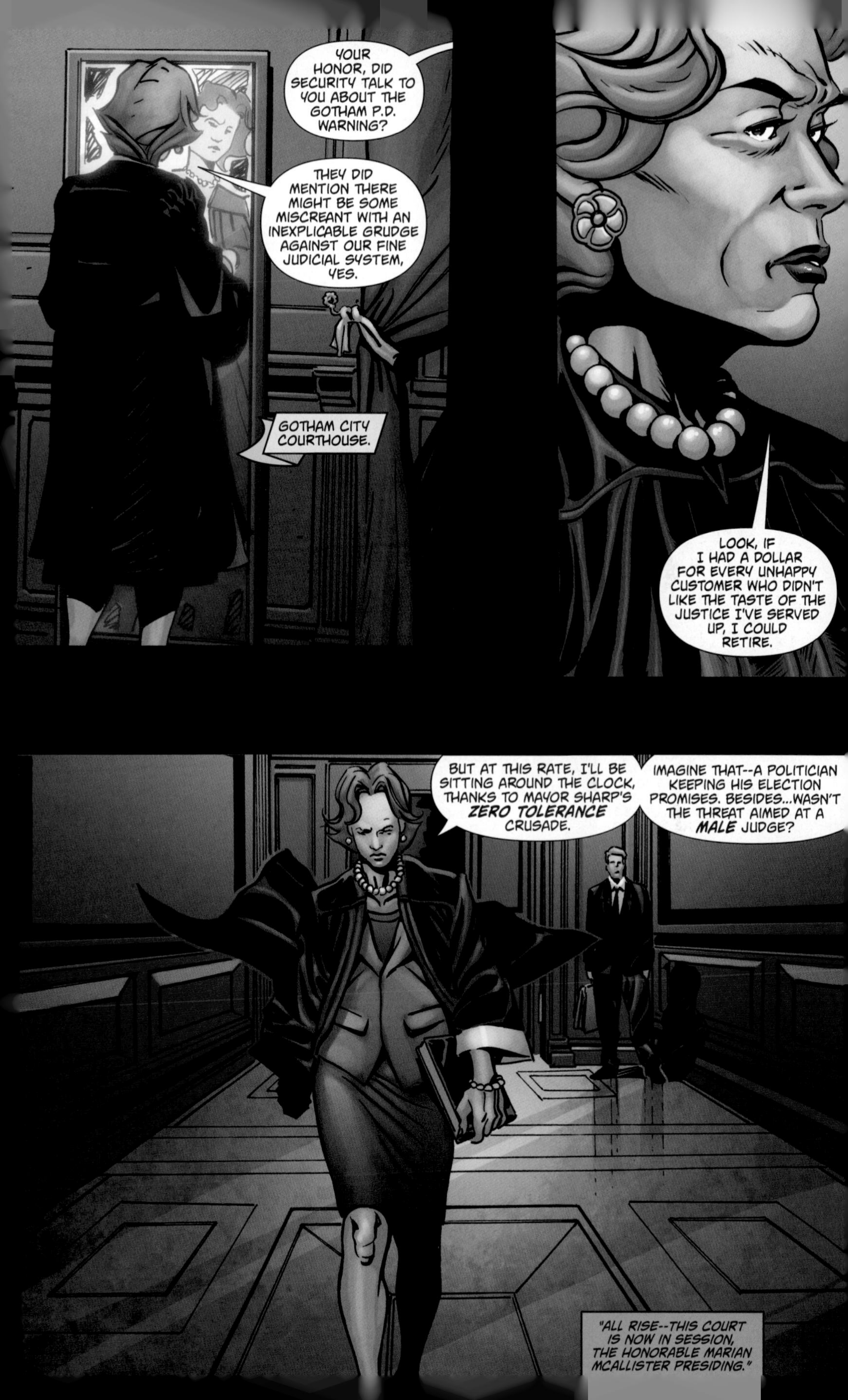
YOUR HONOR, DID SECURITY TALK TO YOU ABOUT THE GOTHAM P.D. WARNING?
THEY DID MENTION THERE MIGHT BE SOME MISCREANT WITH AN INEXPLICABLE GRUDGE AGAINST OUR FINE JUDICIAL SYSTEM, YES.
GOTHAM CITY COURTHOUSE.
LOOK, IF I HAD A DOLLAR FOR EVERY UNHAPPY CUSTOMER WHO DIDN'T LIKE THE TASTE OF THE JUSTICE I'VE SERVED UP, I COULD RETIRE.
BUT AT THIS RATE, I'LL BE SITTING AROUND THE CLOCK, THANKS TO MAYOR SHARP'S *ZERO TOLERANCE* CRUSADE.
IMAGINE THAT--A POLITICIAN KEEPING HIS ELECTION PROMISES. BESIDES...WASN'T THE THREAT AIMED AT A *MALE* JUDGE?
"ALL RISE--THIS COURT IS NOW IN SESSION, THE HONORABLE MARIAN MCALLISTER PRESIDING."

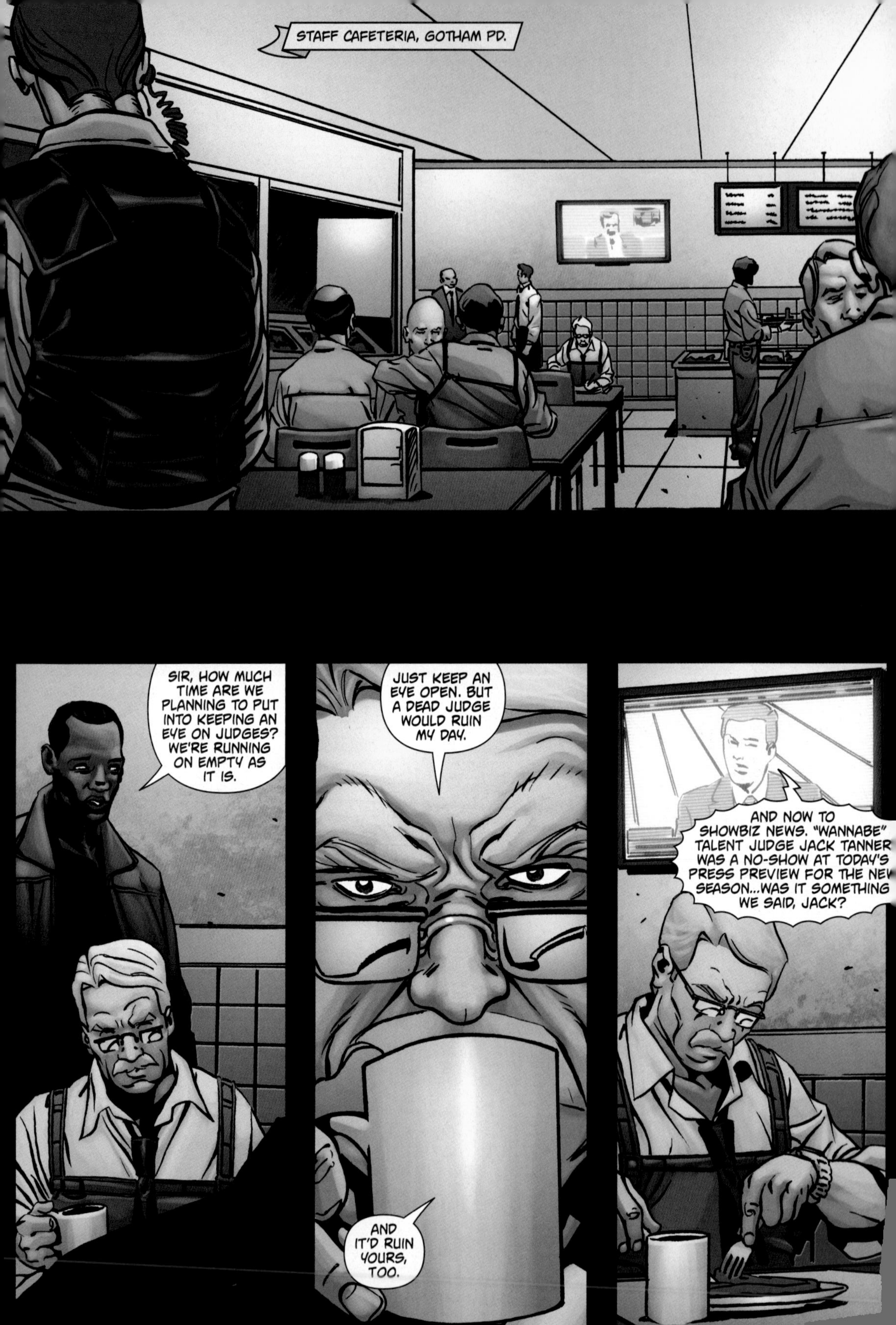
STAFF CAFETERIA, GOTHAM PD.
SIR, HOW MUCH TIME ARE WE PLANNING TO PUT INTO KEEPING AN EYE ON JUDGES? WE'RE RUNNING ON EMPTY AS IT IS.
JUST KEEP AN EYE OPEN. BUT A DEAD JUDGE WOULD RUIN MY DAY.
AND IT'D RUIN YOURS, TOO.
AND NOW TO SHOWBIZ NEWS. "WANNABE" TALENT JUDGE JACK TANNER WAS A NO-SHOW AT TODAY'S PRESS PREVIEW FOR THE NEW SEASON...WAS IT SOMETHING WE SAID, JACK?

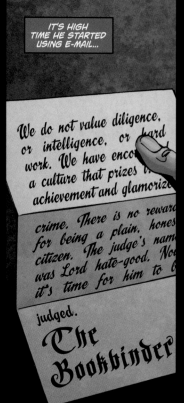

IT'S HIGH TIME HE STARTED USING E-MAIL...

We do not value diligence, or intelligence, or hard work. We have enco... a culture that prizes... achievement and glamorize...

...crime. There is no reward for being a plain, honest citizen. The judge's name was Lord hate-good. Now it's time for him to be judged.

The Bookbinder

WHILE I REMEMBER... BETTER LEAVE A COPY FOR BATMAN.

DEAD LETTER DROP. STILL--CAN'T BE TRACED. CAN'T BE TRACKED. JUST LIKE HIM.

OKAY... OKAY...IT'S ABOUT MONEY. IT'S GOT TO BE ABOUT MONEY...

...OR MAYBE SOME LOSER I DUMPED FROM THE SHOW...

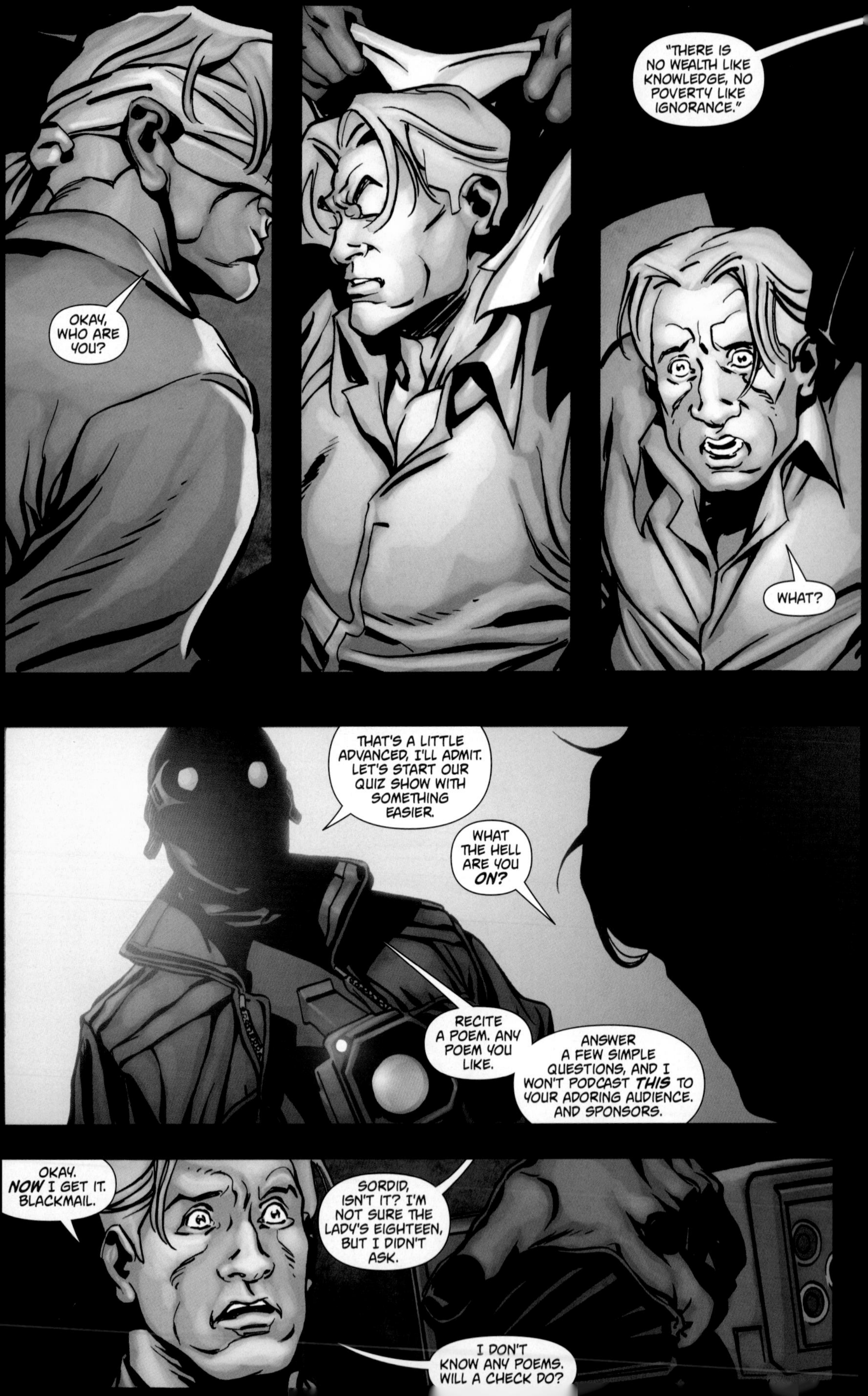
OKAY, WHO ARE YOU?
"THERE IS NO WEALTH LIKE KNOWLEDGE, NO POVERTY LIKE IGNORANCE."
WHAT?
THAT'S A LITTLE ADVANCED, I'LL ADMIT. LET'S START OUR QUIZ SHOW WITH SOMETHING EASIER.
WHAT THE HELL ARE YOU ON?
RECITE A POEM. ANY POEM YOU LIKE.
ANSWER A FEW SIMPLE QUESTIONS, AND I WON'T PODCAST THIS TO YOUR ADORING AUDIENCE. AND SPONSORS.
OKAY. NOW I GET IT. BLACKMAIL.
SORDID, ISN'T IT? I'M NOT SURE THE LADY'S EIGHTEEN, BUT I DIDN'T ASK.
I DON'T KNOW ANY POEMS. WILL A CHECK DO?

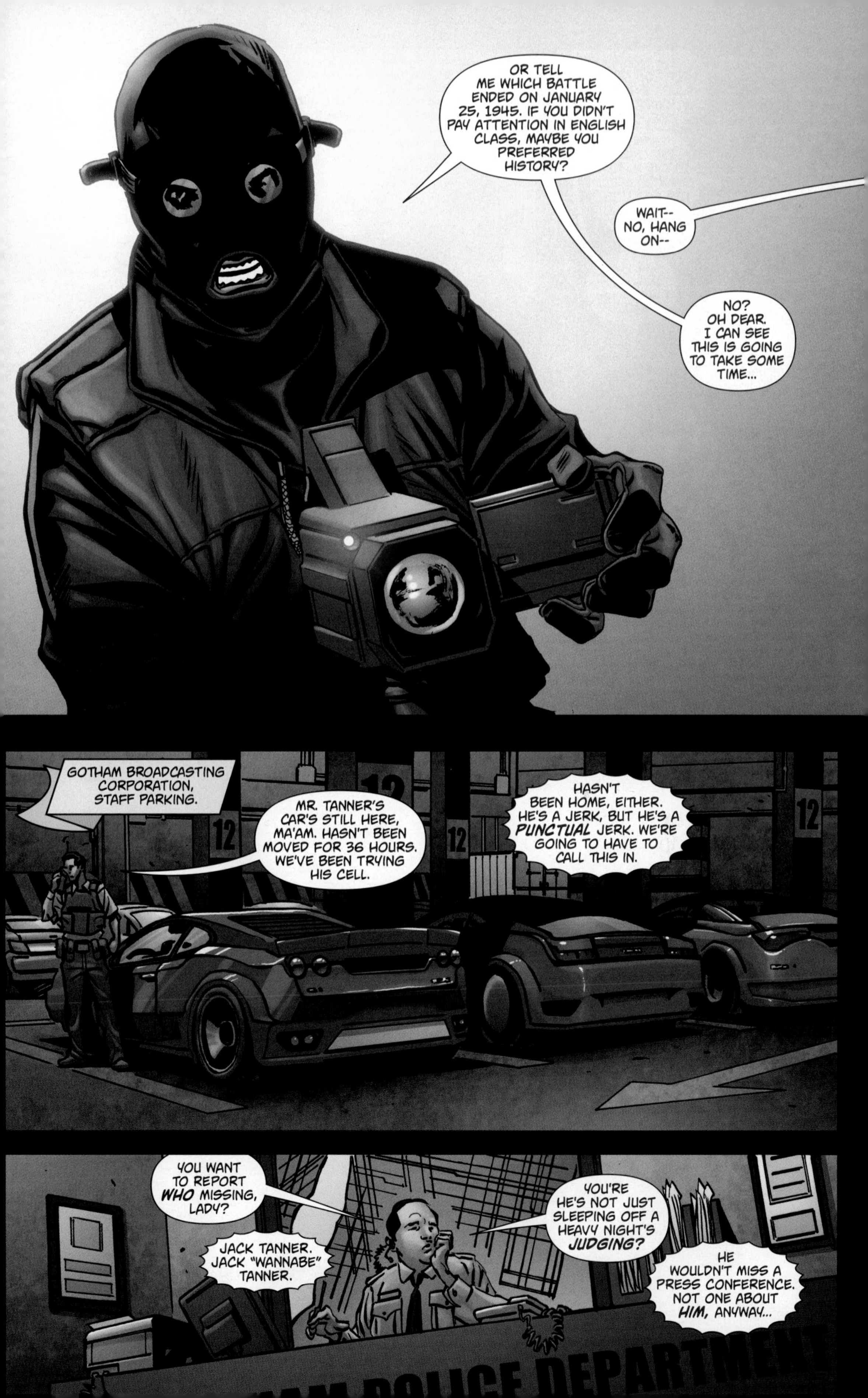
OR TELL ME WHICH BATTLE ENDED ON JANUARY 25, 1945. IF YOU DIDN'T PAY ATTENTION IN ENGLISH CLASS, MAYBE YOU PREFERRED HISTORY?
WAIT-- NO, HANG ON--
NO? OH DEAR. I CAN SEE THIS IS GOING TO TAKE SOME TIME...
GOTHAM BROADCASTING CORPORATION, STAFF PARKING.
12
MR. TANNER'S CAR'S STILL HERE, MA'AM. HASN'T BEEN MOVED FOR 36 HOURS. WE'VE BEEN TRYING HIS CELL.
HASN'T BEEN HOME, EITHER. HE'S A JERK, BUT HE'S A *PUNCTUAL* JERK. WE'RE GOING TO HAVE TO CALL THIS IN.
YOU WANT TO REPORT ***WHO*** MISSING, LADY?
JACK TANNER. JACK "WANNABE" TANNER.
YOU'RE HE'S NOT JUST SLEEPING OFF A HEAVY NIGHT'S ***JUDGING?***
HE WOULDN'T MISS A PRESS CONFERENCE. NOT ONE ABOUT ***HIM,*** ANYWAY...
POLICE

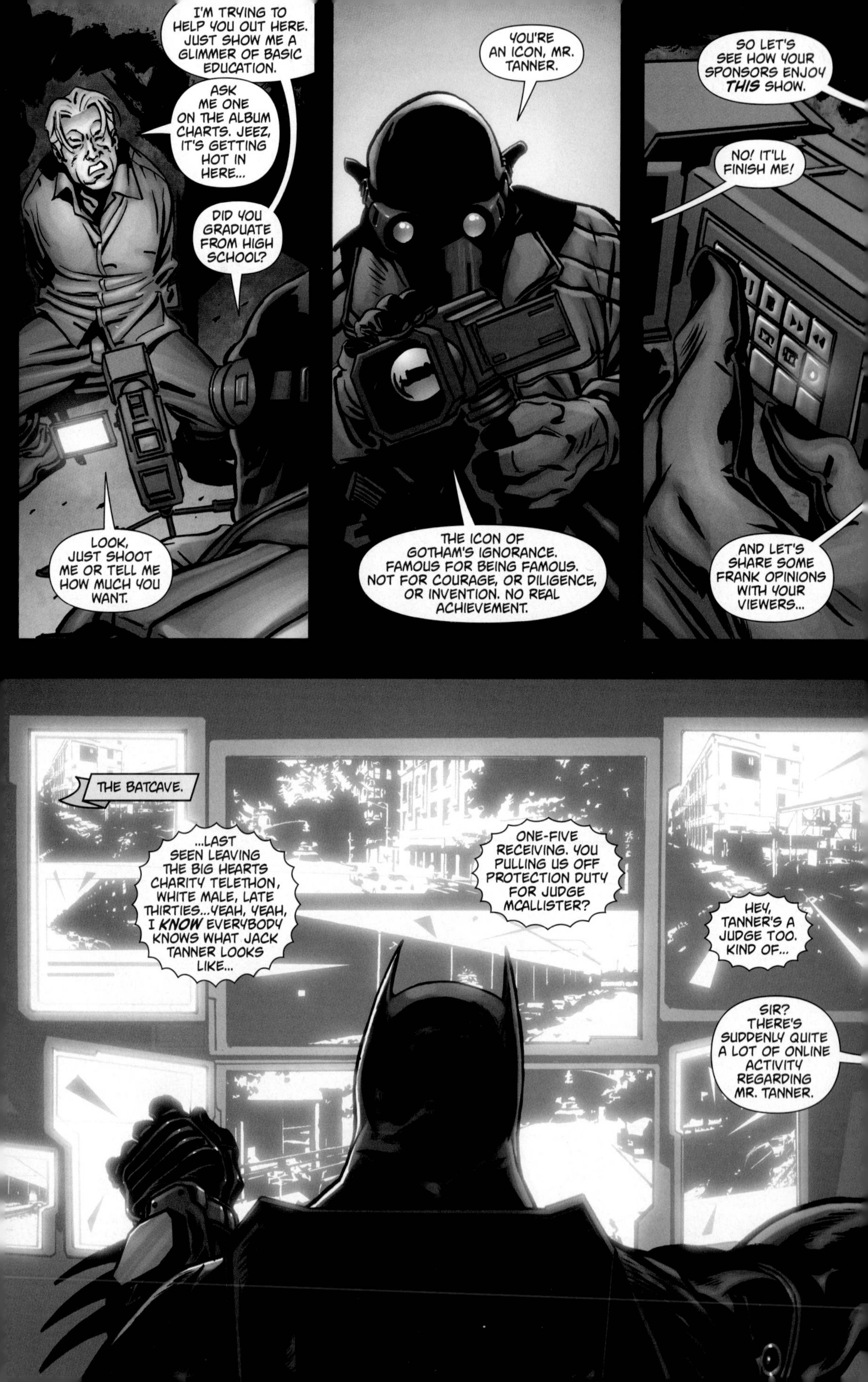
I'M TRYING TO HELP YOU OUT HERE. JUST SHOW ME A GLIMMER OF BASIC EDUCATION.
ASK ME ONE ON THE ALBUM CHARTS. JEEZ, IT'S GETTING HOT IN HERE...
DID YOU GRADUATE FROM HIGH SCHOOL?
LOOK, JUST SHOOT ME OR TELL ME HOW MUCH YOU WANT.
YOU'RE AN ICON, MR. TANNER.
THE ICON OF GOTHAM'S IGNORANCE. FAMOUS FOR BEING FAMOUS. NOT FOR COURAGE, OR DILIGENCE, OR INVENTION. NO REAL ACHIEVEMENT.
SO LET'S SEE HOW YOUR SPONSORS ENJOY THIS SHOW.
NO! IT'LL FINISH ME!
AND LET'S SHARE SOME FRANK OPINIONS WITH YOUR VIEWERS...
THE BATCAVE.
...LAST SEEN LEAVING THE BIG HEARTS CHARITY TELETHON, WHITE MALE, LATE THIRTIES...YEAH, YEAH, I KNOW EVERYBODY KNOWS WHAT JACK TANNER LOOKS LIKE...
ONE-FIVE RECEIVING. YOU PULLING US OFF PROTECTION DUTY FOR JUDGE MCALLISTER?
HEY, TANNER'S A JUDGE TOO. KIND OF...
SIR? THERE'S SUDDENLY QUITE A LOT OF ONLINE ACTIVITY REGARDING MR. TANNER.

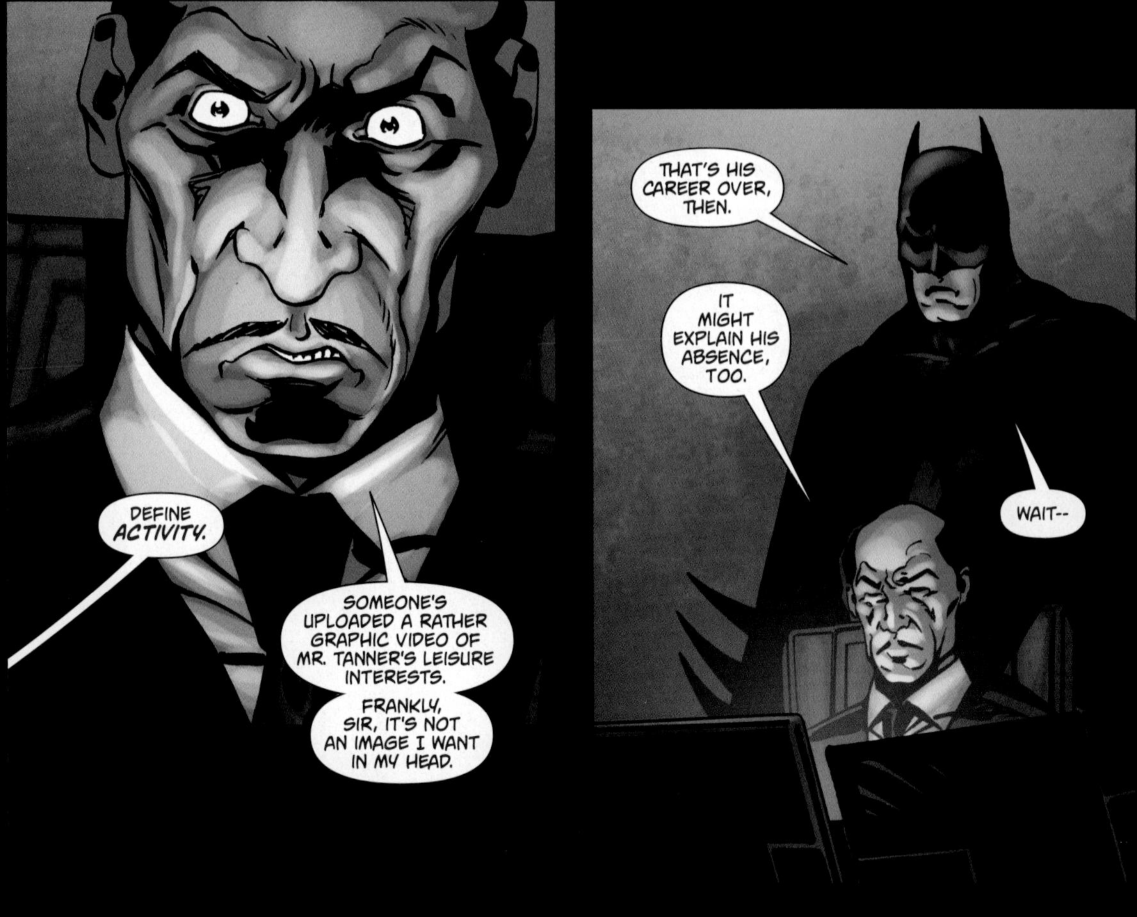
DEFINE ACTIVITY.
SOMEONE'S UPLOADED A RATHER GRAPHIC VIDEO OF MR. TANNER'S LEISURE INTERESTS.
FRANKLY, SIR, IT'S NOT AN IMAGE I WANT IN MY HEAD.
THAT'S HIS CAREER OVER, THEN.
IT MIGHT EXPLAIN HIS ABSENCE, TOO.
WAIT--

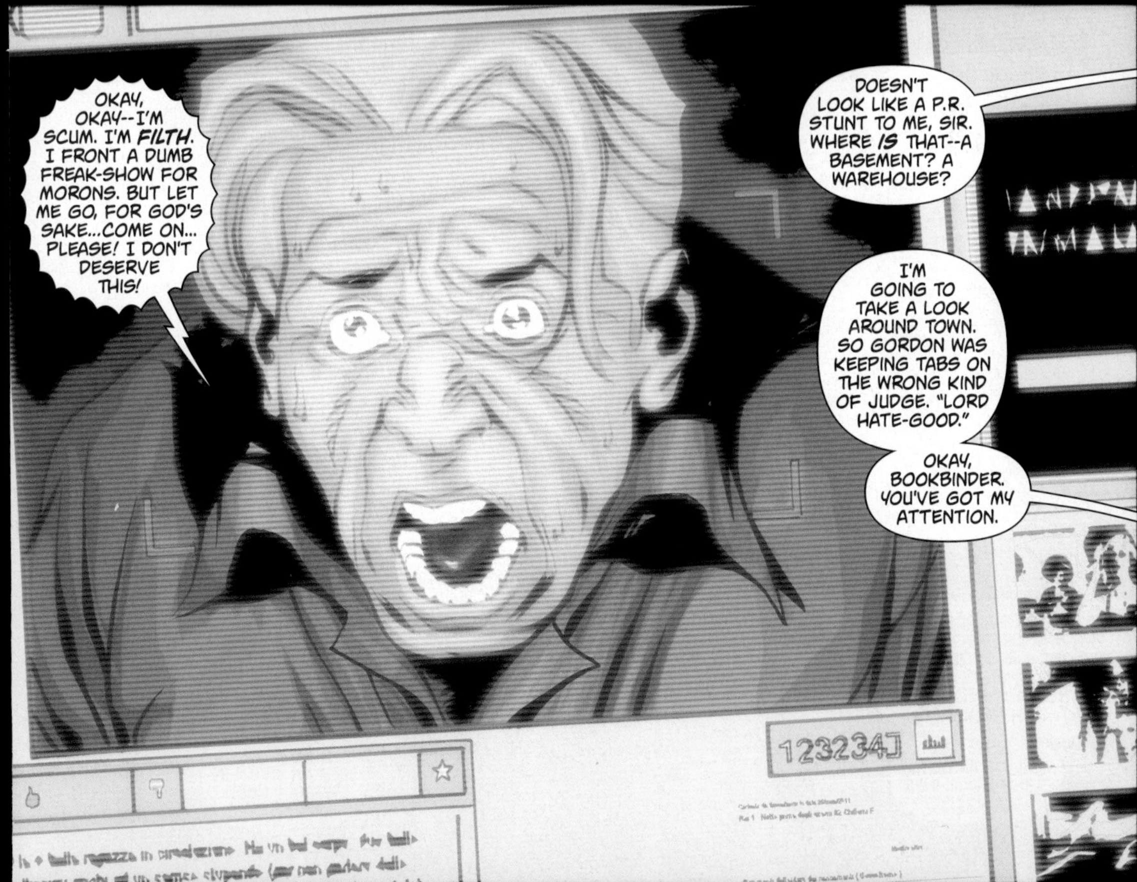
OKAY, OKAY--I'M SCUM. I'M FILTH. I FRONT A DUMB FREAK-SHOW FOR MORONS. BUT LET ME GO, FOR GOD'S SAKE...COME ON... PLEASE! I DON'T DESERVE THIS!
DOESN'T LOOK LIKE A P.R. STUNT TO ME, SIR. WHERE IS THAT--A BASEMENT? A WAREHOUSE?
I'M GOING TO TAKE A LOOK AROUND TOWN. SO GORDON WAS KEEPING TABS ON THE WRONG KIND OF JUDGE. "LORD HATE-GOOD."
OKAY, BOOKBINDER. YOU'VE GOT MY ATTENTION.
123234J

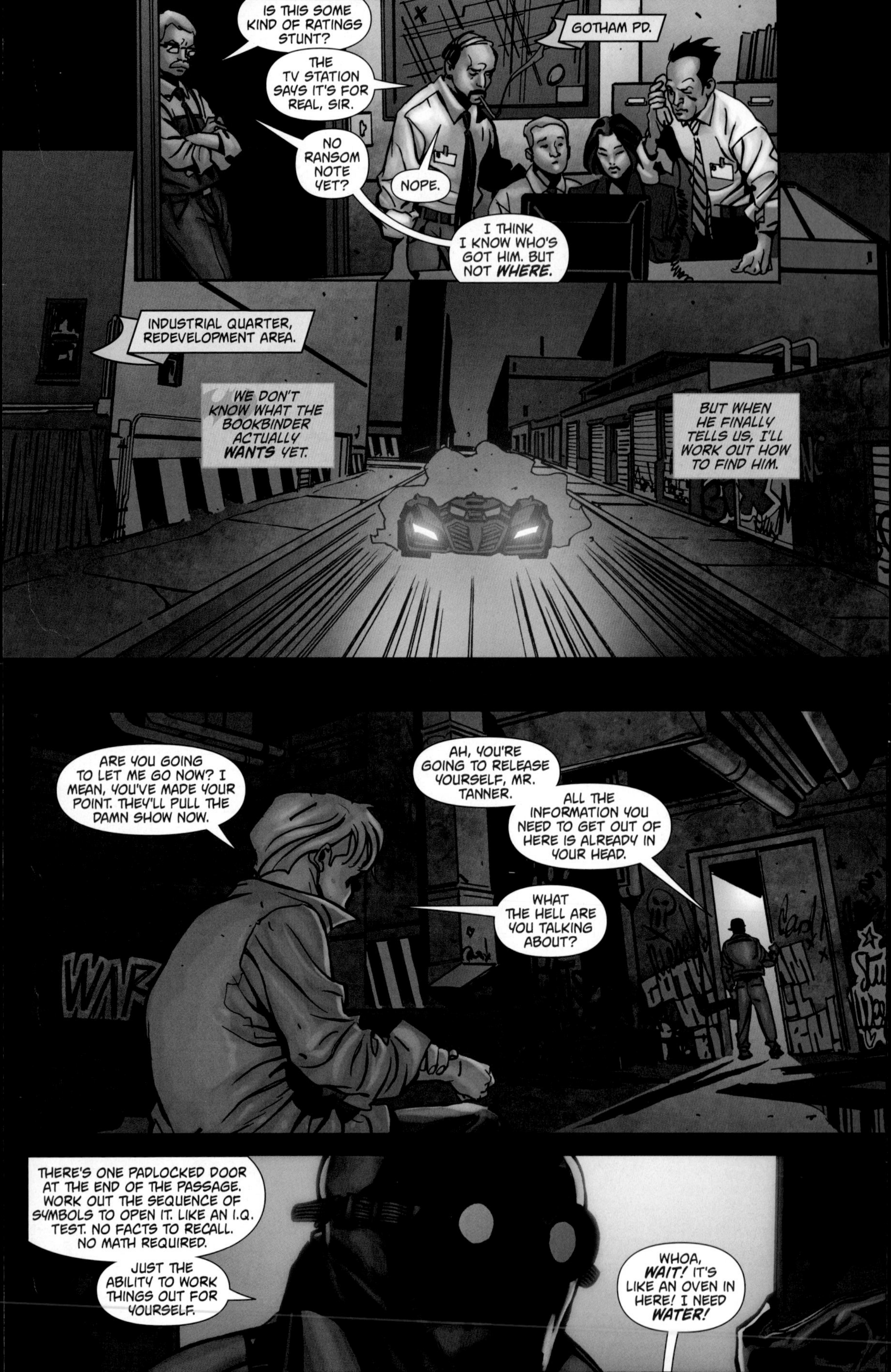
IS THIS SOME KIND OF RATINGS STUNT?
GOTHAM PD.
THE TV STATION SAYS IT'S FOR REAL, SIR.
NO RANSOM NOTE YET?
NOPE.
I THINK I KNOW WHO'S GOT HIM. BUT NOT WHERE.
INDUSTRIAL QUARTER, REDEVELOPMENT AREA.
WE DON'T KNOW WHAT THE BOOKBINDER ACTUALLY WANTS YET.
BUT WHEN HE FINALLY TELLS US, I'LL WORK OUT HOW TO FIND HIM.
ARE YOU GOING TO LET ME GO NOW? I MEAN, YOU'VE MADE YOUR POINT. THEY'LL PULL THE DAMN SHOW NOW.
AH, YOU'RE GOING TO RELEASE YOURSELF, MR. TANNER.
ALL THE INFORMATION YOU NEED TO GET OUT OF HERE IS ALREADY IN YOUR HEAD.
WHAT THE HELL ARE YOU TALKING ABOUT?
THERE'S ONE PADLOCKED DOOR AT THE END OF THE PASSAGE. WORK OUT THE SEQUENCE OF SYMBOLS TO OPEN IT. LIKE AN I.Q. TEST. NO FACTS TO RECALL. NO MATH REQUIRED.
JUST THE ABILITY TO WORK THINGS OUT FOR YOURSELF.
WHOA, WAIT! IT'S LIKE AN OVEN IN HERE! I NEED WATER!

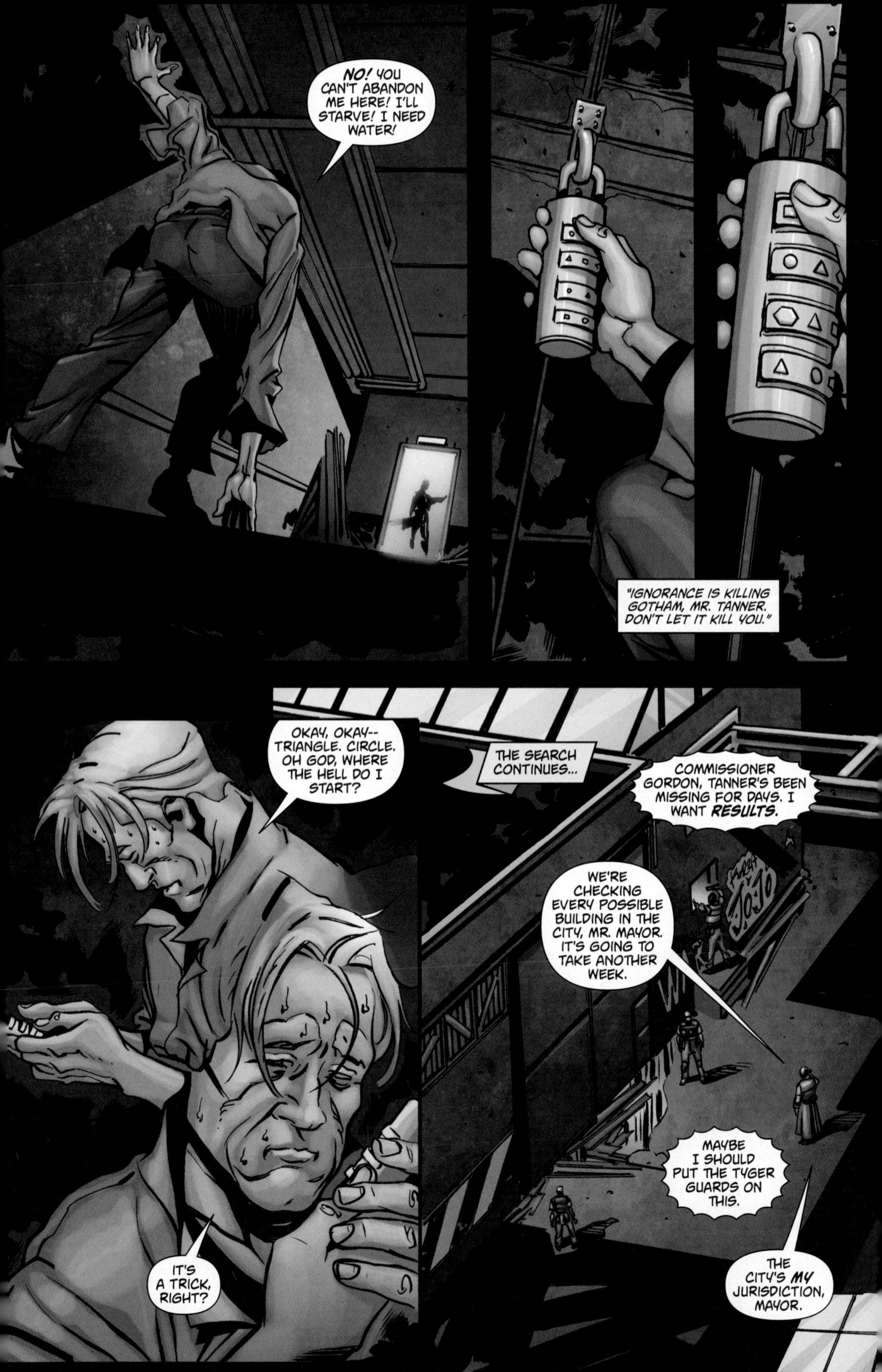
NO! YOU CAN'T ABANDON ME HERE! I'LL STARVE! I NEED WATER!
"IGNORANCE IS KILLING GOTHAM, MR. TANNER. DON'T LET IT KILL YOU."
OKAY, OKAY-- TRIANGLE. CIRCLE. OH GOD, WHERE THE HELL DO I START?
IT'S A TRICK, RIGHT?
THE SEARCH CONTINUES...
COMMISSIONER GORDON, TANNER'S BEEN MISSING FOR DAYS. I WANT RESULTS.
WE'RE CHECKING EVERY POSSIBLE BUILDING IN THE CITY, MR. MAYOR. IT'S GOING TO TAKE ANOTHER WEEK.
MAYBE I SHOULD PUT THE TYGER GUARDS ON THIS.
THE CITY'S MY JURISDICTION, MAYOR.

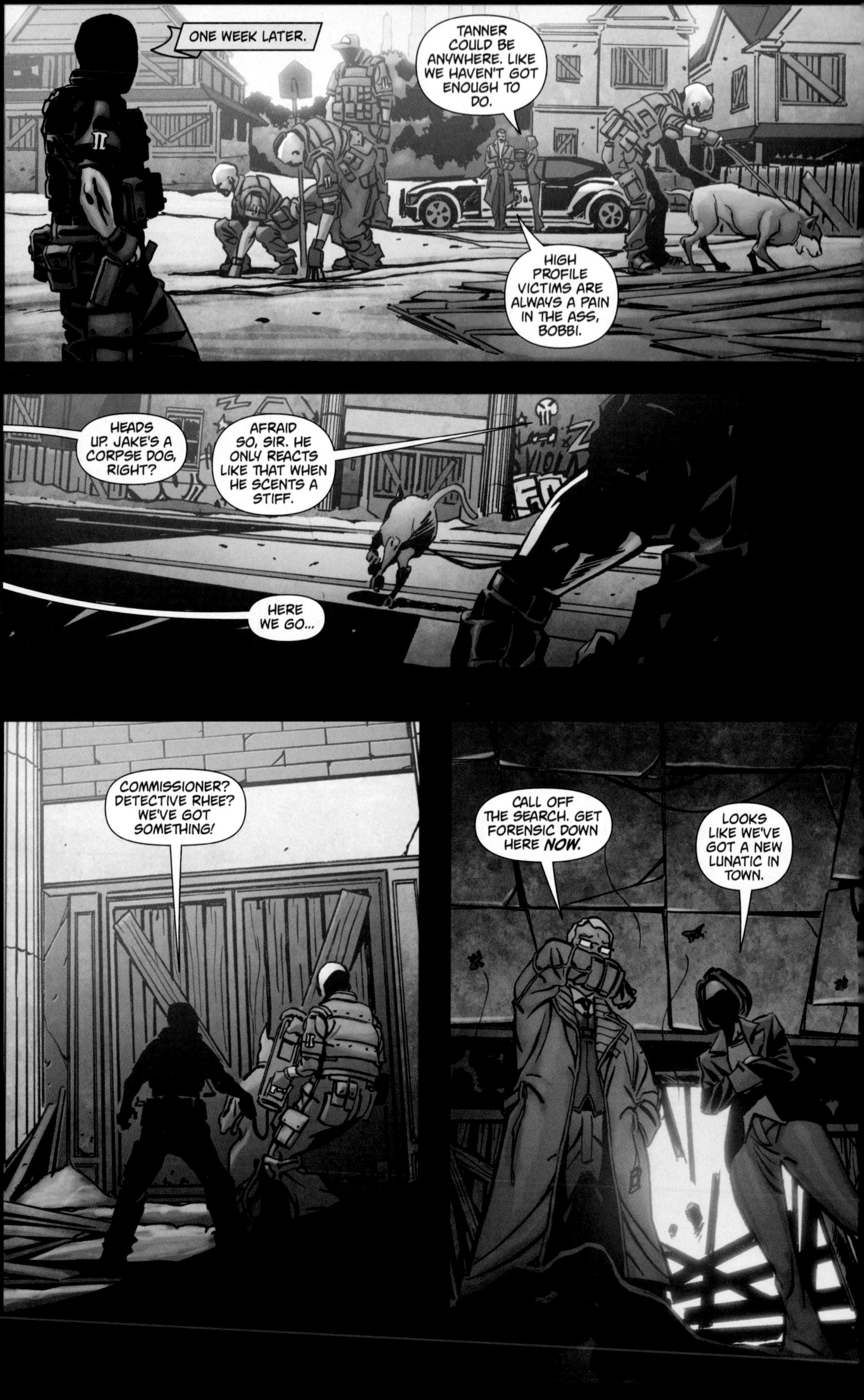
ONE WEEK LATER.
TANNER COULD BE ANYWHERE. LIKE WE HAVEN'T GOT ENOUGH TO DO.
HIGH PROFILE VICTIMS ARE ALWAYS A PAIN IN THE ASS, BOBBI.
HEADS UP. JAKE'S A CORPSE DOG, RIGHT?
AFRAID SO, SIR. HE ONLY REACTS LIKE THAT WHEN HE SCENTS A STIFF.
HERE WE GO...
COMMISSIONER? DETECTIVE RHEE? WE'VE GOT SOMETHING!
CALL OFF THE SEARCH. GET FORENSIC DOWN HERE NOW.
LOOKS LIKE WE'VE GOT A NEW LUNATIC IN TOWN.

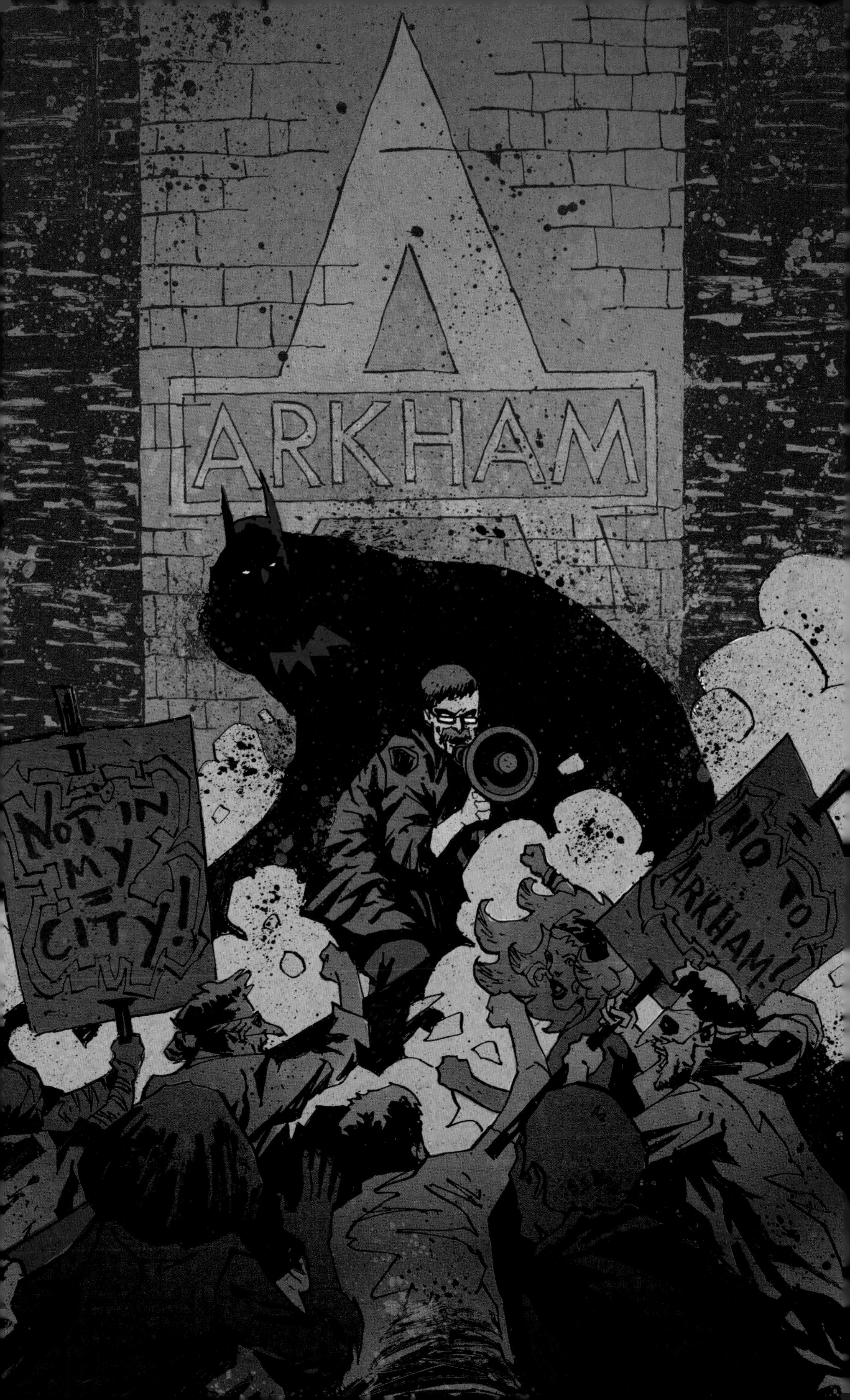
ARKHAM
NOT IN MY CITY!
NO TO ARKHAM!

WELCOME
TO THE SLOUGH OF DESPOND
PART TWO

WRITTEN BY: **KAREN TRAVISS**
ART BY: **CHRISTIAN DUCE**
COLORS BY: ALEJANDRO SANCHEZ
LETTERS BY: TRAVIS LANHAM
COVER BY: CHRIS MITTEN

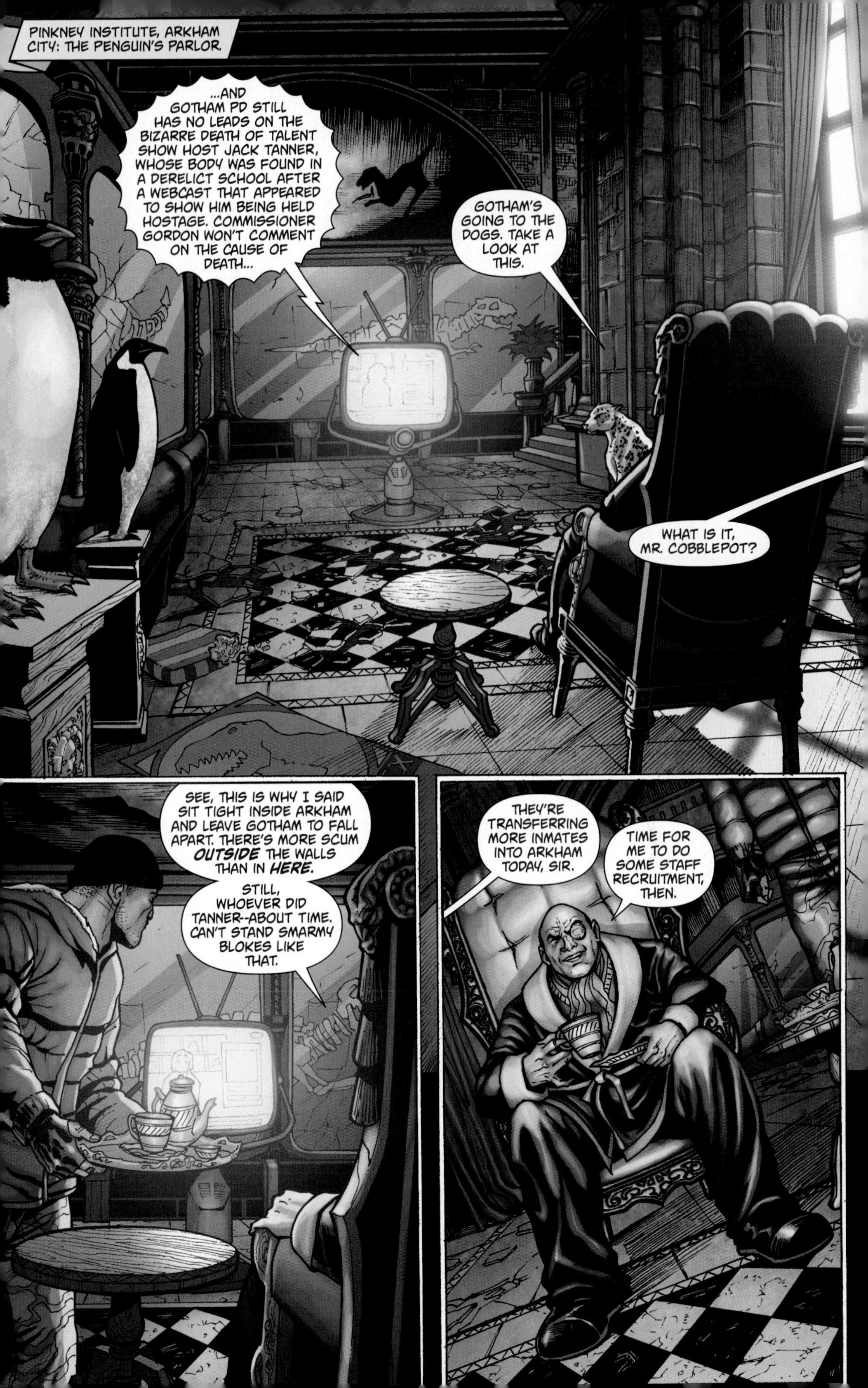
PINKNEY INSTITUTE, ARKHAM CITY: THE PENGUIN'S PARLOR.
...AND GOTHAM PD STILL HAS NO LEADS ON THE BIZARRE DEATH OF TALENT SHOW HOST JACK TANNER, WHOSE BODY WAS FOUND IN A DERELICT SCHOOL AFTER A WEBCAST THAT APPEARED TO SHOW HIM BEING HELD HOSTAGE. COMMISSIONER GORDON WON'T COMMENT ON THE CAUSE OF DEATH...
GOTHAM'S GOING TO THE DOGS. TAKE A LOOK AT THIS.
WHAT IS IT, MR. COBBLEPOT?
SEE, THIS IS WHY I SAID SIT TIGHT INSIDE ARKHAM AND LEAVE GOTHAM TO FALL APART. THERE'S MORE SCUM ***OUTSIDE*** THE WALLS THAN IN ***HERE***.
STILL, WHOEVER DID TANNER--ABOUT TIME. CAN'T STAND SMARMY BLOKES LIKE THAT.
THEY'RE TRANSFERRING MORE INMATES INTO ARKHAM TODAY, SIR.
TIME FOR ME TO DO SOME STAFF RECRUITMENT, THEN.

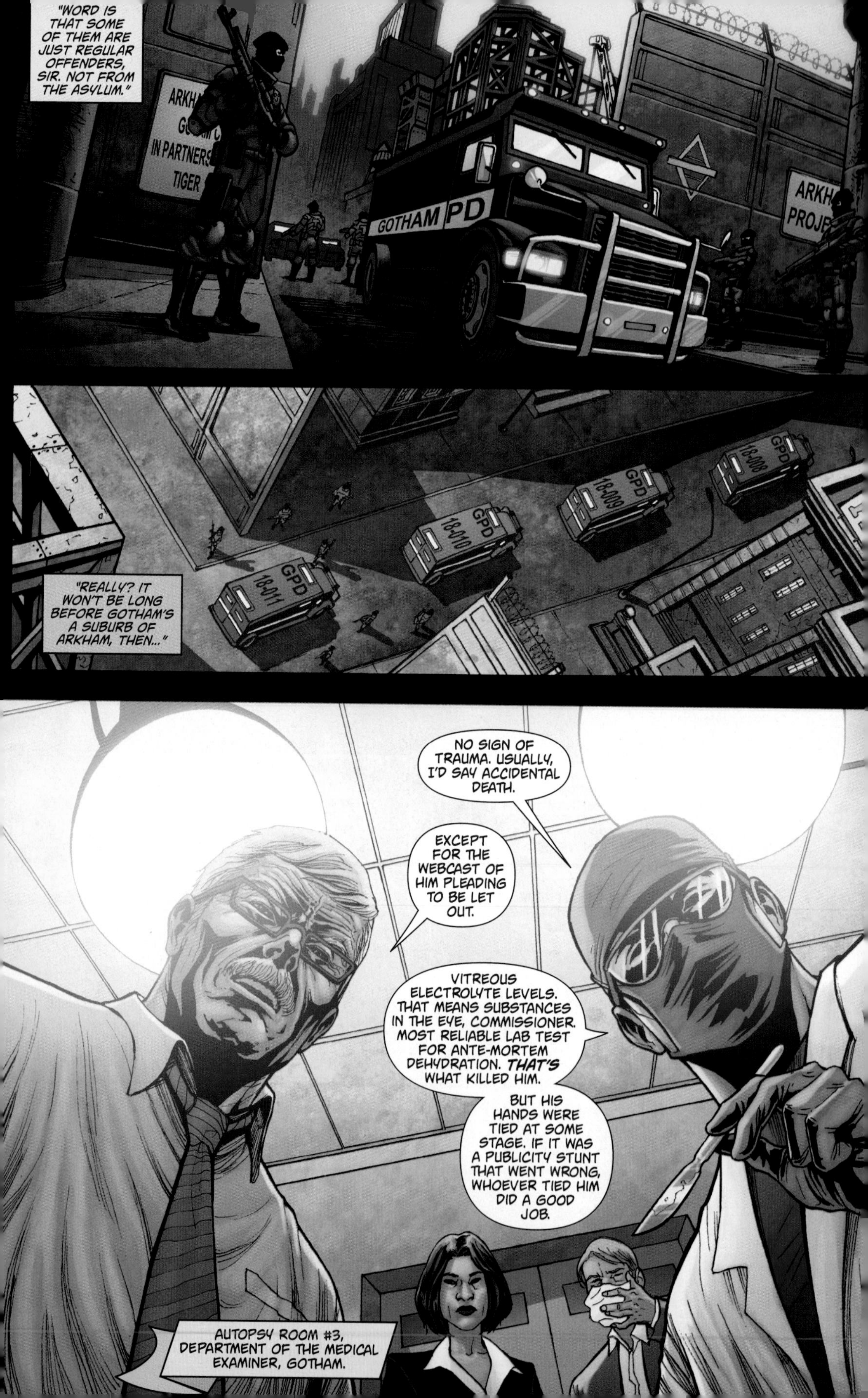
"WORD IS THAT SOME OF THEM ARE JUST REGULAR OFFENDERS, SIR. NOT FROM THE ASYLUM."
GOTHAM PD
GPD 18-008
GPD 18-009
GPD 18-010
GPD 18-011
"REALLY? IT WON'T BE LONG BEFORE GOTHAM'S A SUBURB OF ARKHAM, THEN..."
AUTOPSY ROOM #3, DEPARTMENT OF THE MEDICAL EXAMINER, GOTHAM.
NO SIGN OF TRAUMA. USUALLY, I'D SAY ACCIDENTAL DEATH.
EXCEPT FOR THE WEBCAST OF HIM PLEADING TO BE LET OUT.
VITREOUS ELECTROLYTE LEVELS. THAT MEANS SUBSTANCES IN THE EYE, COMMISSIONER. MOST RELIABLE LAB TEST FOR ANTE-MORTEM DEHYDRATION. THAT'S WHAT KILLED HIM.
BUT HIS HANDS WERE TIED AT SOME STAGE. IF IT WAS A PUBLICITY STUNT THAT WENT WRONG, WHOEVER TIED HIM DID A GOOD JOB.

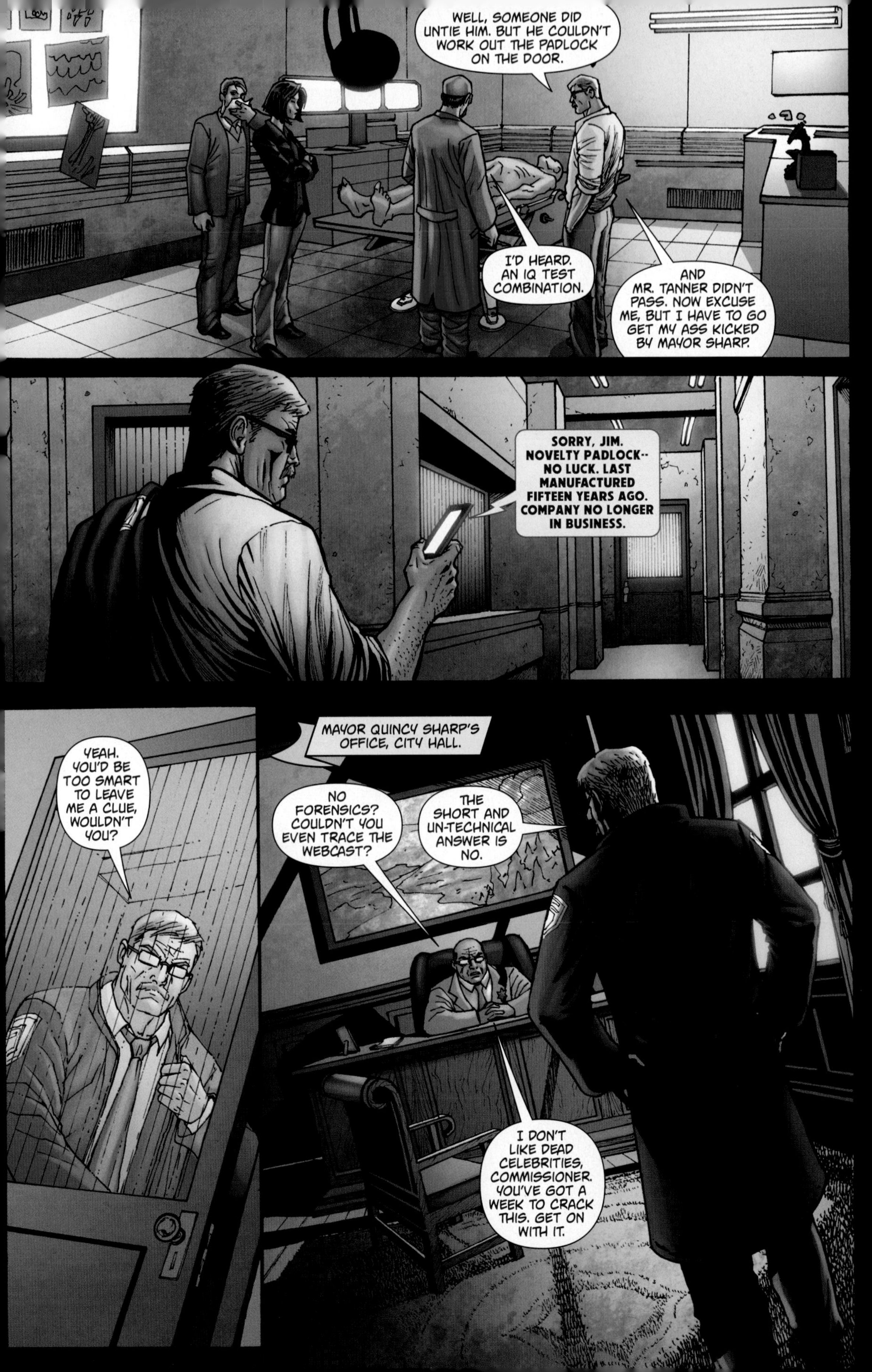
WELL, SOMEONE DID UNTIE HIM. BUT HE COULDN'T WORK OUT THE PADLOCK ON THE DOOR.
I'D HEARD. AN IQ TEST COMBINATION.
AND MR. TANNER DIDN'T PASS. NOW EXCUSE ME, BUT I HAVE TO GO GET MY ASS KICKED BY MAYOR SHARP.
SORRY, JIM. NOVELTY PADLOCK-- NO LUCK. LAST MANUFACTURED FIFTEEN YEARS AGO. COMPANY NO LONGER IN BUSINESS.
YEAH. YOU'D BE TOO SMART TO LEAVE ME A CLUE, WOULDN'T YOU?
MAYOR QUINCY SHARP'S OFFICE, CITY HALL.
NO FORENSICS? COULDN'T YOU EVEN TRACE THE WEBCAST?
THE SHORT AND UN-TECHNICAL ANSWER IS NO.
I DON'T LIKE DEAD CELEBRITIES, COMMISSIONER. YOU'VE GOT A WEEK TO CRACK THIS. GET ON WITH IT.

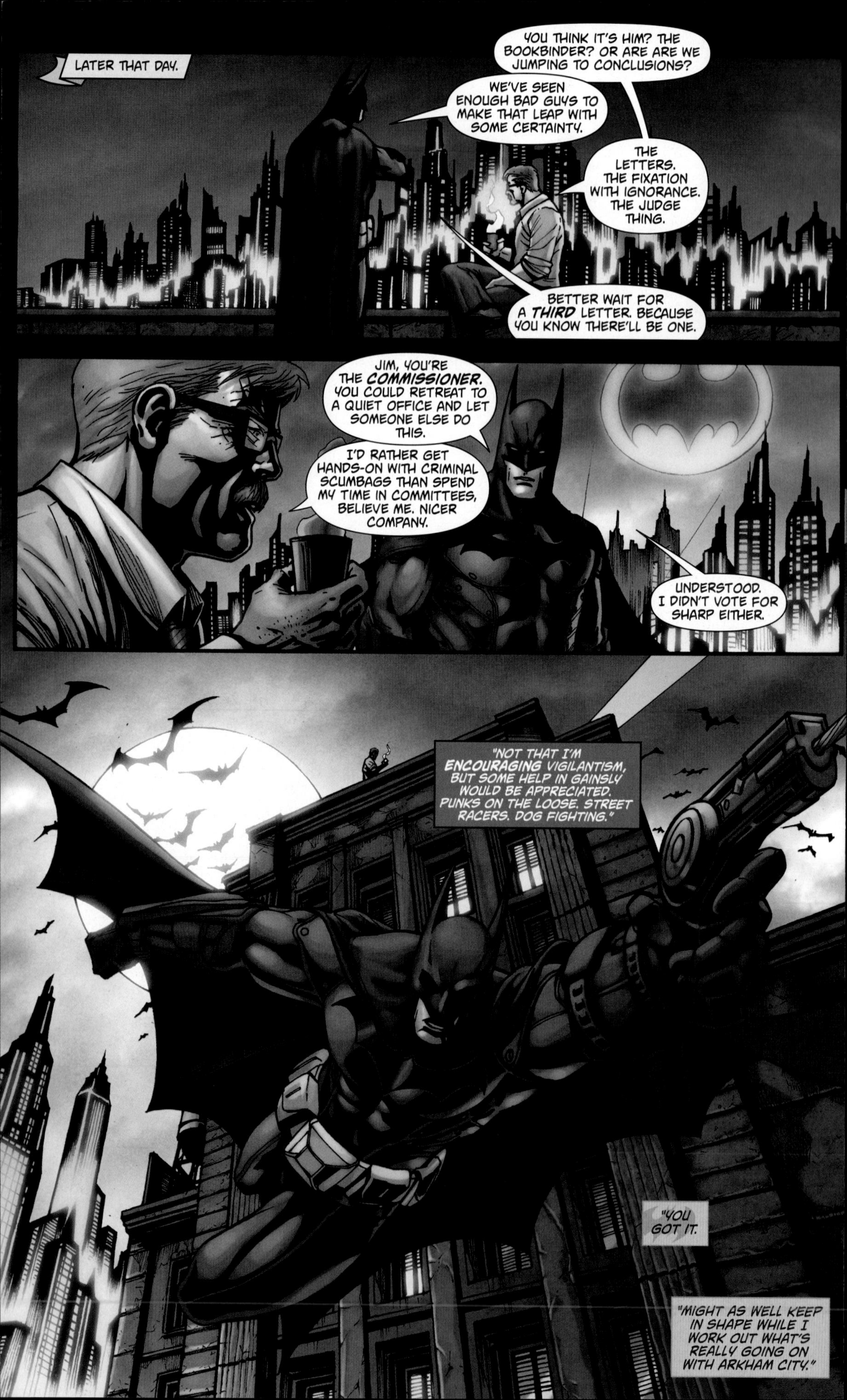
LATER THAT DAY.
YOU THINK IT'S HIM? THE BOOKBINDER? OR ARE ARE WE JUMPING TO CONCLUSIONS?
WE'VE SEEN ENOUGH BAD GUYS TO MAKE THAT LEAP WITH SOME CERTAINTY.
THE LETTERS. THE FIXATION WITH IGNORANCE. THE JUDGE THING.
BETTER WAIT FOR A THIRD LETTER. BECAUSE YOU KNOW THERE'LL BE ONE.
JIM, YOU'RE THE COMMISSIONER. YOU COULD RETREAT TO A QUIET OFFICE AND LET SOMEONE ELSE DO THIS.
I'D RATHER GET HANDS-ON WITH CRIMINAL SCUMBAGS THAN SPEND MY TIME IN COMMITTEES, BELIEVE ME. NICER COMPANY.
UNDERSTOOD. I DIDN'T VOTE FOR SHARP EITHER.
"NOT THAT I'M ENCOURAGING VIGILANTISM, BUT SOME HELP IN GAINSLY WOULD BE APPRECIATED. PUNKS ON THE LOOSE. STREET RACERS. DOG FIGHTING."
"YOU GOT IT.
"MIGHT AS WELL KEEP IN SHAPE WHILE I WORK OUT WHAT'S REALLY GOING ON WITH ARKHAM CITY."

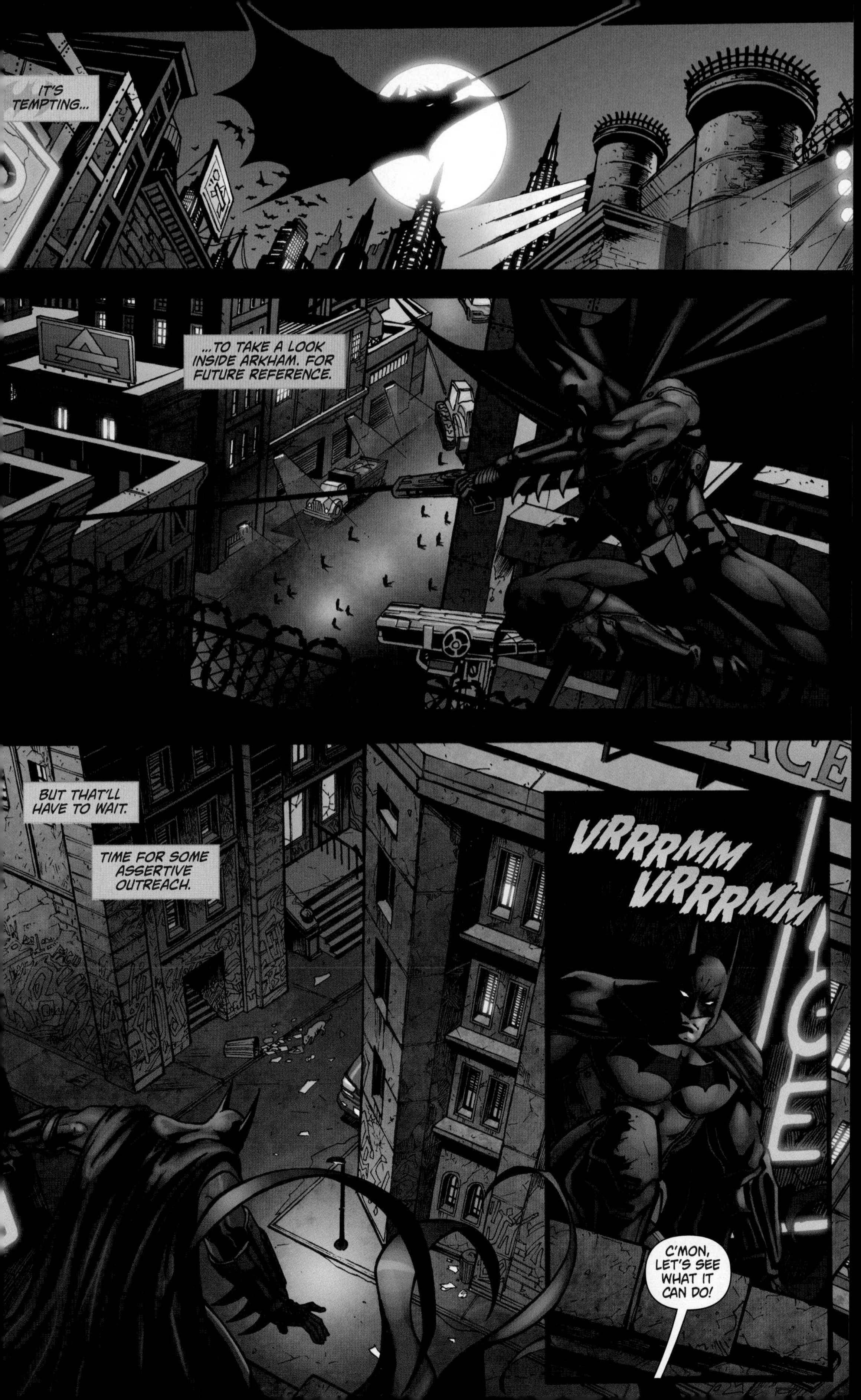
IT'S TEMPTING...
...TO TAKE A LOOK INSIDE ARKHAM. FOR FUTURE REFERENCE.
BUT THAT'LL HAVE TO WAIT.
TIME FOR SOME ASSERTIVE OUTREACH.
VRRRRMM VRRRRMM
C'MON, LET'S SEE WHAT IT CAN DO!

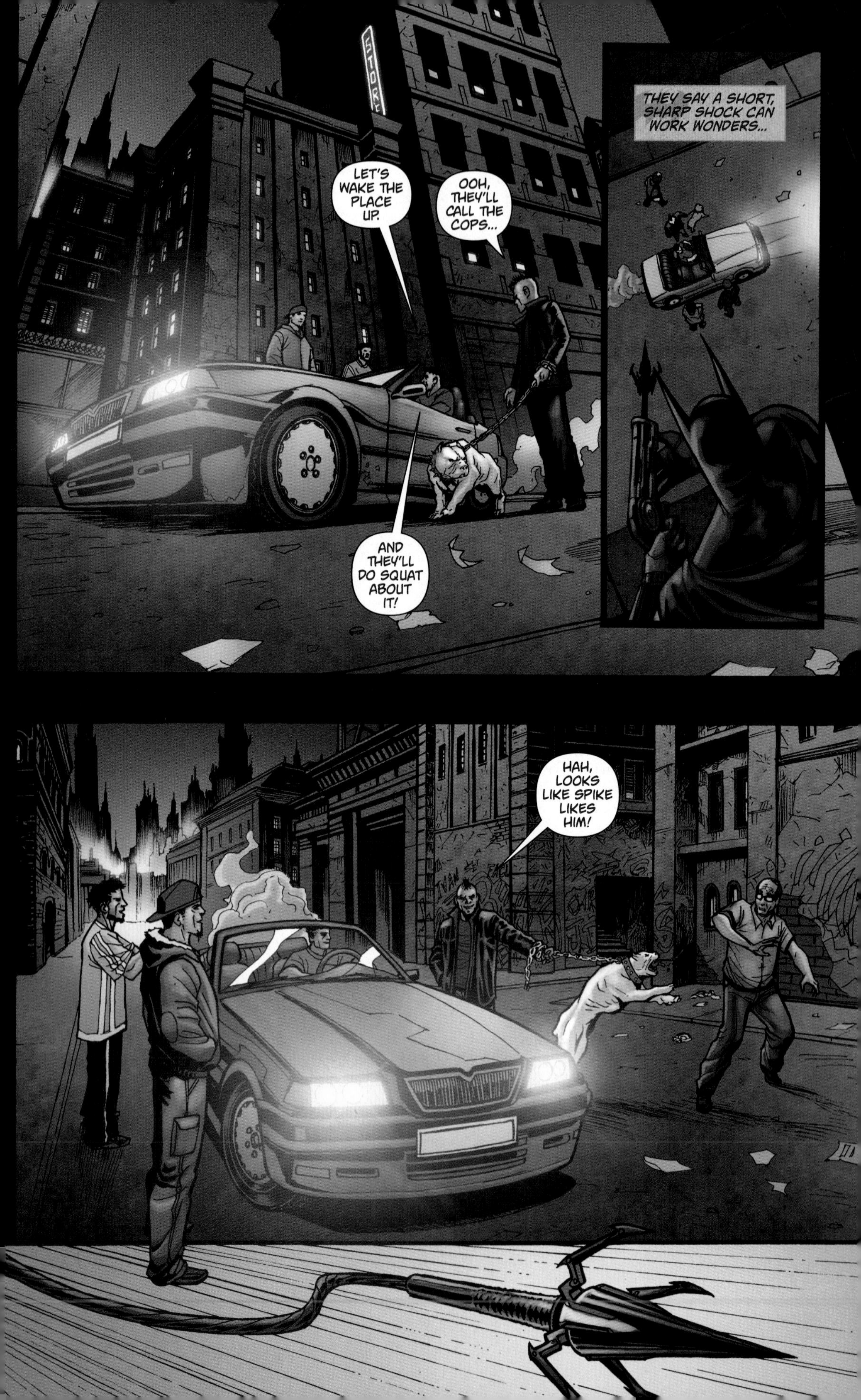
LET'S WAKE THE PLACE UP.
OOH, THEY'LL CALL THE COPS...
AND THEY'LL DO SQUAT ABOUT IT!
THEY SAY A SHORT, SHARP SHOCK CAN WORK WONDERS...
HAH, LOOKS LIKE SPIKE LIKES HIM!

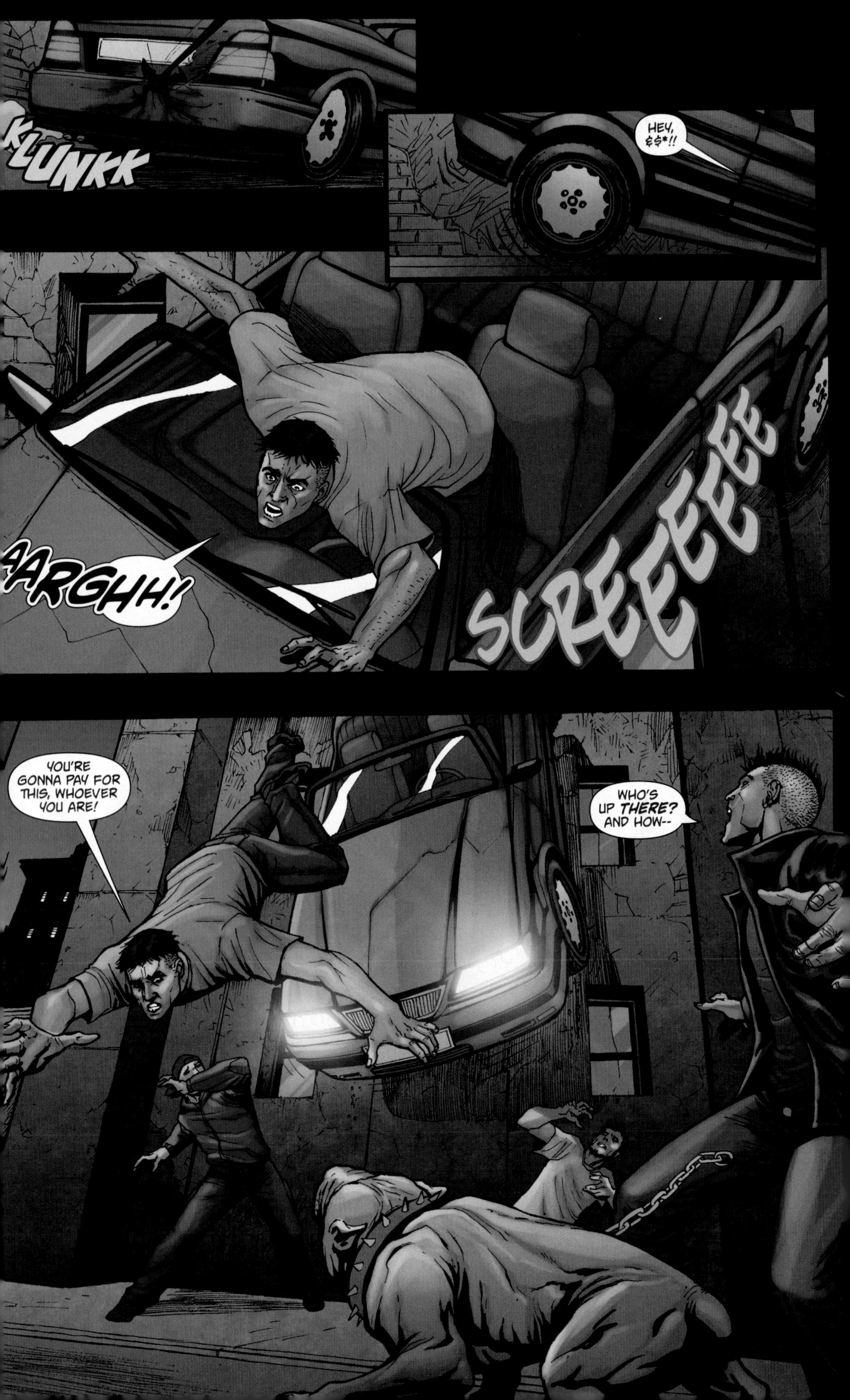
KLUNKK
HEY, $$*!!
AARGHH!
SCREEEEEEE
YOU'RE GONNA PAY FOR THIS, WHOEVER YOU ARE!
WHO'S UP THERE? AND HOW--

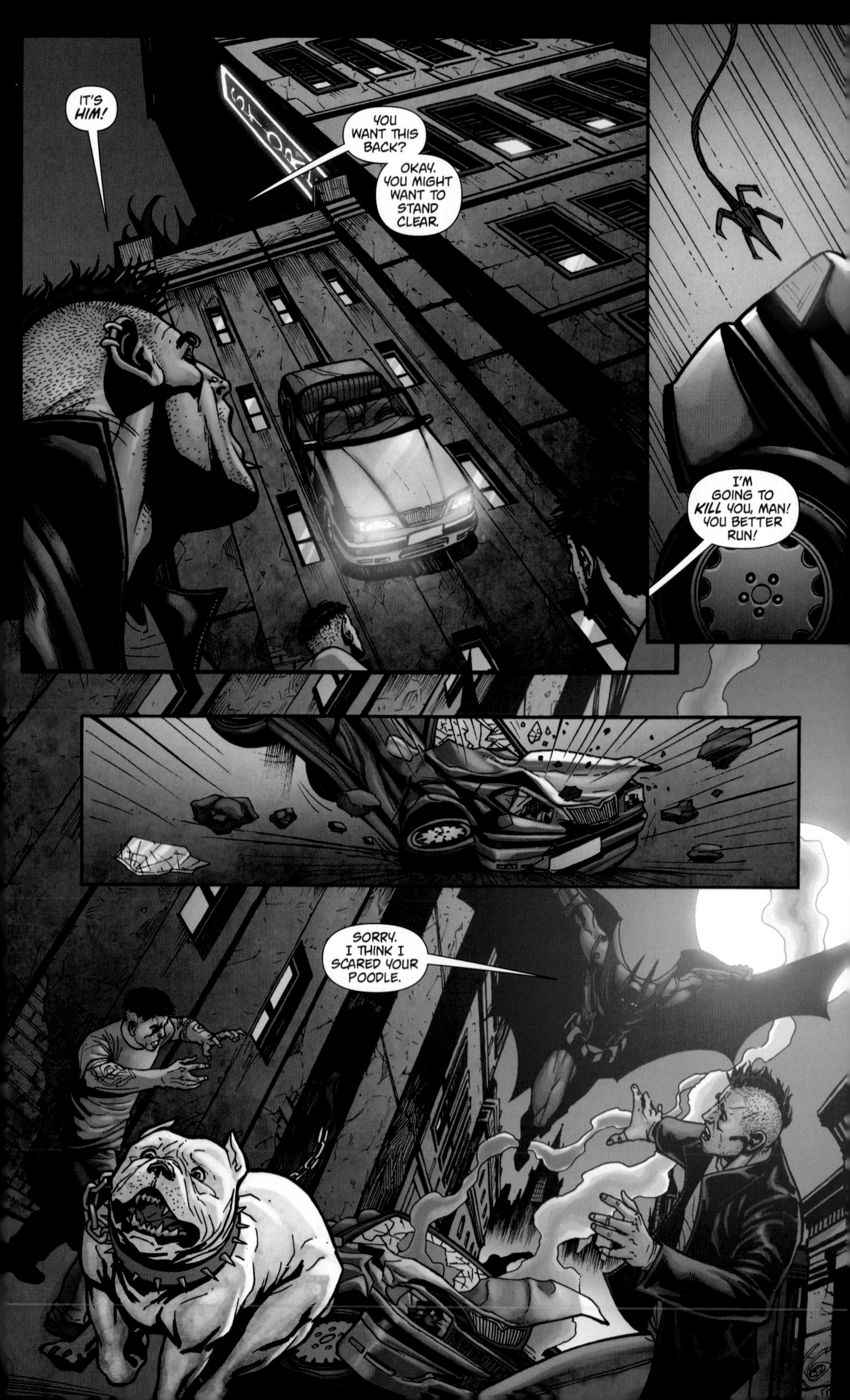
IT'S HIM!
YOU WANT THIS BACK?
OKAY. YOU MIGHT WANT TO STAND CLEAR.
I'M GOING TO KILL YOU, MAN! YOU BETTER RUN!
SORRY. I THINK I SCARED YOUR POODLE.

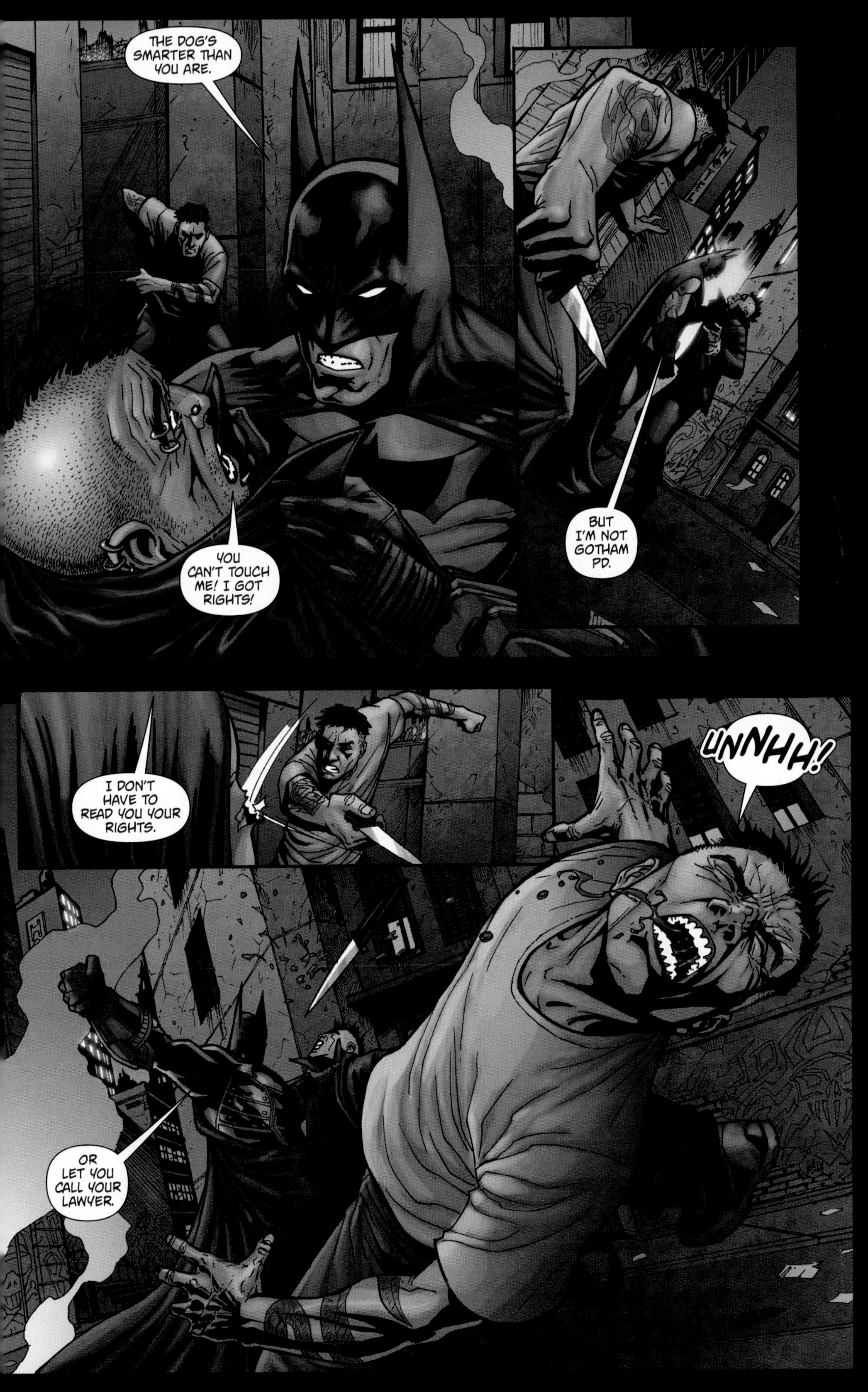
THE DOG'S SMARTER THAN YOU ARE.
YOU CAN'T TOUCH ME! I GOT RIGHTS!
BUT I'M NOT GOTHAM PD.
I DON'T HAVE TO READ YOU YOUR RIGHTS.
UNNHH!
OR LET YOU CALL YOUR LAWYER.

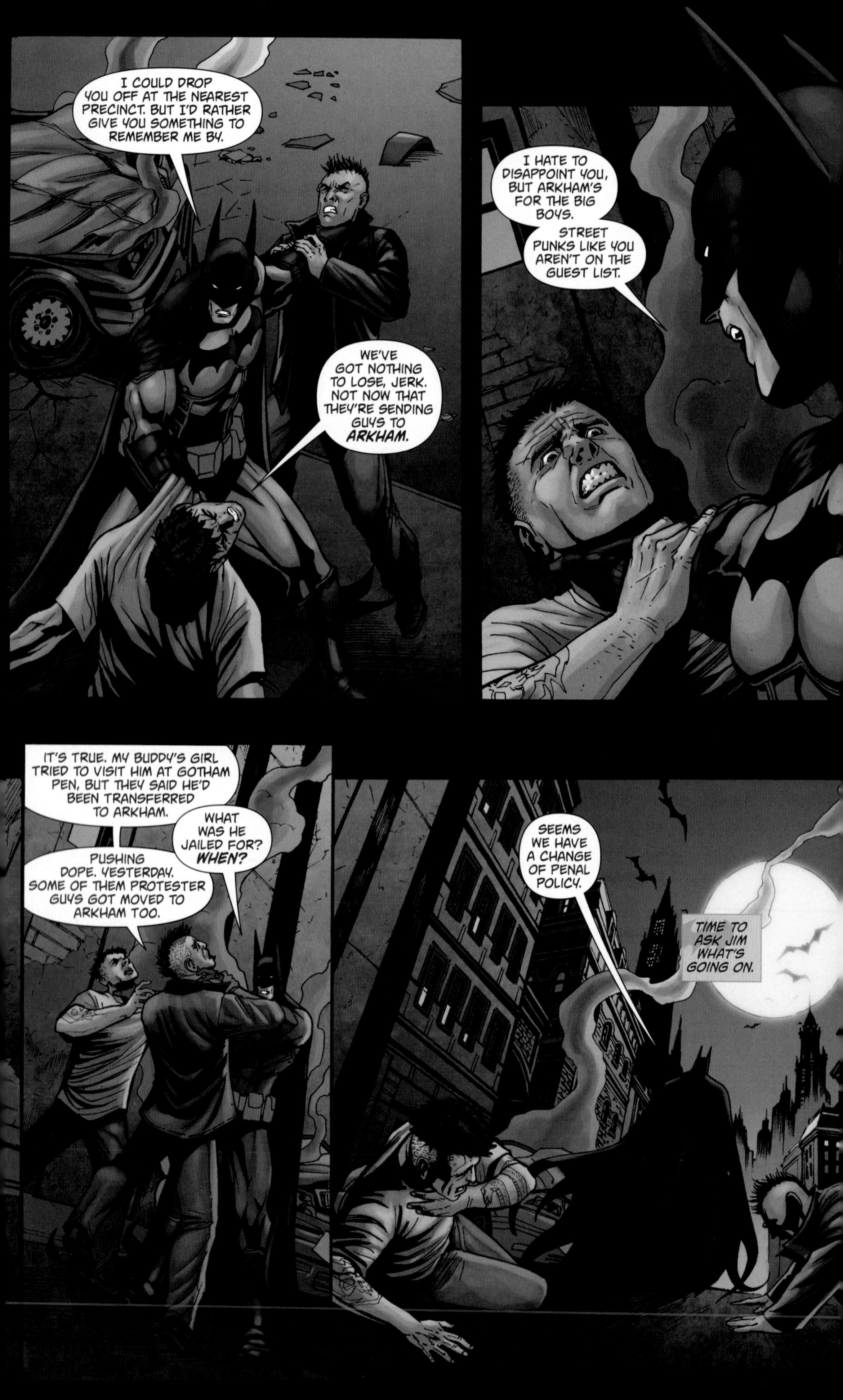

I COULD DROP YOU OFF AT THE NEAREST PRECINCT. BUT I'D RATHER GIVE YOU SOMETHING TO REMEMBER ME BY.
WE'VE GOT NOTHING TO LOSE, JERK. NOT NOW THAT THEY'RE SENDING GUYS TO ARKHAM.
I HATE TO DISAPPOINT YOU, BUT ARKHAM'S FOR THE BIG BOYS.
STREET PUNKS LIKE YOU AREN'T ON THE GUEST LIST.
IT'S TRUE. MY BUDDY'S GIRL TRIED TO VISIT HIM AT GOTHAM PEN, BUT THEY SAID HE'D BEEN TRANSFERRED TO ARKHAM.
WHAT WAS HE JAILED FOR? WHEN?
PUSHING DOPE. YESTERDAY. SOME OF THEM PROTESTER GUYS GOT MOVED TO ARKHAM TOO.
SEEMS WE HAVE A CHANGE OF PENAL POLICY.
TIME TO ASK JIM WHAT'S GOING ON.

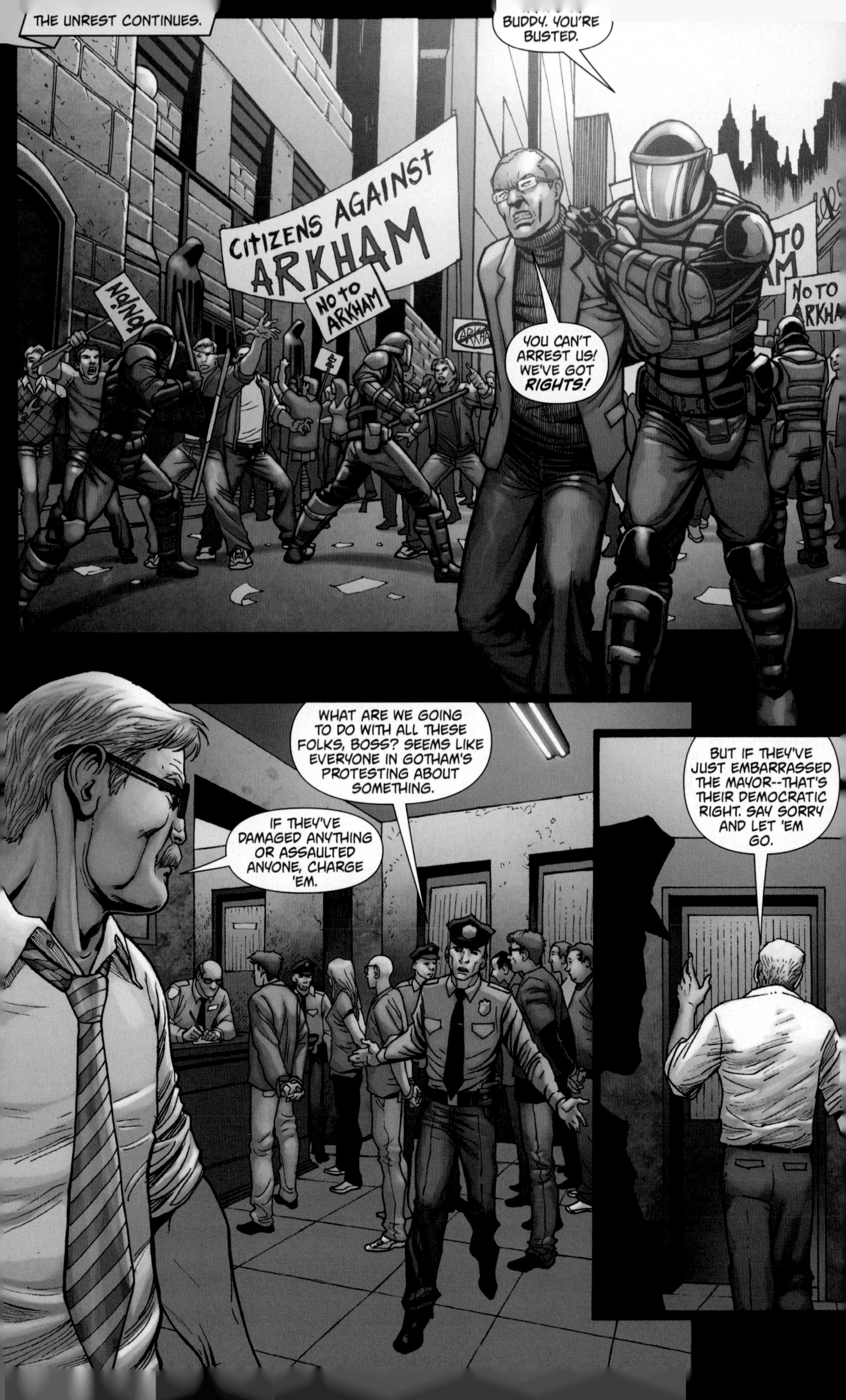

THE UNREST CONTINUES.
BUDDY. YOU'RE BUSTED.
CITIZENS AGAINST ARKHAM
NO TO ARKHAM
YOU CAN'T ARREST US! WE'VE GOT RIGHTS!
WHAT ARE WE GOING TO DO WITH ALL THESE FOLKS, BOSS? SEEMS LIKE EVERYONE IN GOTHAM'S PROTESTING ABOUT SOMETHING.
IF THEY'VE DAMAGED ANYTHING OR ASSAULTED ANYONE, CHARGE 'EM.
BUT IF THEY'VE JUST EMBARRASSED THE MAYOR--THAT'S THEIR DEMOCRATIC RIGHT. SAY SORRY AND LET 'EM GO.

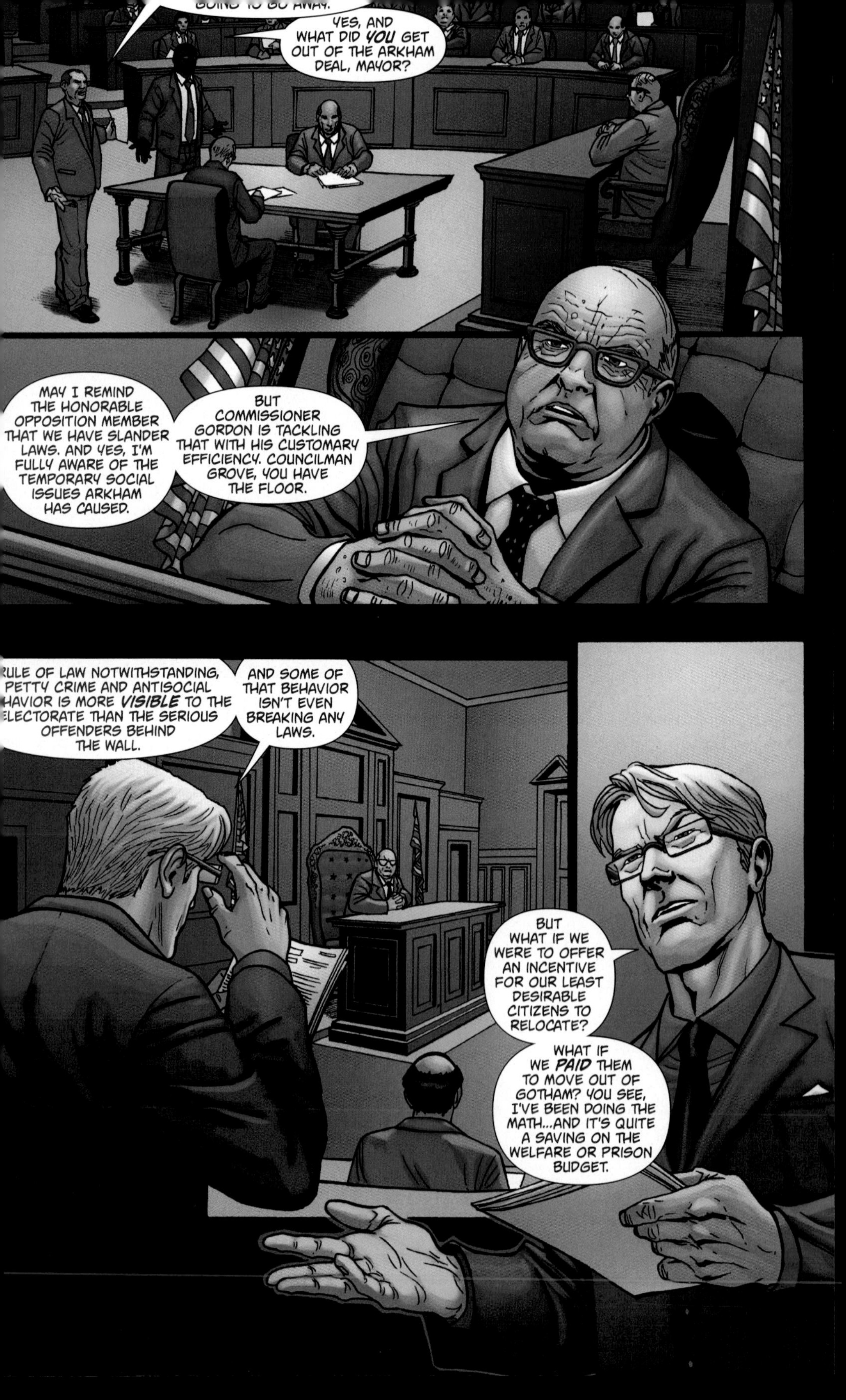
YES, AND WHAT DID YOU GET OUT OF THE ARKHAM DEAL, MAYOR?
MAY I REMIND THE HONORABLE OPPOSITION MEMBER THAT WE HAVE SLANDER LAWS. AND YES, I'M FULLY AWARE OF THE TEMPORARY SOCIAL ISSUES ARKHAM HAS CAUSED.
BUT COMMISSIONER GORDON IS TACKLING THAT WITH HIS CUSTOMARY EFFICIENCY. COUNCILMAN GROVE, YOU HAVE THE FLOOR.
ULE OF LAW NOTWITHSTANDING, PETTY CRIME AND ANTISOCIAL HAVIOR IS MORE VISIBLE TO THE LECTORATE THAN THE SERIOUS OFFENDERS BEHIND THE WALL.
AND SOME OF THAT BEHAVIOR ISN'T EVEN BREAKING ANY LAWS.
BUT WHAT IF WE WERE TO OFFER AN INCENTIVE FOR OUR LEAST DESIRABLE CITIZENS TO RELOCATE?
WHAT IF WE PAID THEM TO MOVE OUT OF GOTHAM? YOU SEE, I'VE BEEN DOING THE MATH...AND IT'S QUITE A SAVING ON THE WELFARE OR PRISON BUDGET.

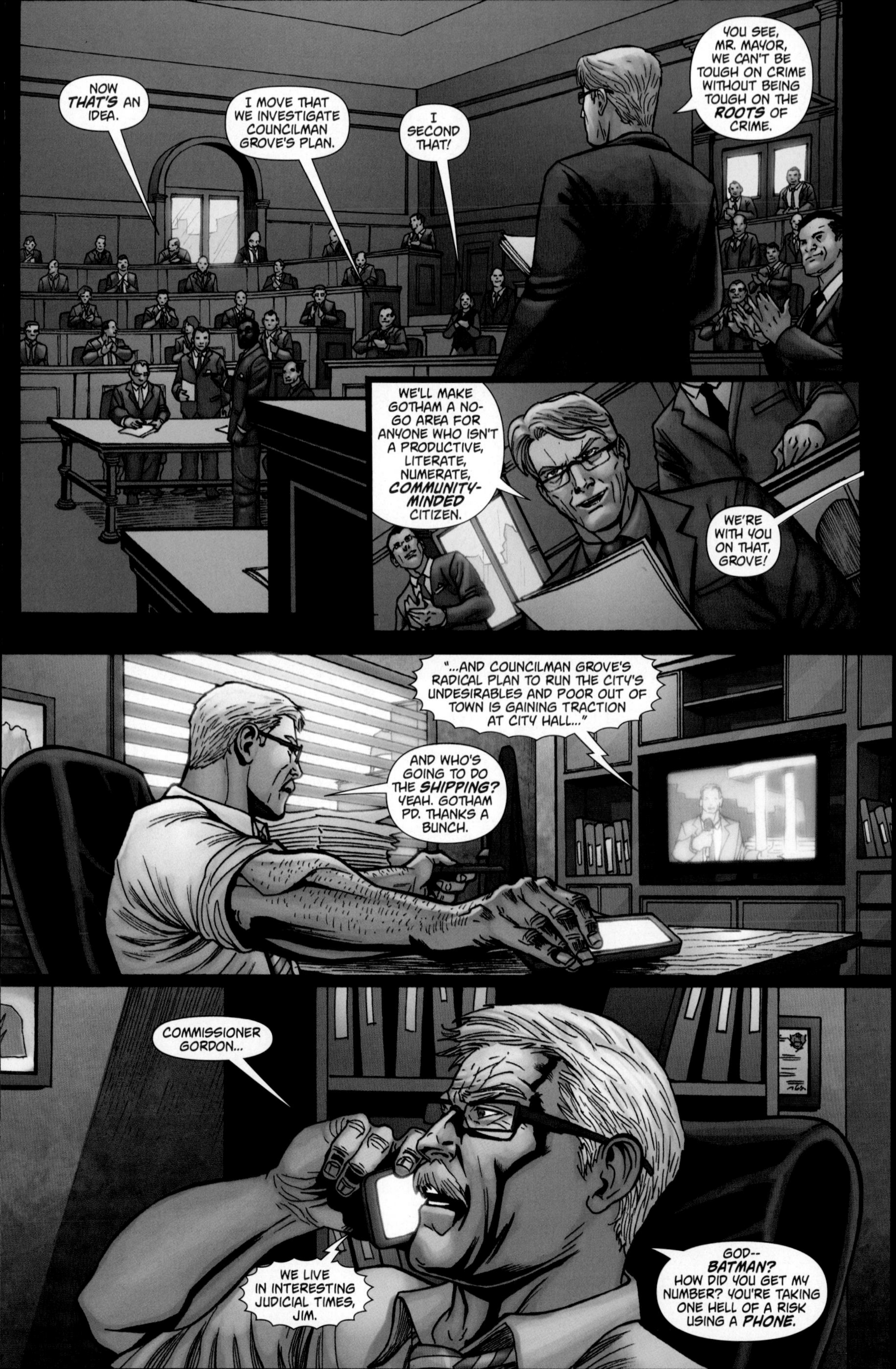
NOW THAT'S AN IDEA.
I MOVE THAT WE INVESTIGATE COUNCILMAN GROVE'S PLAN.
I SECOND THAT!
YOU SEE, MR. MAYOR, WE CAN'T BE TOUGH ON CRIME WITHOUT BEING TOUGH ON THE ROOTS OF CRIME.
WE'LL MAKE GOTHAM A NO-GO AREA FOR ANYONE WHO ISN'T A PRODUCTIVE, LITERATE, NUMERATE, COMMUNITY-MINDED CITIZEN.
WE'RE WITH YOU ON THAT, GROVE!
"...AND COUNCILMAN GROVE'S RADICAL PLAN TO RUN THE CITY'S UNDESIRABLES AND POOR OUT OF TOWN IS GAINING TRACTION AT CITY HALL..."
AND WHO'S GOING TO DO THE SHIPPING? YEAH. GOTHAM PD. THANKS A BUNCH.
COMMISSIONER GORDON...
WE LIVE IN INTERESTING JUDICIAL TIMES, JIM.
GOD-- BATMAN? HOW DID YOU GET MY NUMBER? YOU'RE TAKING ONE HELL OF A RISK USING A PHONE.

THE BATCAVE.

DON'T WORRY. THIS IS UNTRACEABLE. YOU CAN'T DISAPPEAR TO THE ROOF SO OFTEN NOW THAT YOU'VE QUIT SMOKING.

SO, JIM... TELL ME WHY PROTESTERS ARE GETTING CONVICTED AND SENTENCED TO ARKHAM.

AND SINCE WHEN DID HAVING A POLITICAL OPINION LAND YOU IN *JAIL*?

I DIDN'T DAMN WELL KNOW ABOUT *ARKHAM*. AND WE'RE NOT BOOKING PEOPLE JUST FOR PROTESTING.

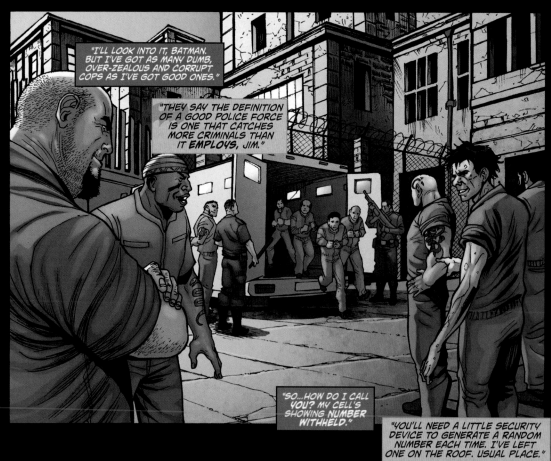

"I'LL LOOK INTO IT, BATMAN. BUT I'VE GOT AS MANY DUMB, OVER-ZEALOUS AND CORRUPT COPS AS I'VE GOT GOOD ONES."

"THEY SAY THE DEFINITION OF A GOOD POLICE FORCE IS ONE THAT CATCHES MORE CRIMINALS THAN IT *EMPLOYS*, JIM."

"SO...HOW DO I CALL *YOU*? MY CELL'S SHOWING *NUMBER WITHHELD*."

"YOU'LL NEED A LITTLE SECURITY DEVICE TO GENERATE A RANDOM NUMBER EACH TIME. I'VE LEFT ONE ON THE ROOF. USUAL PLACE."

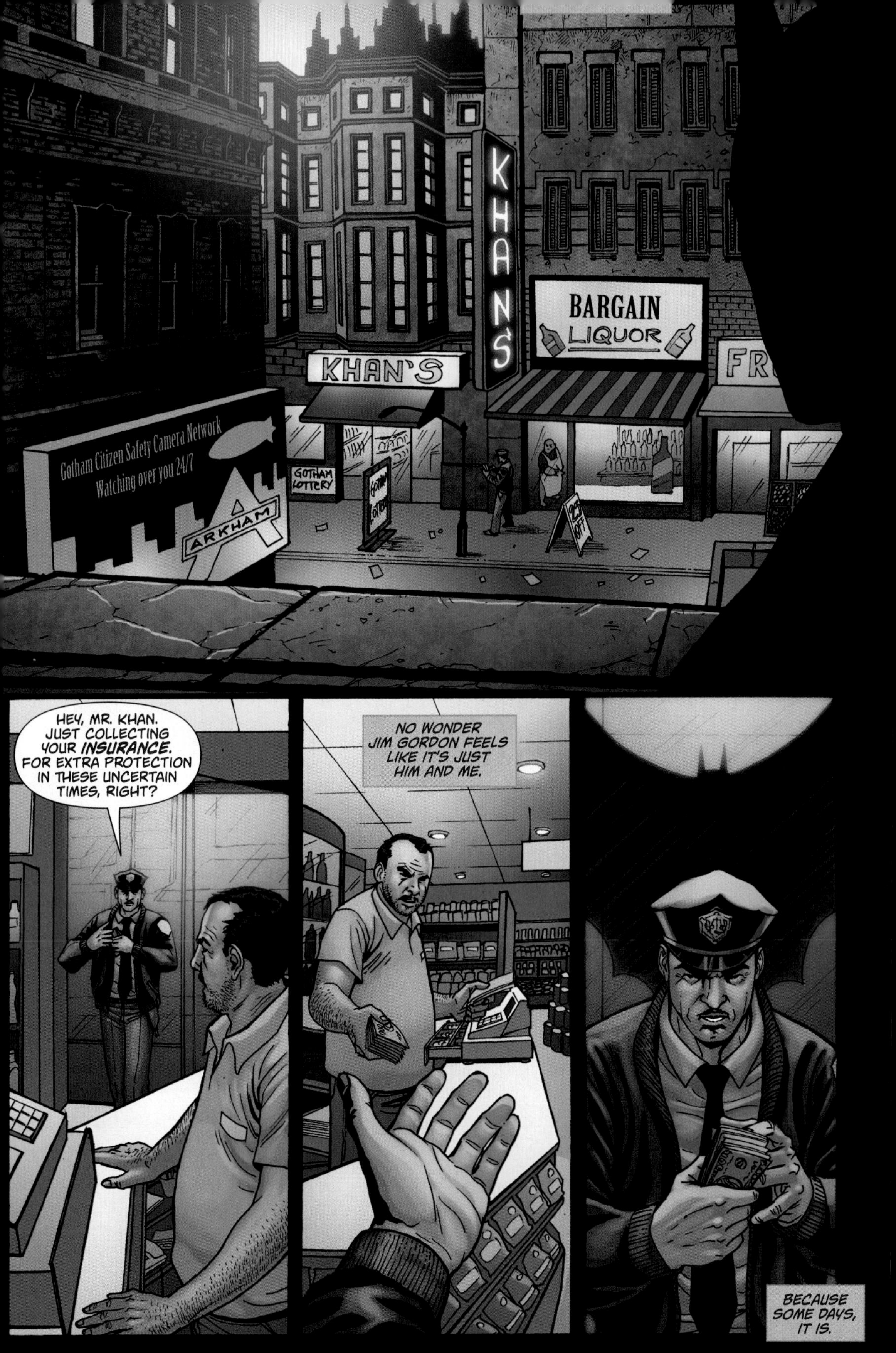
KHAN'S
BARGAIN
LIQUOR
KHAN'S
Gotham Citizen Safety Camera Network
Watching over you 24/7
ARKHAM
GOTHAM LOTTERY
HEY, MR. KHAN. JUST COLLECTING YOUR INSURANCE. FOR EXTRA PROTECTION IN THESE UNCERTAIN TIMES, RIGHT?
NO WONDER JIM GORDON FEELS LIKE IT'S JUST HIM AND ME.
BECAUSE SOME DAYS, IT IS.

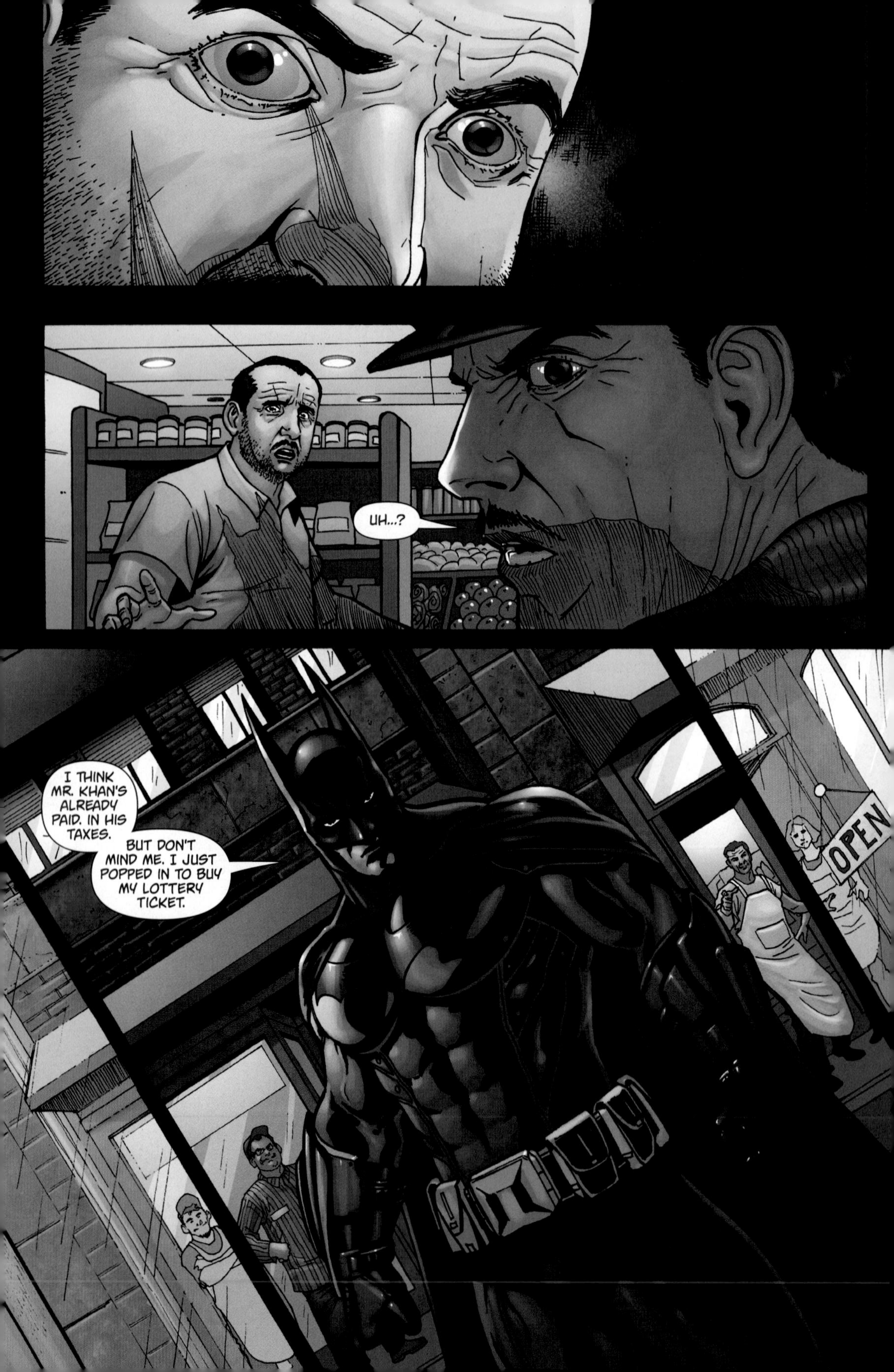
UH...?
I THINK MR. KHAN'S ALREADY PAID. IN HIS TAXES.
BUT DON'T MIND ME. I JUST POPPED IN TO BUY MY LOTTERY TICKET.

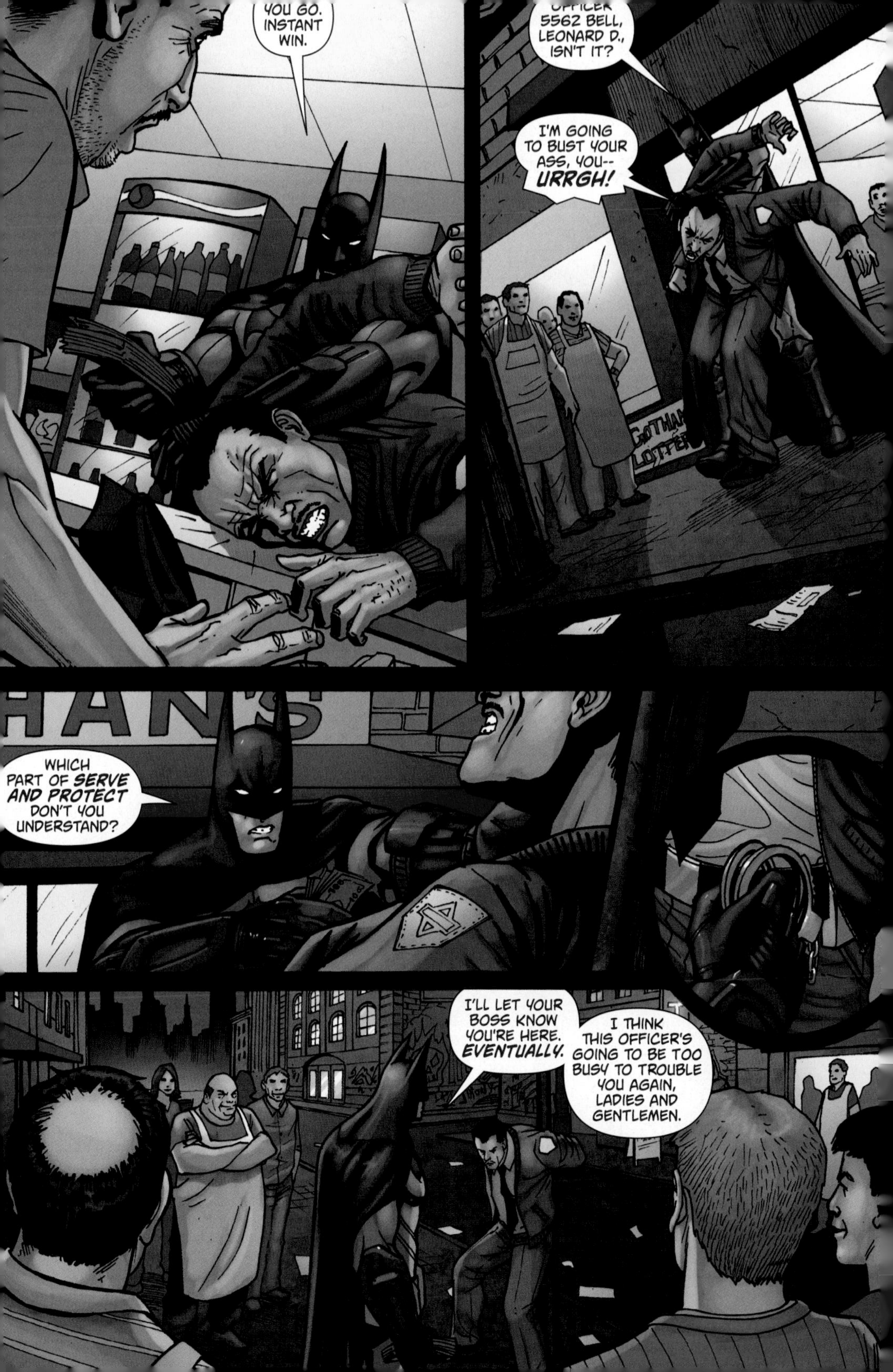

YOU GO. INSTANT WIN.
5562 BELL, LEONARD D., ISN'T IT?
I'M GOING TO BUST YOUR ASS, YOU-- **URRGH!**
WHICH PART OF ***SERVE AND PROTECT*** DON'T YOU UNDERSTAND?
I'LL LET YOUR BOSS KNOW YOU'RE HERE. ***EVENTUALLY.***
I THINK THIS OFFICER'S GOING TO BE TOO BUSY TO TROUBLE YOU AGAIN, LADIES AND GENTLEMEN.

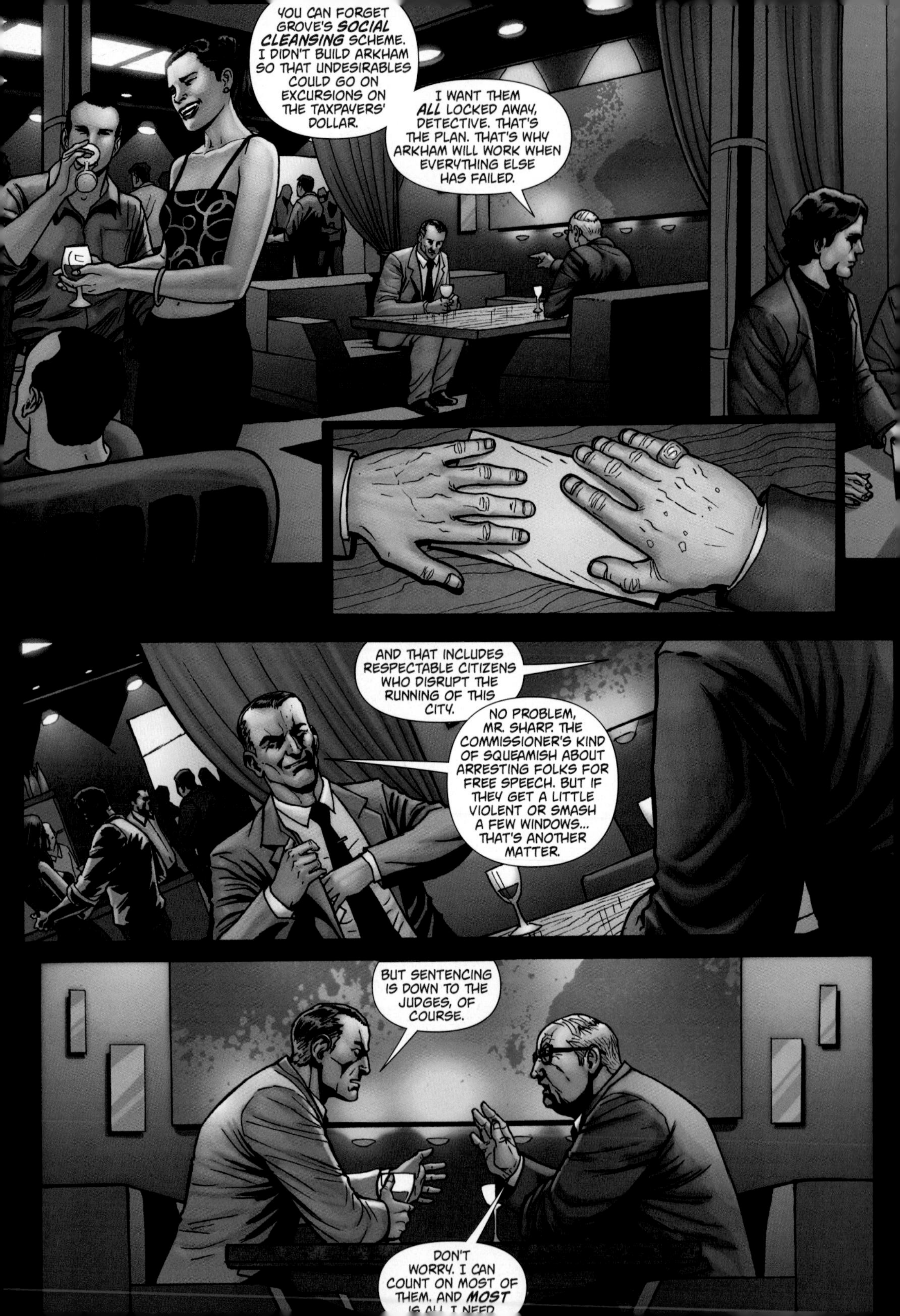
YOU CAN FORGET GROVE'S SOCIAL CLEANSING SCHEME. I DIDN'T BUILD ARKHAM SO THAT UNDESIRABLES COULD GO ON EXCURSIONS ON THE TAXPAYERS' DOLLAR.
I WANT THEM ALL LOCKED AWAY, DETECTIVE. THAT'S THE PLAN. THAT'S WHY ARKHAM WILL WORK WHEN EVERYTHING ELSE HAS FAILED.
AND THAT INCLUDES RESPECTABLE CITIZENS WHO DISRUPT THE RUNNING OF THIS CITY.
NO PROBLEM, MR. SHARP. THE COMMISSIONER'S KIND OF SQUEAMISH ABOUT ARRESTING FOLKS FOR FREE SPEECH. BUT IF THEY GET A LITTLE VIOLENT OR SMASH A FEW WINDOWS... THAT'S ANOTHER MATTER.
BUT SENTENCING IS DOWN TO THE JUDGES, OF COURSE.
DON'T WORRY. I CAN COUNT ON MOST OF THEM. AND MOST

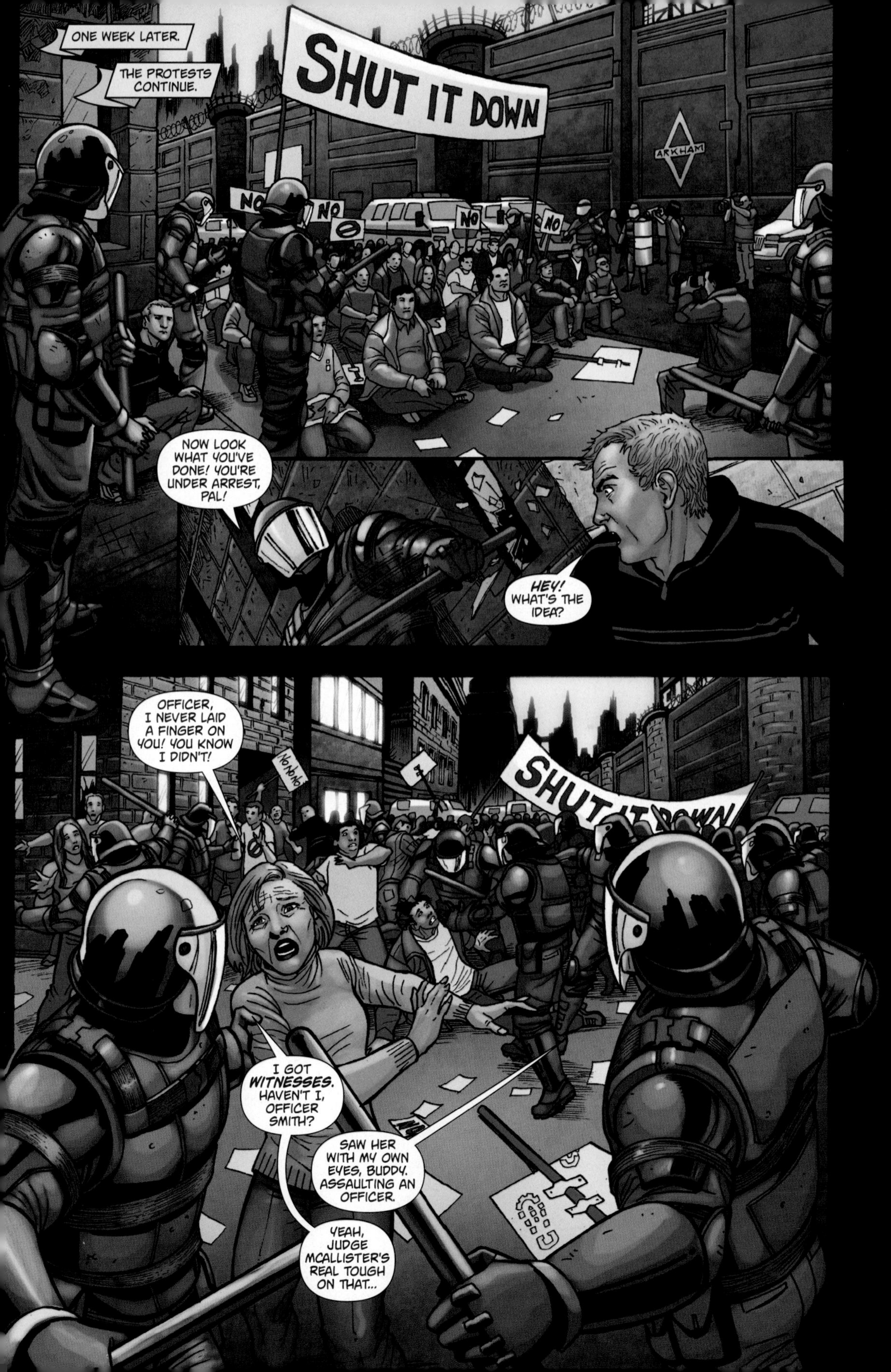
ONE WEEK LATER.
THE PROTESTS CONTINUE.
SHUT IT DOWN
ARKHAM
NO
NO
NO
NO
NO
NOW LOOK WHAT YOU'VE DONE! YOU'RE UNDER ARREST, PAL!
HEY! WHAT'S THE IDEA?
OFFICER, I NEVER LAID A FINGER ON YOU! YOU KNOW I DIDN'T!
SHUT IT DOWN
I GOT WITNESSES. HAVEN'T I, OFFICER SMITH?
SAW HER WITH MY OWN EYES, BUDDY. ASSAULTING AN OFFICER.
YEAH, JUDGE MCALLISTER'S REAL TOUGH ON THAT...

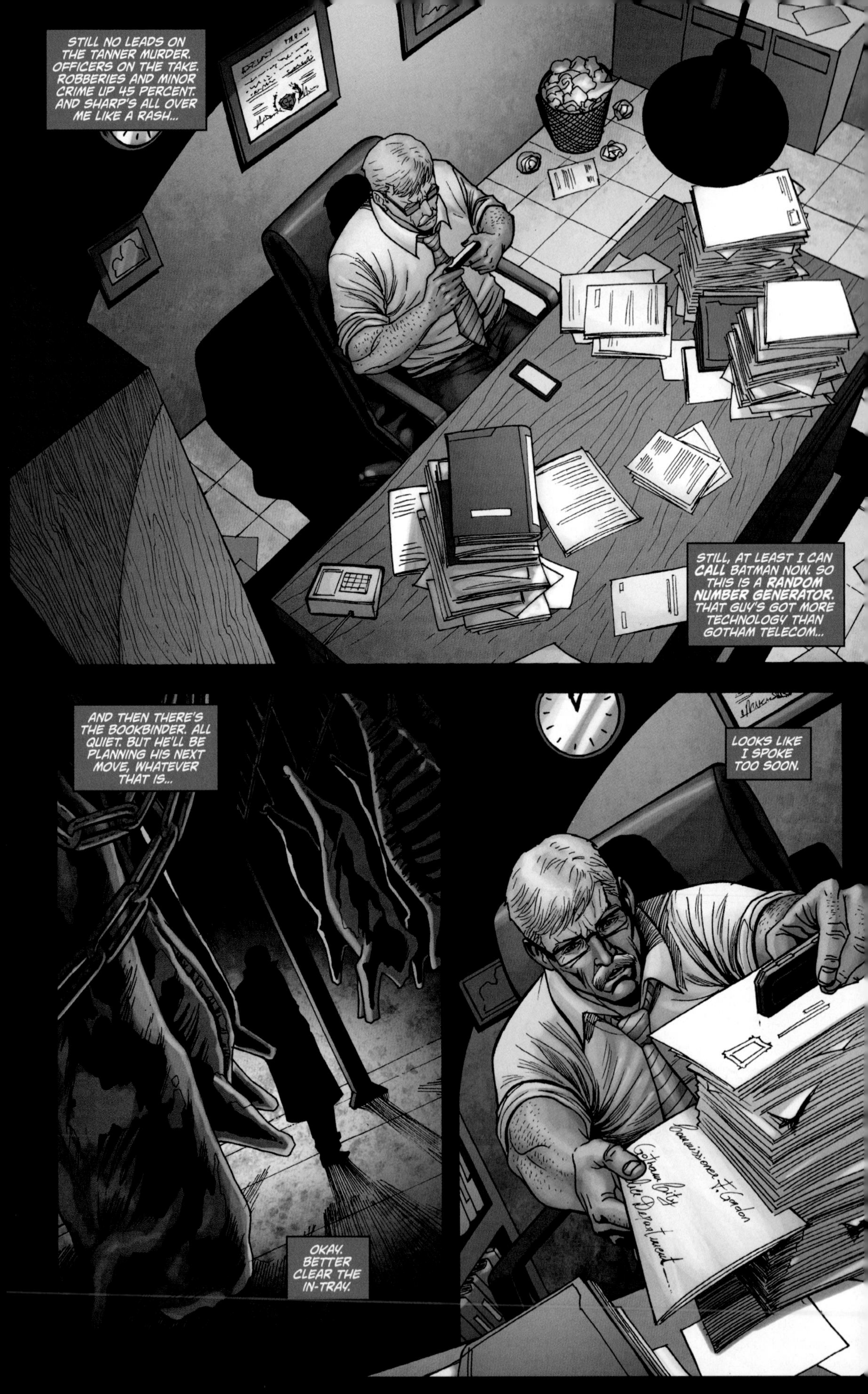

STILL NO LEADS ON THE TANNER MURDER. OFFICERS ON THE TAKE. ROBBERIES AND MINOR CRIME UP 45 PERCENT. AND SHARP'S ALL OVER ME LIKE A RASH...
STILL, AT LEAST I CAN CALL BATMAN NOW. SO THIS IS A RANDOM NUMBER GENERATOR. THAT GUY'S GOT MORE TECHNOLOGY THAN GOTHAM TELECOM...
AND THEN THERE'S THE BOOKBINDER, ALL QUIET. BUT HE'LL BE PLANNING HIS NEXT MOVE, WHATEVER THAT IS...
OKAY. BETTER CLEAR THE IN-TRAY.
LOOKS LIKE I SPOKE TOO SOON.
Commissioner J. Gordon
Gotham City

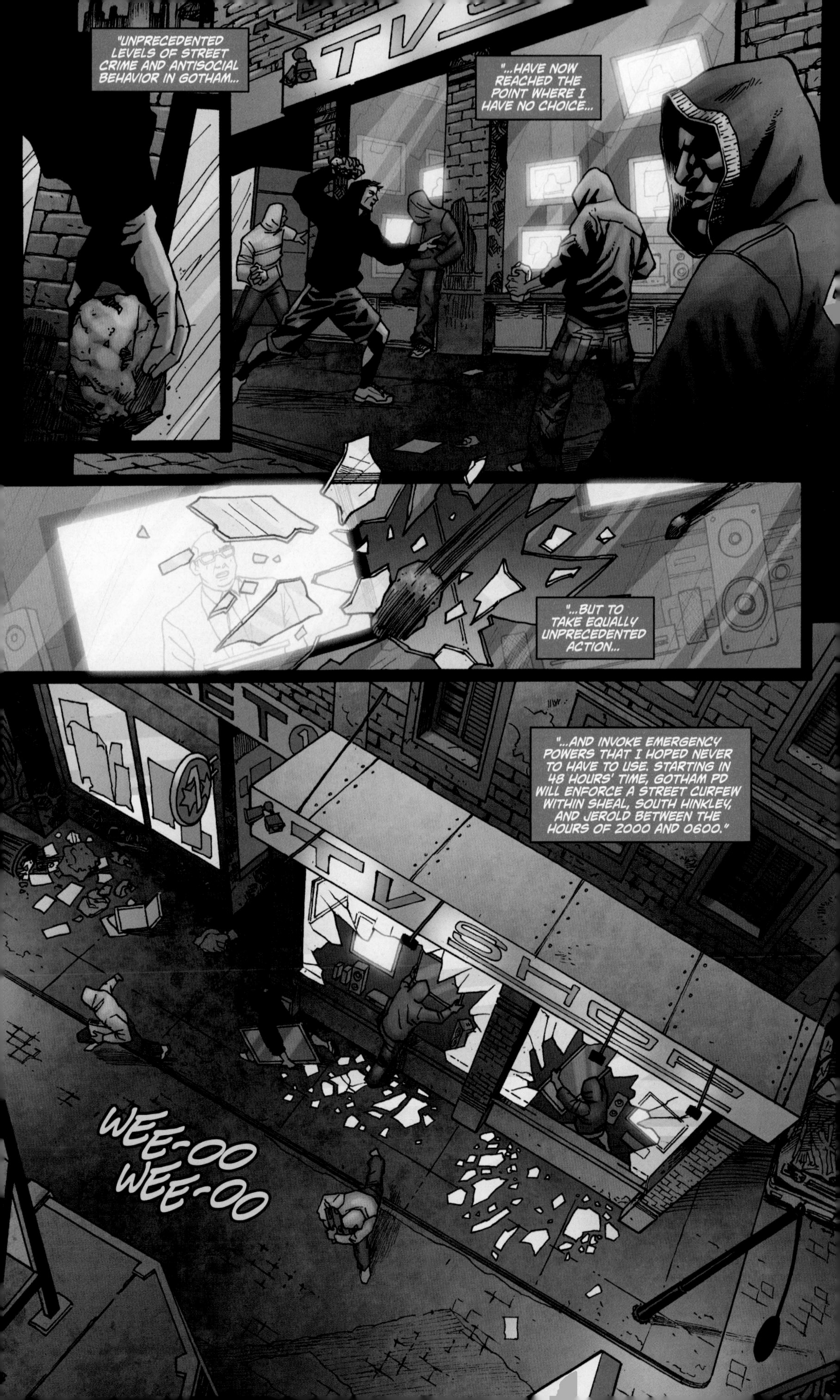
"UNPRECEDENTED LEVELS OF STREET CRIME AND ANTISOCIAL BEHAVIOR IN GOTHAM...
"...HAVE NOW REACHED THE POINT WHERE I HAVE NO CHOICE...
"...BUT TO TAKE EQUALLY UNPRECEDENTED ACTION...
"...AND INVOKE EMERGENCY POWERS THAT I HOPED NEVER TO HAVE TO USE. STARTING IN 48 HOURS' TIME, GOTHAM PD WILL ENFORCE A STREET CURFEW WITHIN SHEAL, SOUTH HINKLEY, AND JEROLD BETWEEN THE HOURS OF 2000 AND 0600."
WEE-OO WEE-OO

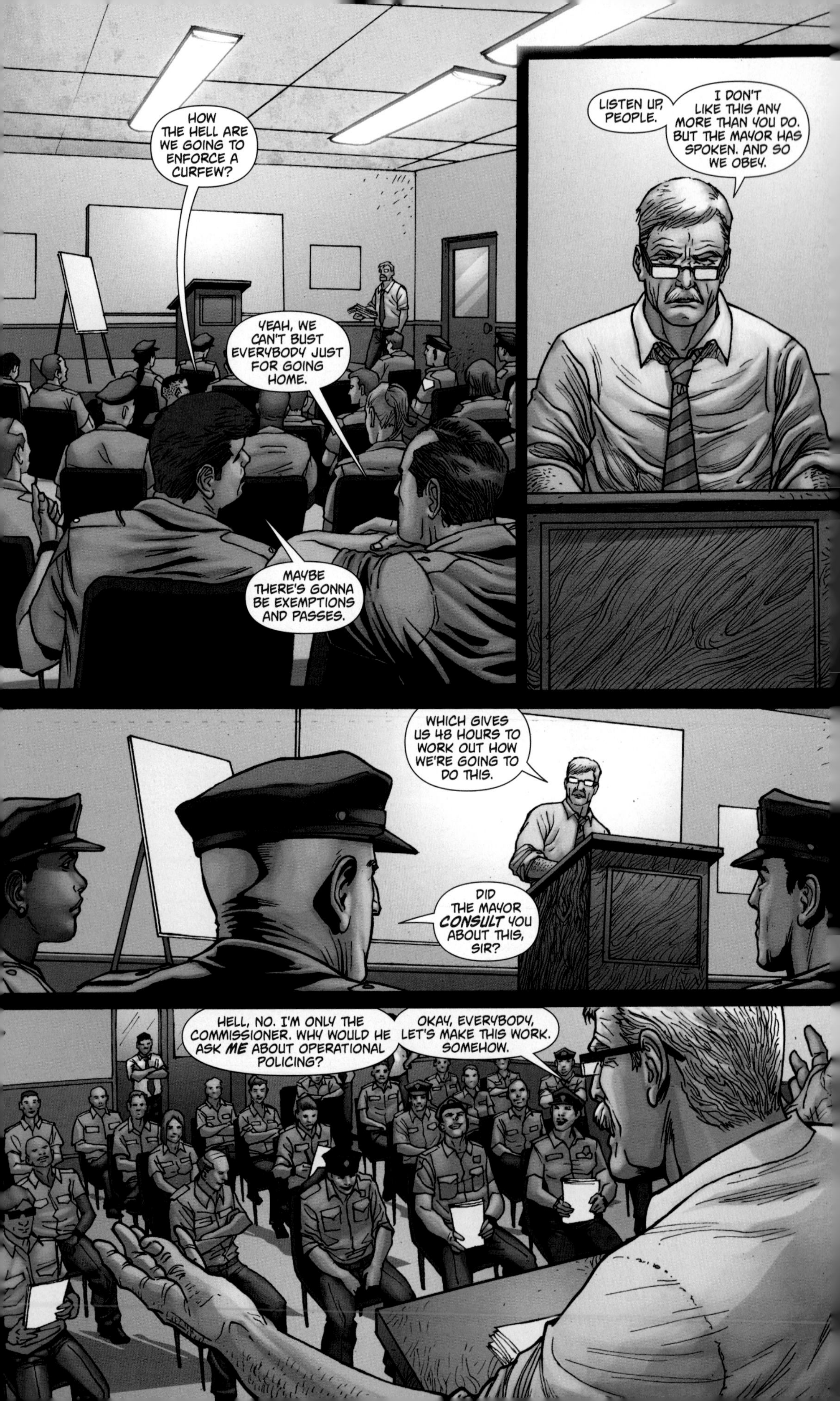
HOW THE HELL ARE WE GOING TO ENFORCE A CURFEW?
YEAH, WE CAN'T BUST EVERYBODY JUST FOR GOING HOME.
MAYBE THERE'S GONNA BE EXEMPTIONS AND PASSES.
LISTEN UP, PEOPLE.
I DON'T LIKE THIS ANY MORE THAN YOU DO. BUT THE MAYOR HAS SPOKEN. AND SO WE OBEY.
WHICH GIVES US 48 HOURS TO WORK OUT HOW WE'RE GOING TO DO THIS.
DID THE MAYOR CONSULT YOU ABOUT THIS, SIR?
HELL, NO. I'M ONLY THE COMMISSIONER. WHY WOULD HE ASK ME ABOUT OPERATIONAL POLICING?
OKAY, EVERYBODY, LET'S MAKE THIS WORK. SOMEHOW.

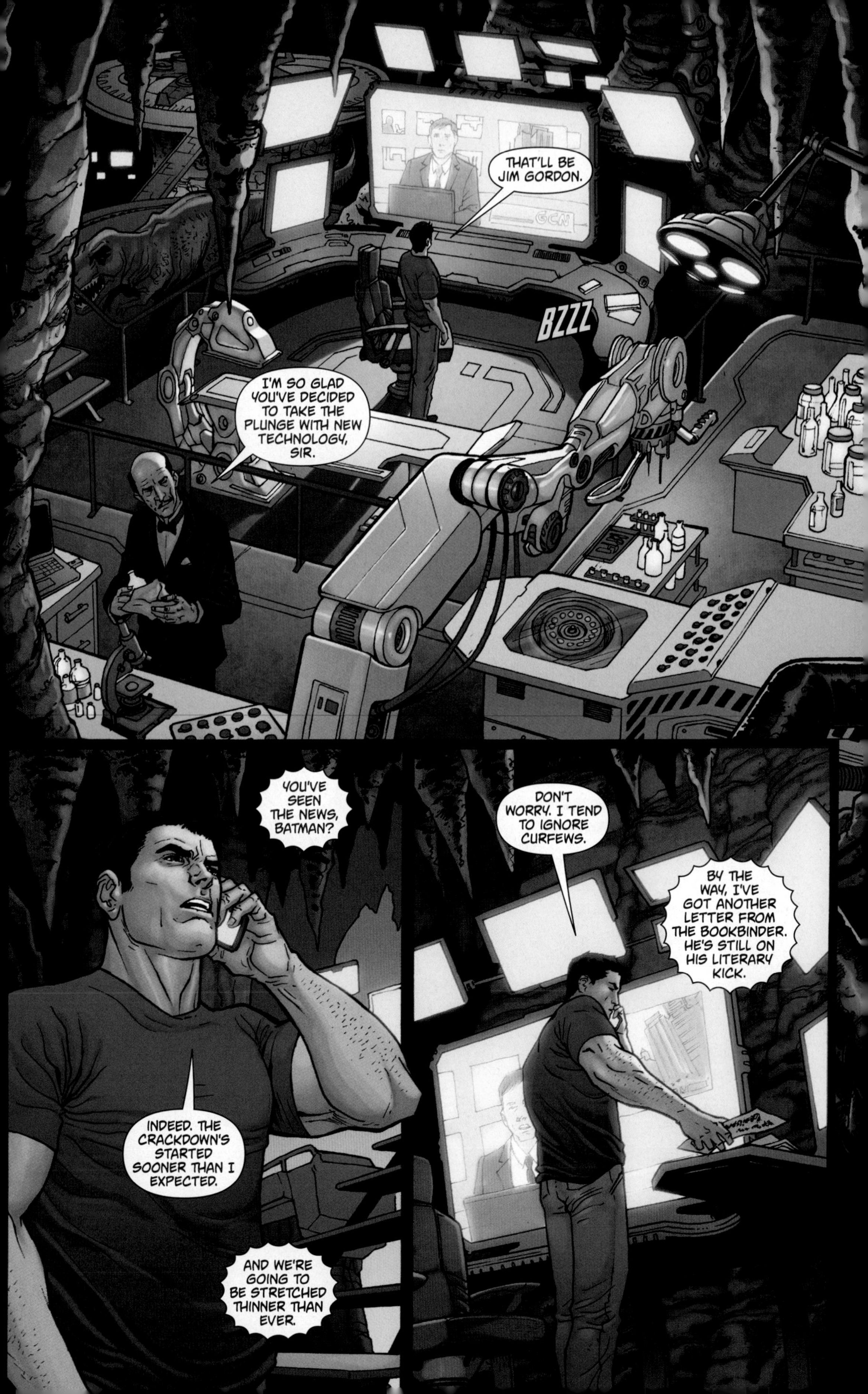
GCN
THAT'LL BE JIM GORDON.
BZZZ
I'M SO GLAD YOU'VE DECIDED TO TAKE THE PLUNGE WITH NEW TECHNOLOGY, SIR.
YOU'VE SEEN THE NEWS, BATMAN?
INDEED. THE CRACKDOWN'S STARTED SOONER THAN I EXPECTED.
AND WE'RE GOING TO BE STRETCHED THINNER THAN EVER.
DON'T WORRY. I TEND TO IGNORE CURFEWS.
BY THE WAY, I'VE GOT ANOTHER LETTER FROM THE BOOKBINDER. HE'S STILL ON HIS LITERARY KICK.

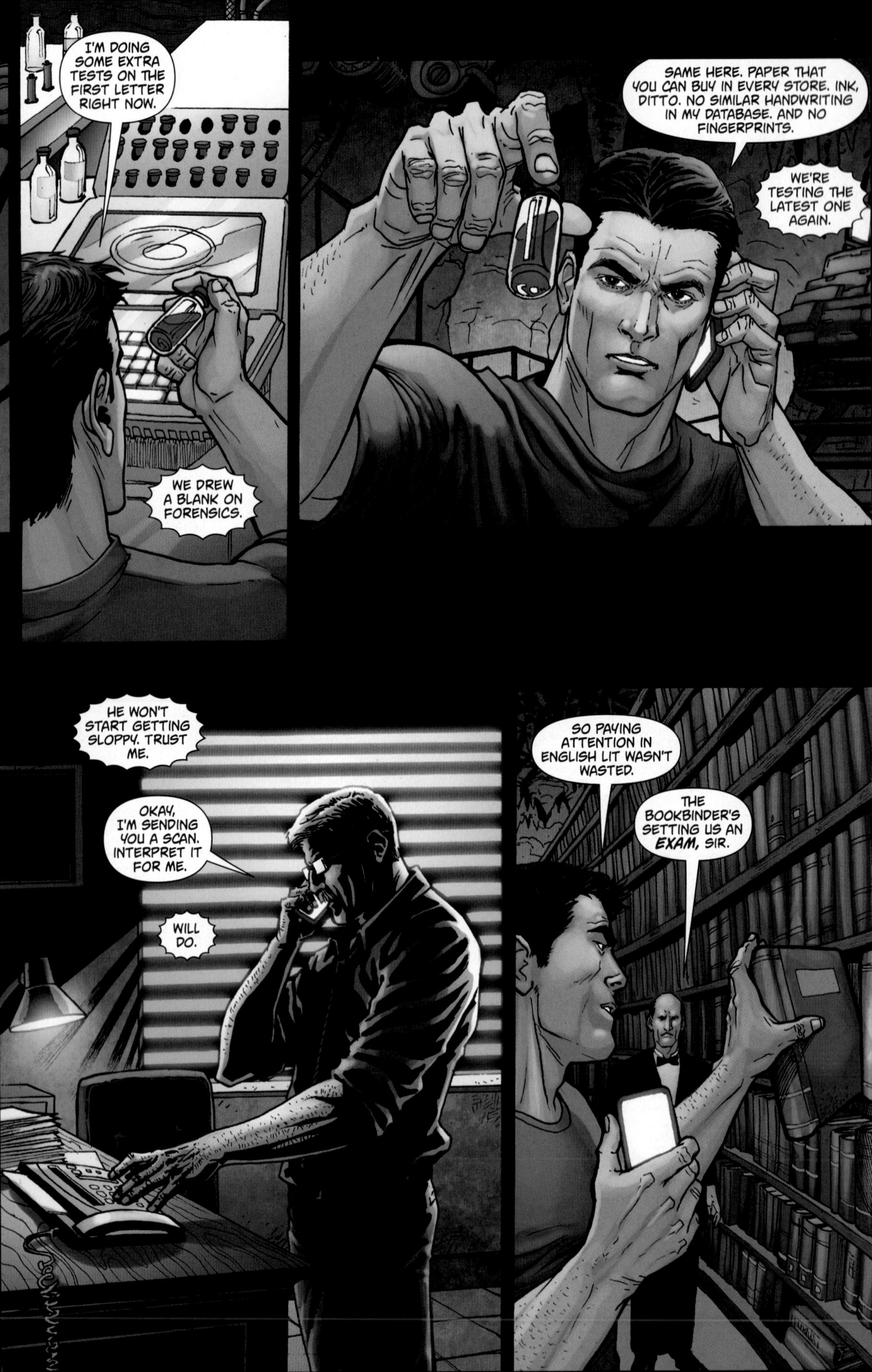
I'M DOING SOME EXTRA TESTS ON THE FIRST LETTER RIGHT NOW.
WE DREW A BLANK ON FORENSICS.
SAME HERE. PAPER THAT YOU CAN BUY IN EVERY STORE. INK, DITTO. NO SIMILAR HANDWRITING IN MY DATABASE. AND NO FINGERPRINTS.
WE'RE TESTING THE LATEST ONE AGAIN.
HE WON'T START GETTING SLOPPY. TRUST ME.
OKAY, I'M SENDING YOU A SCAN. INTERPRET IT FOR ME.
WILL DO.
SO PAYING ATTENTION IN ENGLISH LIT WASN'T WASTED.
THE BOOKBINDER'S SETTING US AN EXAM, SIR.

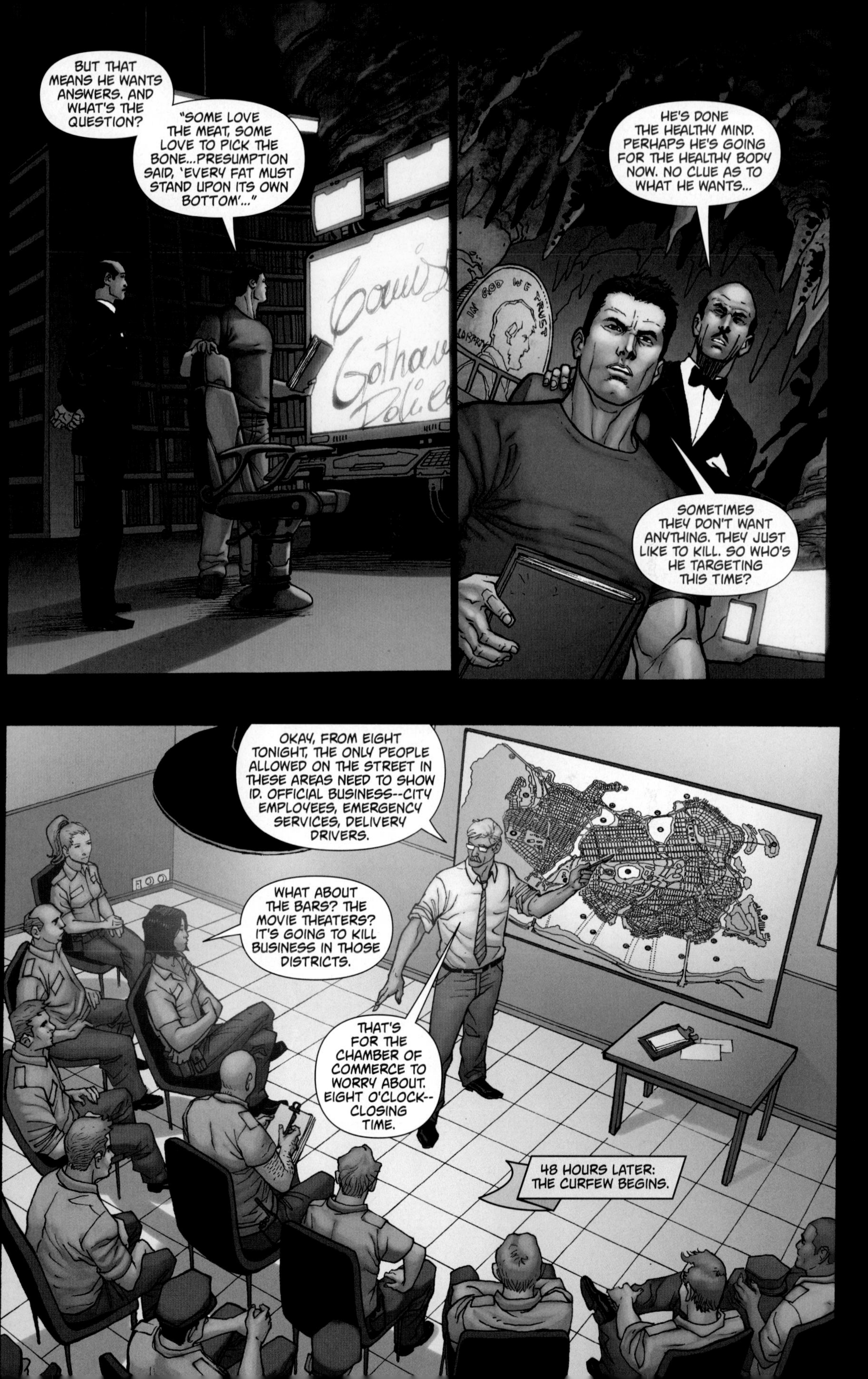
BUT THAT MEANS HE WANTS ANSWERS. AND WHAT'S THE QUESTION?
"SOME LOVE THE MEAT, SOME LOVE TO PICK THE BONE...PRESUMPTION SAID, 'EVERY FAT MUST STAND UPON ITS OWN BOTTOM'..."
HE'S DONE THE HEALTHY MIND. PERHAPS HE'S GOING FOR THE HEALTHY BODY NOW. NO CLUE AS TO WHAT HE WANTS...
SOMETIMES THEY DON'T WANT ANYTHING. THEY JUST LIKE TO KILL. SO WHO'S HE TARGETING THIS TIME?
OKAY, FROM EIGHT TONIGHT, THE ONLY PEOPLE ALLOWED ON THE STREET IN THESE AREAS NEED TO SHOW ID. OFFICIAL BUSINESS--CITY EMPLOYEES, EMERGENCY SERVICES, DELIVERY DRIVERS.
WHAT ABOUT THE BARS? THE MOVIE THEATERS? IT'S GOING TO KILL BUSINESS IN THOSE DISTRICTS.
THAT'S FOR THE CHAMBER OF COMMERCE TO WORRY ABOUT. EIGHT O'CLOCK--CLOSING TIME.
48 HOURS LATER: THE CURFEW BEGINS.

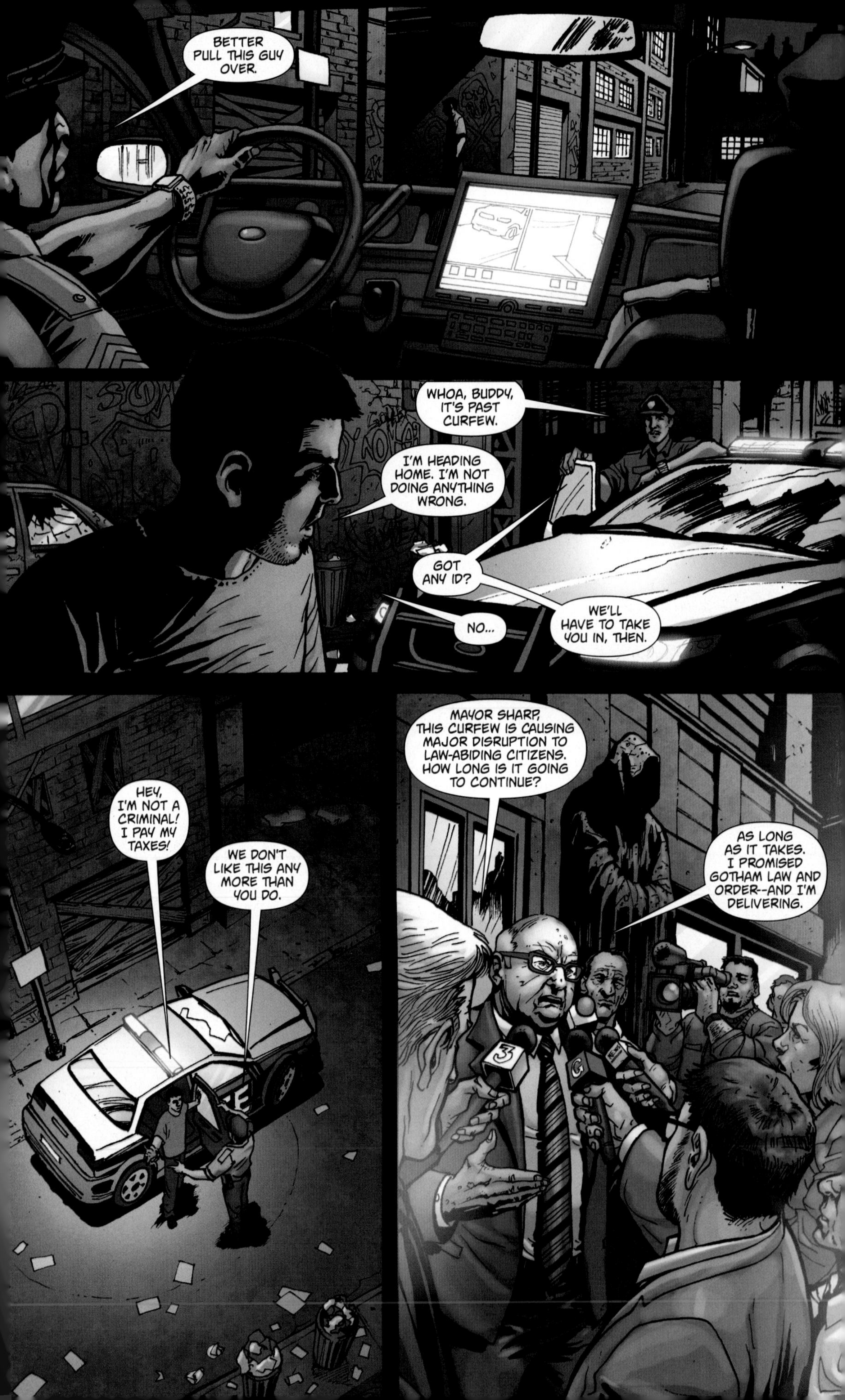
BETTER PULL THIS GUY OVER.
WHOA, BUDDY, IT'S PAST CURFEW.
I'M HEADING HOME. I'M NOT DOING ANYTHING WRONG.
GOT ANY ID?
NO...
WE'LL HAVE TO TAKE YOU IN, THEN.
HEY, I'M NOT A CRIMINAL! I PAY MY TAXES!
WE DON'T LIKE THIS ANY MORE THAN YOU DO.
MAYOR SHARP, THIS CURFEW IS CAUSING MAJOR DISRUPTION TO LAW-ABIDING CITIZENS. HOW LONG IS IT GOING TO CONTINUE?
AS LONG AS IT TAKES. I PROMISED GOTHAM LAW AND ORDER--AND I'M DELIVERING.

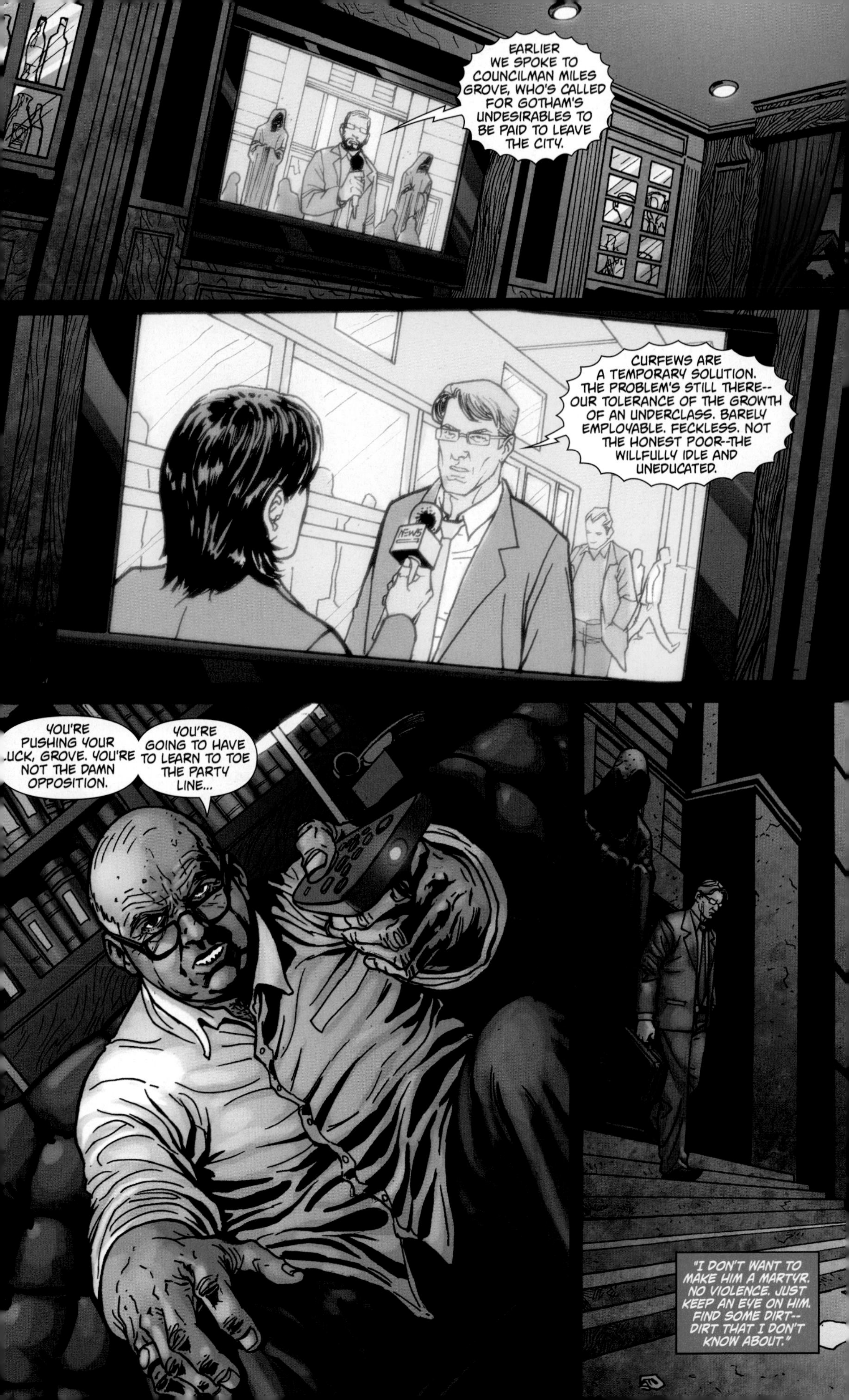
EARLIER WE SPOKE TO COUNCILMAN MILES GROVE, WHO'S CALLED FOR GOTHAM'S UNDESIRABLES TO BE PAID TO LEAVE THE CITY.
CURFEWS ARE A TEMPORARY SOLUTION. THE PROBLEM'S STILL THERE--OUR TOLERANCE OF THE GROWTH OF AN UNDERCLASS. BARELY EMPLOYABLE. FECKLESS. NOT THE HONEST POOR--THE WILLFULLY IDLE AND UNEDUCATED.
NEWS
YOU'RE PUSHING YOUR LUCK, GROVE. YOU'RE NOT THE DAMN OPPOSITION.
YOU'RE GOING TO HAVE TO LEARN TO TOE THE PARTY LINE...
"I DON'T WANT TO MAKE HIM A MARTYR. NO VIOLENCE. JUST KEEP AN EYE ON HIM. FIND SOME DIRT--DIRT THAT I DON'T KNOW ABOUT."

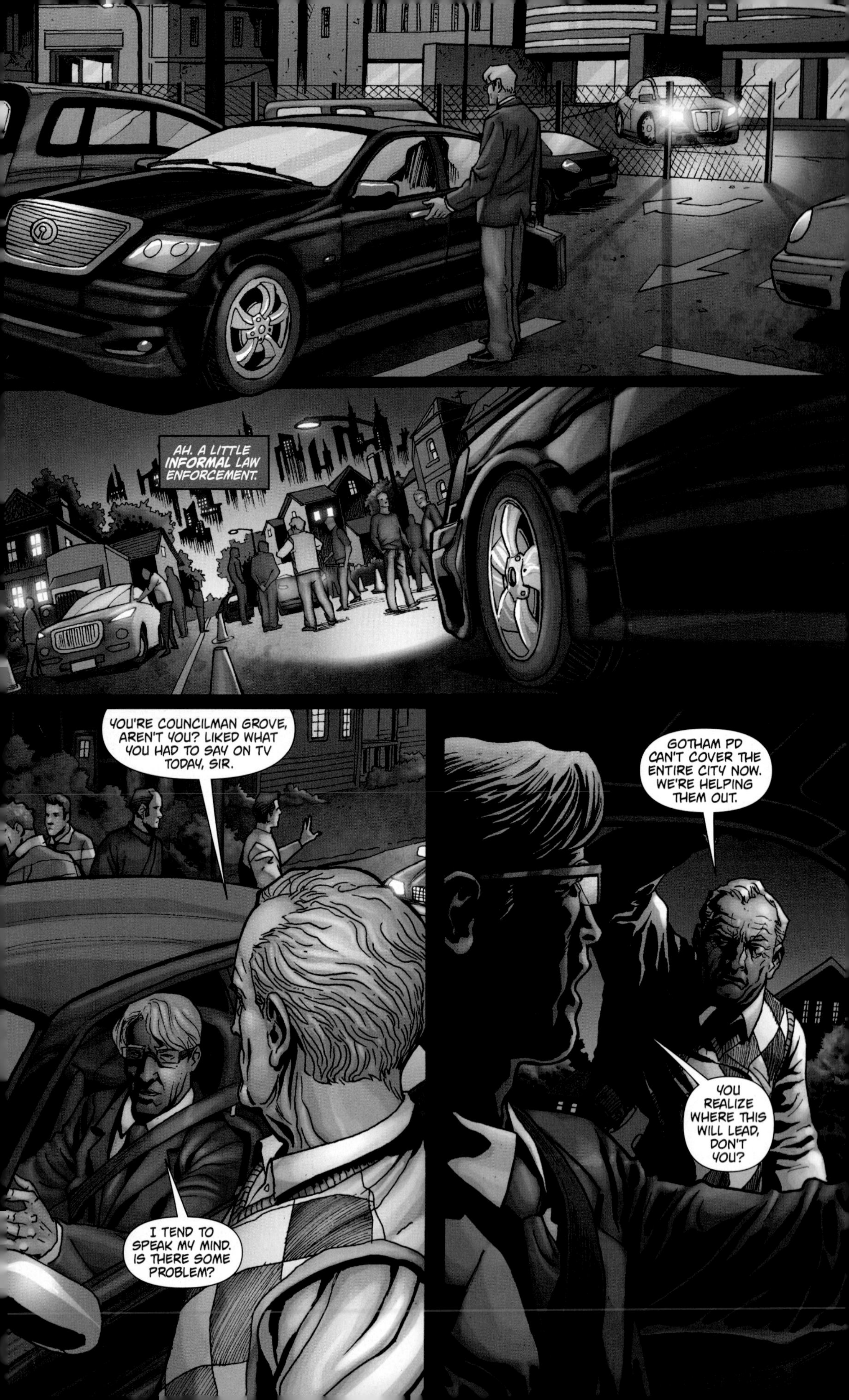
AH. A LITTLE INFORMAL LAW ENFORCEMENT.
YOU'RE COUNCILMAN GROVE, AREN'T YOU? LIKED WHAT YOU HAD TO SAY ON TV TODAY, SIR.
I TEND TO SPEAK MY MIND. IS THERE SOME PROBLEM?
GOTHAM PD CAN'T COVER THE ENTIRE CITY NOW. WE'RE HELPING THEM OUT.
YOU REALIZE WHERE THIS WILL LEAD, DON'T YOU?

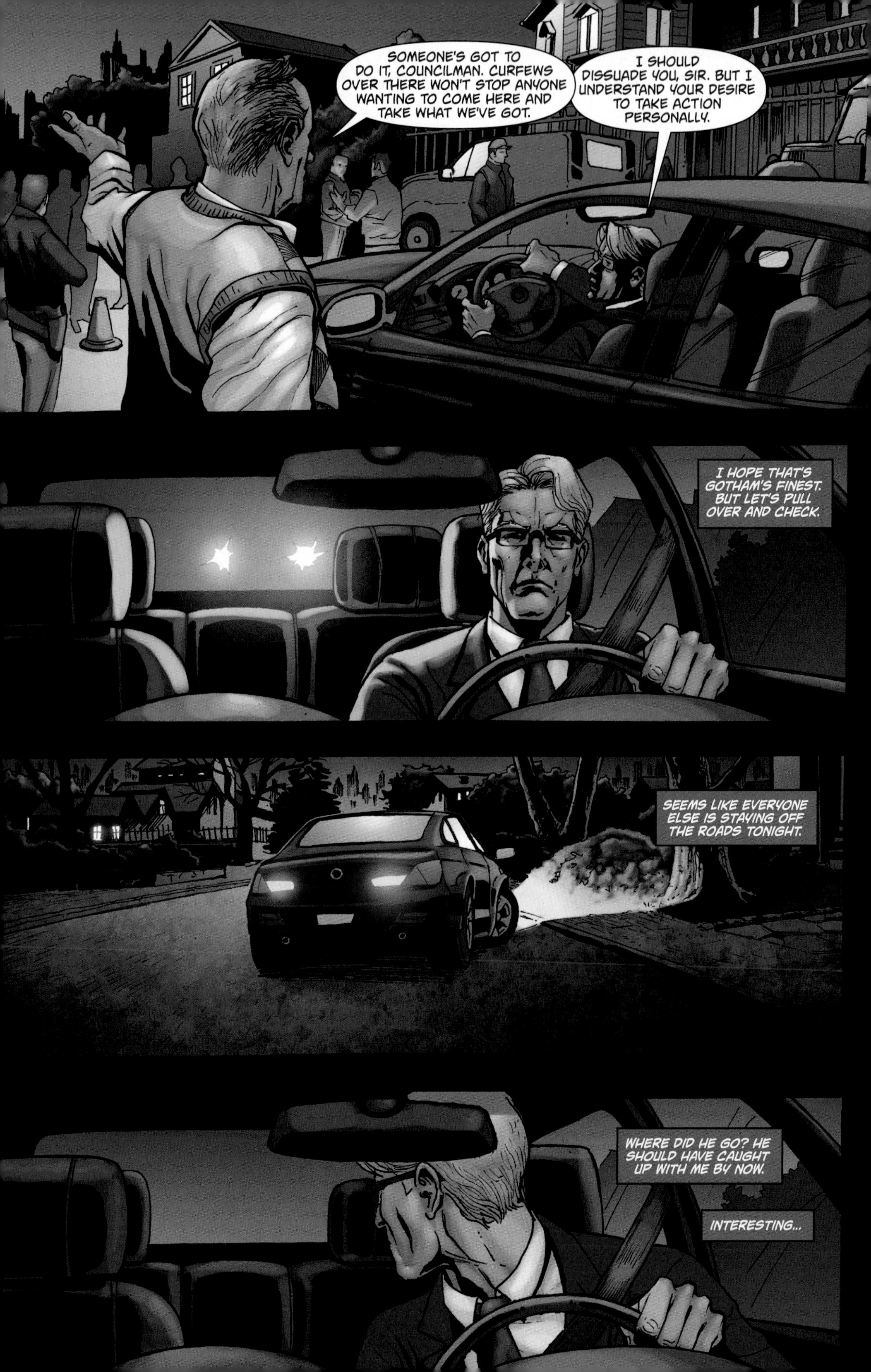
SOMEONE'S GOT TO DO IT, COUNCILMAN. CURFEWS OVER THERE WON'T STOP ANYONE WANTING TO COME HERE AND TAKE WHAT WE'VE GOT.
I SHOULD DISSUADE YOU, SIR. BUT I UNDERSTAND YOUR DESIRE TO TAKE ACTION PERSONALLY.
I HOPE THAT'S GOTHAM'S FINEST. BUT LET'S PULL OVER AND CHECK.
SEEMS LIKE EVERYONE ELSE IS STAYING OFF THE ROADS TONIGHT.
WHERE DID HE GO? HE SHOULD HAVE CAUGHT UP WITH ME BY NOW.
INTERESTING...

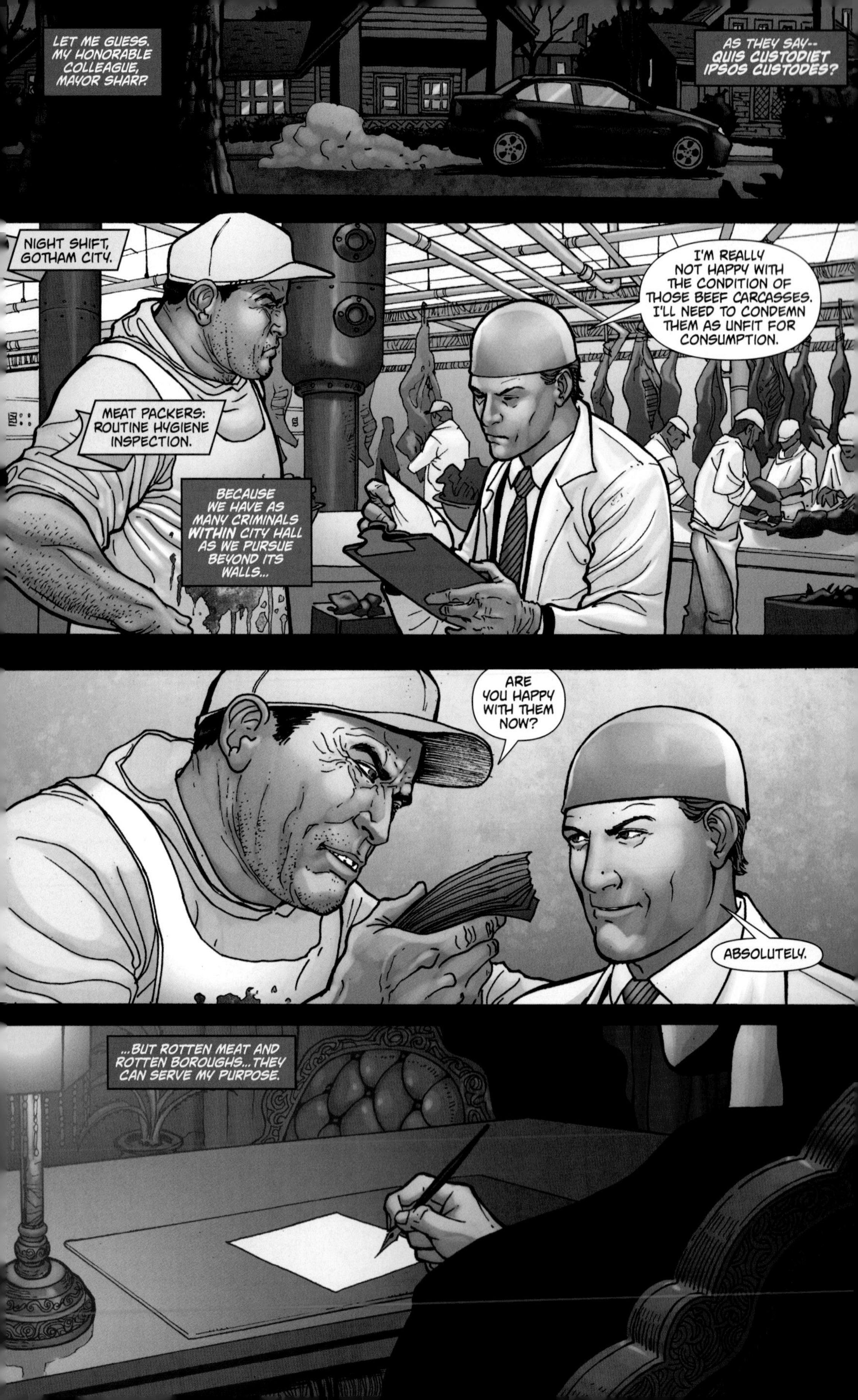

LET ME GUESS. MY HONORABLE COLLEAGUE, MAYOR SHARP.
AS THEY SAY-- QUIS CUSTODIET IPSOS CUSTODES?
NIGHT SHIFT, GOTHAM CITY.
I'M REALLY NOT HAPPY WITH THE CONDITION OF THOSE BEEF CARCASSES. I'LL NEED TO CONDEMN THEM AS UNFIT FOR CONSUMPTION.
MEAT PACKERS: ROUTINE HYGIENE INSPECTION.
BECAUSE WE HAVE AS MANY CRIMINALS WITHIN CITY HALL AS WE PURSUE BEYOND ITS WALLS...
ARE YOU HAPPY WITH THEM NOW?
ABSOLUTELY.
...BUT ROTTEN MEAT AND ROTTEN BOROUGHS...THEY CAN SERVE MY PURPOSE.

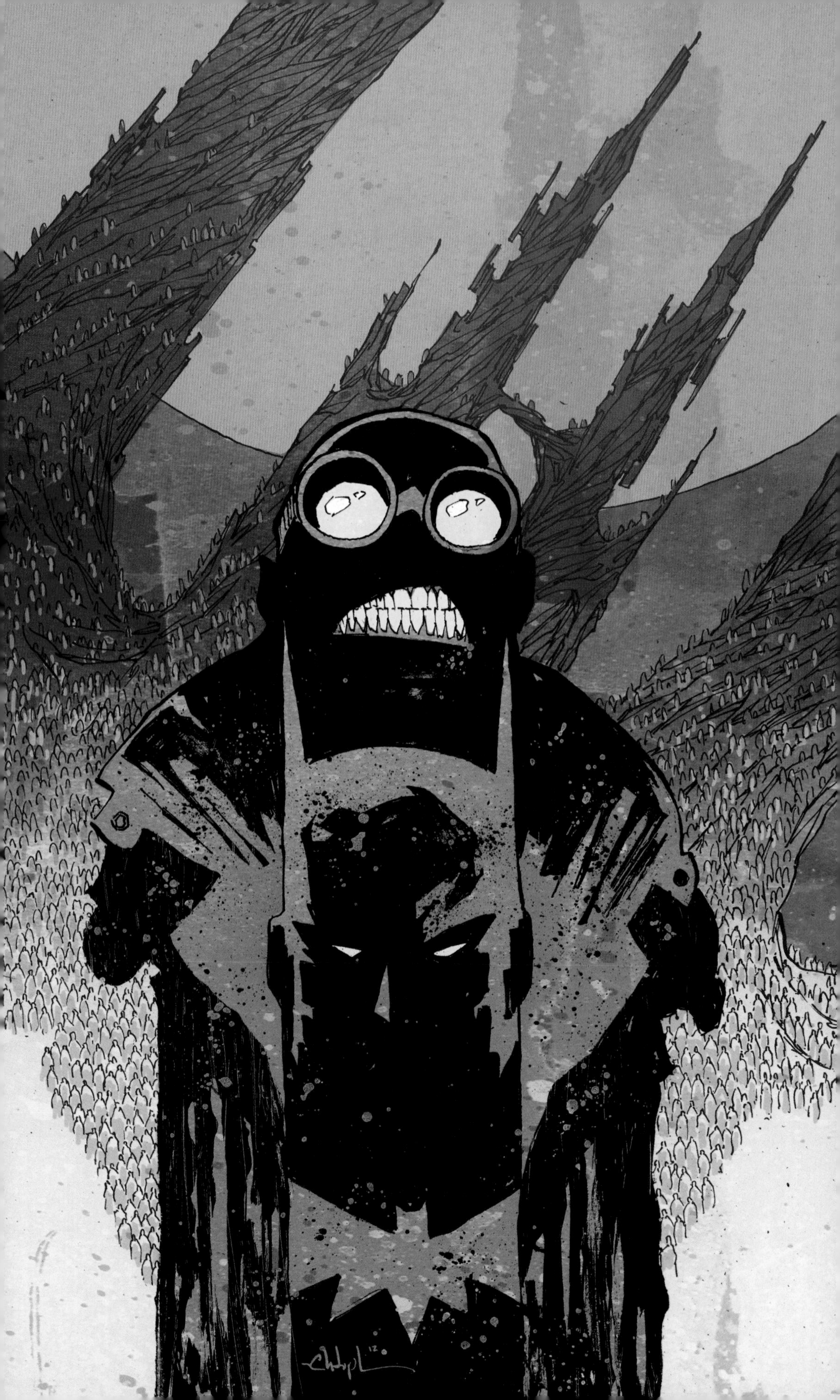

WELCOME
TO THE SLOUGH OF DESPOND
PART THREE

WRITTEN BY: KAREN TRAVISS
ART BY: FEDERICO DALLOCCHIO
COLORS BY: ALEJANDRO SANCHEZ
LETTERS BY: TRAVIS LANHAM
COVER BY: CHRIS MITTEN

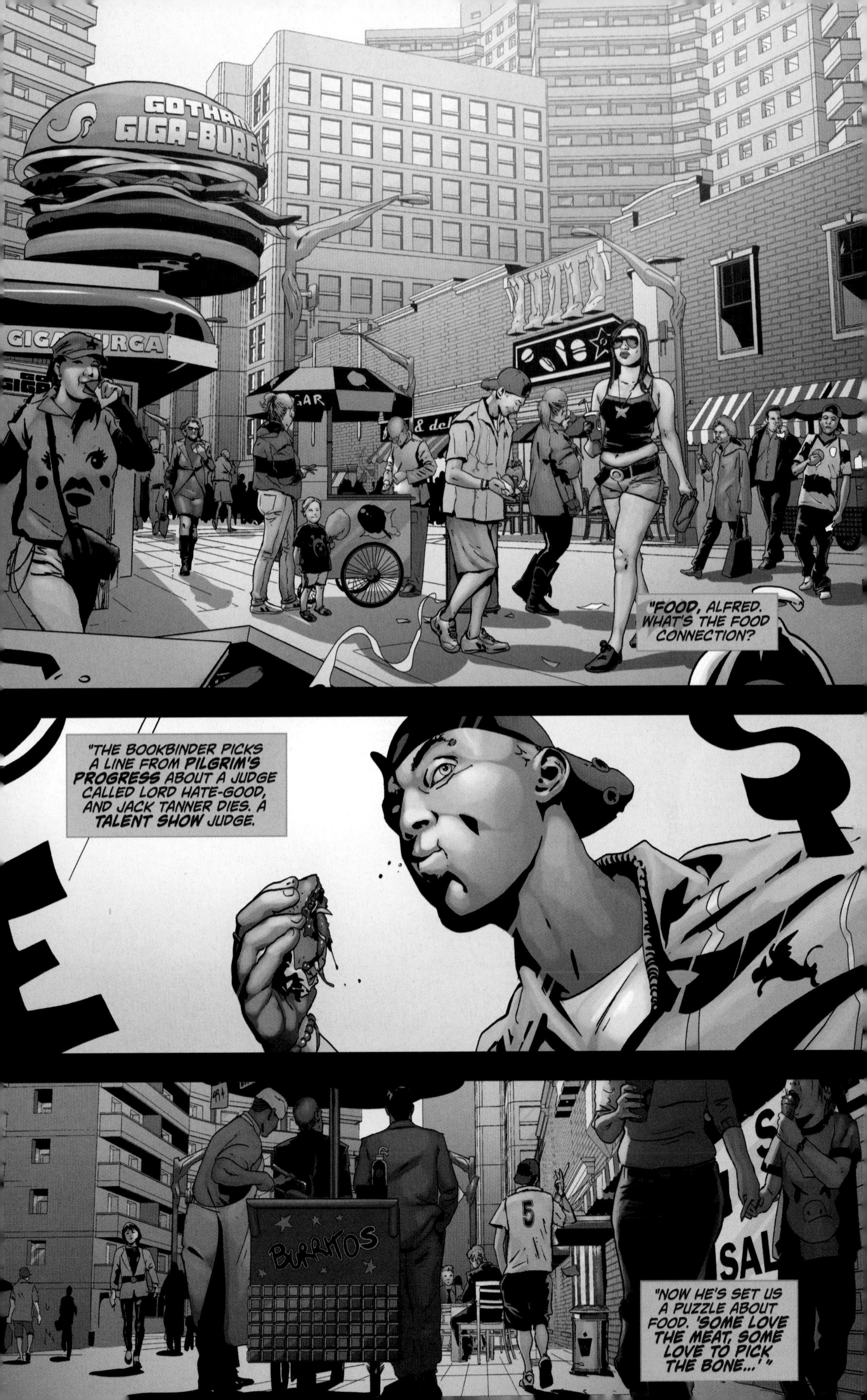
GOTHAM
GIGA-BURGA
GIGABURGA
"FOOD, ALFRED. WHAT'S THE FOOD CONNECTION?
"THE BOOKBINDER PICKS A LINE FROM PILGRIM'S PROGRESS ABOUT A JUDGE CALLED LORD HATE-GOOD, AND JACK TANNER DIES. A TALENT SHOW JUDGE.
BURRITOS
"NOW HE'S SET US A PUZZLE ABOUT FOOD. 'SOME LOVE THE MEAT, SOME LOVE TO PICK THE BONE...'"

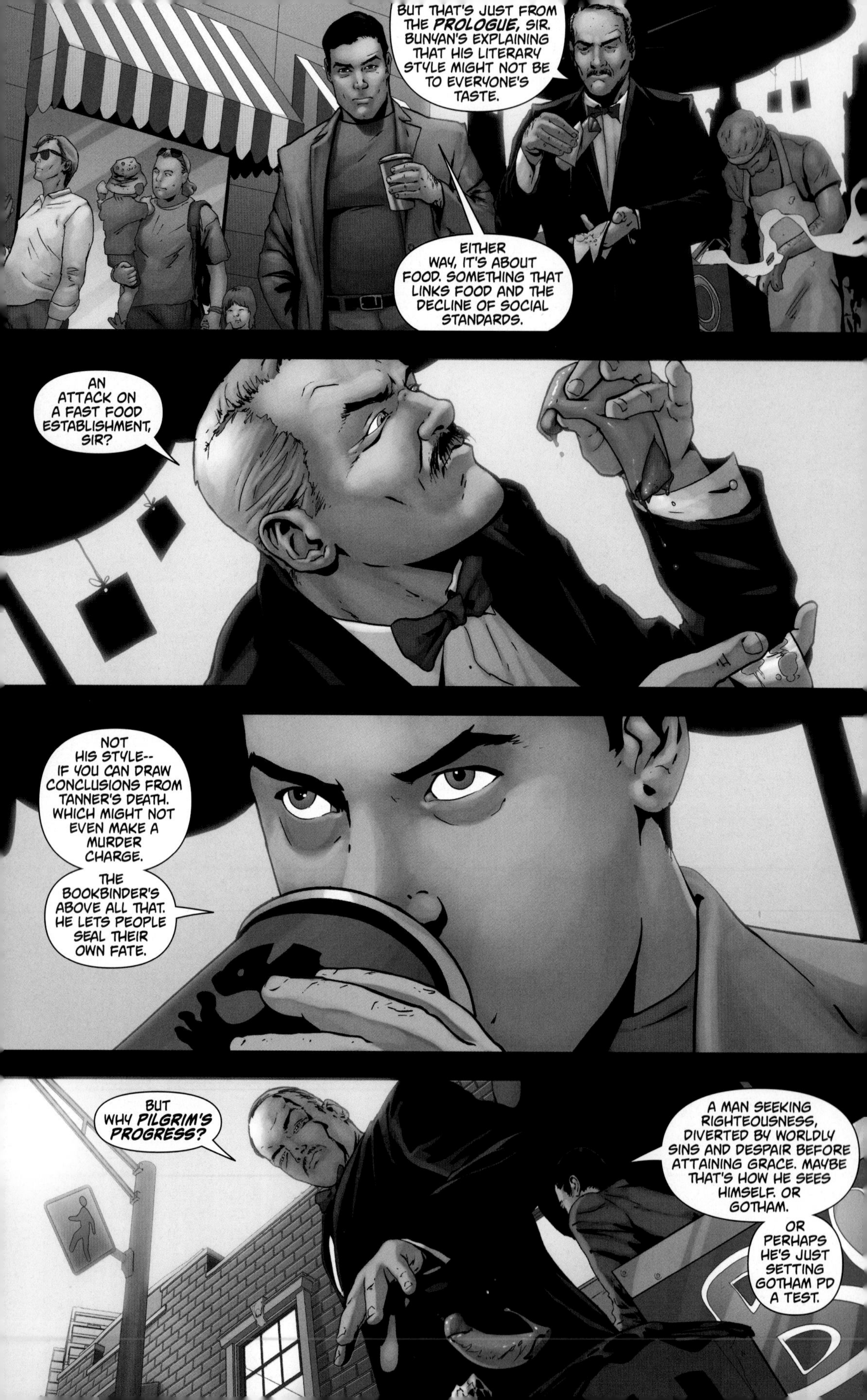
BUT THAT'S JUST FROM THE PROLOGUE, SIR. BUNYAN'S EXPLAINING THAT HIS LITERARY STYLE MIGHT NOT BE TO EVERYONE'S TASTE.
EITHER WAY, IT'S ABOUT FOOD. SOMETHING THAT LINKS FOOD AND THE DECLINE OF SOCIAL STANDARDS.
AN ATTACK ON A FAST FOOD ESTABLISHMENT, SIR?
NOT HIS STYLE-- IF YOU CAN DRAW CONCLUSIONS FROM TANNER'S DEATH. WHICH MIGHT NOT EVEN MAKE A MURDER CHARGE.
THE BOOKBINDER'S ABOVE ALL THAT. HE LETS PEOPLE SEAL THEIR OWN FATE.
BUT WHY PILGRIM'S PROGRESS?
A MAN SEEKING RIGHTEOUSNESS, DIVERTED BY WORLDLY SINS AND DESPAIR BEFORE ATTAINING GRACE. MAYBE THAT'S HOW HE SEES HIMSELF. OR GOTHAM.
OR PERHAPS HE'S JUST SETTING GOTHAM PD A TEST.

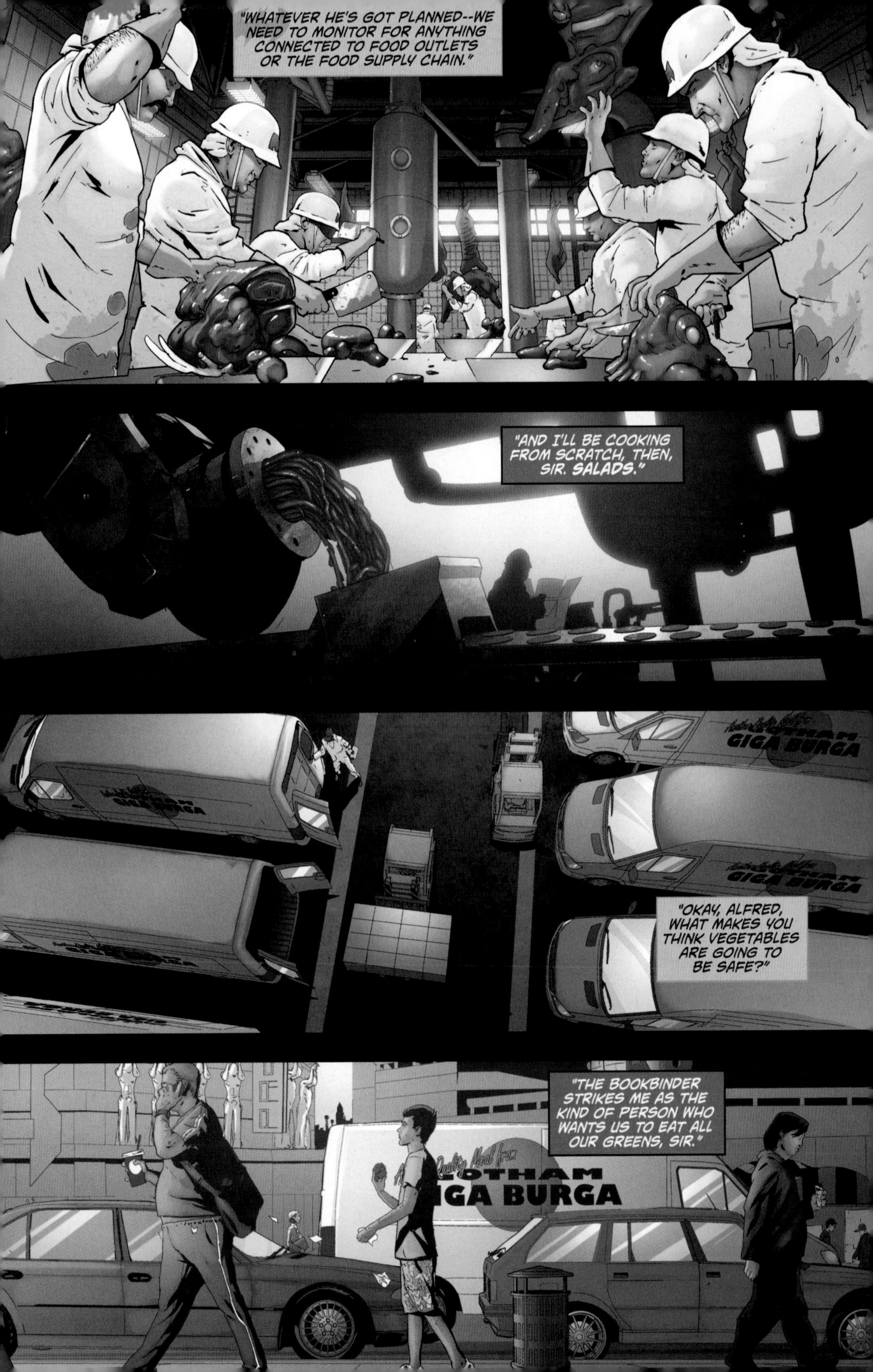
"WHATEVER HE'S GOT PLANNED--WE NEED TO MONITOR FOR ANYTHING CONNECTED TO FOOD OUTLETS OR THE FOOD SUPPLY CHAIN."
"AND I'LL BE COOKING FROM SCRATCH, THEN, SIR. SALADS."
GOTHAM GIGA BURGA
"OKAY, ALFRED, WHAT MAKES YOU THINK VEGETABLES ARE GOING TO BE SAFE?"
"THE BOOKBINDER STRIKES ME AS THE KIND OF PERSON WHO WANTS US TO EAT ALL OUR GREENS, SIR."

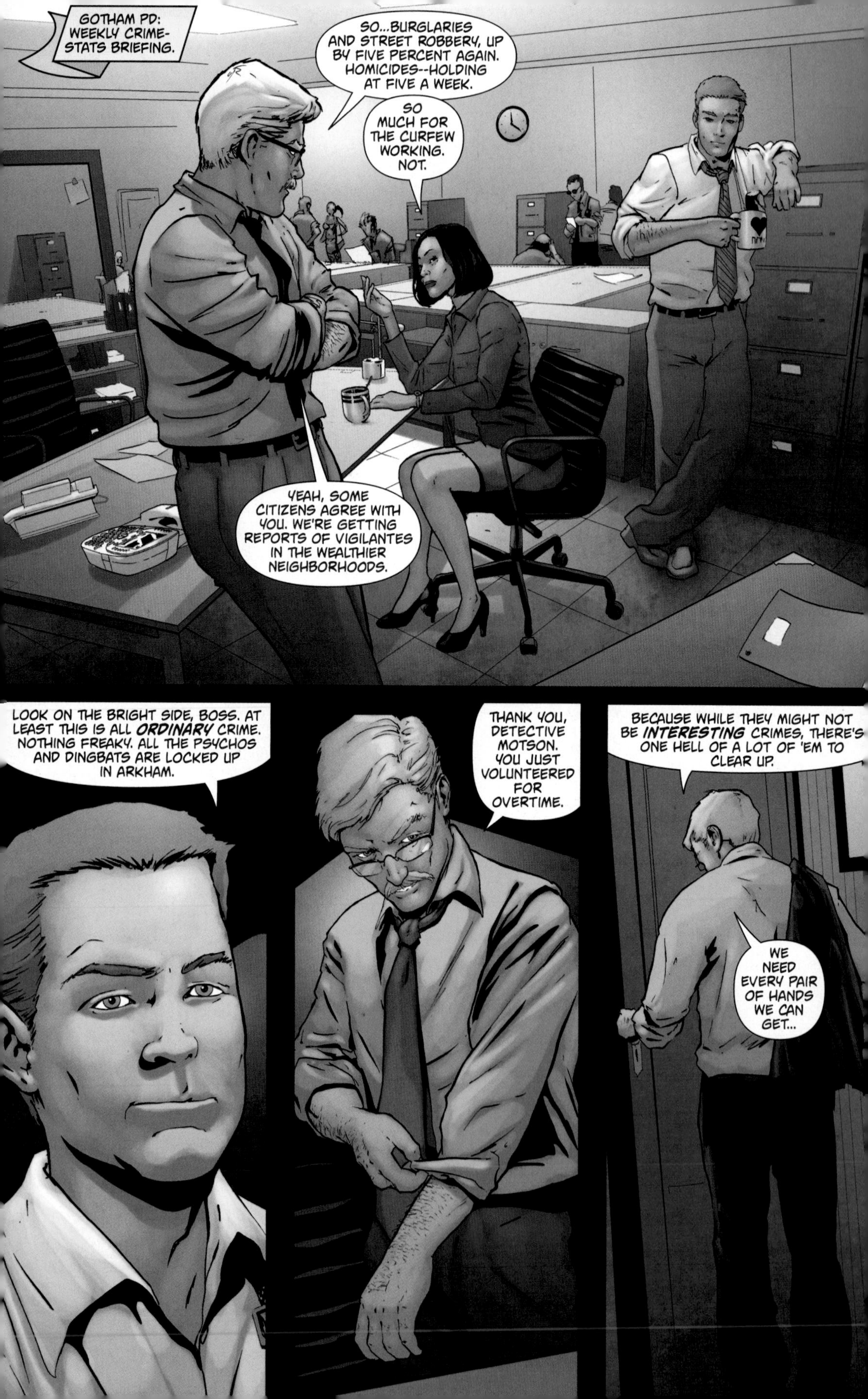
GOTHAM PD: WEEKLY CRIME-STATS BRIEFING.
SO...BURGLARIES AND STREET ROBBERY, UP BY FIVE PERCENT AGAIN. HOMICIDES--HOLDING AT FIVE A WEEK.
SO MUCH FOR THE CURFEW WORKING. NOT.
YEAH, SOME CITIZENS AGREE WITH YOU. WE'RE GETTING REPORTS OF VIGILANTES IN THE WEALTHIER NEIGHBORHOODS.
LOOK ON THE BRIGHT SIDE, BOSS. AT LEAST THIS IS ALL *ORDINARY* CRIME. NOTHING FREAKY. ALL THE PSYCHOS AND DINGBATS ARE LOCKED UP IN ARKHAM.
THANK YOU, DETECTIVE MOTSON. YOU JUST VOLUNTEERED FOR OVERTIME.
BECAUSE WHILE THEY MIGHT NOT BE *INTERESTING* CRIMES, THERE'S ONE HELL OF A LOT OF 'EM TO CLEAR UP.
WE NEED EVERY PAIR OF HANDS WE CAN GET...

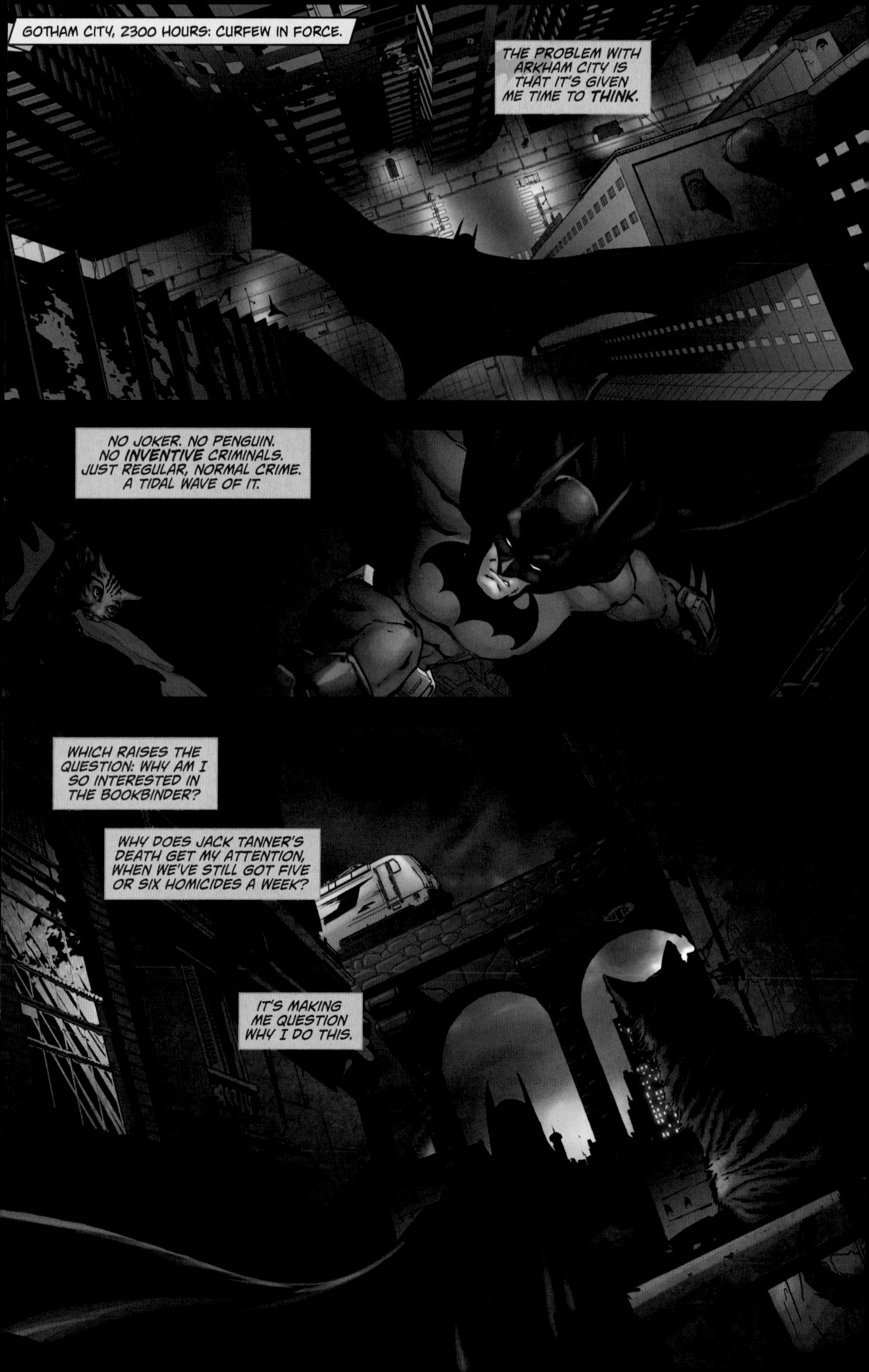
GOTHAM CITY, 2300 HOURS: CURFEW IN FORCE.
THE PROBLEM WITH ARKHAM CITY IS THAT IT'S GIVEN ME TIME TO THINK.
NO JOKER. NO PENGUIN. NO INVENTIVE CRIMINALS. JUST REGULAR, NORMAL CRIME. A TIDAL WAVE OF IT.
WHICH RAISES THE QUESTION: WHY AM I SO INTERESTED IN THE BOOKBINDER?
WHY DOES JACK TANNER'S DEATH GET MY ATTENTION, WHEN WE'VE STILL GOT FIVE OR SIX HOMICIDES A WEEK?
IT'S MAKING ME QUESTION WHY I DO THIS.

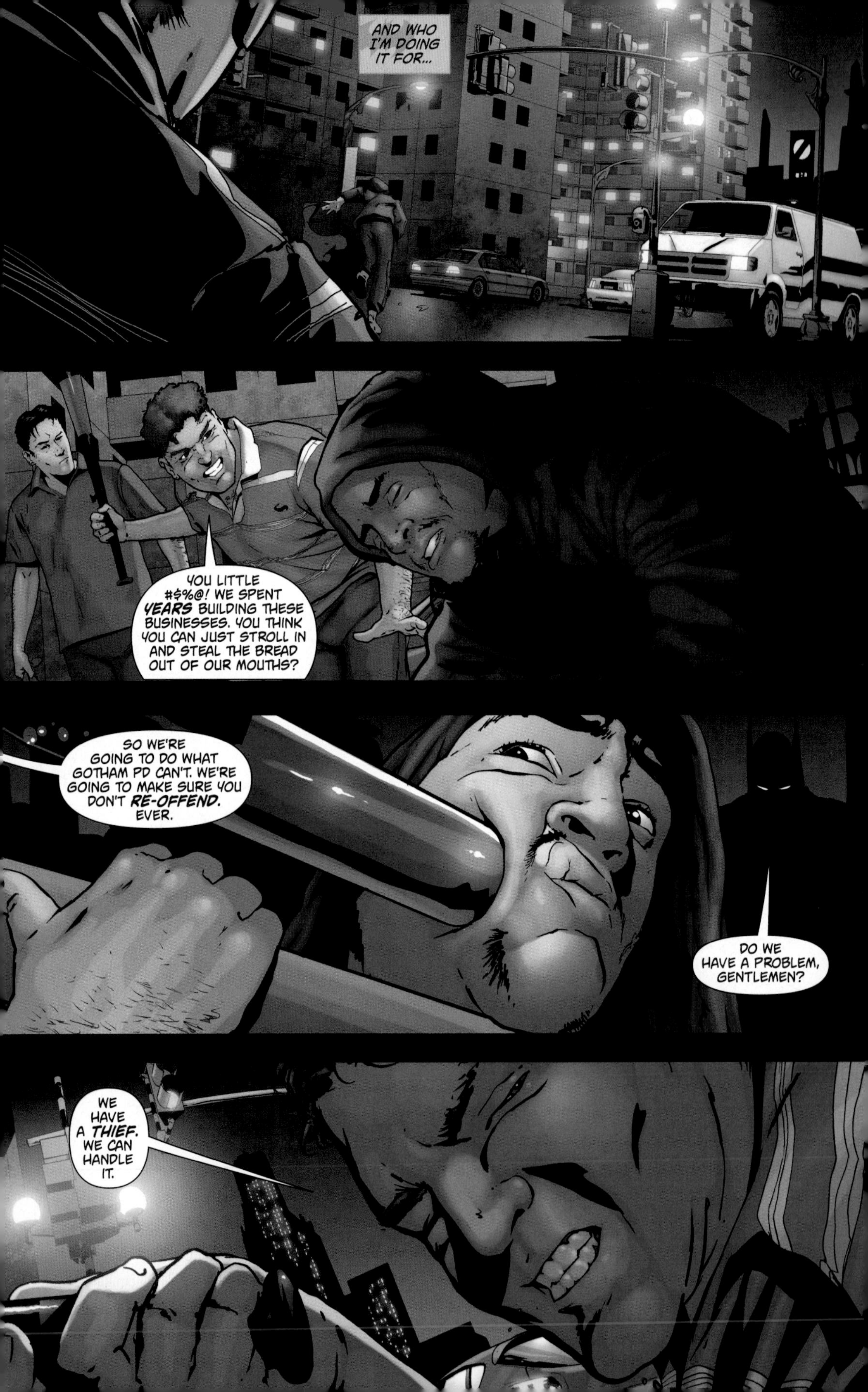
AND WHO I'M DOING IT FOR...
YOU LITTLE #$%@! WE SPENT YEARS BUILDING THESE BUSINESSES. YOU THINK YOU CAN JUST STROLL IN AND STEAL THE BREAD OUT OF OUR MOUTHS?
SO WE'RE GOING TO DO WHAT GOTHAM PD CAN'T. WE'RE GOING TO MAKE SURE YOU DON'T RE-OFFEND. EVER.
DO WE HAVE A PROBLEM, GENTLEMEN?
WE HAVE A THIEF. WE CAN HANDLE IT.

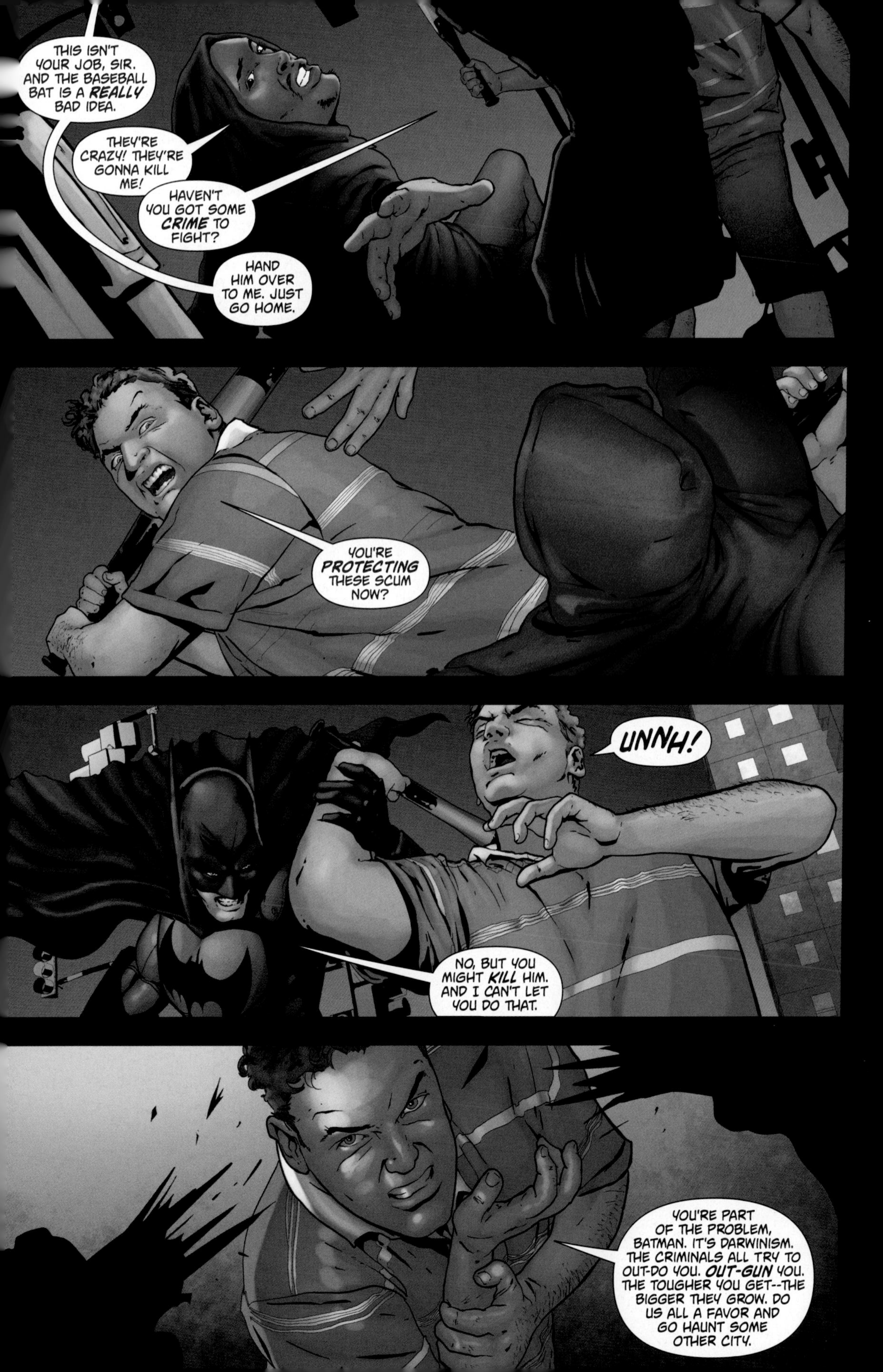
THIS ISN'T YOUR JOB, SIR. AND THE BASEBALL BAT IS A *REALLY* BAD IDEA.
THEY'RE CRAZY! THEY'RE GONNA KILL ME!
HAVEN'T YOU GOT SOME *CRIME* TO FIGHT?
HAND HIM OVER TO ME. JUST GO HOME.
YOU'RE *PROTECTING* THESE SCUM NOW?
UNNH!
NO, BUT YOU MIGHT *KILL* HIM. AND I CAN'T LET YOU DO THAT.
YOU'RE PART OF THE PROBLEM, BATMAN. IT'S DARWINISM. THE CRIMINALS ALL TRY TO OUT-DO YOU. *OUT-GUN* YOU. THE TOUGHER YOU GET--THE BIGGER THEY GROW. DO US ALL A FAVOR AND GO HAUNT SOME OTHER CITY.

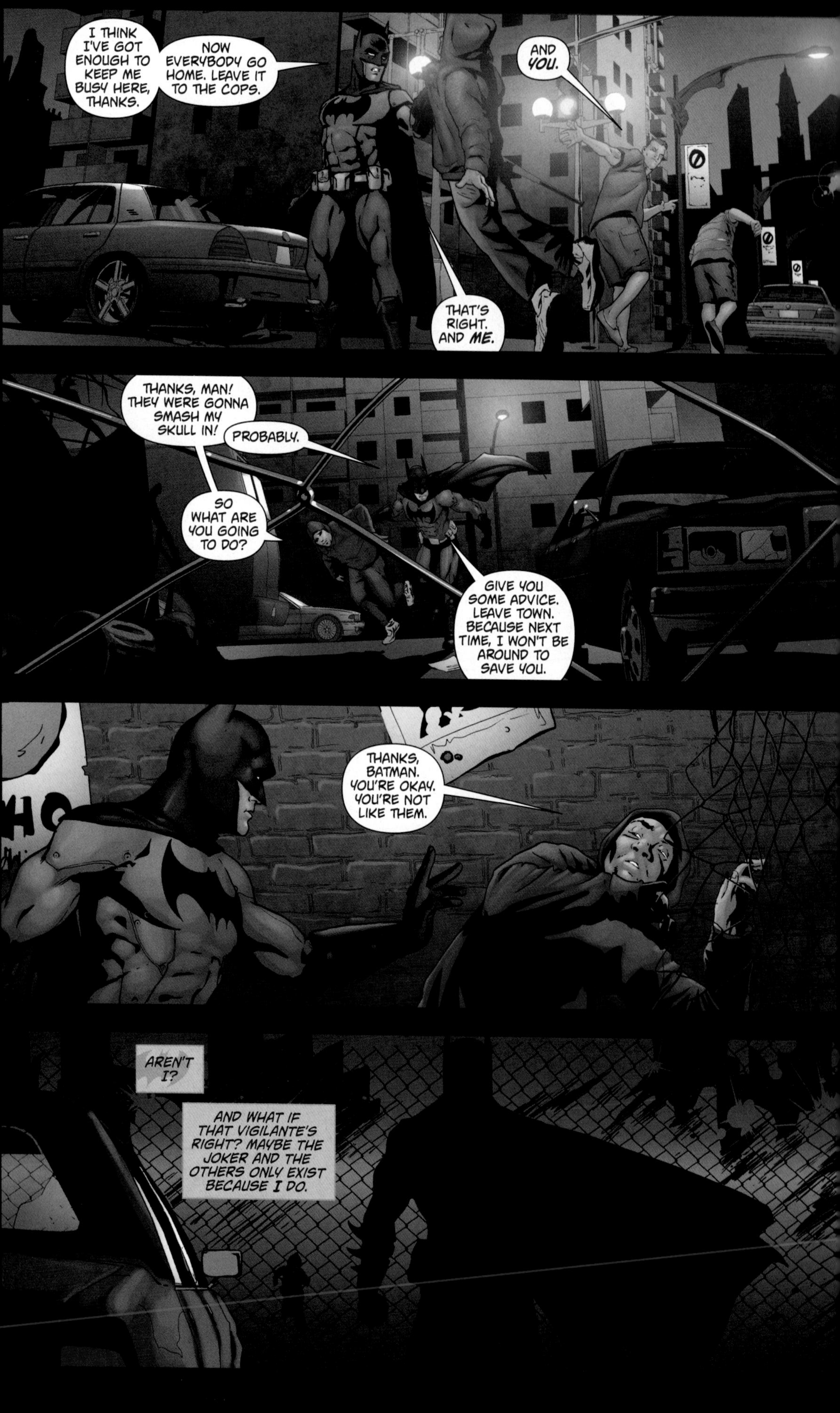
I THINK I'VE GOT ENOUGH TO KEEP ME BUSY HERE, THANKS.
NOW EVERYBODY GO HOME. LEAVE IT TO THE COPS.
AND YOU.
THAT'S RIGHT. AND ME.
THANKS, MAN! THEY WERE GONNA SMASH MY SKULL IN!
PROBABLY.
SO WHAT ARE YOU GOING TO DO?
GIVE YOU SOME ADVICE. LEAVE TOWN. BECAUSE NEXT TIME, I WON'T BE AROUND TO SAVE YOU.
THANKS, BATMAN. YOU'RE OKAY. YOU'RE NOT LIKE THEM.
AREN'T I?
AND WHAT IF THAT VIGILANTE'S RIGHT? MAYBE THE JOKER AND THE OTHERS ONLY EXIST BECAUSE I DO.

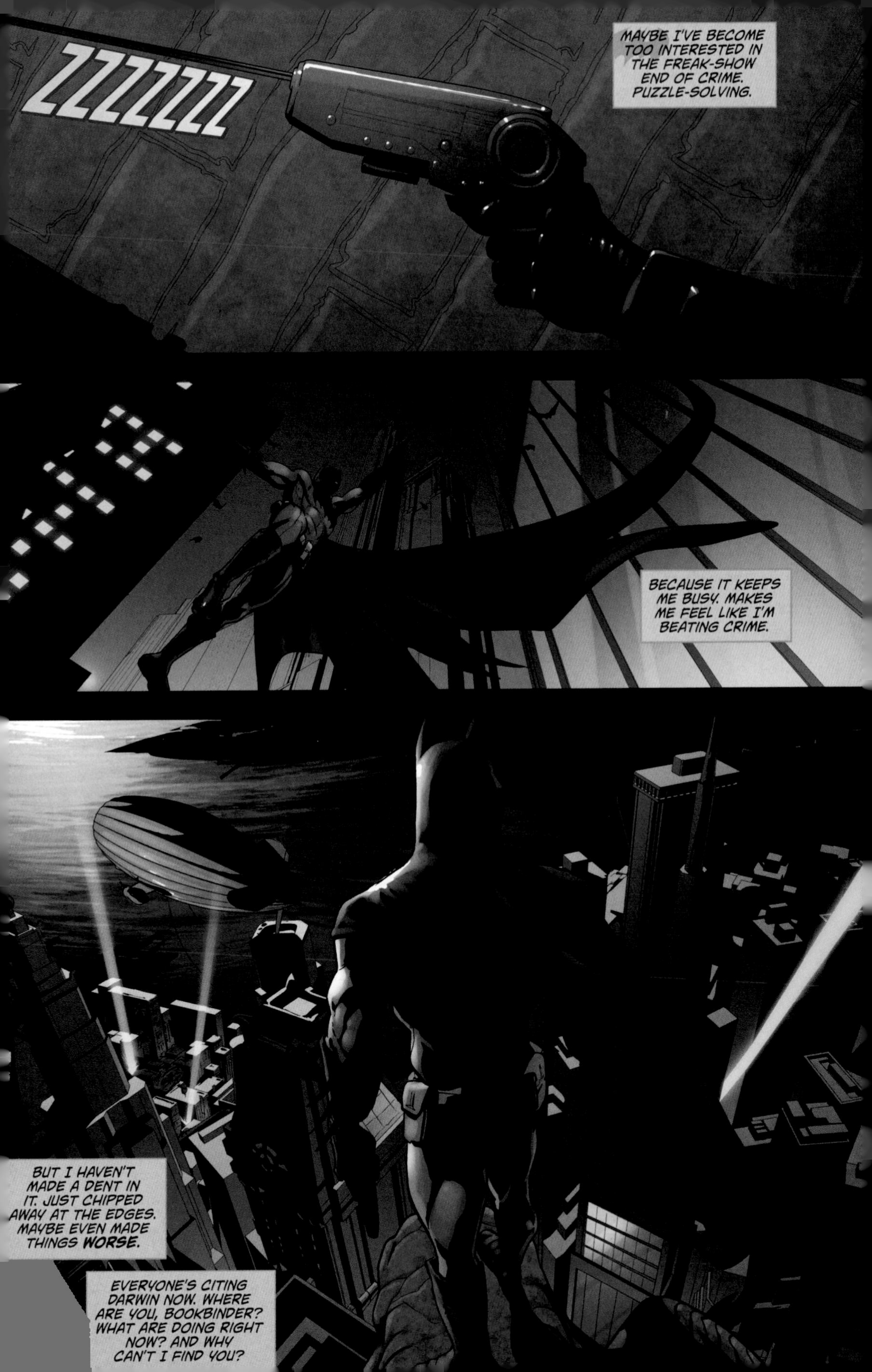
ZZZZZZZZ
MAYBE I'VE BECOME TOO INTERESTED IN THE FREAK-SHOW END OF CRIME. PUZZLE-SOLVING.
BECAUSE IT KEEPS ME BUSY. MAKES ME FEEL LIKE I'M BEATING CRIME.
BUT I HAVEN'T MADE A DENT IN IT. JUST CHIPPED AWAY AT THE EDGES. MAYBE EVEN MADE THINGS WORSE.
EVERYONE'S CITING DARWIN NOW. WHERE ARE YOU, BOOKBINDER? WHAT ARE DOING RIGHT NOW? AND WHY CAN'T I FIND YOU?

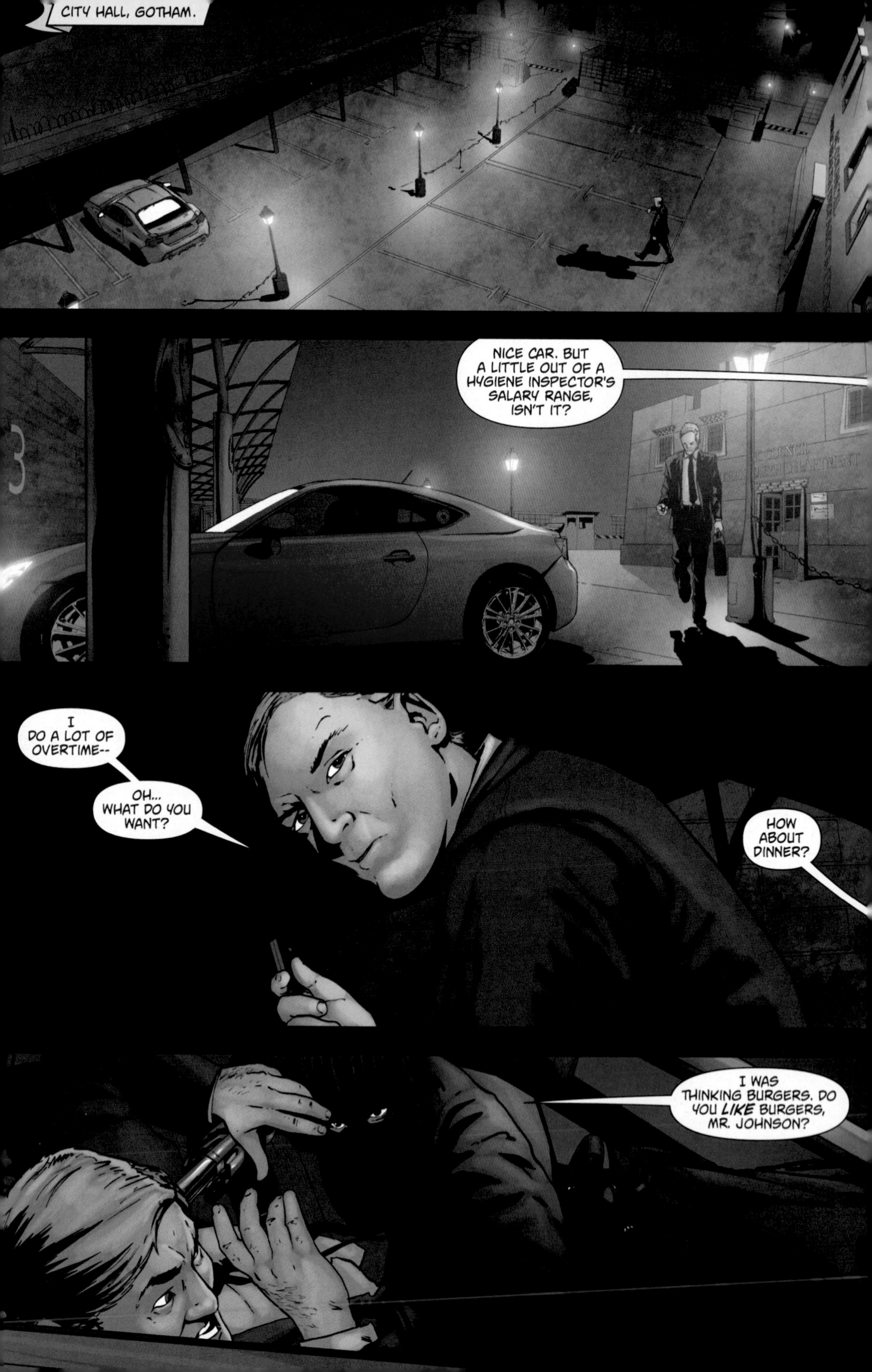
CITY HALL, GOTHAM.
NICE CAR. BUT A LITTLE OUT OF A HYGIENE INSPECTOR'S SALARY RANGE, ISN'T IT?
I DO A LOT OF OVERTIME--
OH... WHAT DO YOU WANT?
HOW ABOUT DINNER?
I WAS THINKING BURGERS. DO YOU *LIKE* BURGERS, MR. JOHNSON?

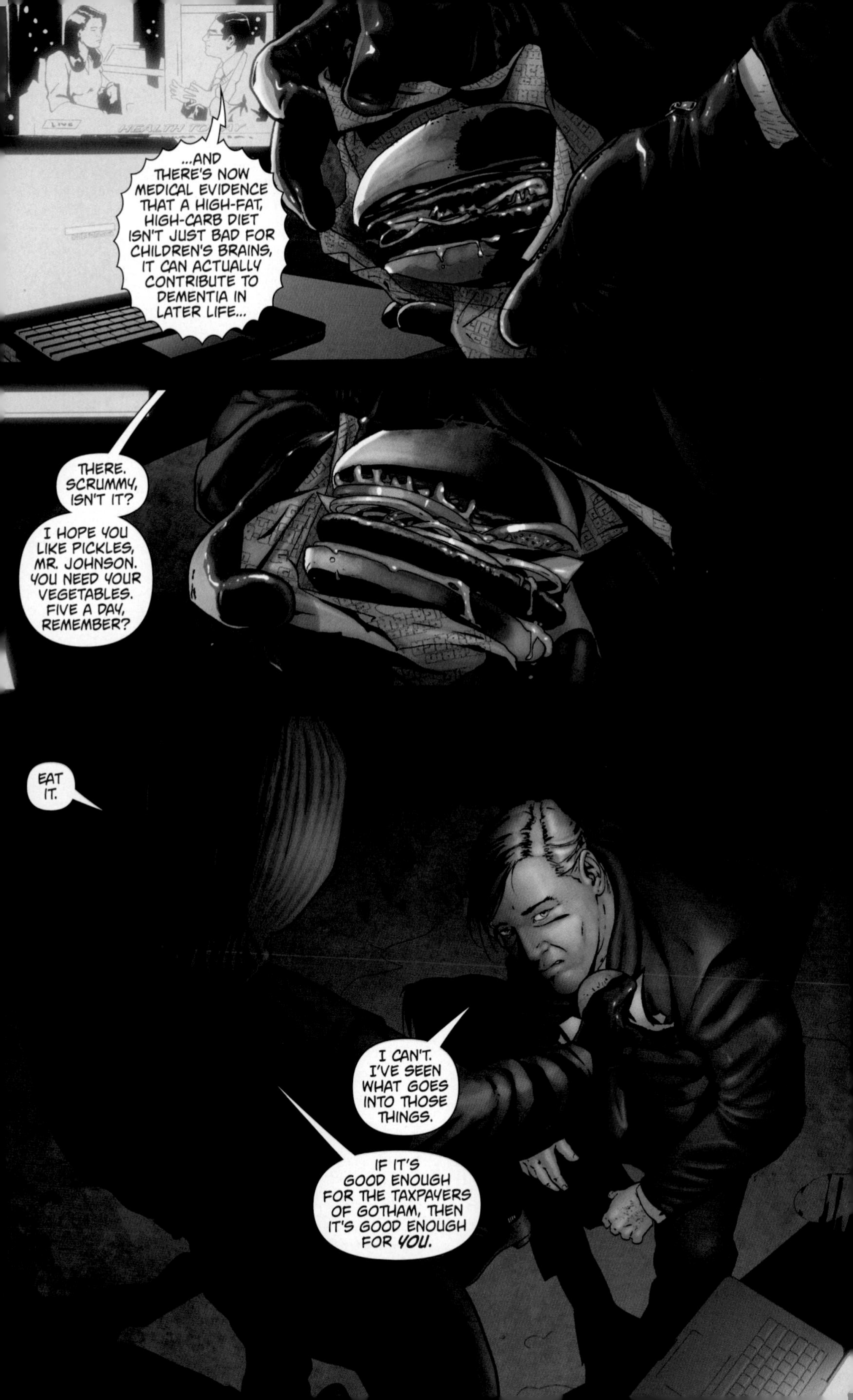
LIVE
HEALTH TODAY
...AND THERE'S NOW MEDICAL EVIDENCE THAT A HIGH-FAT, HIGH-CARB DIET ISN'T JUST BAD FOR CHILDREN'S BRAINS, IT CAN ACTUALLY CONTRIBUTE TO DEMENTIA IN LATER LIFE...
THERE. SCRUMMY, ISN'T IT?
I HOPE YOU LIKE PICKLES, MR. JOHNSON. YOU NEED YOUR VEGETABLES. FIVE A DAY, REMEMBER?
EAT IT.
I CAN'T. I'VE SEEN WHAT GOES INTO THOSE THINGS.
IF IT'S GOOD ENOUGH FOR THE TAXPAYERS OF GOTHAM, THEN IT'S GOOD ENOUGH FOR *YOU*.

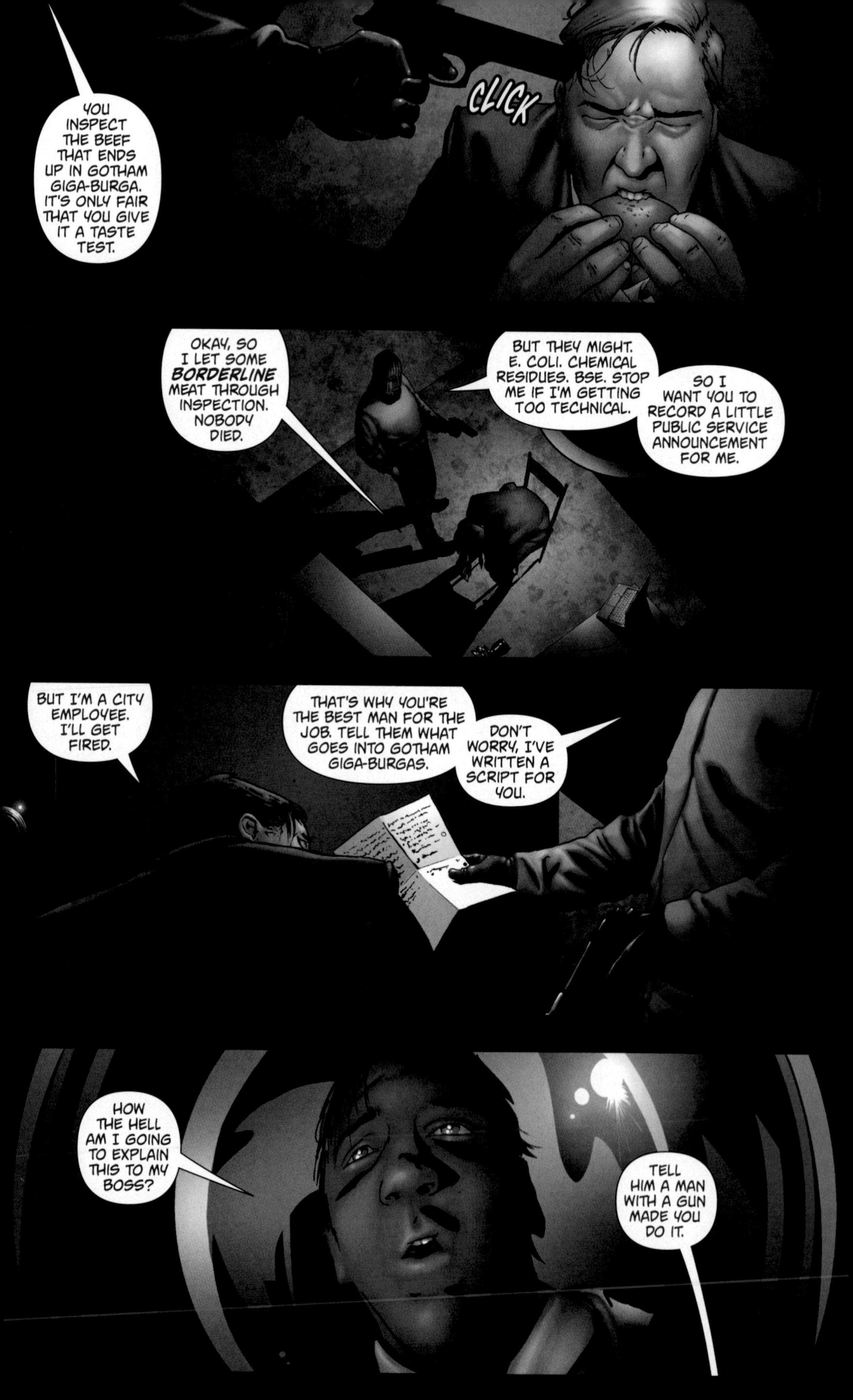

YOU INSPECT THE BEEF THAT ENDS UP IN GOTHAM GIGA-BURGA. IT'S ONLY FAIR THAT YOU GIVE IT A TASTE TEST.
CLICK
OKAY, SO I LET SOME BORDERLINE MEAT THROUGH INSPECTION. NOBODY DIED.
BUT THEY MIGHT. E. COLI. CHEMICAL RESIDUES. BSE. STOP ME IF I'M GETTING TOO TECHNICAL.
SO I WANT YOU TO RECORD A LITTLE PUBLIC SERVICE ANNOUNCEMENT FOR ME.
BUT I'M A CITY EMPLOYEE. I'LL GET FIRED.
THAT'S WHY YOU'RE THE BEST MAN FOR THE JOB. TELL THEM WHAT GOES INTO GOTHAM GIGA-BURGAS.
DON'T WORRY, I'VE WRITTEN A SCRIPT FOR YOU.
HOW THE HELL AM I GOING TO EXPLAIN THIS TO MY BOSS?
TELL HIM A MAN WITH A GUN MADE YOU DO IT.

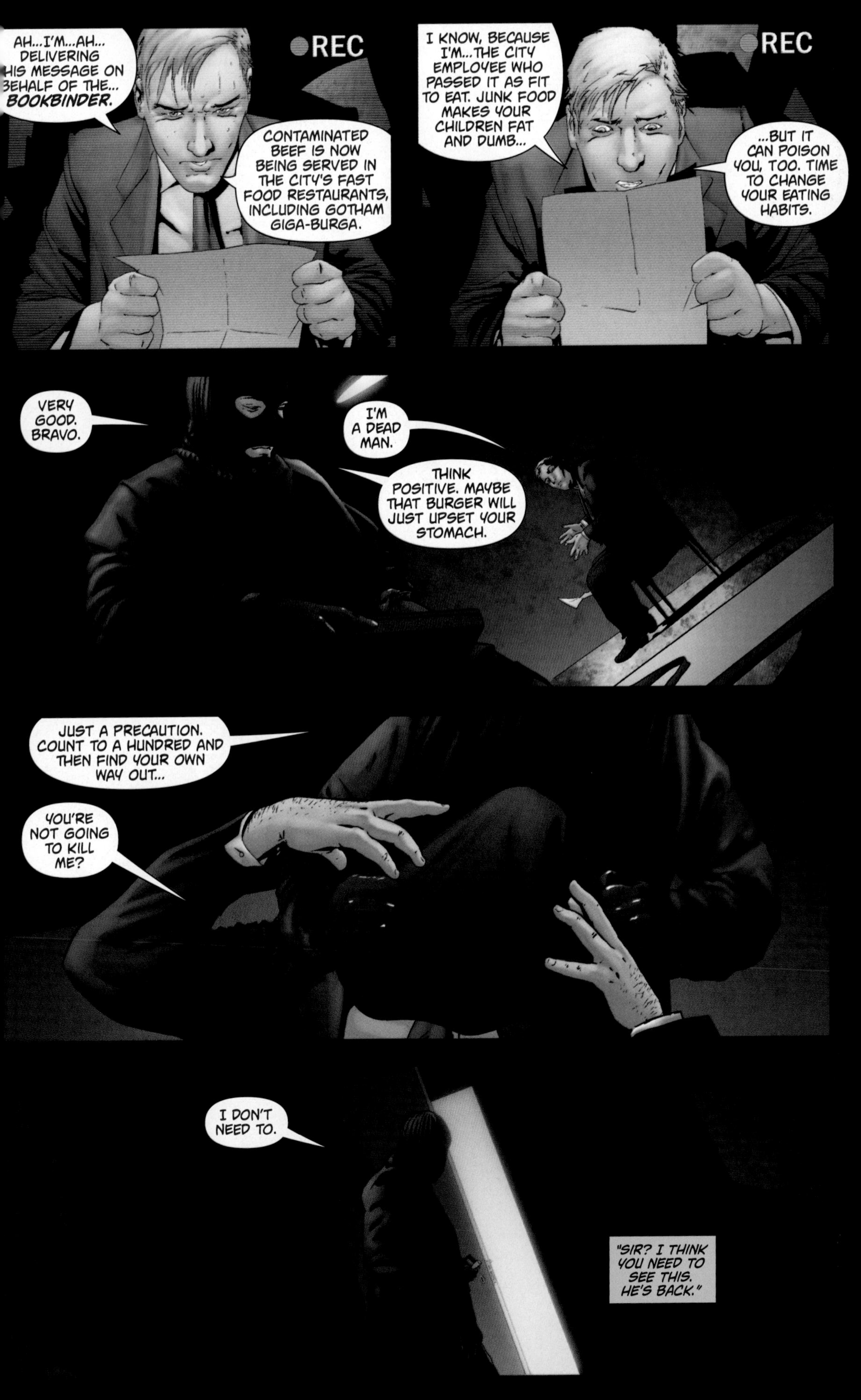
REC
AH...I'M...AH... DELIVERING HIS MESSAGE ON BEHALF OF THE... **BOOKBINDER**.
CONTAMINATED BEEF IS NOW BEING SERVED IN THE CITY'S FAST FOOD RESTAURANTS, INCLUDING GOTHAM GIGA-BURGA.
REC
I KNOW, BECAUSE I'M...THE CITY EMPLOYEE WHO PASSED IT AS FIT TO EAT. JUNK FOOD MAKES YOUR CHILDREN FAT AND DUMB...
...BUT IT CAN POISON YOU, TOO. TIME TO CHANGE YOUR EATING HABITS.
VERY GOOD. BRAVO.
I'M A DEAD MAN.
THINK POSITIVE. MAYBE THAT BURGER WILL JUST UPSET YOUR STOMACH.
JUST A PRECAUTION. COUNT TO A HUNDRED AND THEN FIND YOUR OWN WAY OUT...
YOU'RE NOT GOING TO KILL ME?
I DON'T NEED TO.
"SIR? I THINK YOU NEED TO SEE THIS. HE'S BACK."

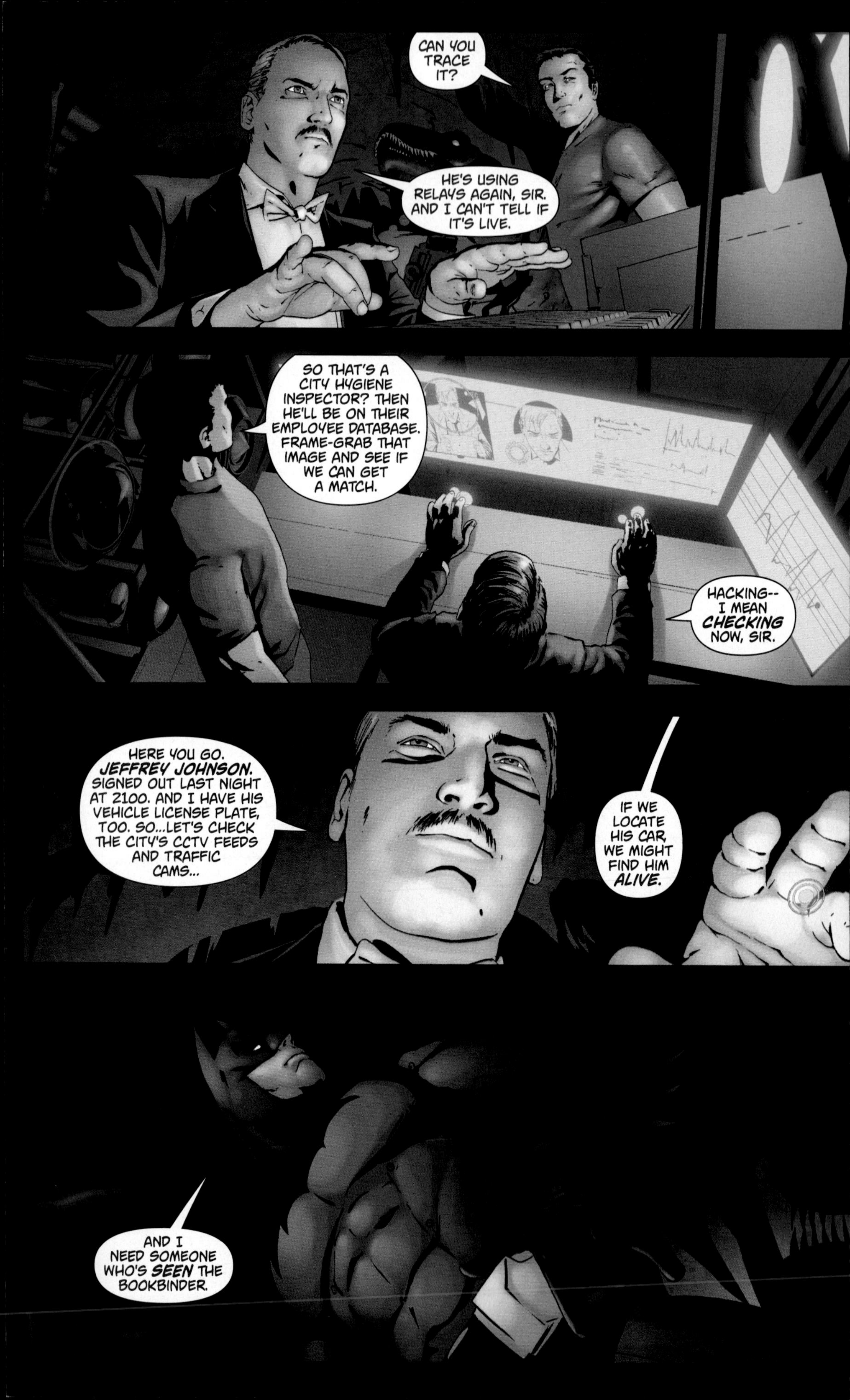
CAN YOU TRACE IT?
HE'S USING RELAYS AGAIN, SIR. AND I CAN'T TELL IF IT'S LIVE.
SO THAT'S A CITY HYGIENE INSPECTOR? THEN HE'LL BE ON THEIR EMPLOYEE DATABASE. FRAME-GRAB THAT IMAGE AND SEE IF WE CAN GET A MATCH.
HACKING-- I MEAN CHECKING NOW, SIR.
HERE YOU GO. JEFFREY JOHNSON. SIGNED OUT LAST NIGHT AT 2100. AND I HAVE HIS VEHICLE LICENSE PLATE, TOO. SO...LET'S CHECK THE CITY'S CCTV FEEDS AND TRAFFIC CAMS...
IF WE LOCATE HIS CAR, WE MIGHT FIND HIM ALIVE.
AND I NEED SOMEONE WHO'S SEEN THE BOOKBINDER.

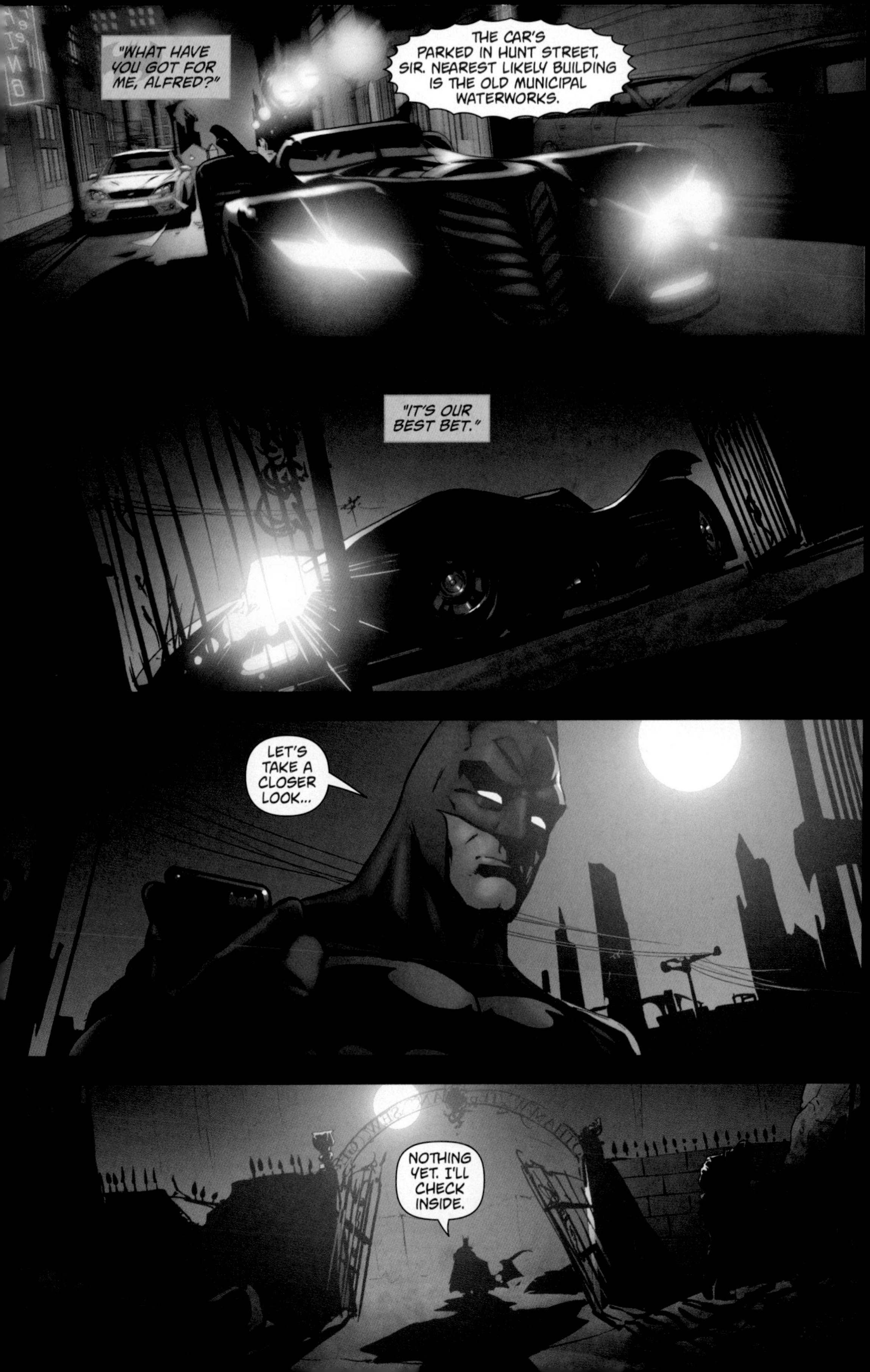
"WHAT HAVE YOU GOT FOR ME, ALFRED?"
THE CAR'S PARKED IN HUNT STREET, SIR. NEAREST LIKELY BUILDING IS THE OLD MUNICIPAL WATERWORKS.
"IT'S OUR BEST BET."
LET'S TAKE A CLOSER LOOK...
NOTHING YET. I'LL CHECK INSIDE.

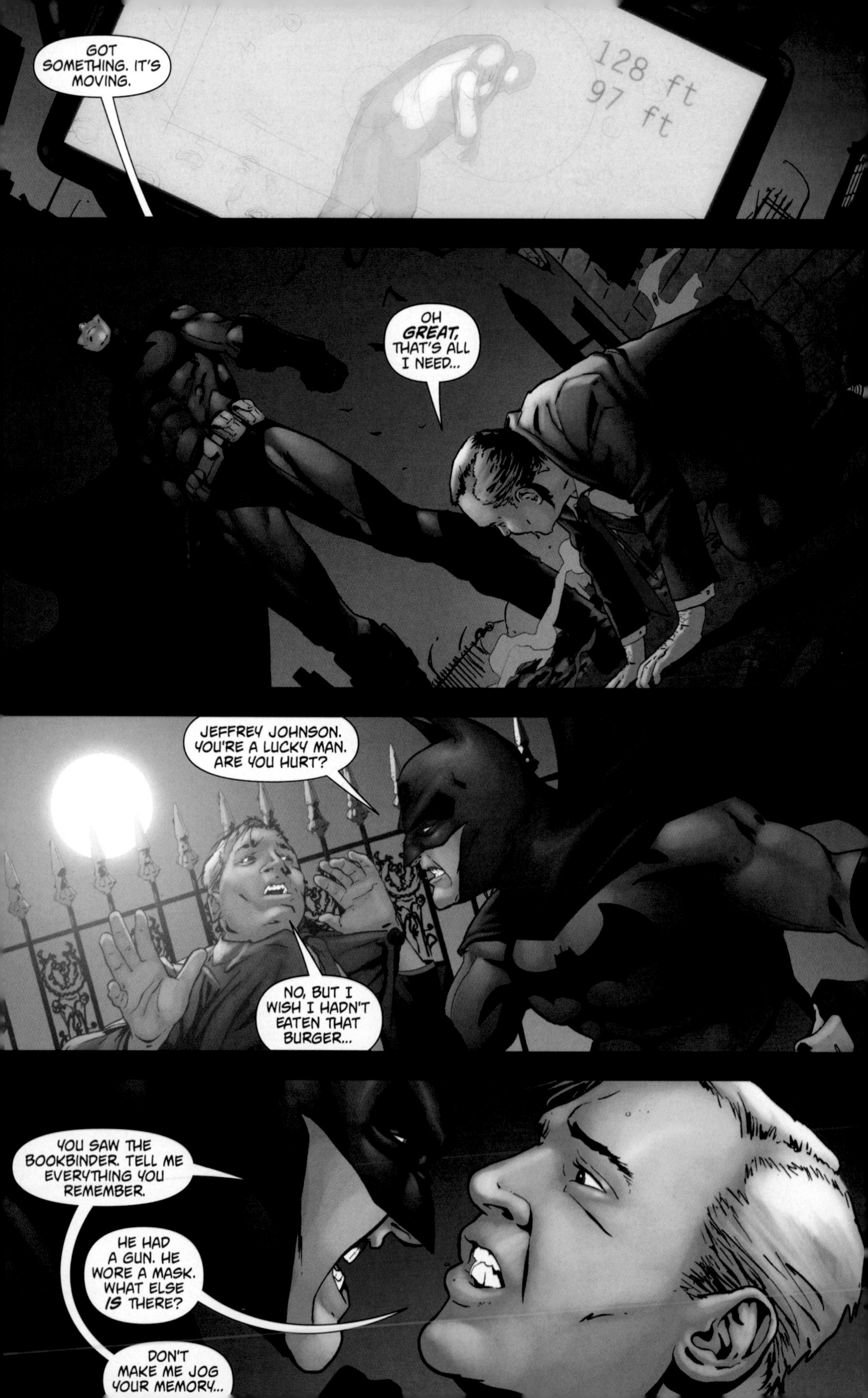
GOT SOMETHING. IT'S MOVING.
128 ft
97 ft
OH GREAT, THAT'S ALL I NEED...
JEFFREY JOHNSON. YOU'RE A LUCKY MAN. ARE YOU HURT?
NO, BUT I WISH I HADN'T EATEN THAT BURGER...
YOU SAW THE BOOKBINDER. TELL ME EVERYTHING YOU REMEMBER.
HE HAD A GUN. HE WORE A MASK. WHAT ELSE IS THERE?
DON'T MAKE ME JOG YOUR MEMORY...

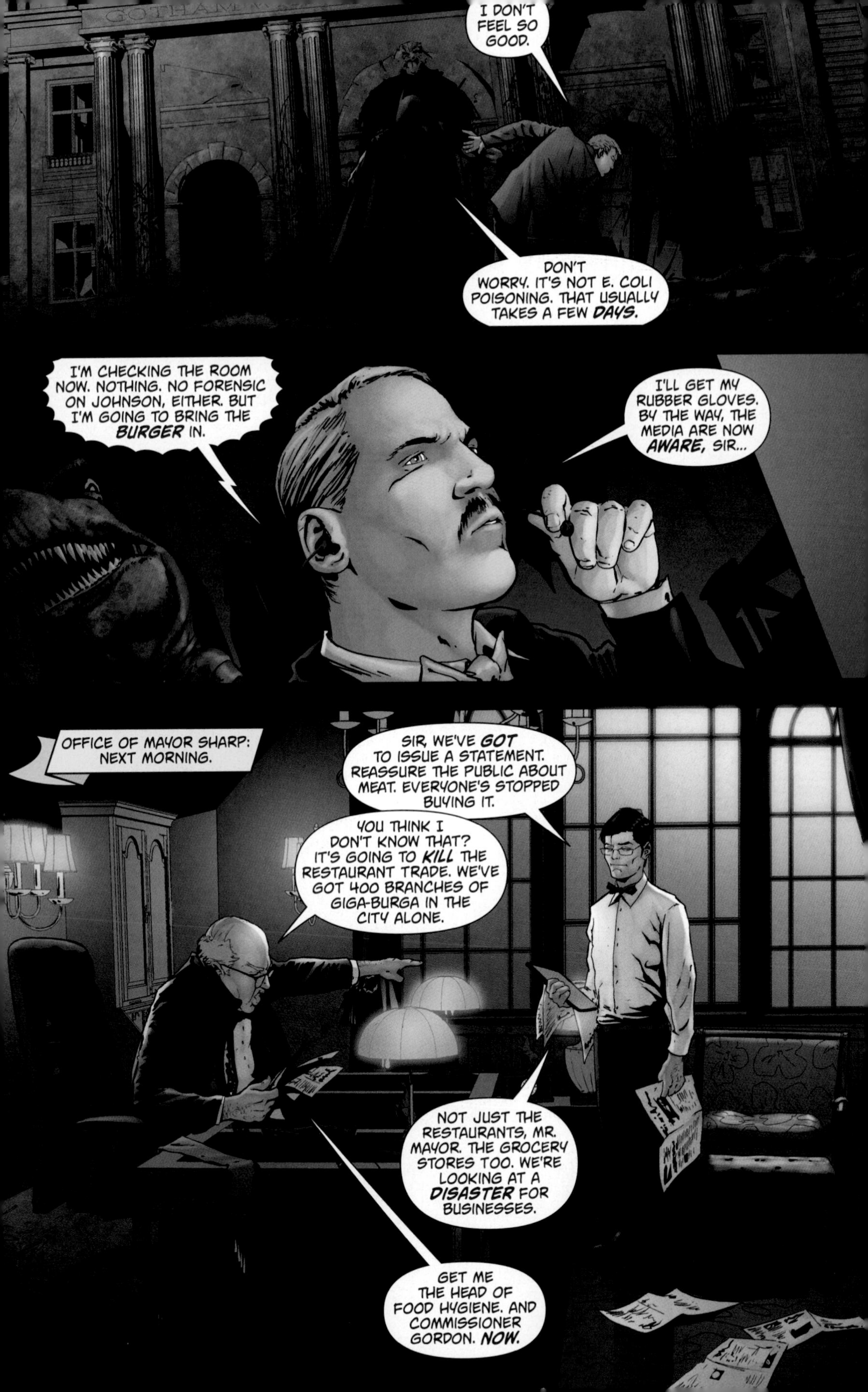
GOTHAM
I DON'T FEEL SO GOOD.
DON'T WORRY. IT'S NOT E. COLI POISONING. THAT USUALLY TAKES A FEW DAYS.
I'M CHECKING THE ROOM NOW. NOTHING. NO FORENSIC ON JOHNSON, EITHER. BUT I'M GOING TO BRING THE BURGER IN.
I'LL GET MY RUBBER GLOVES. BY THE WAY, THE MEDIA ARE NOW AWARE, SIR...
OFFICE OF MAYOR SHARP: NEXT MORNING.
SIR, WE'VE GOT TO ISSUE A STATEMENT. REASSURE THE PUBLIC ABOUT MEAT. EVERYONE'S STOPPED BUYING IT.
YOU THINK I DON'T KNOW THAT? IT'S GOING TO KILL THE RESTAURANT TRADE. WE'VE GOT 400 BRANCHES OF GIGA-BURGA IN THE CITY ALONE.
NOT JUST THE RESTAURANTS, MR. MAYOR. THE GROCERY STORES TOO. WE'RE LOOKING AT A DISASTER FOR BUSINESSES.
GET ME THE HEAD OF FOOD HYGIENE. AND COMMISSIONER GORDON. NOW.

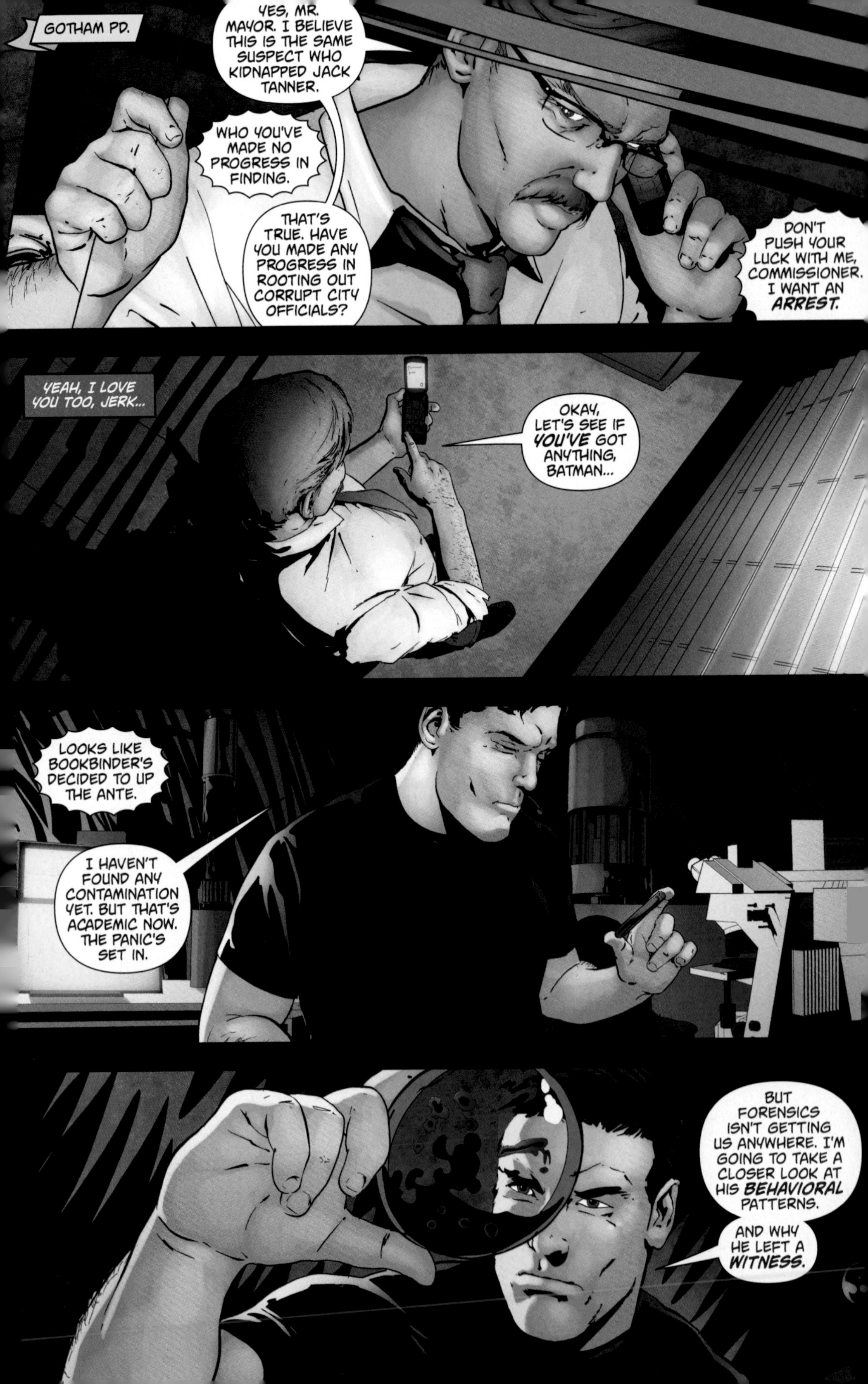
GOTHAM PD.
YES, MR. MAYOR. I BELIEVE THIS IS THE SAME SUSPECT WHO KIDNAPPED JACK TANNER.
WHO YOU'VE MADE NO PROGRESS IN FINDING.
THAT'S TRUE. HAVE YOU MADE ANY PROGRESS IN ROOTING OUT CORRUPT CITY OFFICIALS?
DON'T PUSH YOUR LUCK WITH ME, COMMISSIONER. I WANT AN ARREST.
YEAH, I LOVE YOU TOO, JERK...
OKAY, LET'S SEE IF YOU'VE GOT ANYTHING, BATMAN...
LOOKS LIKE BOOKBINDER'S DECIDED TO UP THE ANTE.
I HAVEN'T FOUND ANY CONTAMINATION YET. BUT THAT'S ACADEMIC NOW. THE PANIC'S SET IN.
BUT FORENSICS ISN'T GETTING US ANYWHERE. I'M GOING TO TAKE A CLOSER LOOK AT HIS BEHAVIORAL PATTERNS.
AND WHY HE LEFT A WITNESS.

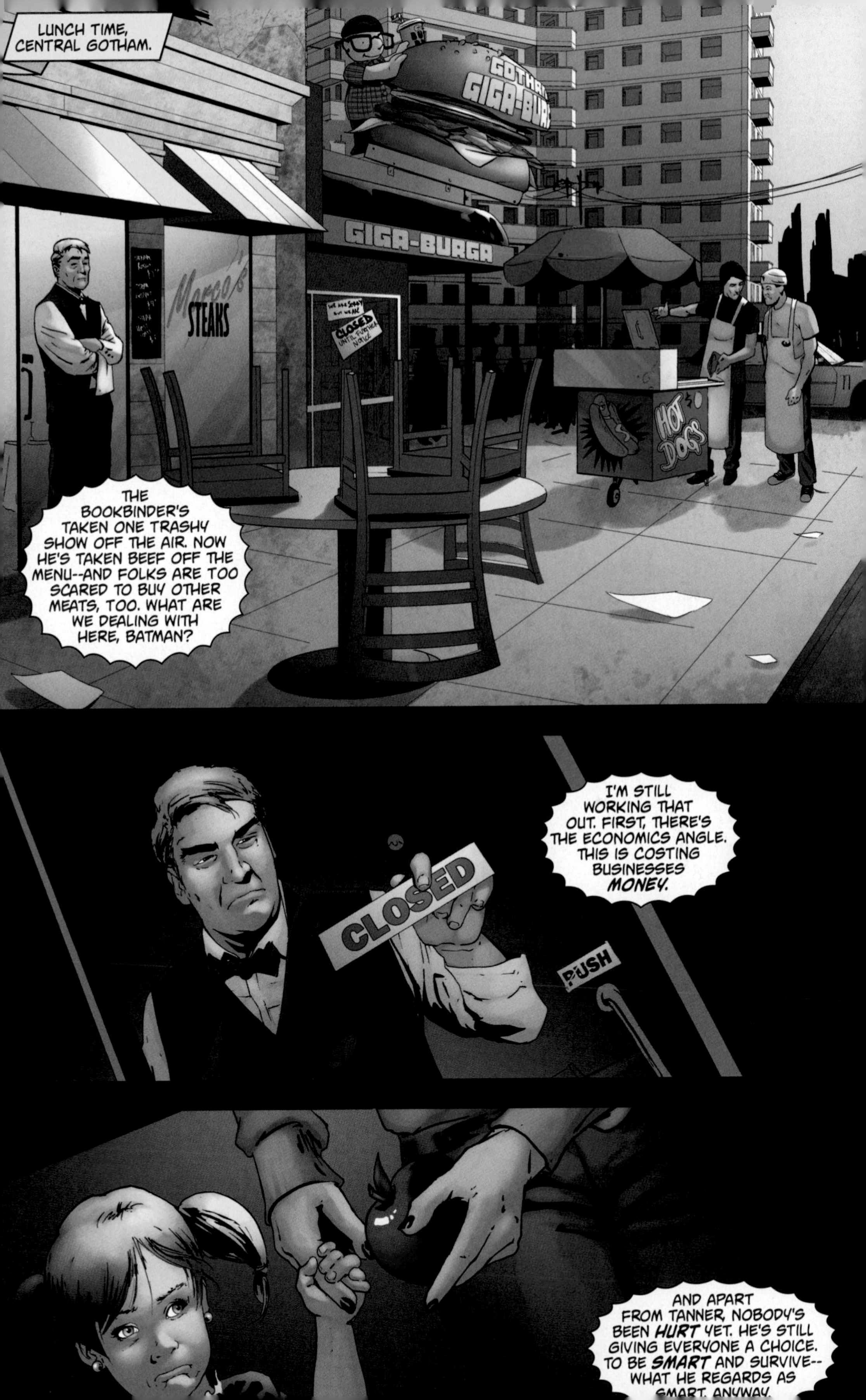

LUNCH TIME, CENTRAL GOTHAM.
GIGA-BURGA
Marco's STEAKS
CLOSED UNTIL FURTHER NOTICE
HOT DOGS
THE BOOKBINDER'S TAKEN ONE TRASHY SHOW OFF THE AIR. NOW HE'S TAKEN BEEF OFF THE MENU--AND FOLKS ARE TOO SCARED TO BUY OTHER MEATS, TOO. WHAT ARE WE DEALING WITH HERE, BATMAN?
I'M STILL WORKING THAT OUT. FIRST, THERE'S THE ECONOMICS ANGLE. THIS IS COSTING BUSINESSES *MONEY.*
CLOSED
PUSH
AND APART FROM TANNER, NOBODY'S BEEN *HURT* YET. HE'S STILL GIVING EVERYONE A CHOICE. TO BE *SMART* AND SURVIVE--WHAT HE REGARDS AS SMART, ANYWAY.

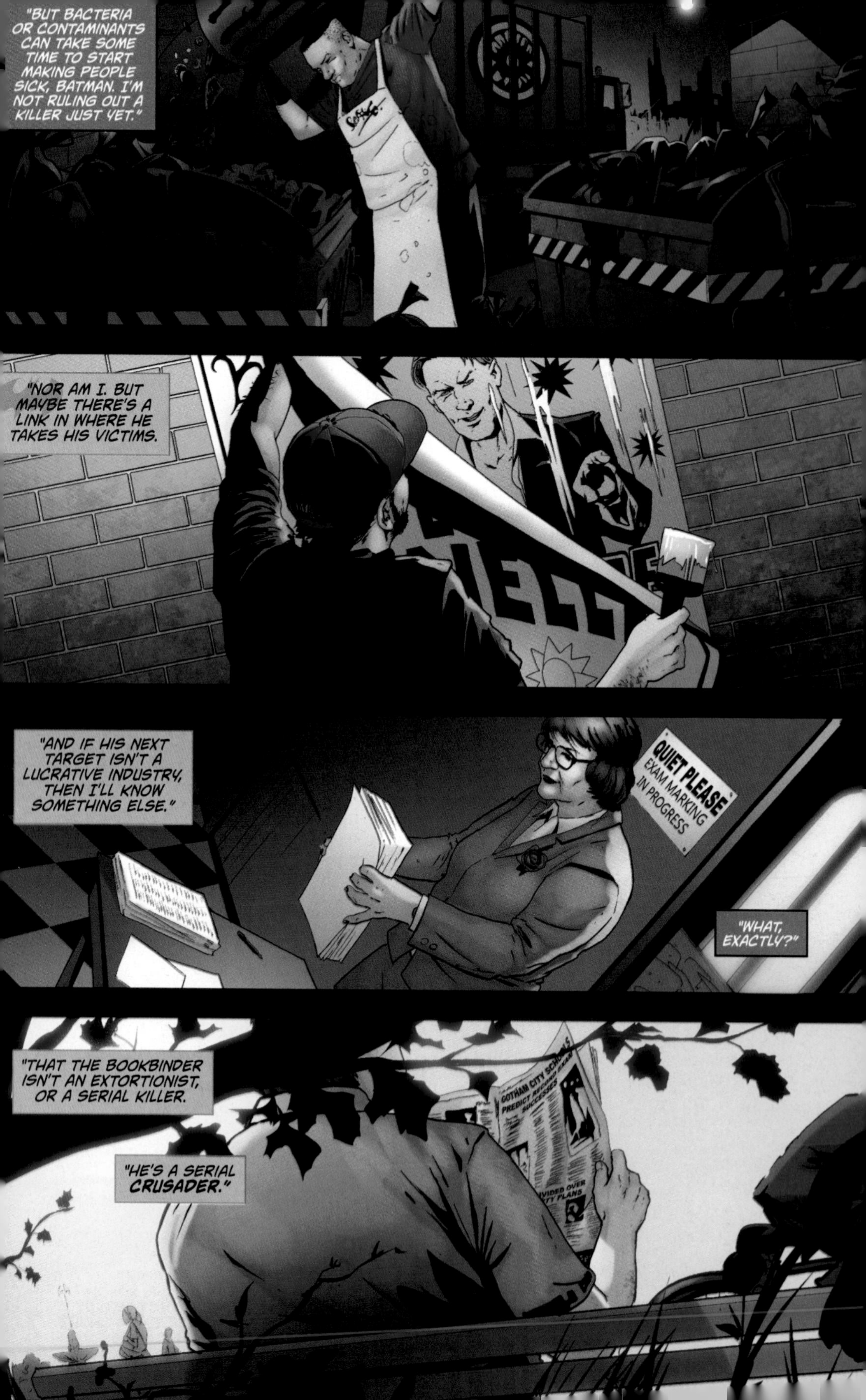
"BUT BACTERIA OR CONTAMINANTS CAN TAKE SOME TIME TO START MAKING PEOPLE SICK, BATMAN. I'M NOT RULING OUT A KILLER JUST YET."
"NOR AM I. BUT MAYBE THERE'S A LINK IN WHERE HE TAKES HIS VICTIMS.
"AND IF HIS NEXT TARGET ISN'T A LUCRATIVE INDUSTRY, THEN I'LL KNOW SOMETHING ELSE."
QUIET PLEASE
EXAM MARKING IN PROGRESS
"WHAT, EXACTLY?"
"THAT THE BOOKBINDER ISN'T AN EXTORTIONIST, OR A SERIAL KILLER.
"HE'S A SERIAL CRUSADER."
GOTHAM CITY SCHOOLS PREDICT RECORD EXAM SUCCESSES

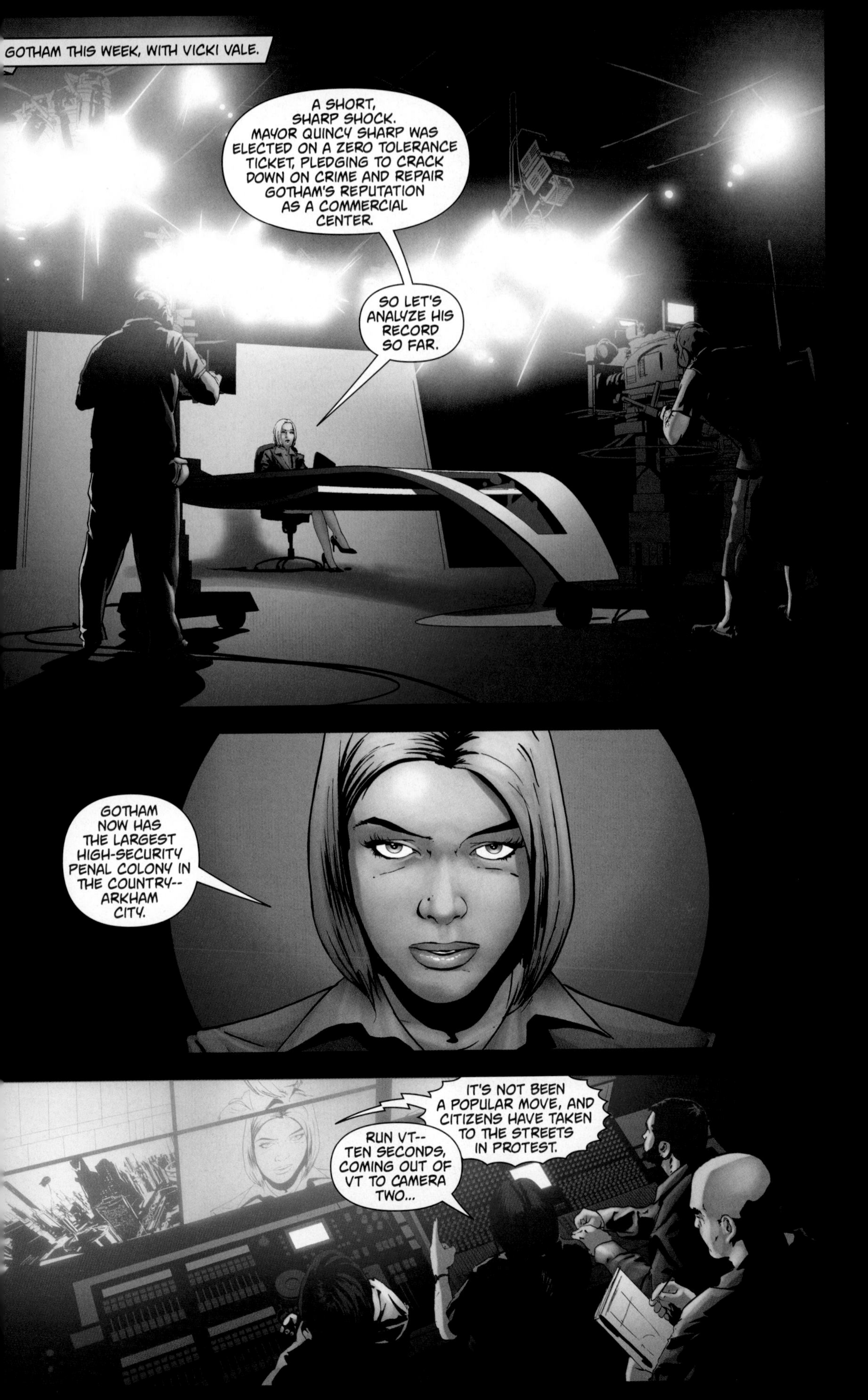
GOTHAM THIS WEEK, WITH VICKI VALE.
A SHORT, SHARP SHOCK. MAYOR QUINCY SHARP WAS ELECTED ON A ZERO TOLERANCE TICKET, PLEDGING TO CRACK DOWN ON CRIME AND REPAIR GOTHAM'S REPUTATION AS A COMMERCIAL CENTER.
SO LET'S ANALYZE HIS RECORD SO FAR.
GOTHAM NOW HAS THE LARGEST HIGH-SECURITY PENAL COLONY IN THE COUNTRY-- ARKHAM CITY.
IT'S NOT BEEN A POPULAR MOVE, AND CITIZENS HAVE TAKEN TO THE STREETS IN PROTEST.
RUN VT-- TEN SECONDS, COMING OUT OF VT TO CAMERA TWO...

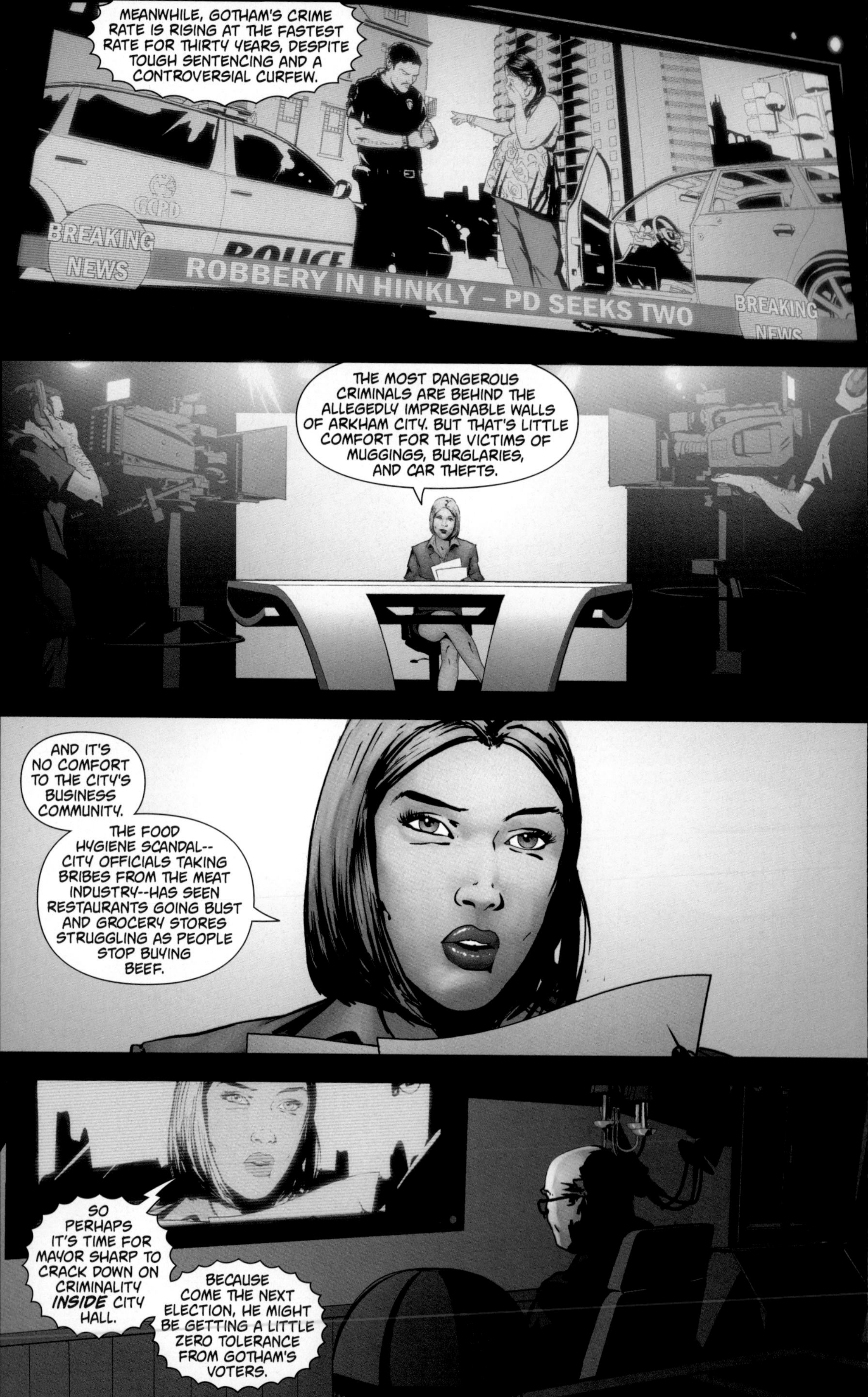
MEANWHILE, GOTHAM'S CRIME RATE IS RISING AT THE FASTEST RATE FOR THIRTY YEARS, DESPITE TOUGH SENTENCING AND A CONTROVERSIAL CURFEW.
GCPD
BREAKING NEWS
ROBBERY IN HINKLY – PD SEEKS TWO
BREAKING NEWS
THE MOST DANGEROUS CRIMINALS ARE BEHIND THE ALLEGEDLY IMPREGNABLE WALLS OF ARKHAM CITY. BUT THAT'S LITTLE COMFORT FOR THE VICTIMS OF MUGGINGS, BURGLARIES, AND CAR THEFTS.
AND IT'S NO COMFORT TO THE CITY'S BUSINESS COMMUNITY.
THE FOOD HYGIENE SCANDAL--CITY OFFICIALS TAKING BRIBES FROM THE MEAT INDUSTRY--HAS SEEN RESTAURANTS GOING BUST AND GROCERY STORES STRUGGLING AS PEOPLE STOP BUYING BEEF.
SO PERHAPS IT'S TIME FOR MAYOR SHARP TO CRACK DOWN ON CRIMINALITY *INSIDE* CITY HALL.
BECAUSE COME THE NEXT ELECTION, HE MIGHT BE GETTING A LITTLE ZERO TOLERANCE FROM GOTHAM'S VOTERS.

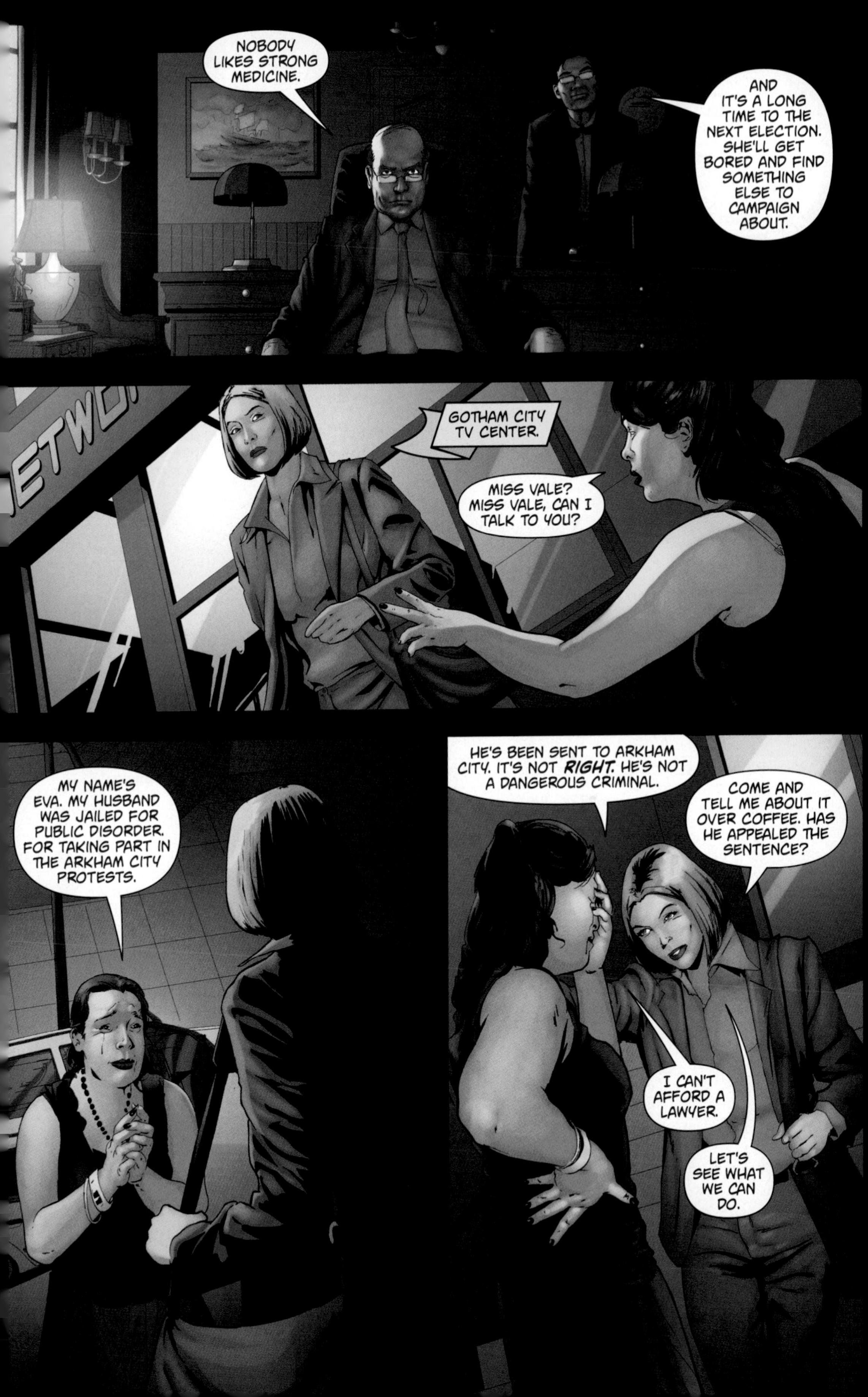
NOBODY LIKES STRONG MEDICINE.
AND IT'S A LONG TIME TO THE NEXT ELECTION. SHE'LL GET BORED AND FIND SOMETHING ELSE TO CAMPAIGN ABOUT.
NETWO
GOTHAM CITY TV CENTER.
MISS VALE? MISS VALE, CAN I TALK TO YOU?
MY NAME'S EVA. MY HUSBAND WAS JAILED FOR PUBLIC DISORDER. FOR TAKING PART IN THE ARKHAM CITY PROTESTS.
HE'S BEEN SENT TO ARKHAM CITY. IT'S NOT RIGHT. HE'S NOT A DANGEROUS CRIMINAL.
COME AND TELL ME ABOUT IT OVER COFFEE. HAS HE APPEALED THE SENTENCE?
I CAN'T AFFORD A LAWYER.
LET'S SEE WHAT WE CAN DO.

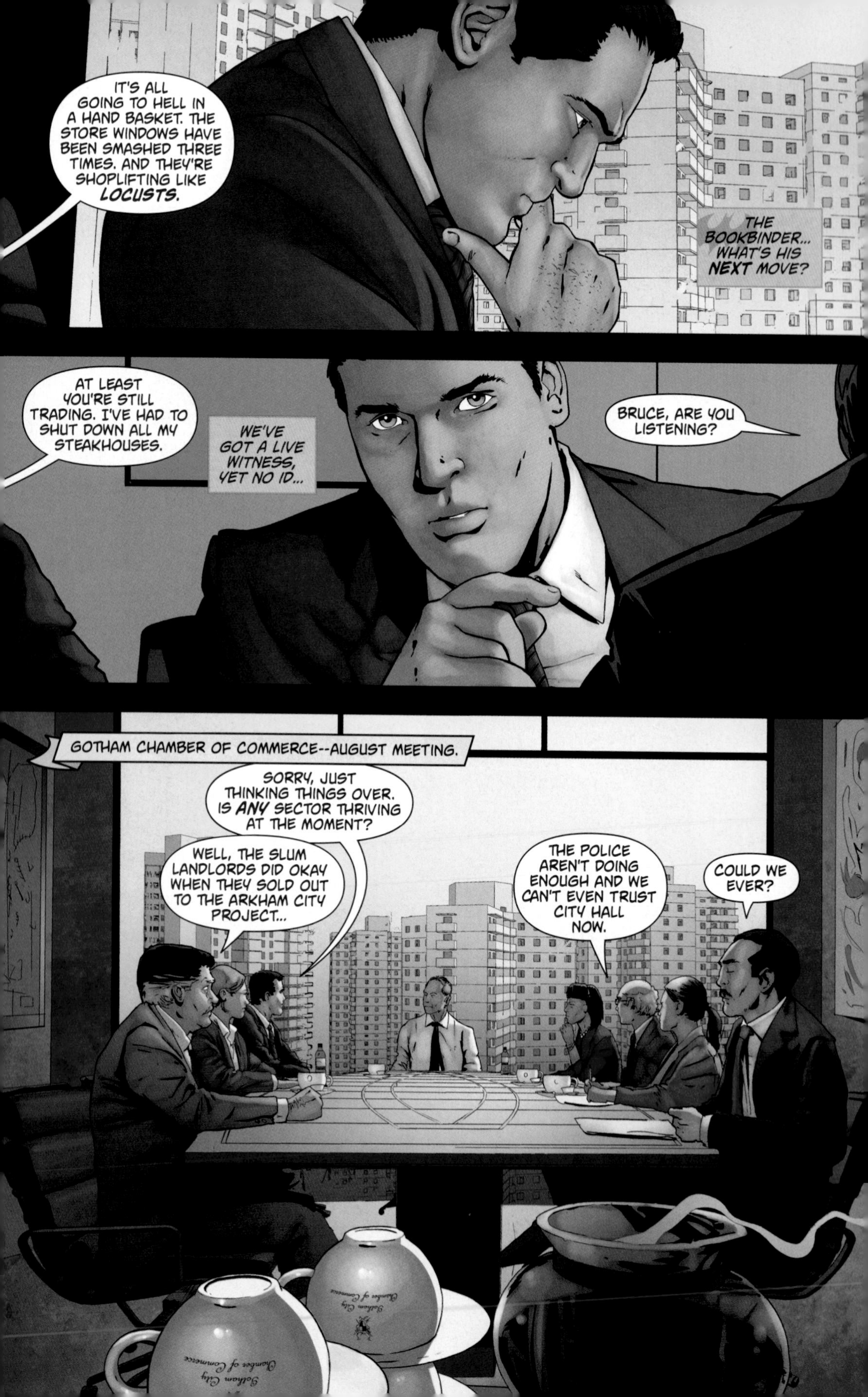
IT'S ALL GOING TO HELL IN A HAND BASKET. THE STORE WINDOWS HAVE BEEN SMASHED THREE TIMES. AND THEY'RE SHOPLIFTING LIKE LOCUSTS.
THE BOOKBINDER... WHAT'S HIS NEXT MOVE?
AT LEAST YOU'RE STILL TRADING. I'VE HAD TO SHUT DOWN ALL MY STEAKHOUSES.
WE'VE GOT A LIVE WITNESS, YET NO ID...
BRUCE, ARE YOU LISTENING?
GOTHAM CHAMBER OF COMMERCE--AUGUST MEETING.
SORRY, JUST THINKING THINGS OVER. IS ANY SECTOR THRIVING AT THE MOMENT?
WELL, THE SLUM LANDLORDS DID OKAY WHEN THEY SOLD OUT TO THE ARKHAM CITY PROJECT...
THE POLICE AREN'T DOING ENOUGH AND WE CAN'T EVEN TRUST CITY HALL NOW.
COULD WE EVER?

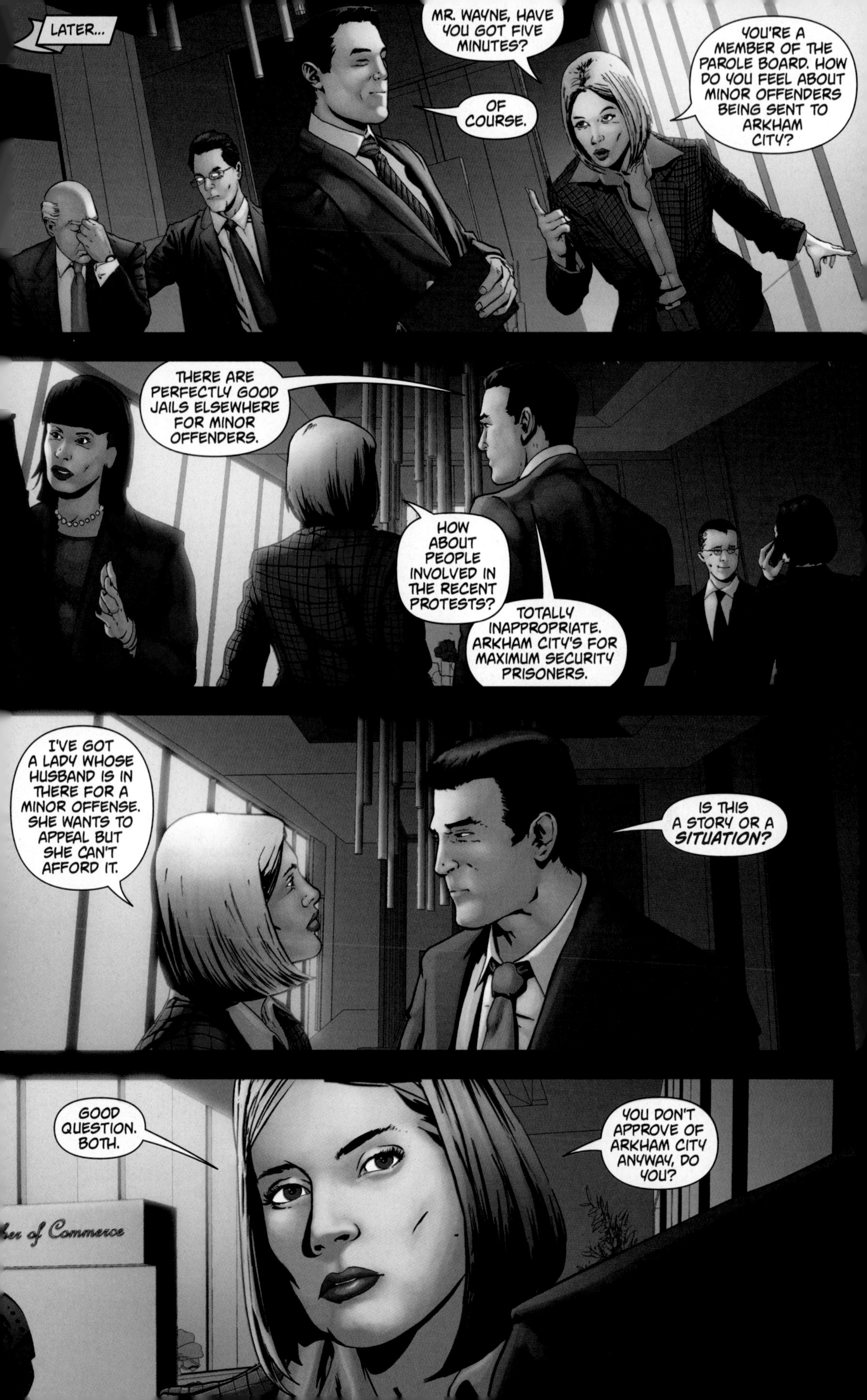
LATER...
MR. WAYNE, HAVE YOU GOT FIVE MINUTES?
OF COURSE.
YOU'RE A MEMBER OF THE PAROLE BOARD. HOW DO YOU FEEL ABOUT MINOR OFFENDERS BEING SENT TO ARKHAM CITY?
THERE ARE PERFECTLY GOOD JAILS ELSEWHERE FOR MINOR OFFENDERS.
HOW ABOUT PEOPLE INVOLVED IN THE RECENT PROTESTS?
TOTALLY INAPPROPRIATE. ARKHAM CITY'S FOR MAXIMUM SECURITY PRISONERS.
I'VE GOT A LADY WHOSE HUSBAND IS IN THERE FOR A MINOR OFFENSE. SHE WANTS TO APPEAL BUT SHE CAN'T AFFORD IT.
IS THIS A STORY OR A *SITUATION?*
GOOD QUESTION. BOTH.
YOU DON'T APPROVE OF ARKHAM CITY ANYWAY, DO YOU?
ber of Commerce

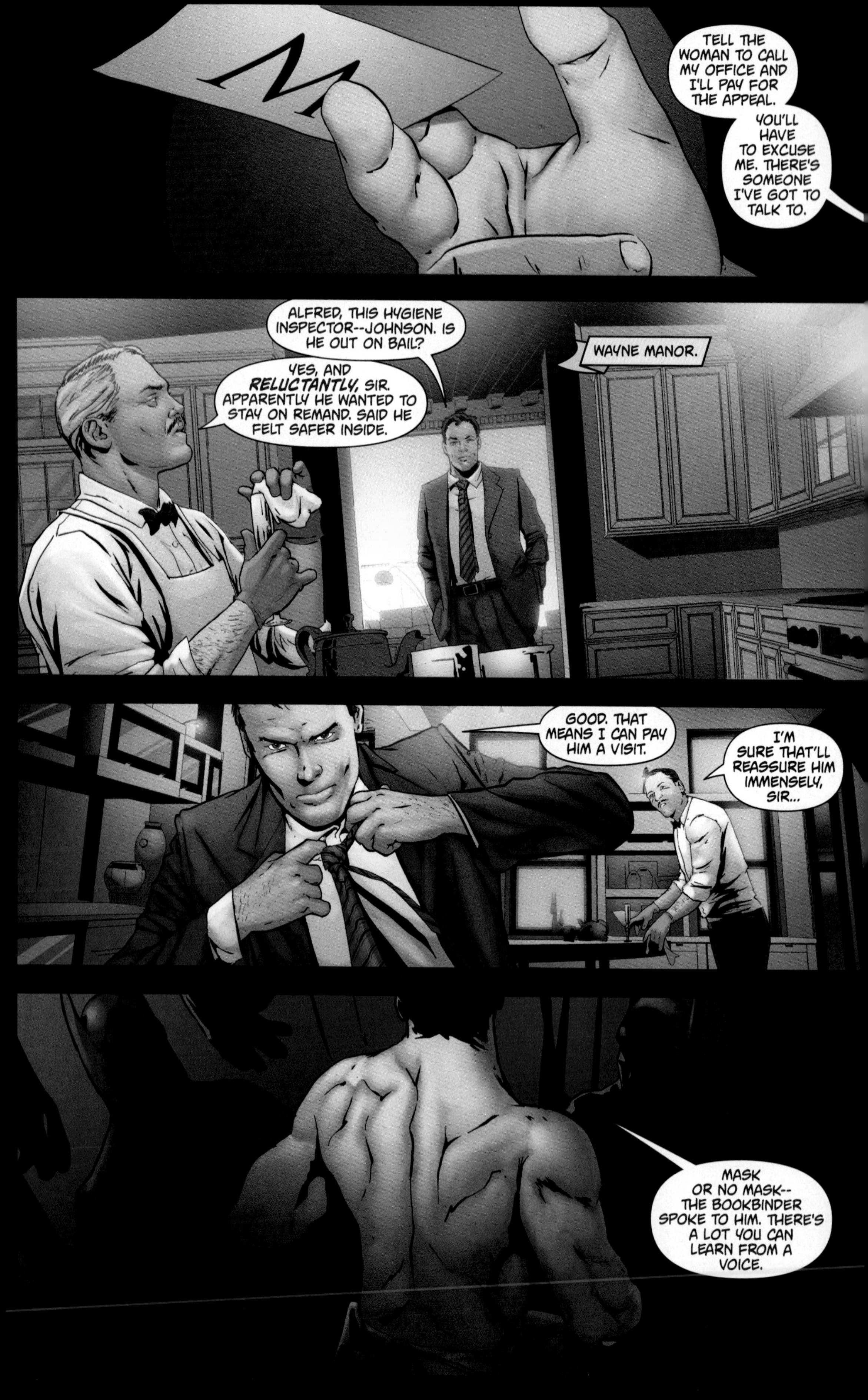
TELL THE WOMAN TO CALL MY OFFICE AND I'LL PAY FOR THE APPEAL.
YOU'LL HAVE TO EXCUSE ME. THERE'S SOMEONE I'VE GOT TO TALK TO.
WAYNE MANOR.
ALFRED, THIS HYGIENE INSPECTOR--JOHNSON. IS HE OUT ON BAIL?
YES, AND **RELUCTANTLY**, SIR. APPARENTLY HE WANTED TO STAY ON REMAND. SAID HE FELT SAFER INSIDE.
GOOD. THAT MEANS I CAN PAY HIM A VISIT.
I'M SURE THAT'LL REASSURE HIM IMMENSELY, SIR...
MASK OR NO MASK--THE BOOKBINDER SPOKE TO HIM. THERE'S A LOT YOU CAN LEARN FROM A VOICE.

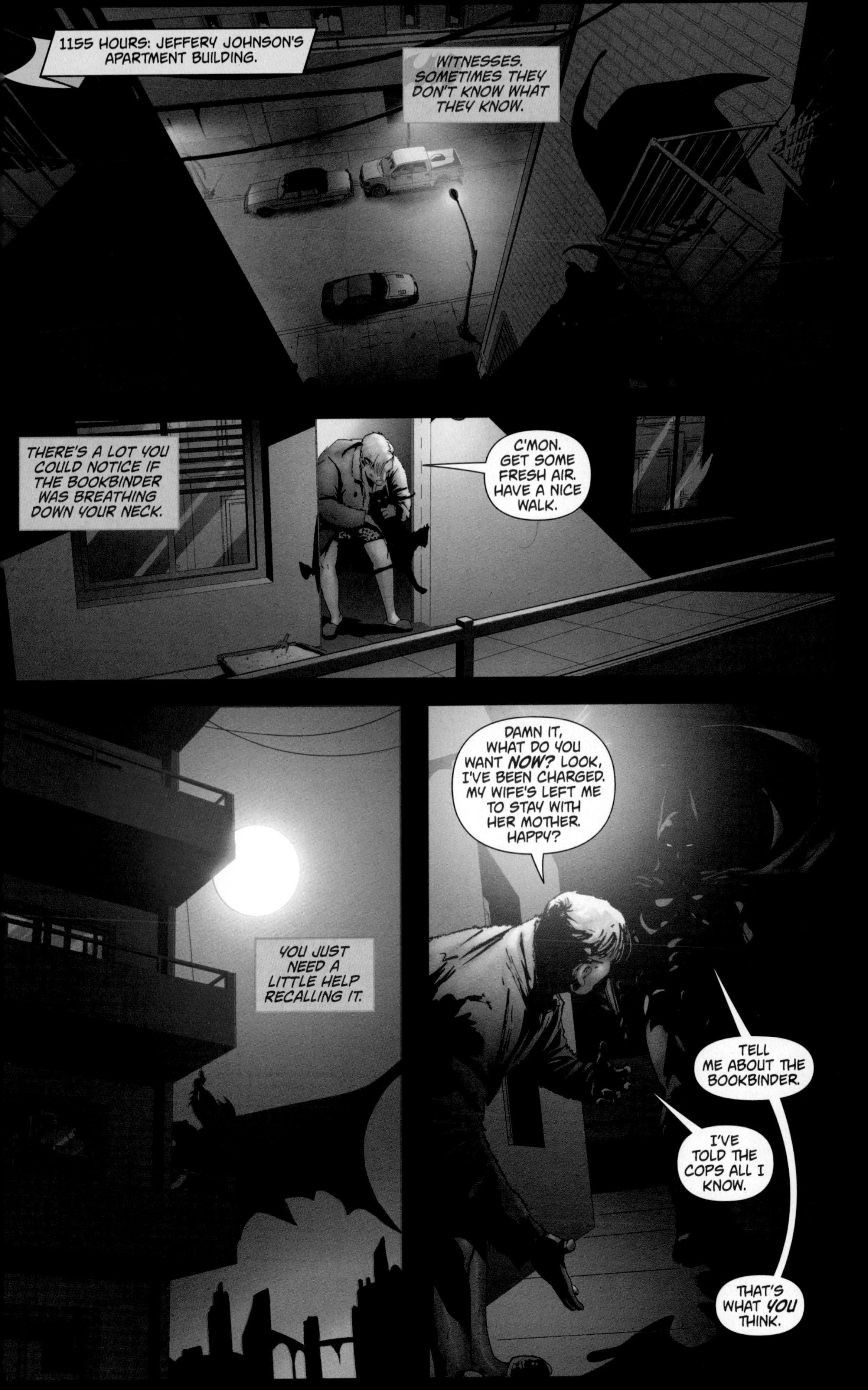
1155 HOURS: JEFFERY JOHNSON'S APARTMENT BUILDING.
WITNESSES. SOMETIMES THEY DON'T KNOW WHAT THEY KNOW.
THERE'S A LOT YOU COULD NOTICE IF THE BOOKBINDER WAS BREATHING DOWN YOUR NECK.
C'MON. GET SOME FRESH AIR. HAVE A NICE WALK.
YOU JUST NEED A LITTLE HELP RECALLING IT.
DAMN IT, WHAT DO YOU WANT NOW? LOOK, I'VE BEEN CHARGED. MY WIFE'S LEFT ME TO STAY WITH HER MOTHER. HAPPY?
TELL ME ABOUT THE BOOKBINDER.
I'VE TOLD THE COPS ALL I KNOW.
THAT'S WHAT YOU THINK.

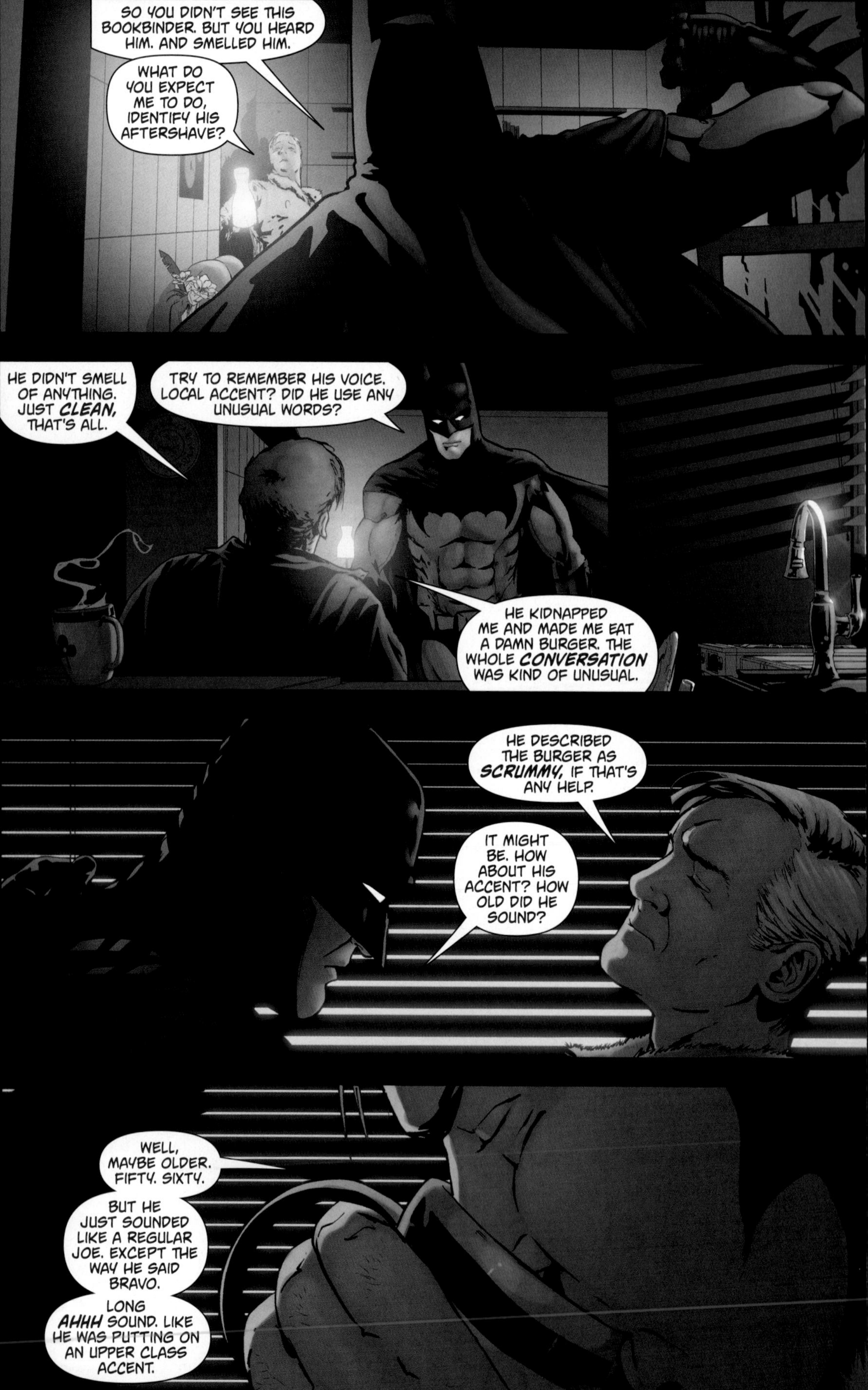
SO YOU DIDN'T SEE THIS BOOKBINDER. BUT YOU HEARD HIM. AND SMELLED HIM.
WHAT DO YOU EXPECT ME TO DO, IDENTIFY HIS AFTERSHAVE?
HE DIDN'T SMELL OF ANYTHING. JUST CLEAN, THAT'S ALL.
TRY TO REMEMBER HIS VOICE. LOCAL ACCENT? DID HE USE ANY UNUSUAL WORDS?
HE KIDNAPPED ME AND MADE ME EAT A DAMN BURGER. THE WHOLE CONVERSATION WAS KIND OF UNUSUAL.
HE DESCRIBED THE BURGER AS SCRUMMY, IF THAT'S ANY HELP.
IT MIGHT BE. HOW ABOUT HIS ACCENT? HOW OLD DID HE SOUND?
WELL, MAYBE OLDER. FIFTY. SIXTY.
BUT HE JUST SOUNDED LIKE A REGULAR JOE. EXCEPT THE WAY HE SAID BRAVO.
LONG AHHH SOUND. LIKE HE WAS PUTTING ON AN UPPER CLASS ACCENT.

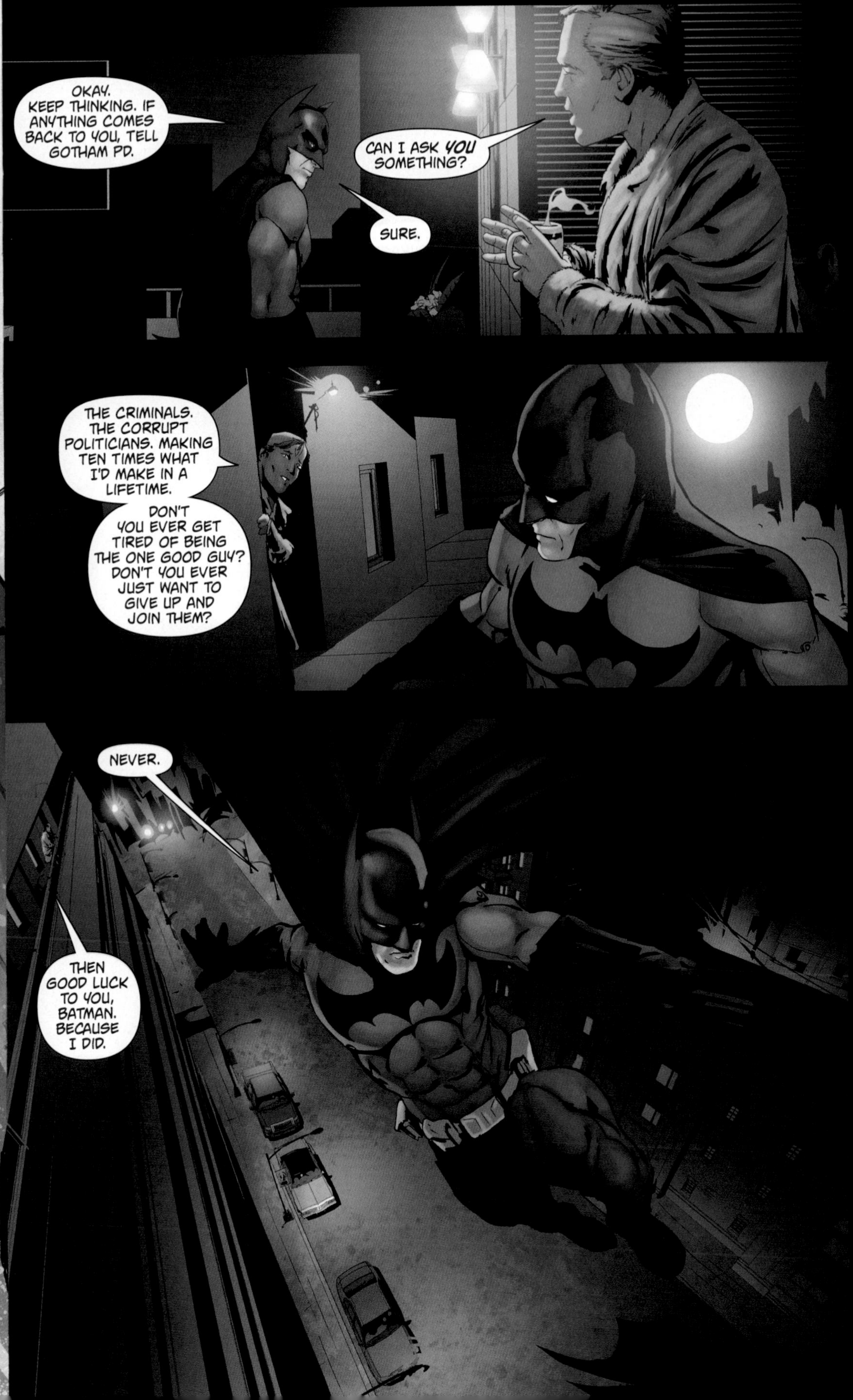
OKAY. KEEP THINKING. IF ANYTHING COMES BACK TO YOU, TELL GOTHAM PD.
CAN I ASK *YOU* SOMETHING?
SURE.
THE CRIMINALS. THE CORRUPT POLITICIANS. MAKING TEN TIMES WHAT I'D MAKE IN A LIFETIME.
DON'T YOU EVER GET TIRED OF BEING THE ONE GOOD GUY? DON'T YOU EVER JUST WANT TO GIVE UP AND JOIN THEM?
NEVER.
THEN GOOD LUCK TO YOU, BATMAN. BECAUSE I DID.

WELCOME
TO THE SLOUGH OF DESPOND
PART FOUR

WRITTEN BY: KAREN TRAVISS
ART BY: TONY SHASTEEN
COLORS BY: ALLEN PASSALAQUA
LETTERS BY: TRAVIS LANHAM
COVER BY: CHRIS MITTEN

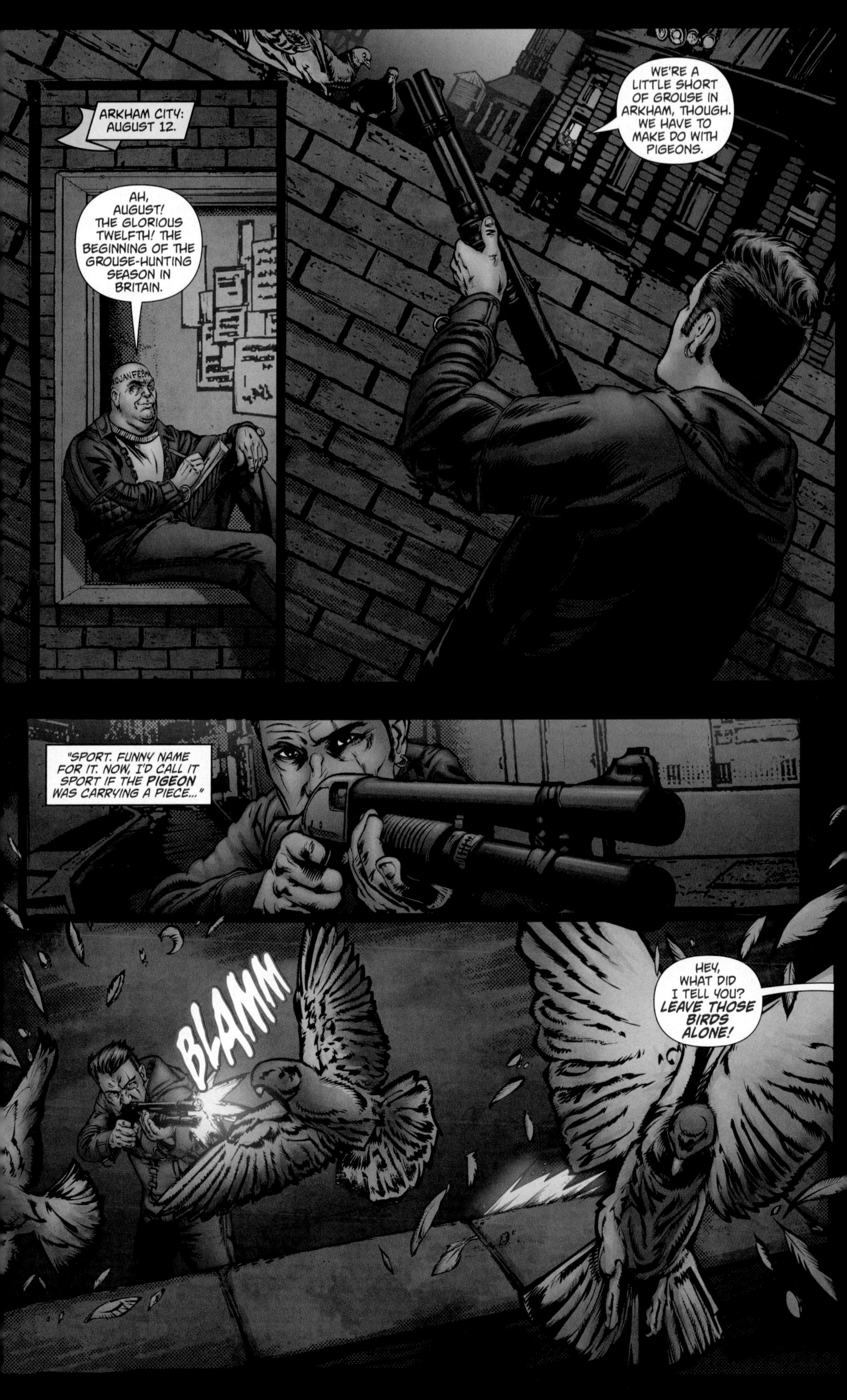
ARKHAM CITY: AUGUST 12.
AH, AUGUST! THE GLORIOUS TWELFTH! THE BEGINNING OF THE GROUSE-HUNTING SEASON IN BRITAIN.
WE'RE A LITTLE SHORT OF GROUSE IN ARKHAM, THOUGH. WE HAVE TO MAKE DO WITH PIGEONS.
"SPORT. FUNNY NAME FOR IT. NOW, I'D CALL IT SPORT IF THE PIGEON WAS CARRYING A PIECE..."
BLAMM
HEY, WHAT DID I TELL YOU? LEAVE THOSE BIRDS ALONE!

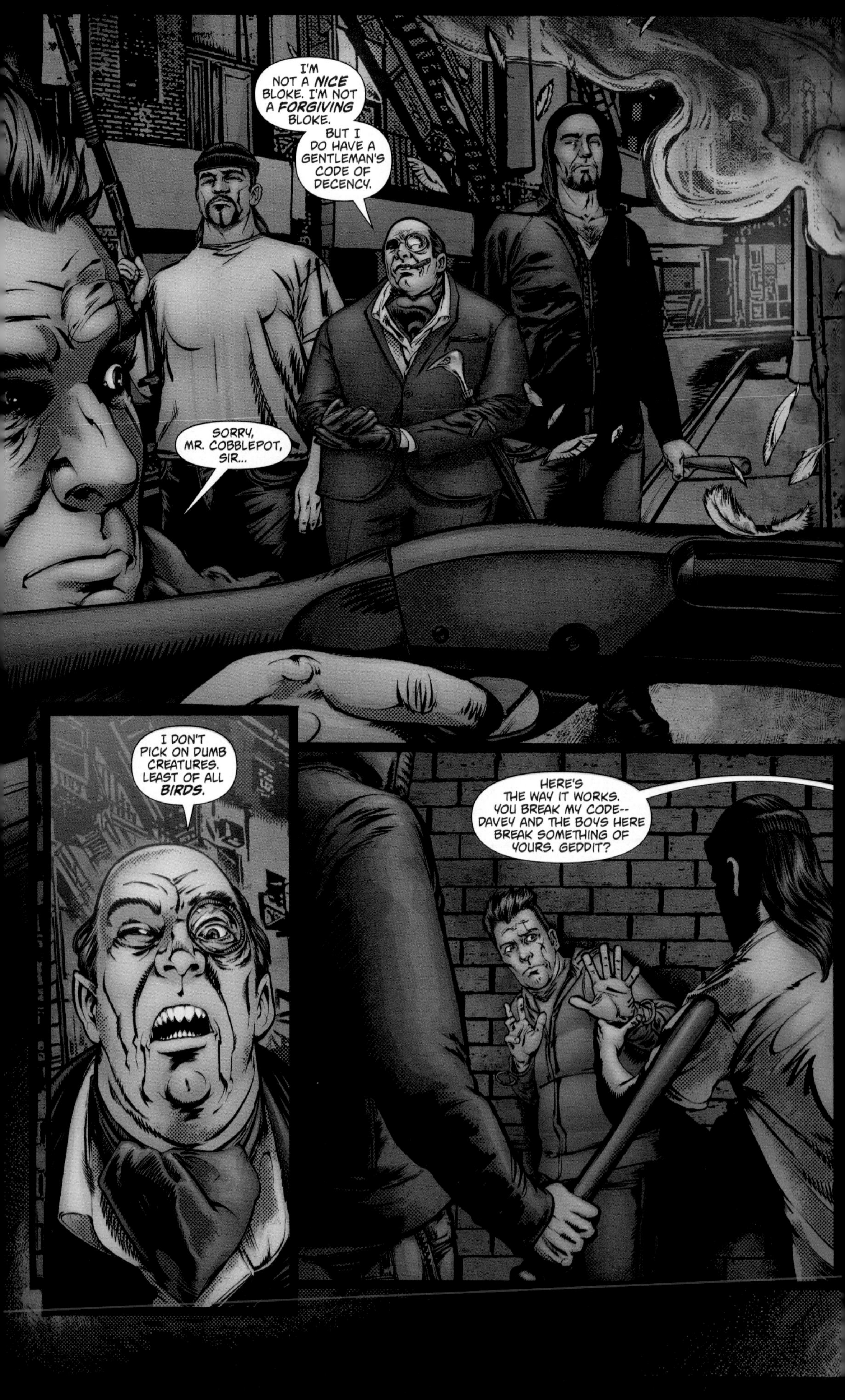
I'M NOT A NICE BLOKE. I'M NOT A FORGIVING BLOKE.
BUT I DO HAVE A GENTLEMAN'S CODE OF DECENCY.
SORRY, MR. COBBLEPOT, SIR...
I DON'T PICK ON DUMB CREATURES. LEAST OF ALL BIRDS.
HERE'S THE WAY IT WORKS. YOU BREAK MY CODE-- DAVEY AND THE BOYS HERE BREAK SOMETHING OF YOURS. GEDDIT?

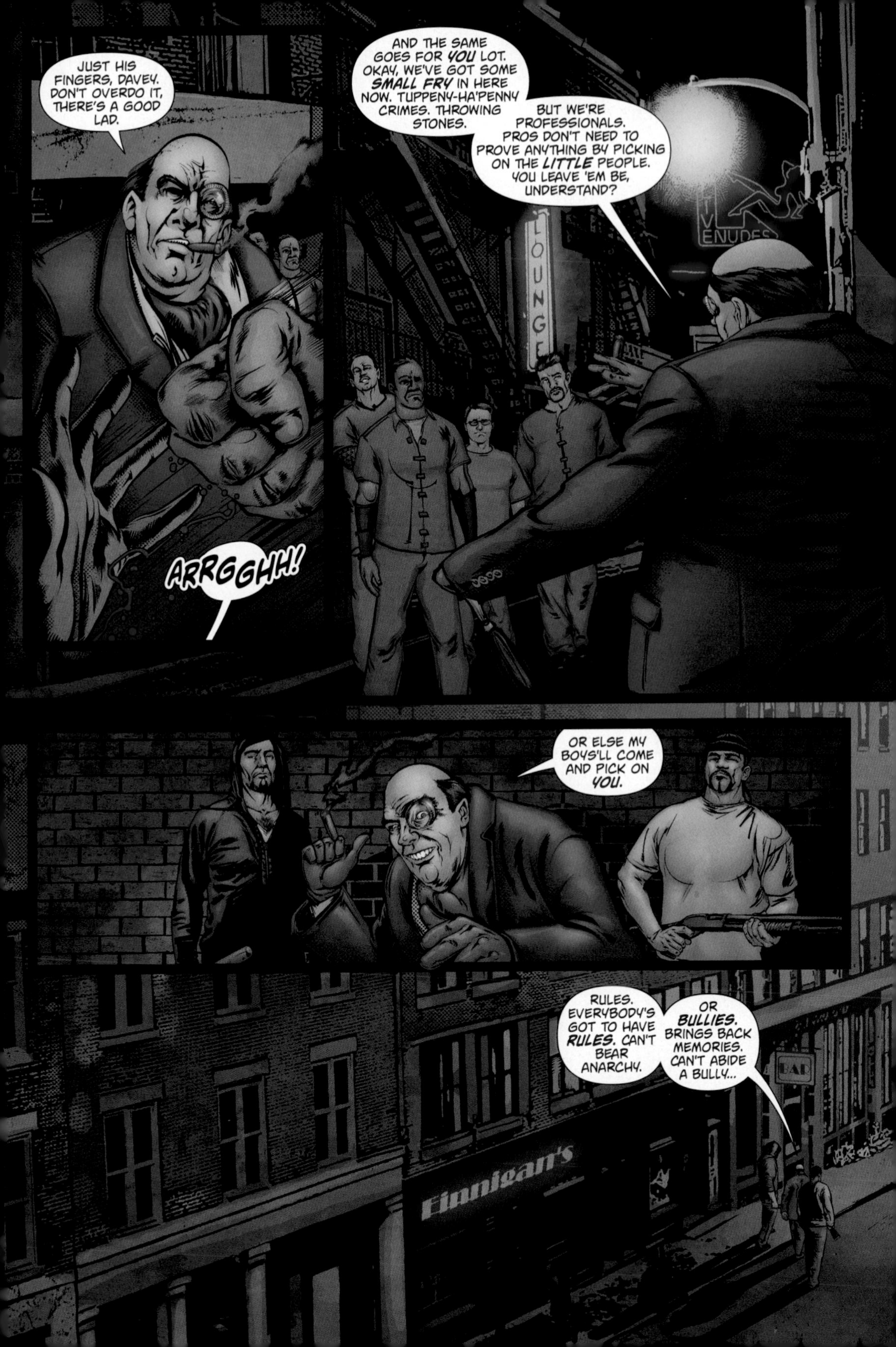
JUST HIS FINGERS, DAVEY. DON'T OVERDO IT, THERE'S A GOOD LAD.
ARRGGHH!
AND THE SAME GOES FOR YOU LOT. OKAY, WE'VE GOT SOME SMALL FRY IN HERE NOW. TUPPENY-HA'PENNY CRIMES. THROWING STONES.
BUT WE'RE PROFESSIONALS. PROS DON'T NEED TO PROVE ANYTHING BY PICKING ON THE LITTLE PEOPLE. YOU LEAVE 'EM BE, UNDERSTAND?
LOUNGE
NUDES
OR ELSE MY BOYS'LL COME AND PICK ON YOU.
RULES. EVERYBODY'S GOT TO HAVE RULES. CAN'T BEAR ANARCHY.
OR BULLIES. BRINGS BACK MEMORIES. CAN'T ABIDE A BULLY...
BAR
Finnigan's

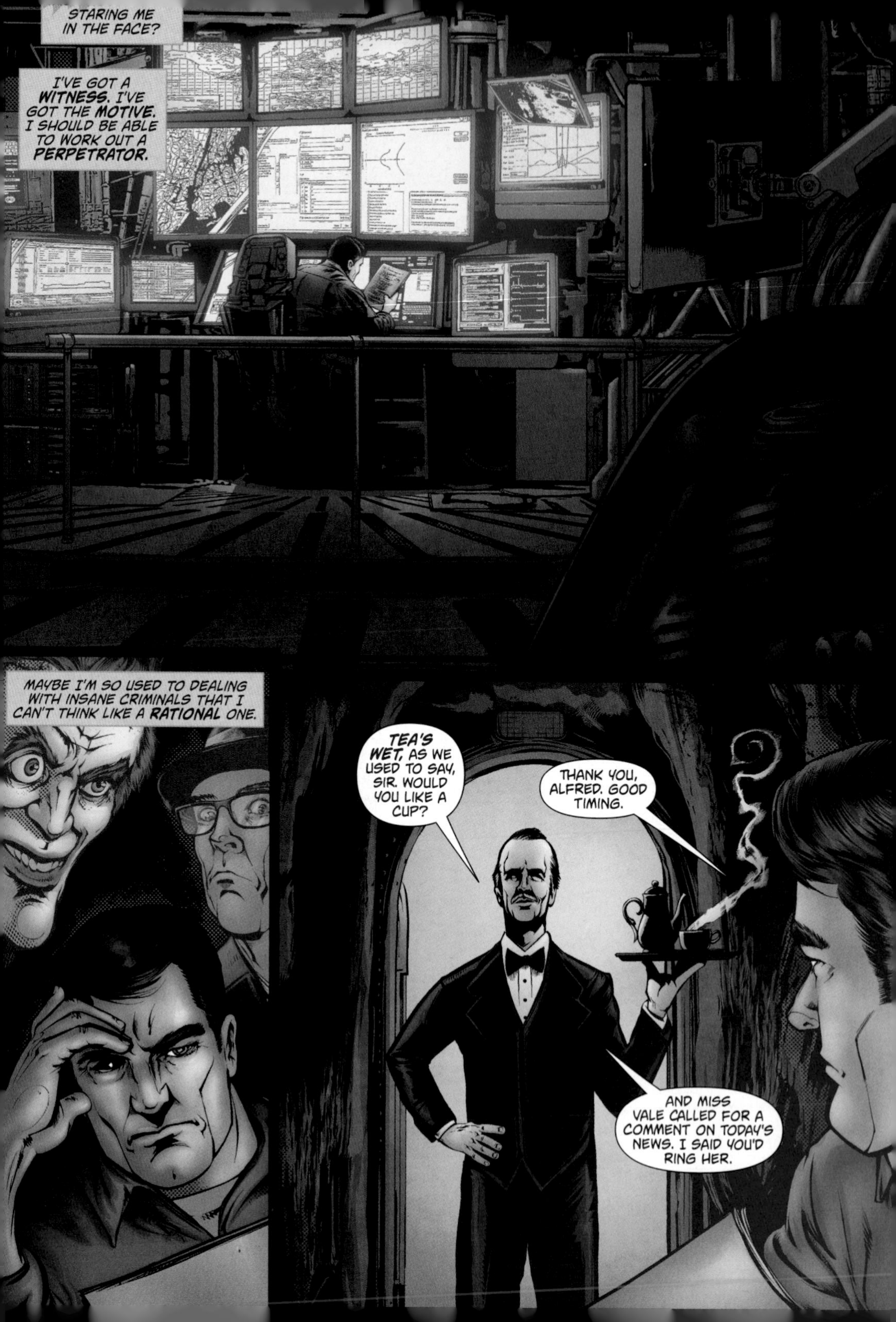
STARING ME IN THE FACE?
I'VE GOT A WITNESS. I'VE GOT THE MOTIVE. I SHOULD BE ABLE TO WORK OUT A PERPETRATOR.
MAYBE I'M SO USED TO DEALING WITH INSANE CRIMINALS THAT I CAN'T THINK LIKE A RATIONAL ONE.
TEA'S WET, AS WE USED TO SAY, SIR. WOULD YOU LIKE A CUP?
THANK YOU, ALFRED. GOOD TIMING.
AND MISS VALE CALLED FOR A COMMENT ON TODAY'S NEWS. I SAID YOU'D RING HER.

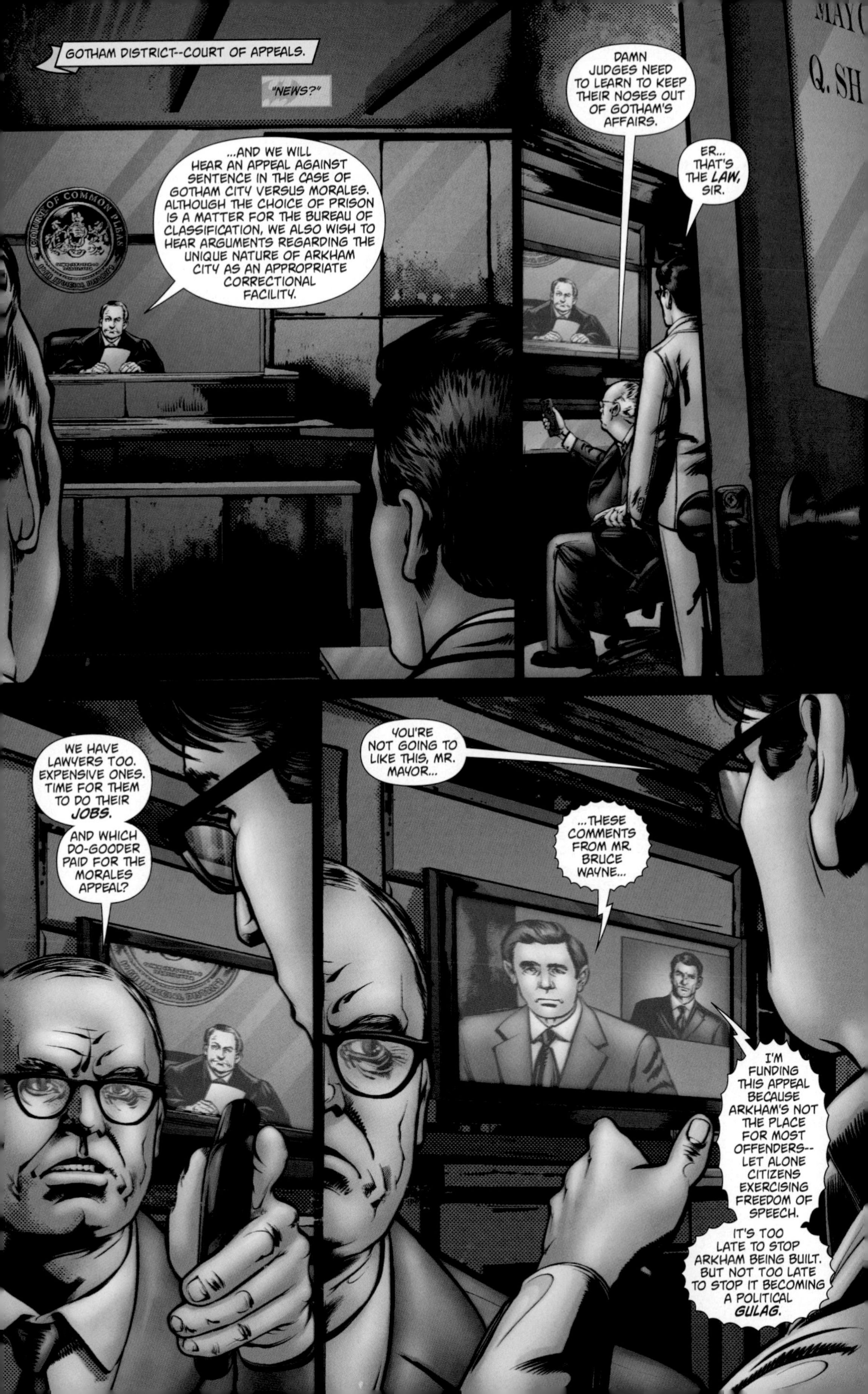
GOTHAM DISTRICT--COURT OF APPEALS.
"NEWS?"
...AND WE WILL HEAR AN APPEAL AGAINST SENTENCE IN THE CASE OF GOTHAM CITY VERSUS MORALES. ALTHOUGH THE CHOICE OF PRISON IS A MATTER FOR THE BUREAU OF CLASSIFICATION, WE ALSO WISH TO HEAR ARGUMENTS REGARDING THE UNIQUE NATURE OF ARKHAM CITY AS AN APPROPRIATE CORRECTIONAL FACILITY.
COURT OF COMMON PLEAS
MAYO
Q. SH
DAMN JUDGES NEED TO LEARN TO KEEP THEIR NOSES OUT OF GOTHAM'S AFFAIRS.
ER... THAT'S THE LAW, SIR.
WE HAVE LAWYERS TOO. EXPENSIVE ONES. TIME FOR THEM TO DO THEIR JOBS.
AND WHICH DO-GOODER PAID FOR THE MORALES APPEAL?
YOU'RE NOT GOING TO LIKE THIS, MR. MAYOR...
...THESE COMMENTS FROM MR. BRUCE WAYNE...
I'M FUNDING THIS APPEAL BECAUSE ARKHAM'S NOT THE PLACE FOR MOST OFFENDERS-- LET ALONE CITIZENS EXERCISING FREEDOM OF SPEECH.
IT'S TOO LATE TO STOP ARKHAM BEING BUILT. BUT NOT TOO LATE TO STOP IT BECOMING A POLITICAL GULAG.

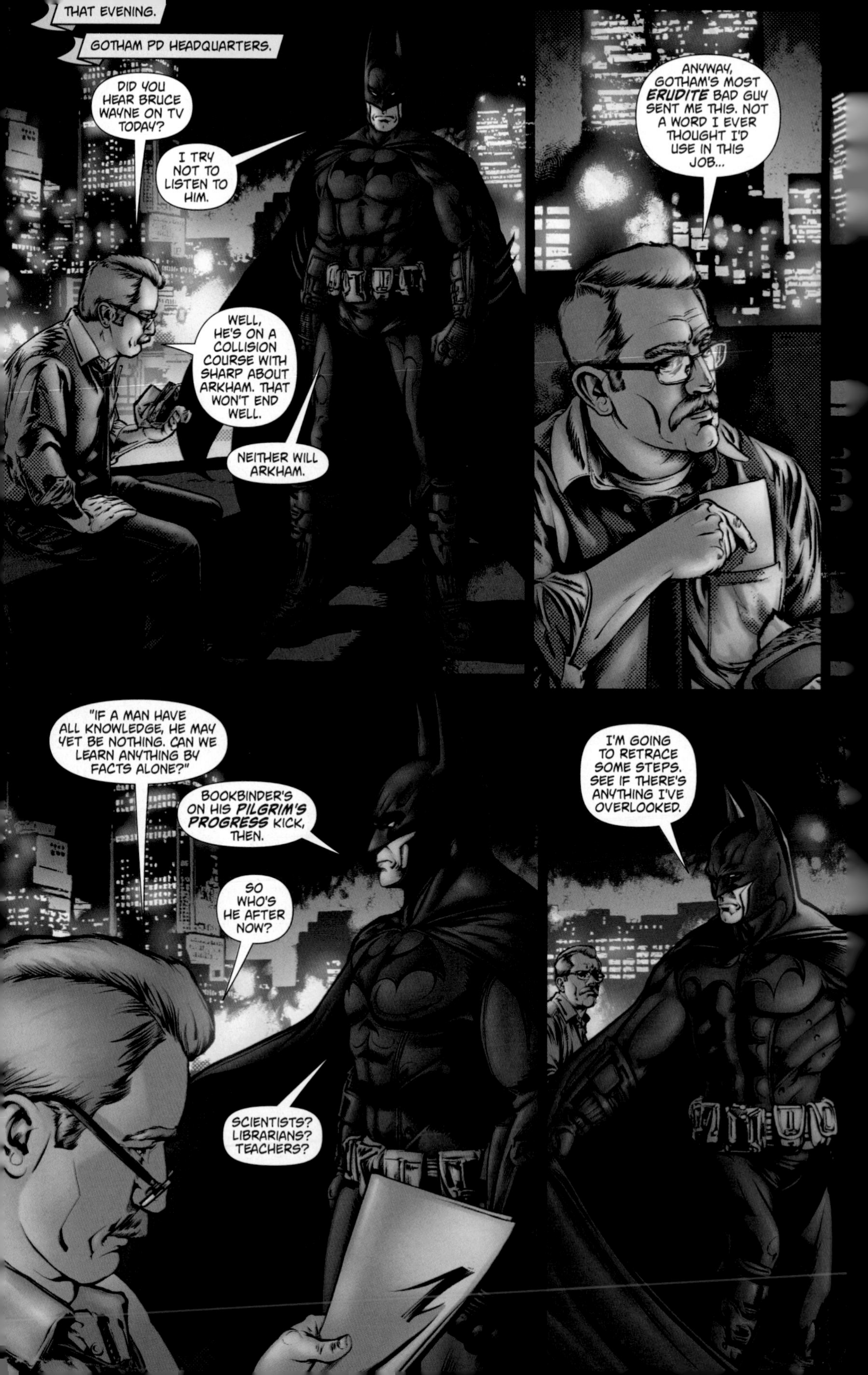
THAT EVENING.
GOTHAM PD HEADQUARTERS.
DID YOU HEAR BRUCE WAYNE ON TV TODAY?
I TRY NOT TO LISTEN TO HIM.
WELL, HE'S ON A COLLISION COURSE WITH SHARP ABOUT ARKHAM. THAT WON'T END WELL.
NEITHER WILL ARKHAM.
ANYWAY, GOTHAM'S MOST ERUDITE BAD GUY SENT ME THIS. NOT A WORD I EVER THOUGHT I'D USE IN THIS JOB...
"IF A MAN HAVE ALL KNOWLEDGE, HE MAY YET BE NOTHING. CAN WE LEARN ANYTHING BY FACTS ALONE?"
BOOKBINDER'S ON HIS PILGRIM'S PROGRESS KICK, THEN.
SO WHO'S HE AFTER NOW?
SCIENTISTS? LIBRARIANS? TEACHERS?
I'M GOING TO RETRACE SOME STEPS. SEE IF THERE'S ANYTHING I'VE OVERLOOKED.

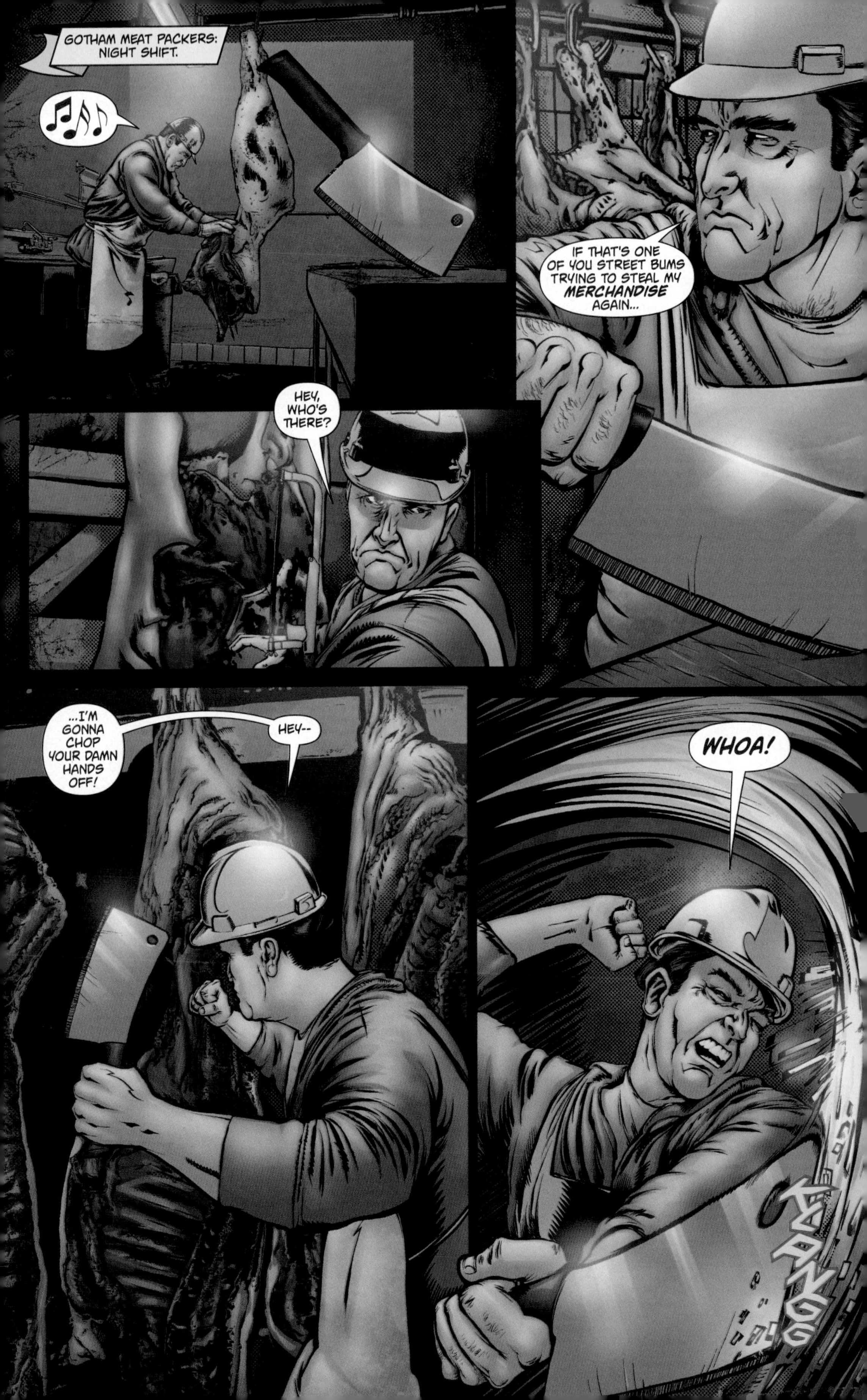
GOTHAM MEAT PACKERS: NIGHT SHIFT.
♫♫♪
HEY, WHO'S THERE?
IF THAT'S ONE OF YOU STREET BUMS TRYING TO STEAL MY MERCHANDISE AGAIN...
...I'M GONNA CHOP YOUR DAMN HANDS OFF!
HEY--
WHOA!
KLANGG

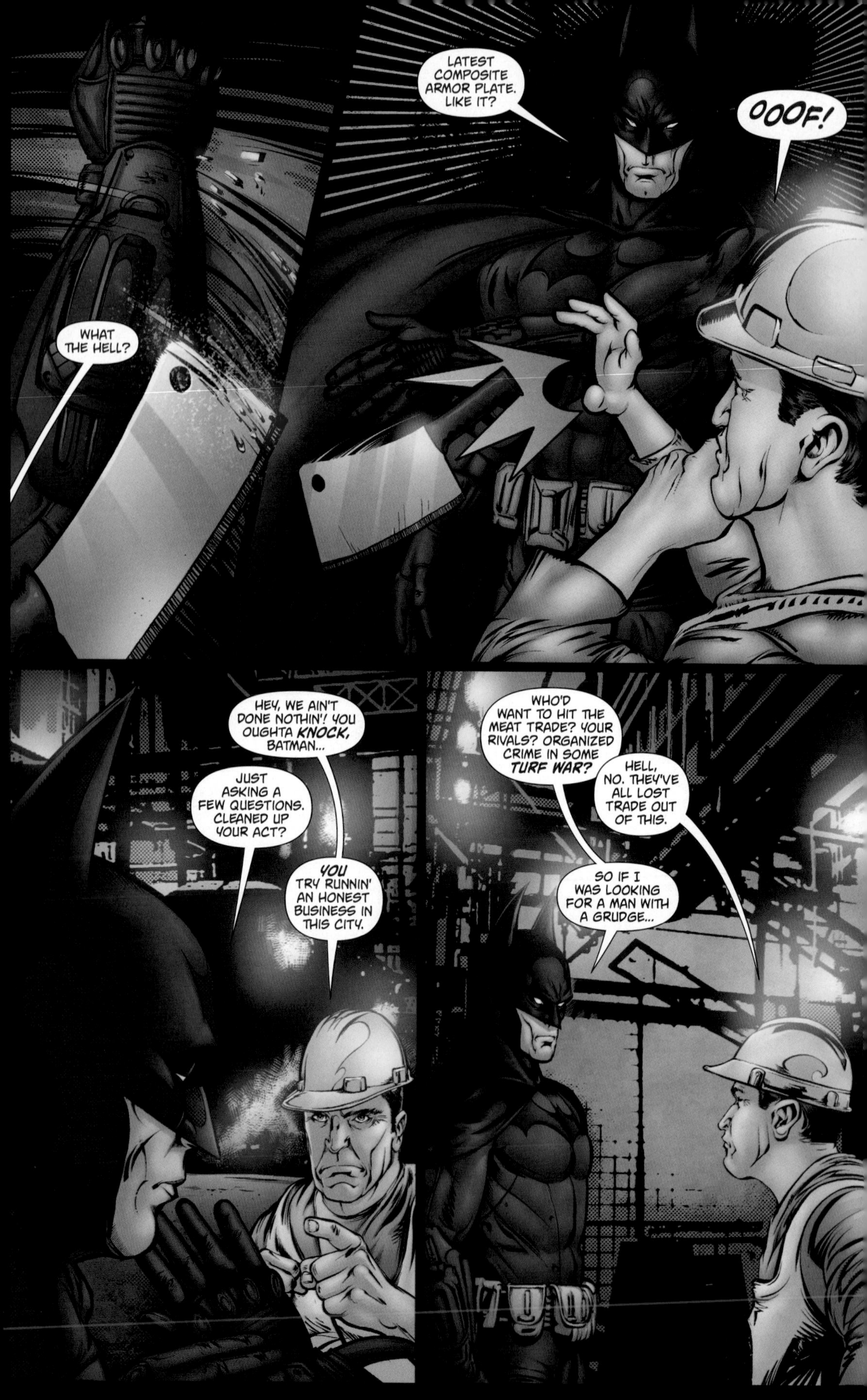
LATEST COMPOSITE ARMOR PLATE. LIKE IT?
OOOF!
WHAT THE HELL?
HEY, WE AIN'T DONE NOTHIN'! YOU OUGHTA KNOCK, BATMAN...
JUST ASKING A FEW QUESTIONS. CLEANED UP YOUR ACT?
YOU TRY RUNNIN' AN HONEST BUSINESS IN THIS CITY.
WHO'D WANT TO HIT THE MEAT TRADE? YOUR RIVALS? ORGANIZED CRIME IN SOME TURF WAR?
HELL, NO. THEY'VE ALL LOST TRADE OUT OF THIS.
SO IF I WAS LOOKING FOR A MAN WITH A GRUDGE...

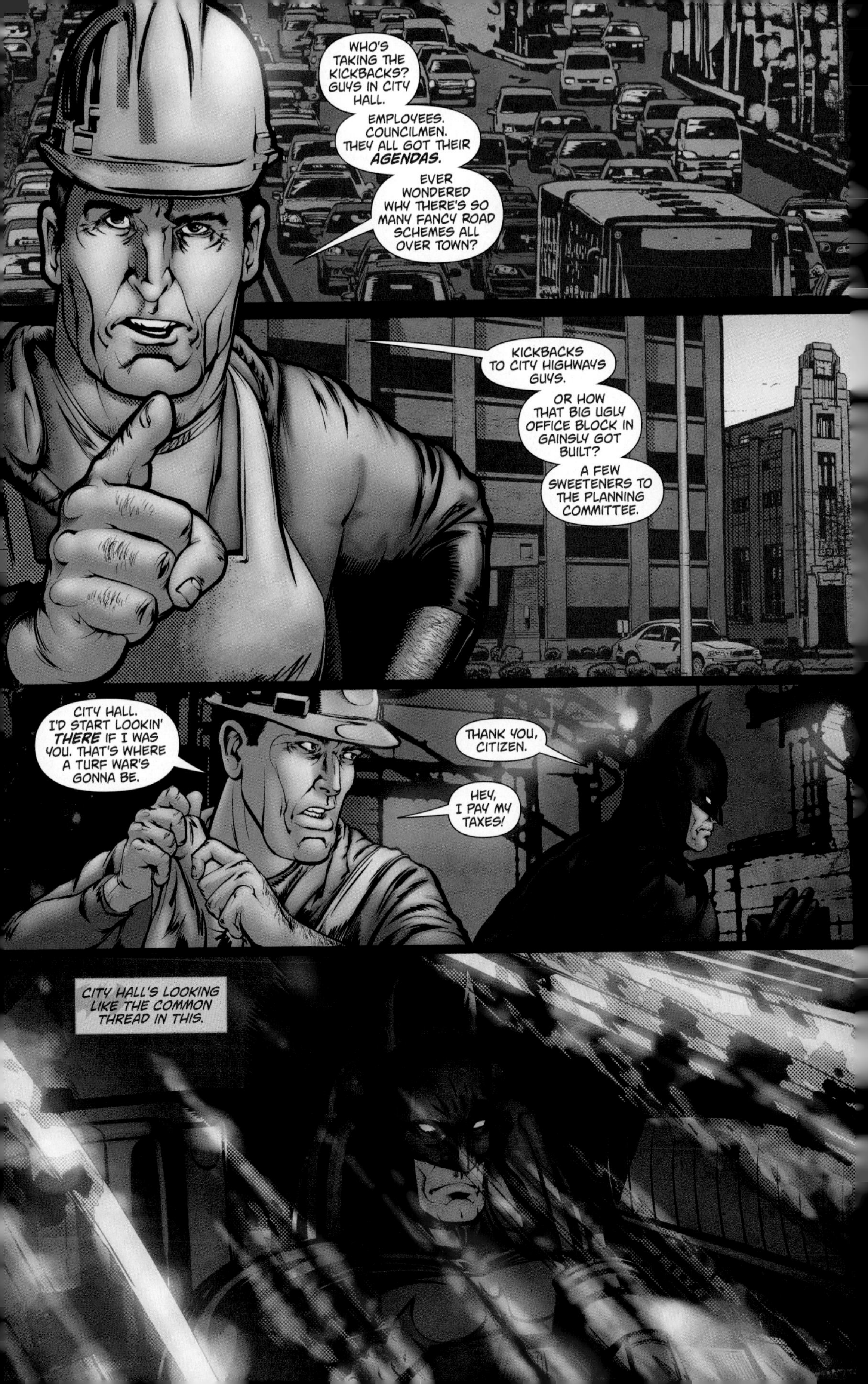
WHO'S TAKING THE KICKBACKS? GUYS IN CITY HALL.
EMPLOYEES. COUNCILMEN. THEY ALL GOT THEIR AGENDAS.
EVER WONDERED WHY THERE'S SO MANY FANCY ROAD SCHEMES ALL OVER TOWN?
KICKBACKS TO CITY HIGHWAYS GUYS.
OR HOW THAT BIG UGLY OFFICE BLOCK IN GAINSLY GOT BUILT?
A FEW SWEETENERS TO THE PLANNING COMMITTEE.
CITY HALL. I'D START LOOKIN' THERE IF I WAS YOU. THAT'S WHERE A TURF WAR'S GONNA BE.
THANK YOU, CITIZEN.
HEY, I PAY MY TAXES!
CITY HALL'S LOOKING LIKE THE COMMON THREAD IN THIS.

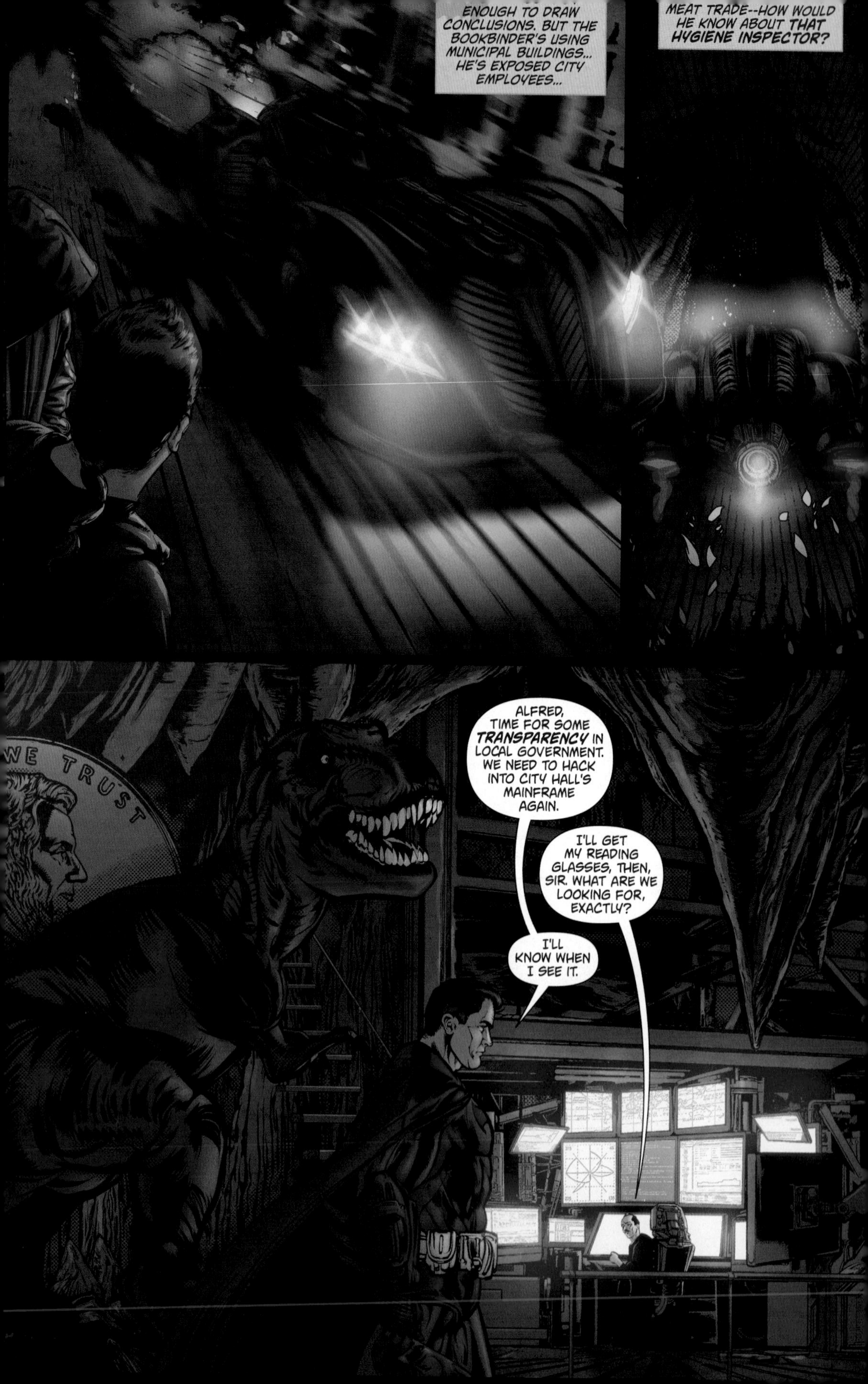
ENOUGH TO DRAW CONCLUSIONS. BUT THE BOOKBINDER'S USING MUNICIPAL BUILDINGS... HE'S EXPOSED CITY EMPLOYEES...
MEAT TRADE--HOW WOULD HE KNOW ABOUT THAT HYGIENE INSPECTOR?
WE TRUST
ALFRED, TIME FOR SOME TRANSPARENCY IN LOCAL GOVERNMENT. WE NEED TO HACK INTO CITY HALL'S MAINFRAME AGAIN.
I'LL GET MY READING GLASSES, THEN, SIR. WHAT ARE WE LOOKING FOR, EXACTLY?
I'LL KNOW WHEN I SEE IT.

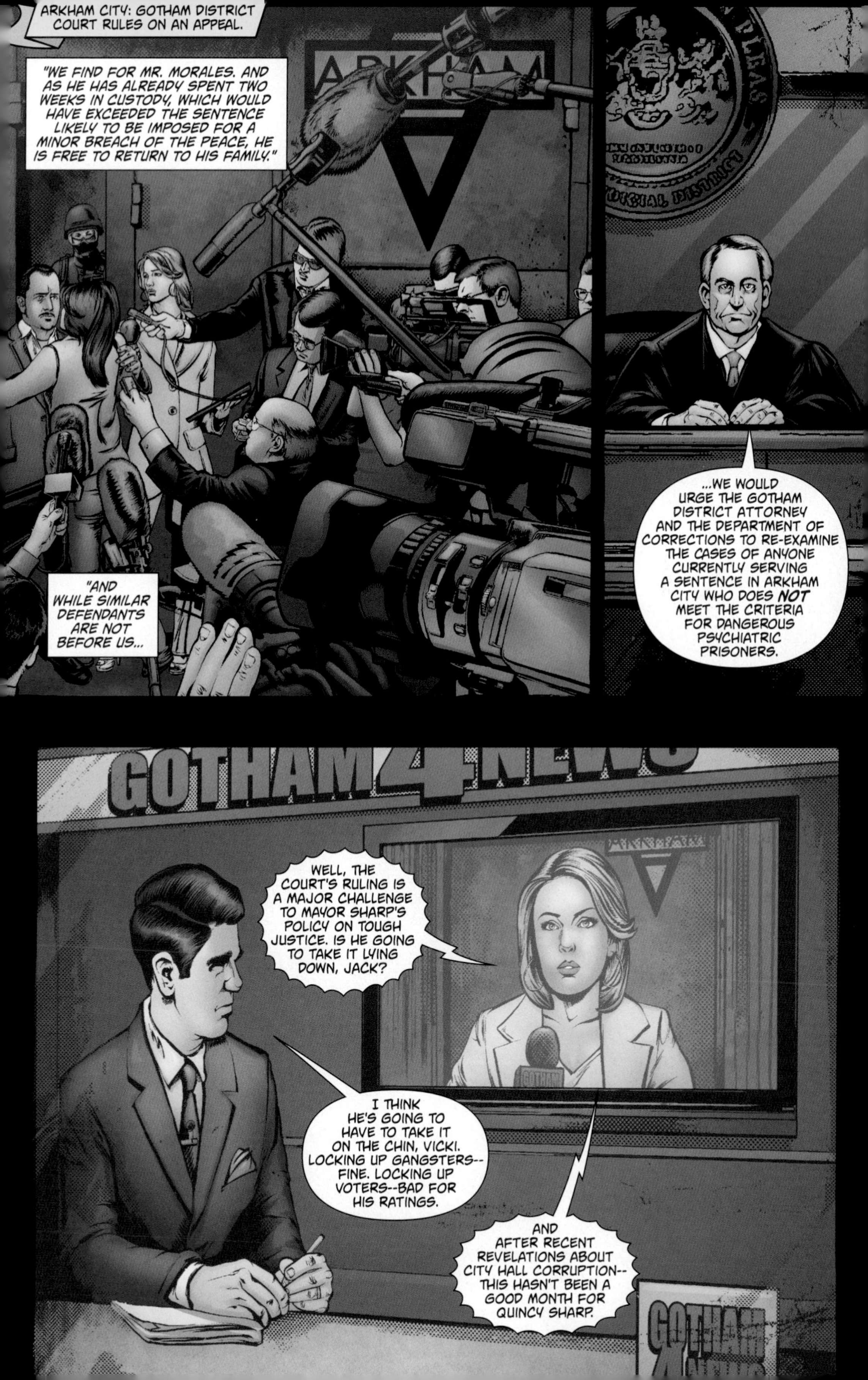

ARKHAM CITY: GOTHAM DISTRICT COURT RULES ON AN APPEAL.
"WE FIND FOR MR. MORALES. AND AS HE HAS ALREADY SPENT TWO WEEKS IN CUSTODY, WHICH WOULD HAVE EXCEEDED THE SENTENCE LIKELY TO BE IMPOSED FOR A MINOR BREACH OF THE PEACE, HE IS FREE TO RETURN TO HIS FAMILY."
ARKHAM
"AND WHILE SIMILAR DEFENDANTS ARE NOT BEFORE US...
...WE WOULD URGE THE GOTHAM DISTRICT ATTORNEY AND THE DEPARTMENT OF CORRECTIONS TO RE-EXAMINE THE CASES OF ANYONE CURRENTLY SERVING A SENTENCE IN ARKHAM CITY WHO DOES *NOT* MEET THE CRITERIA FOR DANGEROUS PSYCHIATRIC PRISONERS.
GOTHAM 4
WELL, THE COURT'S RULING IS A MAJOR CHALLENGE TO MAYOR SHARP'S POLICY ON TOUGH JUSTICE. IS HE GOING TO TAKE IT LYING DOWN, JACK?
I THINK HE'S GOING TO HAVE TO TAKE IT ON THE CHIN, VICKI. LOCKING UP GANGSTERS--FINE. LOCKING UP VOTERS--BAD FOR HIS RATINGS.
AND AFTER RECENT REVELATIONS ABOUT CITY HALL CORRUPTION--THIS HASN'T BEEN A GOOD MONTH FOR QUINCY SHARP.
GOTHAM

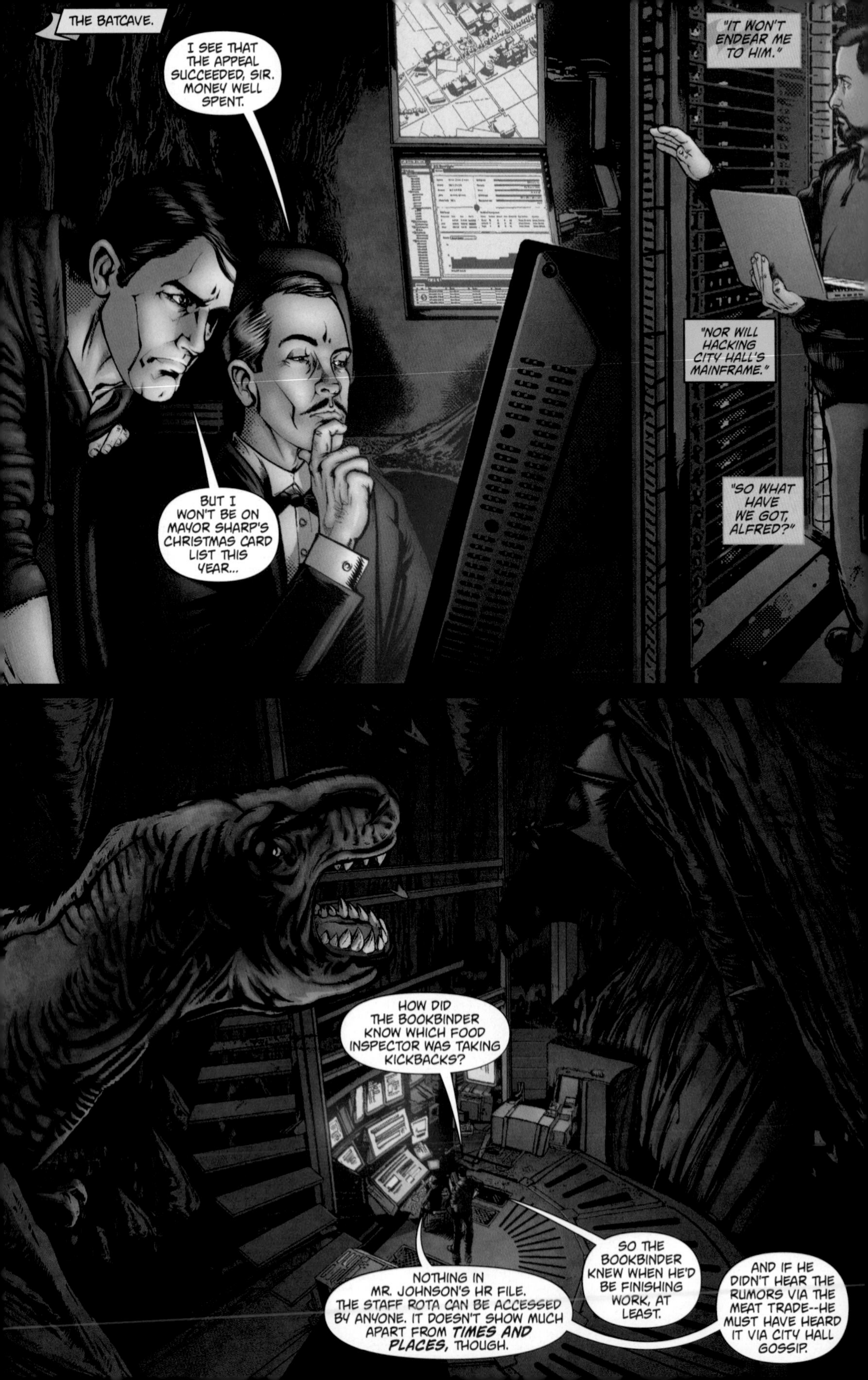
THE BATCAVE.
I SEE THAT THE APPEAL SUCCEEDED, SIR. MONEY WELL SPENT.
BUT I WON'T BE ON MAYOR SHARP'S CHRISTMAS CARD LIST THIS YEAR...
"IT WON'T ENDEAR ME TO HIM."
"NOR WILL HACKING CITY HALL'S MAINFRAME."
"SO WHAT HAVE WE GOT, ALFRED?"
HOW DID THE BOOKBINDER KNOW WHICH FOOD INSPECTOR WAS TAKING KICKBACKS?
NOTHING IN MR. JOHNSON'S HR FILE. THE STAFF ROTA CAN BE ACCESSED BY ANYONE. IT DOESN'T SHOW MUCH APART FROM TIMES AND PLACES, THOUGH.
SO THE BOOKBINDER KNEW WHEN HE'D BE FINISHING WORK, AT LEAST.
AND IF HE DIDN'T HEAR THE RUMORS VIA THE MEAT TRADE--HE MUST HAVE HEARD IT VIA CITY HALL GOSSIP.

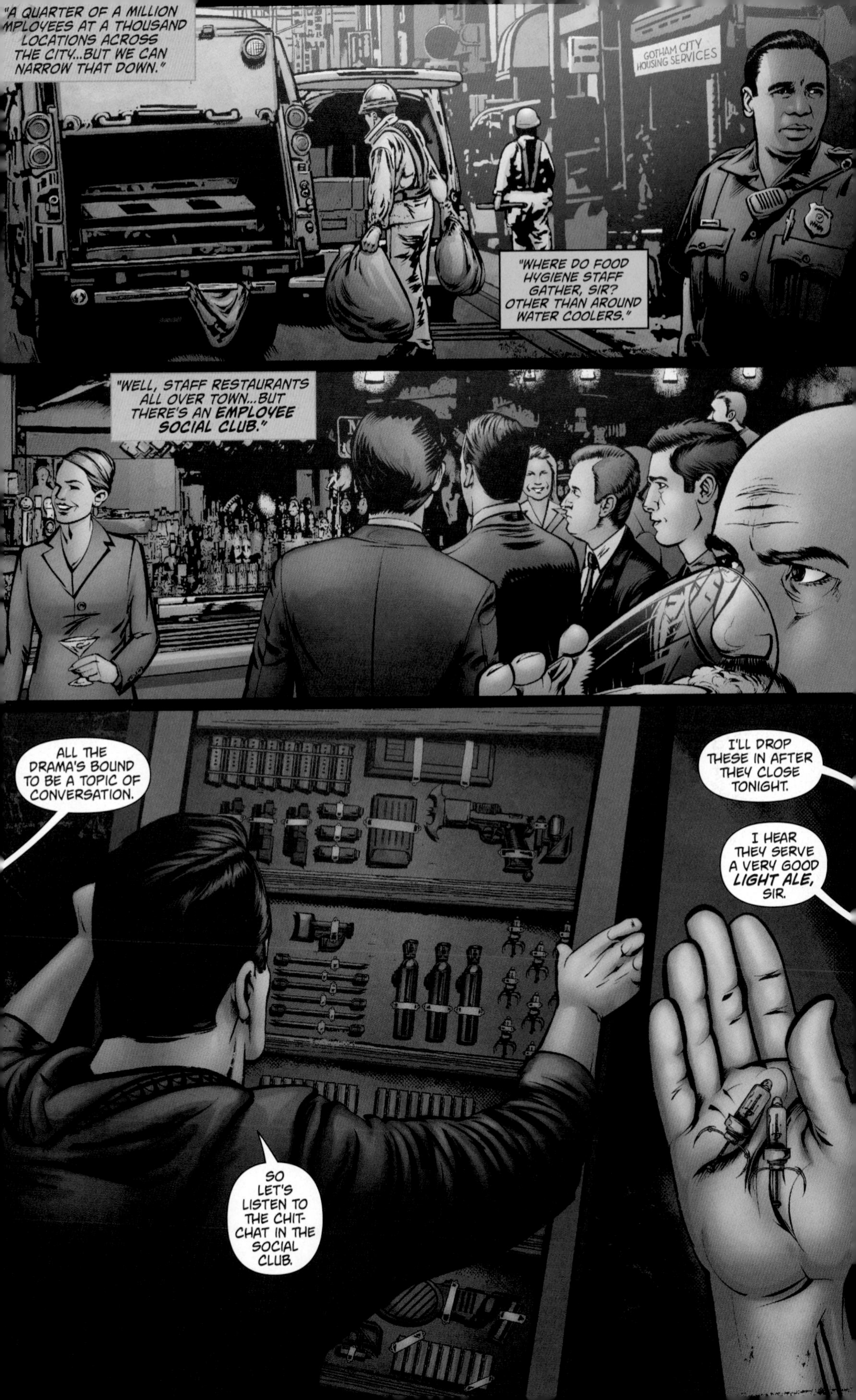
"A QUARTER OF A MILLION EMPLOYEES AT A THOUSAND LOCATIONS ACROSS THE CITY...BUT WE CAN NARROW THAT DOWN."
GOTHAM CITY HOUSING SERVICES
"WHERE DO FOOD HYGIENE STAFF GATHER, SIR? OTHER THAN AROUND WATER COOLERS."
"WELL, STAFF RESTAURANTS ALL OVER TOWN...BUT THERE'S AN EMPLOYEE SOCIAL CLUB."
ALL THE DRAMA'S BOUND TO BE A TOPIC OF CONVERSATION.
SO LET'S LISTEN TO THE CHIT-CHAT IN THE SOCIAL CLUB.
I'LL DROP THESE IN AFTER THEY CLOSE TONIGHT.
I HEAR THEY SERVE A VERY GOOD LIGHT ALE, SIR.

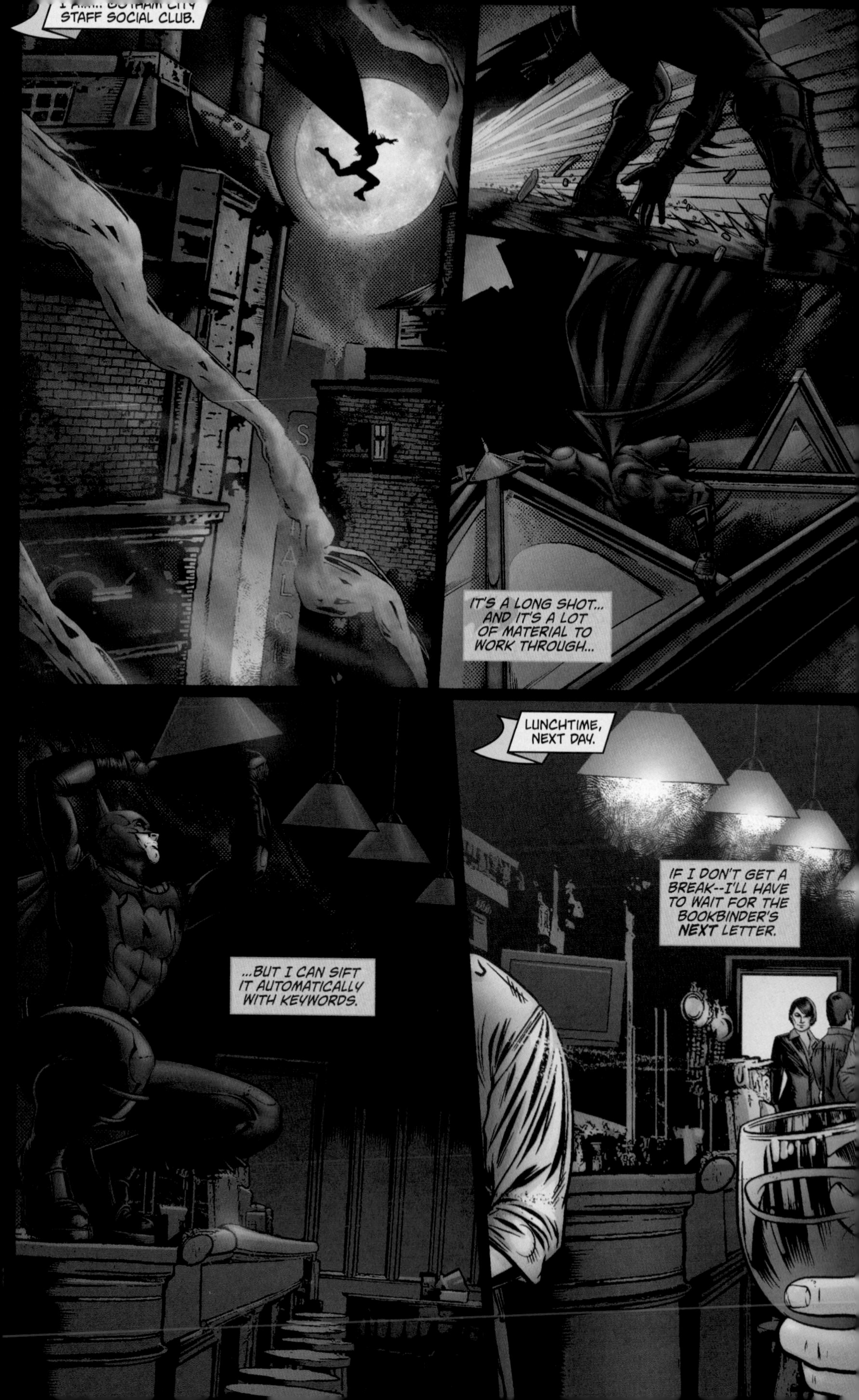

STAFF SOCIAL CLUB.
IT'S A LONG SHOT... AND IT'S A LOT OF MATERIAL TO WORK THROUGH...
...BUT I CAN SIFT IT AUTOMATICALLY WITH KEYWORDS.
LUNCHTIME, NEXT DAY.
IF I DON'T GET A BREAK--I'LL HAVE TO WAIT FOR THE BOOKBINDER'S **NEXT** LETTER.

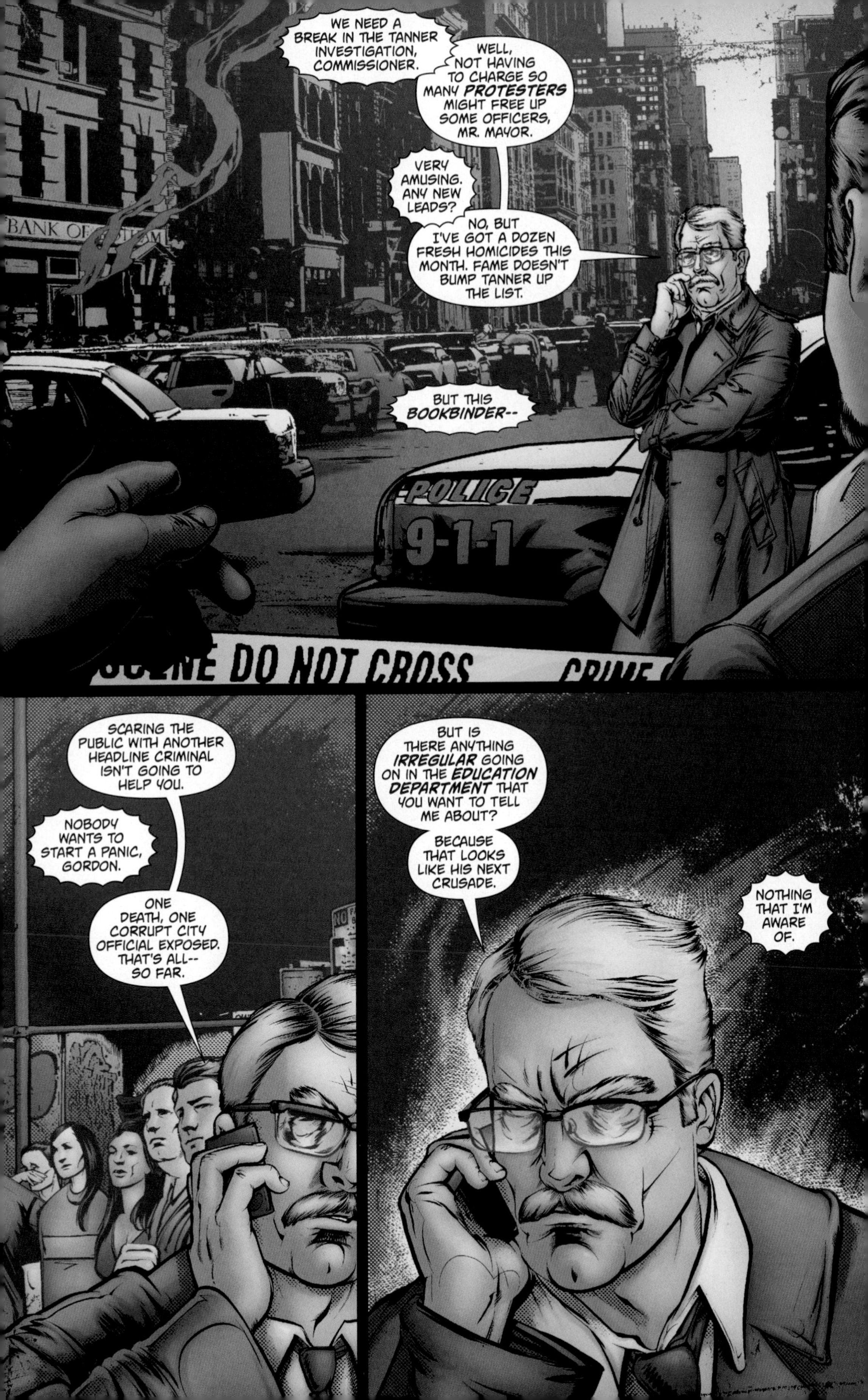
WE NEED A BREAK IN THE TANNER INVESTIGATION, COMMISSIONER.
WELL, NOT HAVING TO CHARGE SO MANY PROTESTERS MIGHT FREE UP SOME OFFICERS, MR. MAYOR.
VERY AMUSING. ANY NEW LEADS?
NO, BUT I'VE GOT A DOZEN FRESH HOMICIDES THIS MONTH. FAME DOESN'T BUMP TANNER UP THE LIST.
BUT THIS BOOKBINDER--
POLICE
9-1-1
DO NOT CROSS
SCARING THE PUBLIC WITH ANOTHER HEADLINE CRIMINAL ISN'T GOING TO HELP YOU.
NOBODY WANTS TO START A PANIC, GORDON.
ONE DEATH, ONE CORRUPT CITY OFFICIAL EXPOSED. THAT'S ALL-- SO FAR.
BUT IS THERE ANYTHING IRREGULAR GOING ON IN THE EDUCATION DEPARTMENT THAT YOU WANT TO TELL ME ABOUT?
BECAUSE THAT LOOKS LIKE HIS NEXT CRUSADE.
NOTHING THAT I'M AWARE OF.

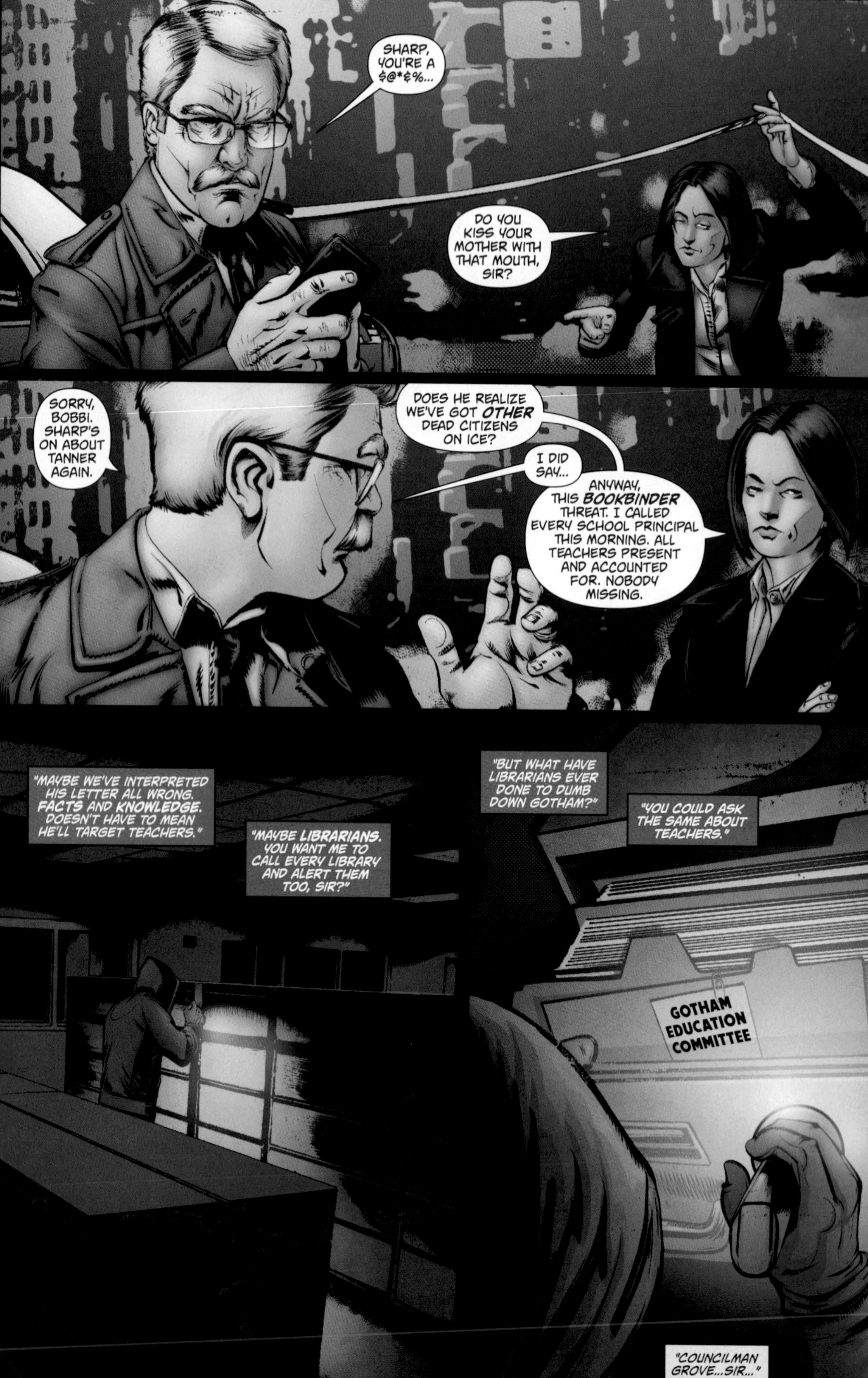
SHARP, YOU'RE A $@*&%...
DO YOU KISS YOUR MOTHER WITH THAT MOUTH, SIR?
SORRY, BOBBI. SHARP'S ON ABOUT TANNER AGAIN.
DOES HE REALIZE WE'VE GOT **OTHER** DEAD CITIZENS ON ICE?
I DID SAY...
ANYWAY, THIS **BOOKBINDER** THREAT. I CALLED EVERY SCHOOL PRINCIPAL THIS MORNING. ALL TEACHERS PRESENT AND ACCOUNTED FOR. NOBODY MISSING.
"MAYBE WE'VE INTERPRETED HIS LETTER ALL WRONG. **FACTS** AND **KNOWLEDGE**. DOESN'T HAVE TO MEAN HE'LL TARGET TEACHERS."
"MAYBE **LIBRARIANS**. YOU WANT ME TO CALL EVERY LIBRARY AND ALERT THEM TOO, SIR?"
"BUT WHAT HAVE LIBRARIANS EVER DONE TO DUMB DOWN GOTHAM?"
"YOU COULD ASK THE SAME ABOUT TEACHERS."
GOTHAM EDUCATION COMMITTEE
"COUNCILMAN GROVE...SIR..."

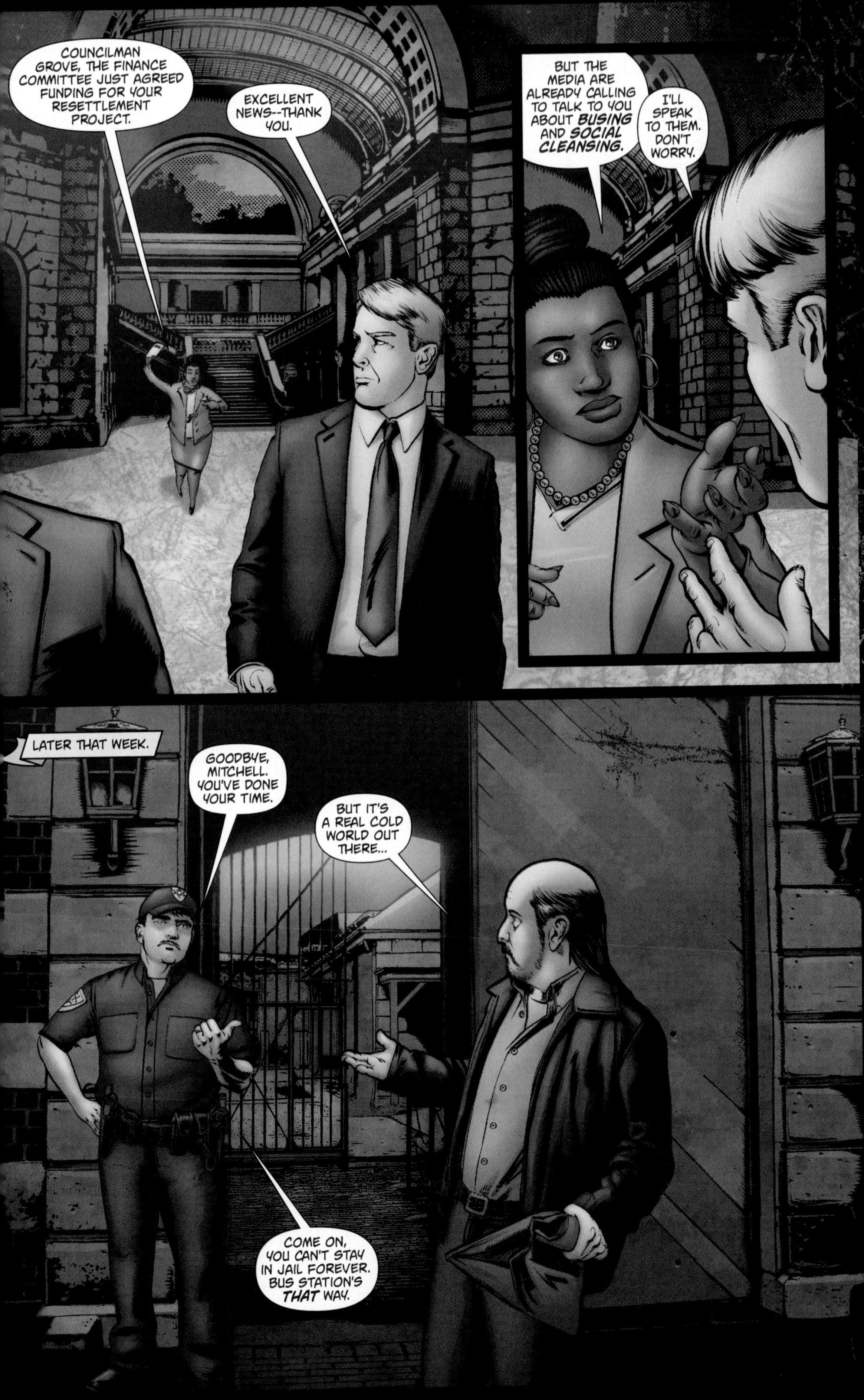
COUNCILMAN GROVE, THE FINANCE COMMITTEE JUST AGREED FUNDING FOR YOUR RESETTLEMENT PROJECT.
EXCELLENT NEWS--THANK YOU.
BUT THE MEDIA ARE ALREADY CALLING TO TALK TO YOU ABOUT BUSING AND SOCIAL CLEANSING.
I'LL SPEAK TO THEM. DON'T WORRY.
LATER THAT WEEK.
GOODBYE, MITCHELL. YOU'VE DONE YOUR TIME.
BUT IT'S A REAL COLD WORLD OUT THERE...
COME ON, YOU CAN'T STAY IN JAIL FOREVER. BUS STATION'S THAT WAY.

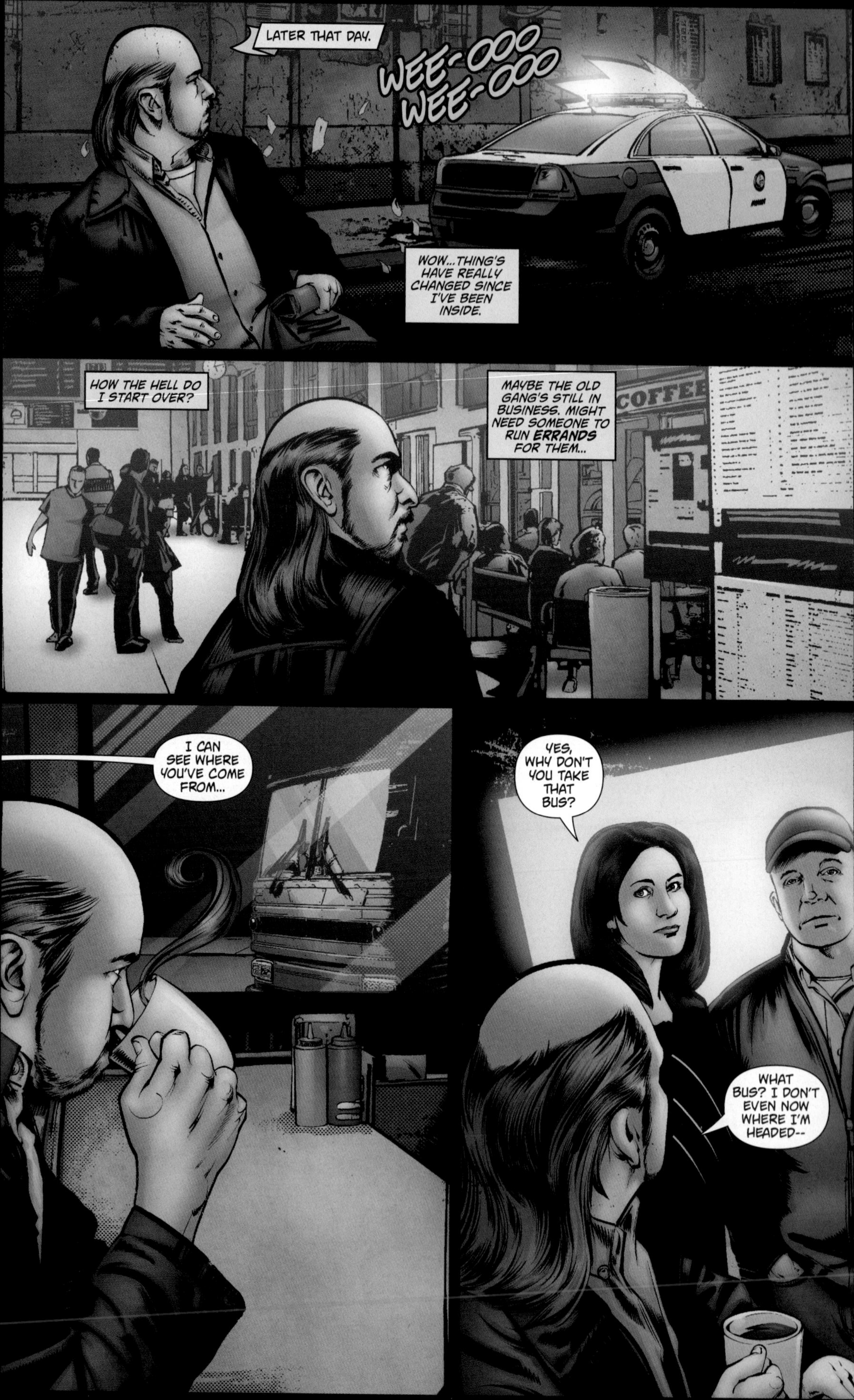
LATER THAT DAY.
WEE-OOO WEE-OOO
WOW...THING'S HAVE REALLY CHANGED SINCE I'VE BEEN INSIDE.
HOW THE HELL DO I START OVER?
MAYBE THE OLD GANG'S STILL IN BUSINESS. MIGHT NEED SOMEONE TO RUN ERRANDS FOR THEM...
COFFEE
I CAN SEE WHERE YOU'VE COME FROM...
YES, WHY DON'T YOU TAKE THAT BUS?
WHAT BUS? I DON'T EVEN NOW WHERE I'M HEADED--

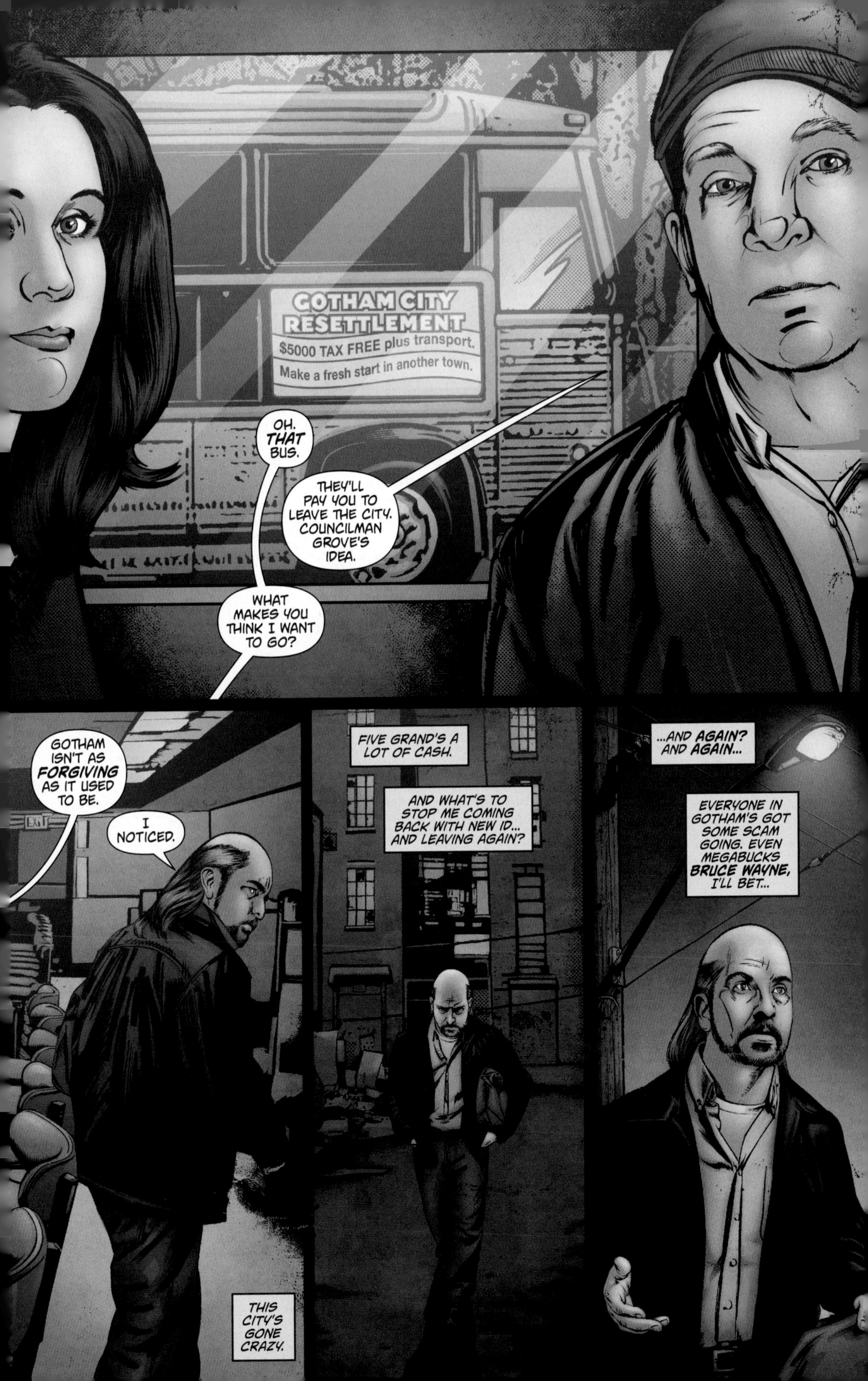
GOTHAM CITY RESETTLEMENT
$5000 TAX FREE plus transport.
Make a fresh start in another town.
OH. THAT BUS.
THEY'LL PAY YOU TO LEAVE THE CITY. COUNCILMAN GROVE'S IDEA.
WHAT MAKES YOU THINK I WANT TO GO?
GOTHAM ISN'T AS FORGIVING AS IT USED TO BE.
I NOTICED.
FIVE GRAND'S A LOT OF CASH.
AND WHAT'S TO STOP ME COMING BACK WITH NEW ID... AND LEAVING AGAIN?
...AND AGAIN? AND AGAIN...
EVERYONE IN GOTHAM'S GOT SOME SCAM GOING. EVEN MEGABUCKS BRUCE WAYNE, I'LL BET...
THIS CITY'S GONE CRAZY.

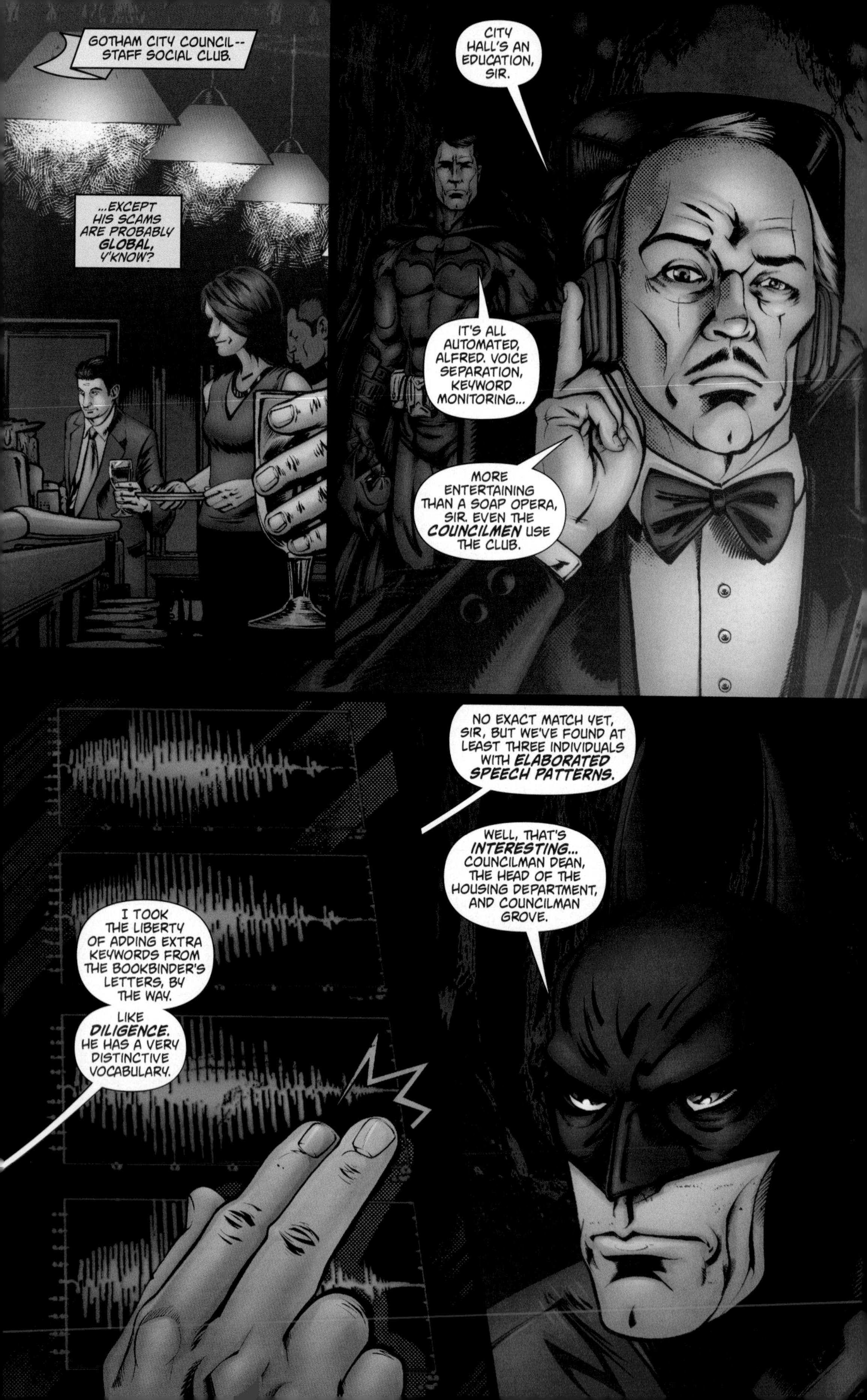

GOTHAM CITY COUNCIL--
STAFF SOCIAL CLUB.
...EXCEPT HIS SCAMS ARE PROBABLY GLOBAL, Y'KNOW?
CITY HALL'S AN EDUCATION, SIR.
IT'S ALL AUTOMATED, ALFRED. VOICE SEPARATION, KEYWORD MONITORING...
MORE ENTERTAINING THAN A SOAP OPERA, SIR. EVEN THE COUNCILMEN USE THE CLUB.
NO EXACT MATCH YET, SIR, BUT WE'VE FOUND AT LEAST THREE INDIVIDUALS WITH ELABORATED SPEECH PATTERNS.
WELL, THAT'S INTERESTING... COUNCILMAN DEAN, THE HEAD OF THE HOUSING DEPARTMENT, AND COUNCILMAN GROVE.
I TOOK THE LIBERTY OF ADDING EXTRA KEYWORDS FROM THE BOOKBINDER'S LETTERS, BY THE WAY.
LIKE DILIGENCE. HE HAS A VERY DISTINCTIVE VOCABULARY.

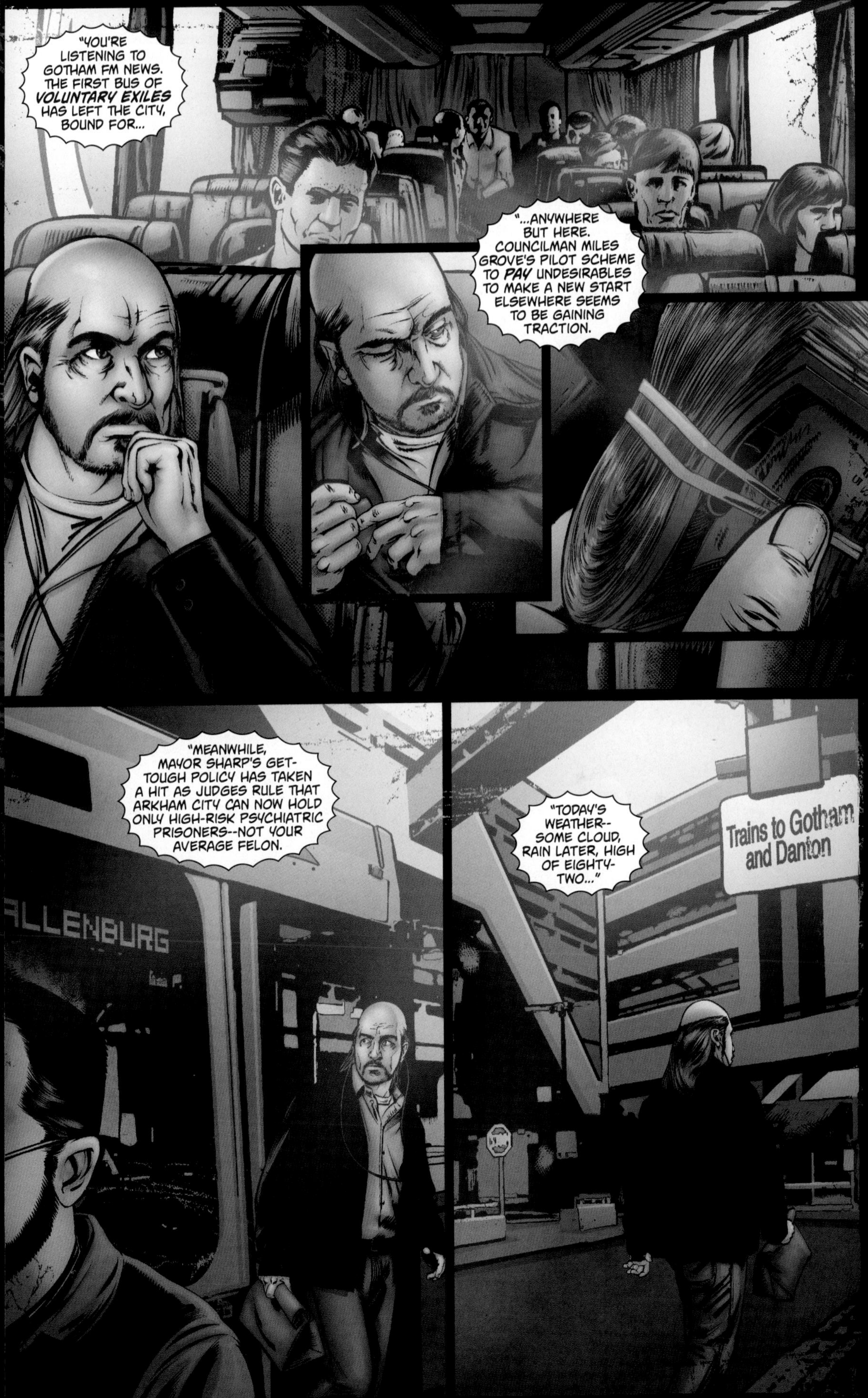
"YOU'RE LISTENING TO GOTHAM FM NEWS. THE FIRST BUS OF VOLUNTARY EXILES HAS LEFT THE CITY, BOUND FOR...
"...ANYWHERE BUT HERE. COUNCILMAN MILES GROVE'S PILOT SCHEME TO PAY UNDESIRABLES TO MAKE A NEW START ELSEWHERE SEEMS TO BE GAINING TRACTION.
"MEANWHILE, MAYOR SHARP'S GET-TOUGH POLICY HAS TAKEN A HIT AS JUDGES RULE THAT ARKHAM CITY CAN NOW HOLD ONLY HIGH-RISK PSYCHIATRIC PRISONERS--NOT YOUR AVERAGE FELON.
ALLENBURG
"TODAY'S WEATHER--SOME CLOUD, RAIN LATER, HIGH OF EIGHTY-TWO..."
Trains to Gotham and Danton

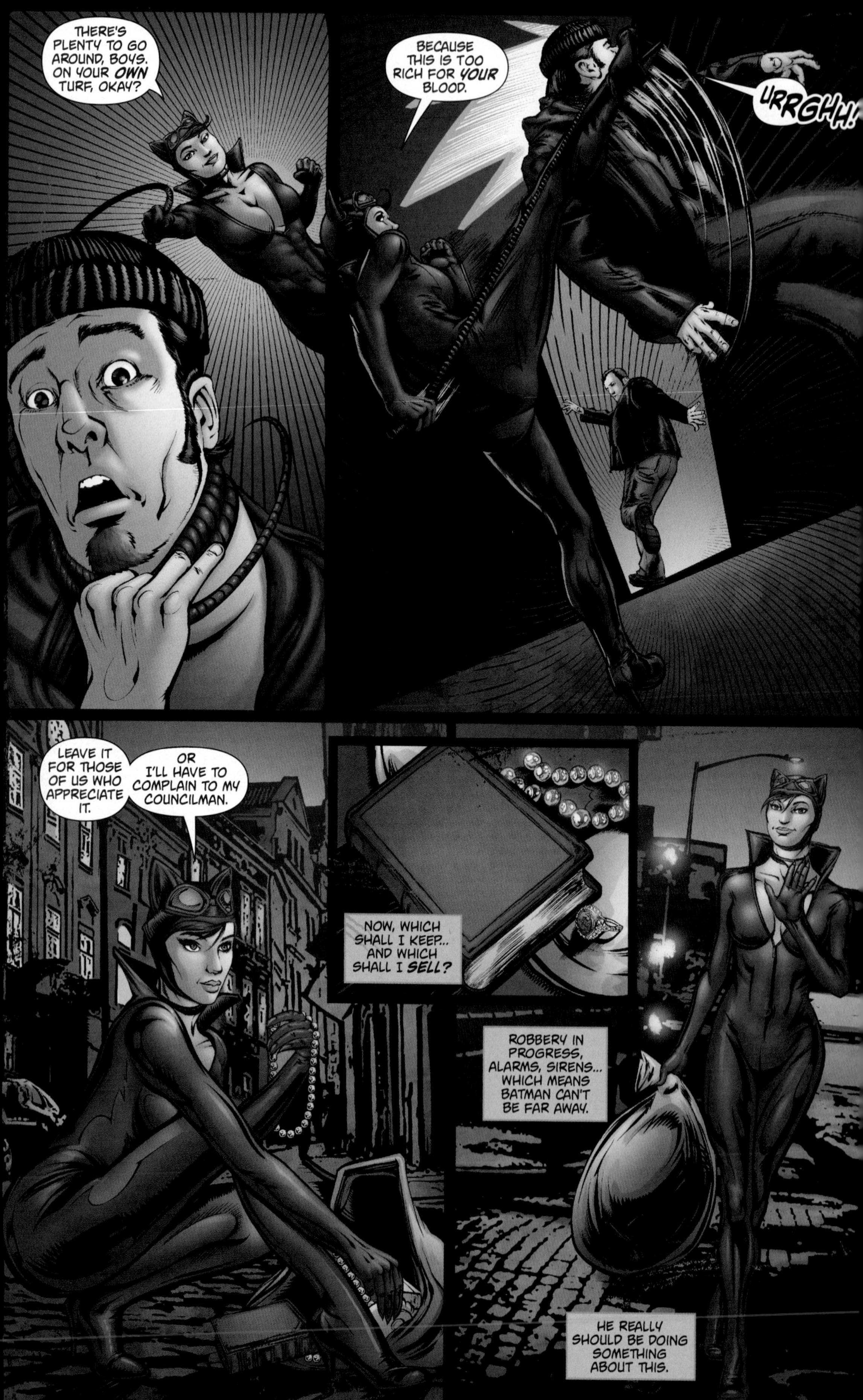
THERE'S PLENTY TO GO AROUND, BOYS. ON YOUR OWN TURF, OKAY?
BECAUSE THIS IS TOO RICH FOR YOUR BLOOD.
URRGHH!
LEAVE IT FOR THOSE OF US WHO APPRECIATE IT.
OR I'LL HAVE TO COMPLAIN TO MY COUNCILMAN.
NOW, WHICH SHALL I KEEP... AND WHICH SHALL I SELL?
ROBBERY IN PROGRESS, ALARMS, SIRENS... WHICH MEANS BATMAN CAN'T BE FAR AWAY.
HE REALLY SHOULD BE DOING SOMETHING ABOUT THIS.

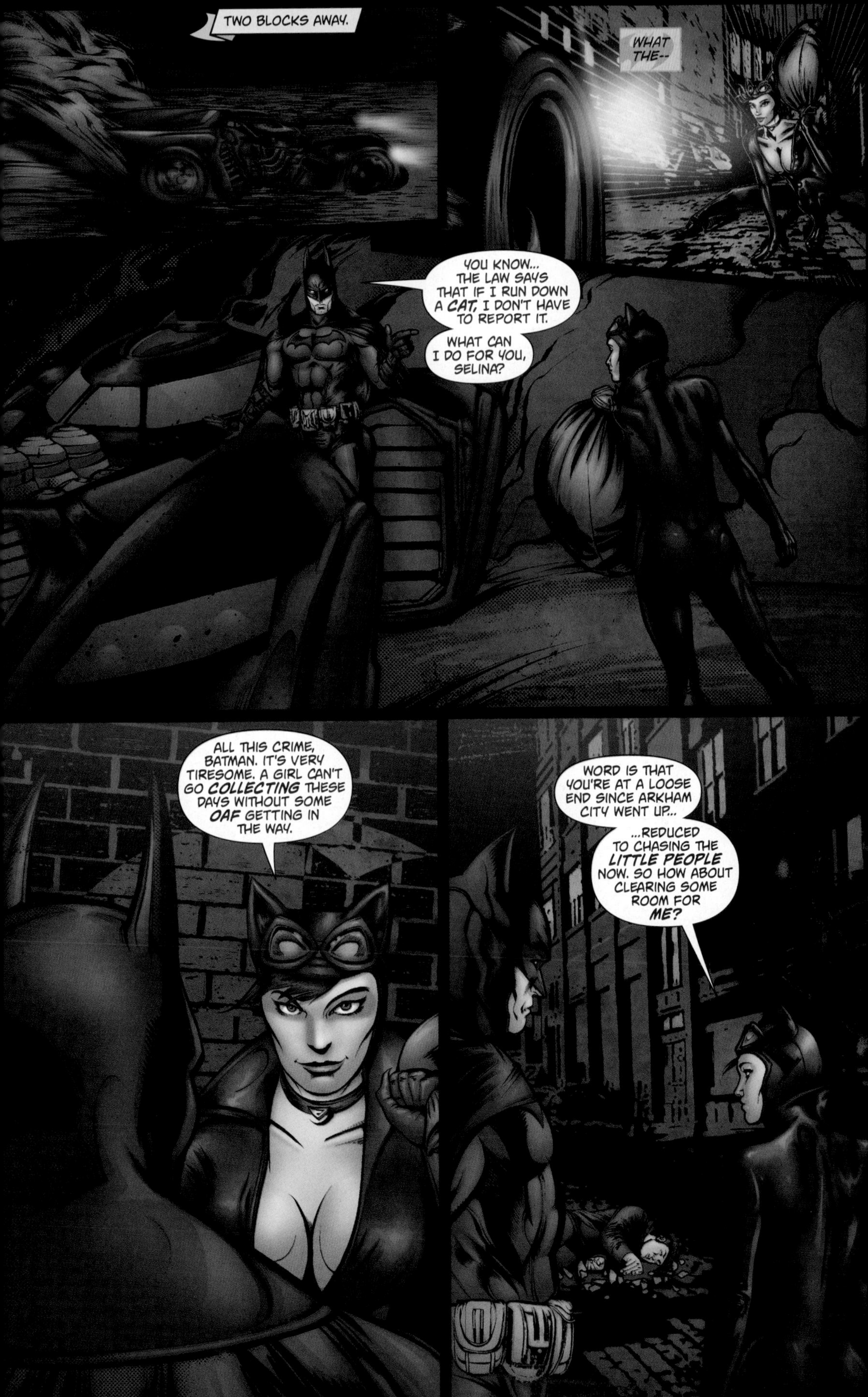
TWO BLOCKS AWAY.
WHAT THE--
YOU KNOW... THE LAW SAYS THAT IF I RUN DOWN A CAT, I DON'T HAVE TO REPORT IT.
WHAT CAN I DO FOR YOU, SELINA?
ALL THIS CRIME, BATMAN. IT'S VERY TIRESOME. A GIRL CAN'T GO COLLECTING THESE DAYS WITHOUT SOME OAF GETTING IN THE WAY.
WORD IS THAT YOU'RE AT A LOOSE END SINCE ARKHAM CITY WENT UP...
...REDUCED TO CHASING THE LITTLE PEOPLE NOW. SO HOW ABOUT CLEARING SOME ROOM FOR ME?

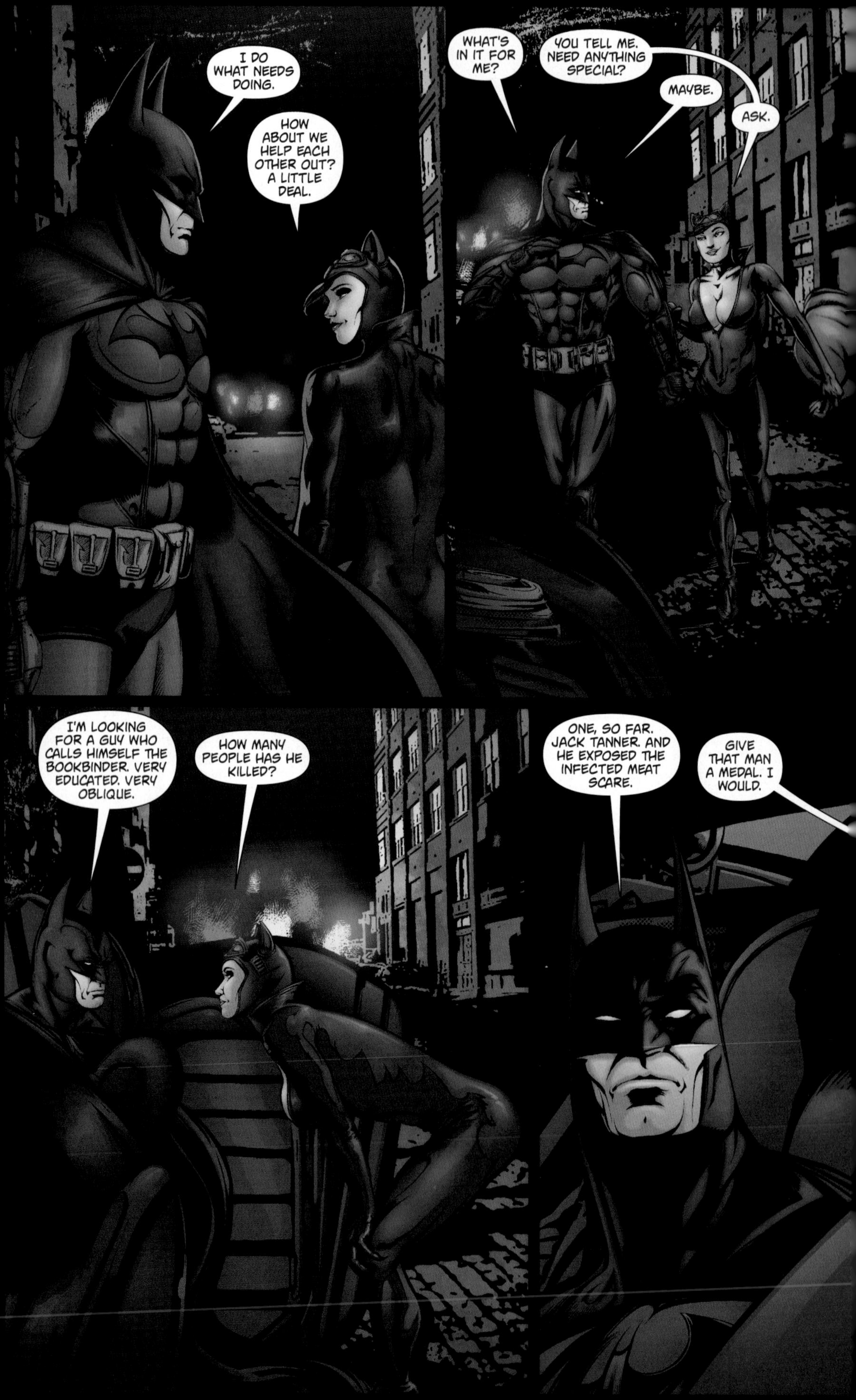
I DO WHAT NEEDS DOING.
HOW ABOUT WE HELP EACH OTHER OUT? A LITTLE DEAL.
WHAT'S IN IT FOR ME?
YOU TELL ME. NEED ANYTHING SPECIAL?
MAYBE.
ASK.
I'M LOOKING FOR A GUY WHO CALLS HIMSELF THE BOOKBINDER. VERY EDUCATED. VERY OBLIQUE.
HOW MANY PEOPLE HAS HE KILLED?
ONE, SO FAR. JACK TANNER. AND HE EXPOSED THE INFECTED MEAT SCARE.
GIVE THAT MAN A MEDAL. I WOULD.

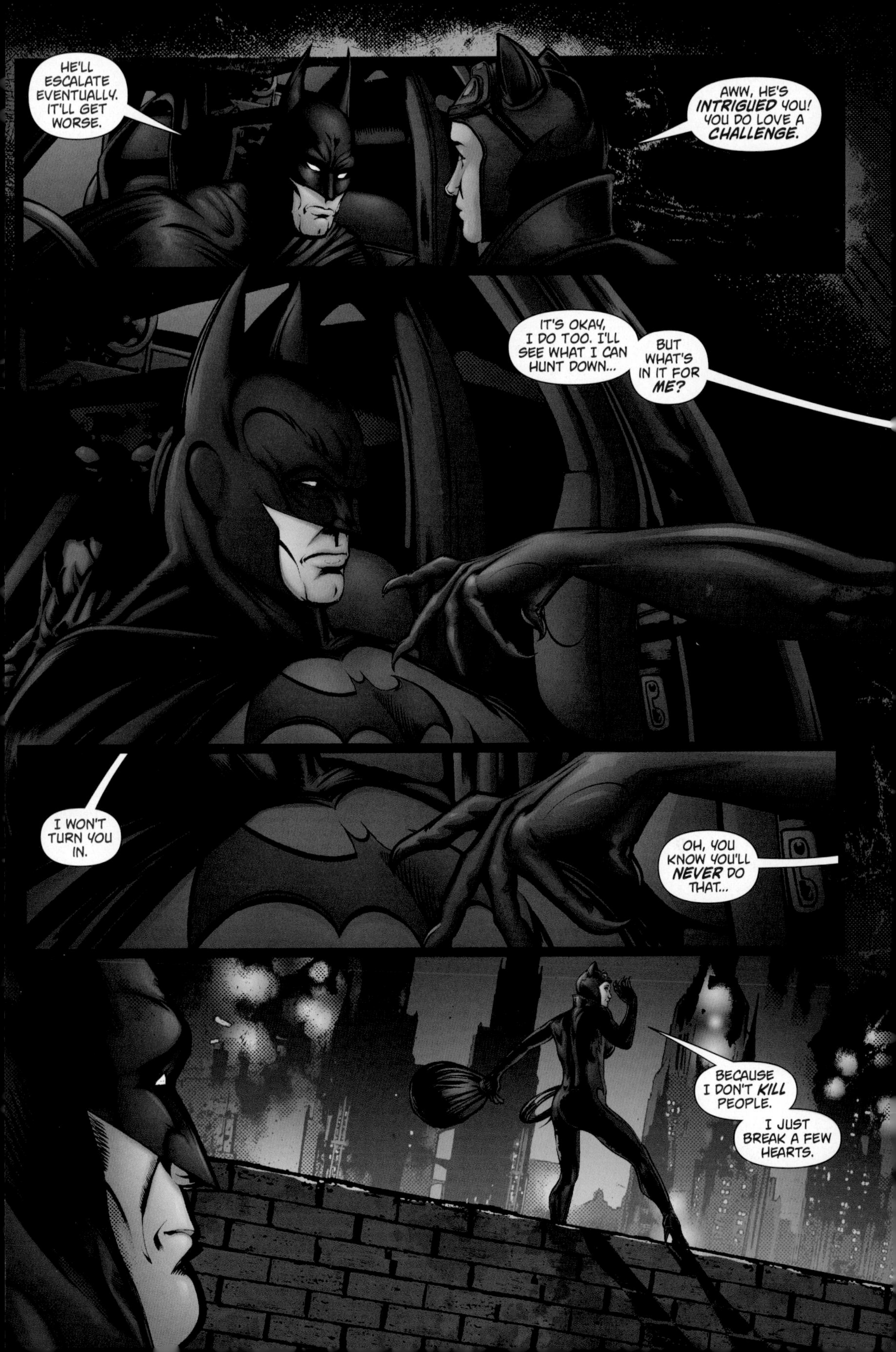
HE'LL ESCALATE EVENTUALLY. IT'LL GET WORSE.
AWW, HE'S **INTRIGUED** YOU! YOU DO LOVE A **CHALLENGE**.
IT'S OKAY, I DO TOO. I'LL SEE WHAT I CAN HUNT DOWN...
BUT WHAT'S IN IT FOR **ME?**
I WON'T TURN YOU IN.
OH, YOU KNOW YOU'LL **NEVER** DO THAT...
BECAUSE I DON'T **KILL** PEOPLE.
I JUST BREAK A FEW HEARTS.

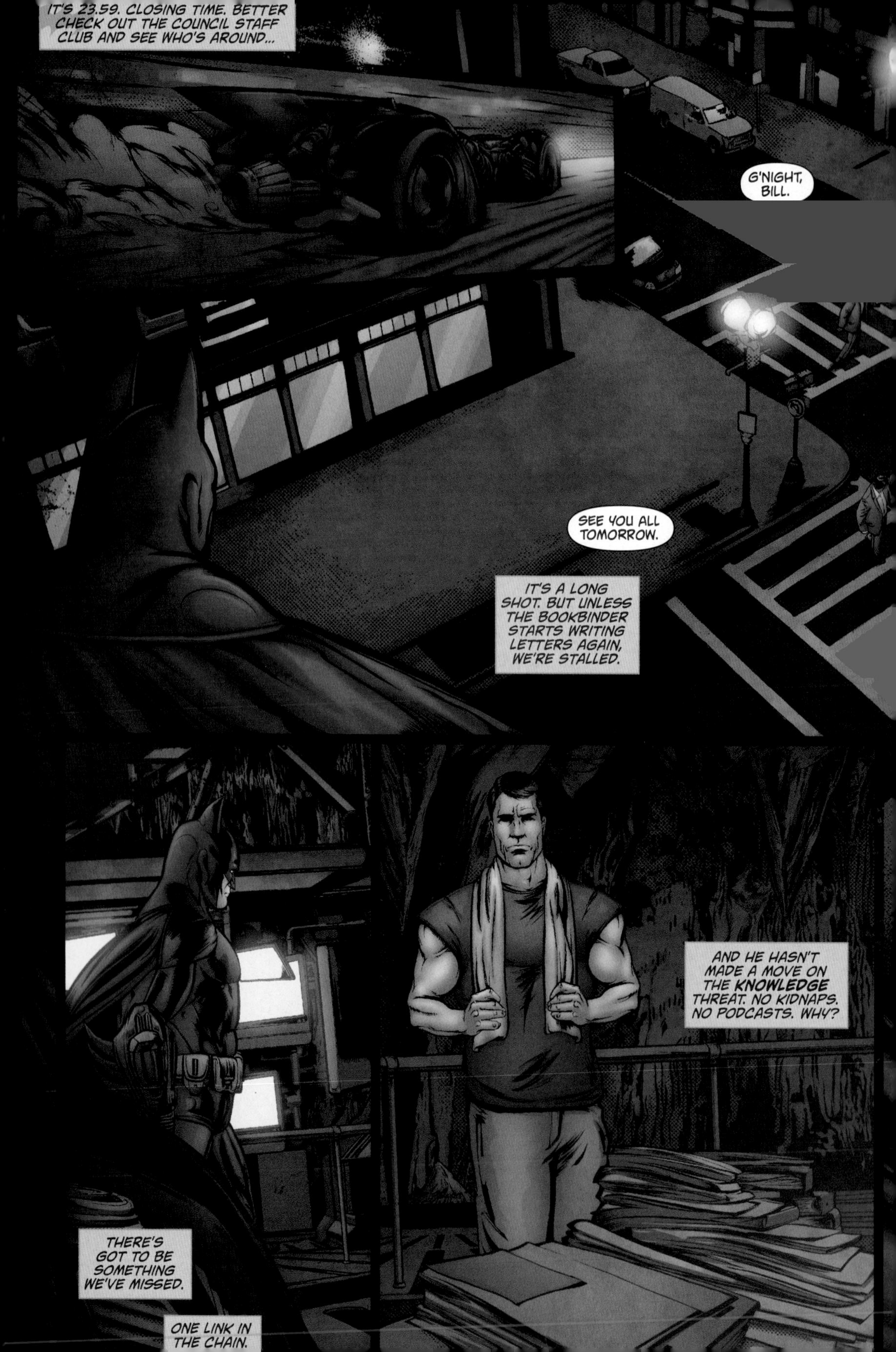
IT'S 23.59. CLOSING TIME. BETTER CHECK OUT THE COUNCIL STAFF CLUB AND SEE WHO'S AROUND...
G'NIGHT, BILL.
SEE YOU ALL TOMORROW.
IT'S A LONG SHOT. BUT UNLESS THE BOOKBINDER STARTS WRITING LETTERS AGAIN, WE'RE STALLED.
AND HE HASN'T MADE A MOVE ON THE **KNOWLEDGE** THREAT. NO KIDNAPS. NO PODCASTS. WHY?
THERE'S GOT TO BE SOMETHING WE'VE MISSED.
ONE LINK IN THE CHAIN.

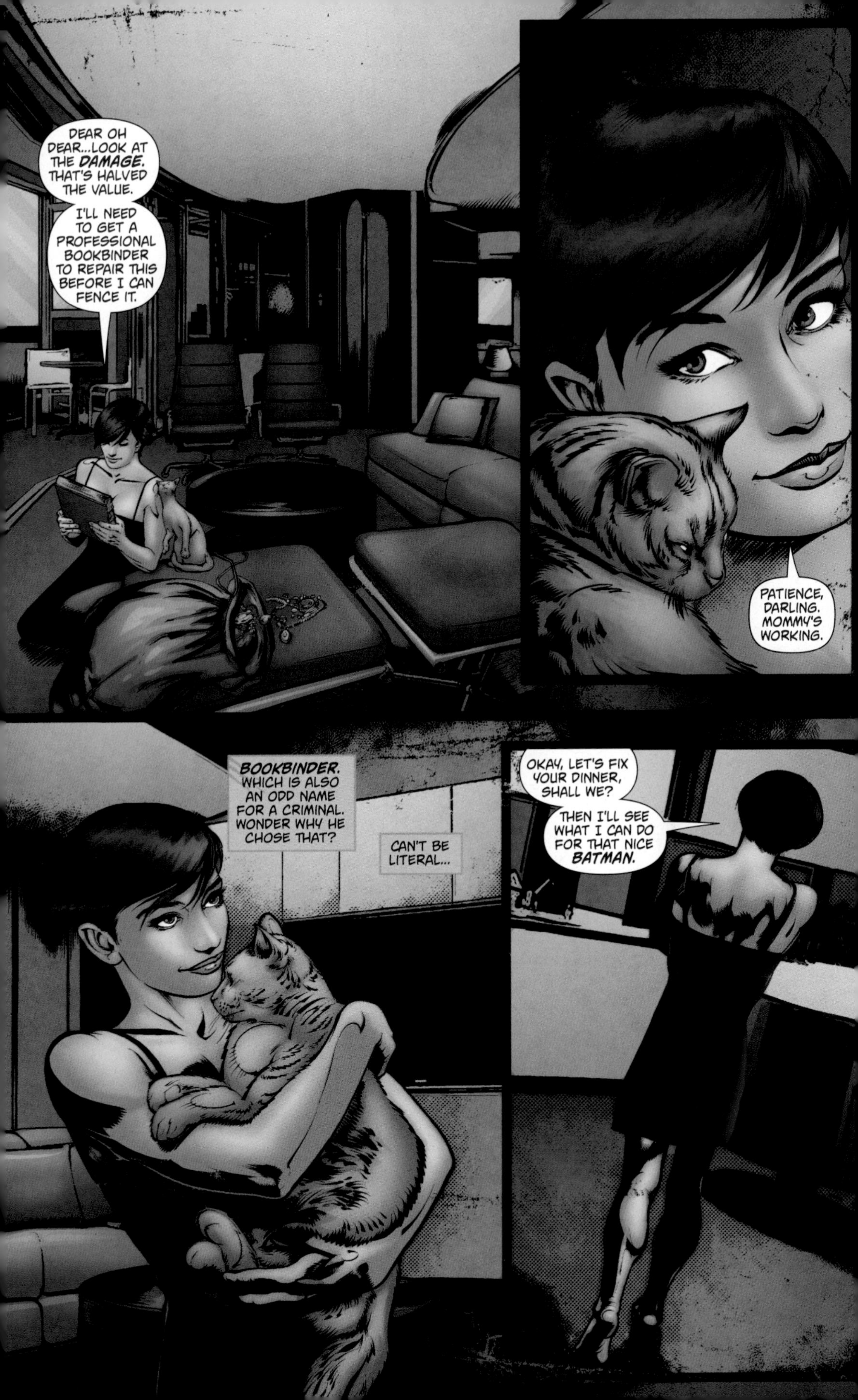
DEAR OH DEAR...LOOK AT THE DAMAGE. THAT'S HALVED THE VALUE.
I'LL NEED TO GET A PROFESSIONAL BOOKBINDER TO REPAIR THIS BEFORE I CAN FENCE IT.
PATIENCE, DARLING. MOMMY'S WORKING.
BOOKBINDER. WHICH IS ALSO AN ODD NAME FOR A CRIMINAL. WONDER WHY HE CHOSE THAT?
CAN'T BE LITERAL...
OKAY, LET'S FIX YOUR DINNER, SHALL WE?
THEN I'LL SEE WHAT I CAN DO FOR THAT NICE BATMAN.

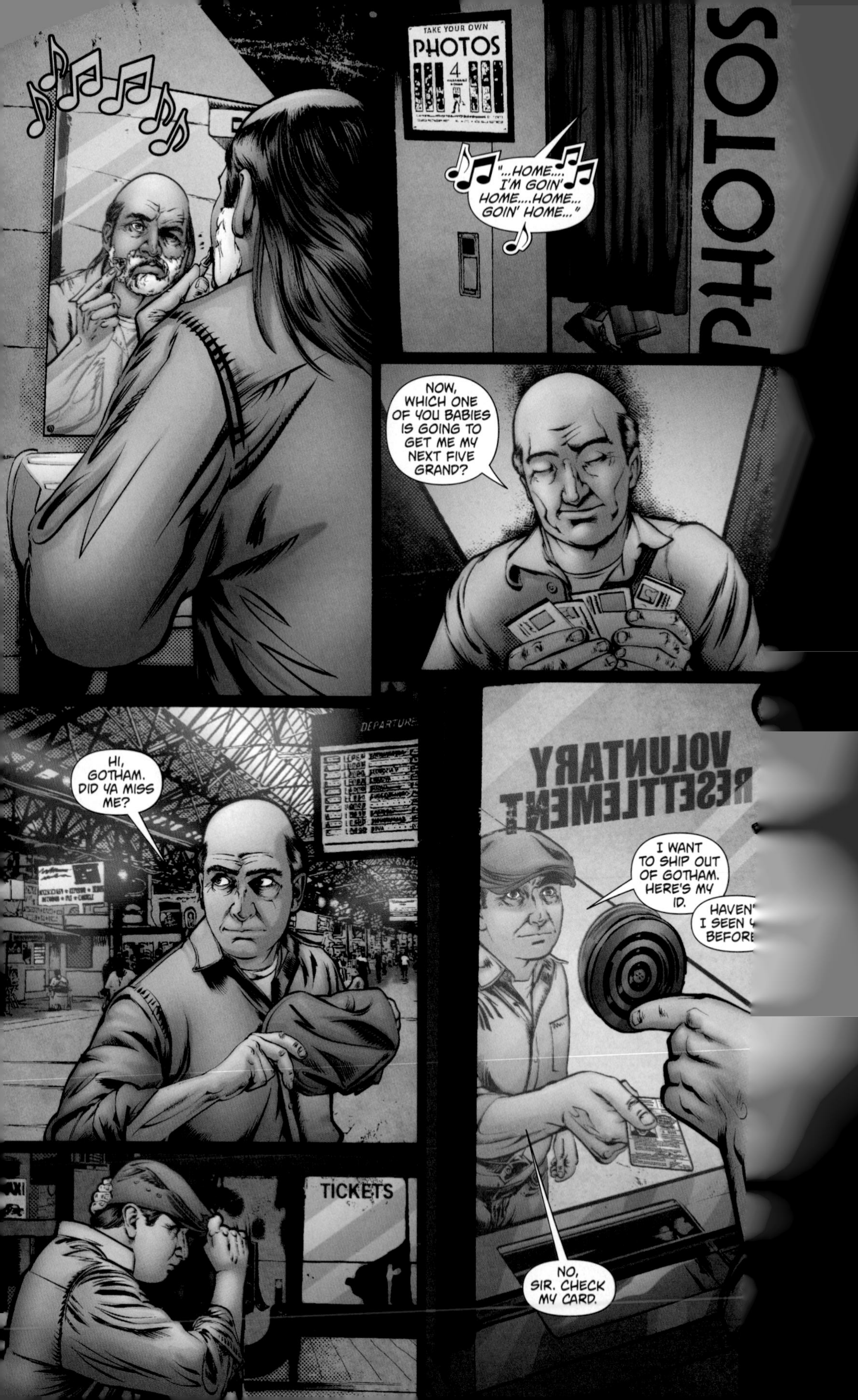
TAKE YOUR OWN
PHOTOS
4
"...HOME... I'M GOIN' HOME....HOME... GOIN' HOME..."
PHOTOS
NOW, WHICH ONE OF YOU BABIES IS GOING TO GET ME MY NEXT FIVE GRAND?
DEPARTURE
HI, GOTHAM. DID YA MISS ME?
VOLUNTARY RESETTLEMENT
I WANT TO SHIP OUT OF GOTHAM. HERE'S MY ID.
HAVEN'T I SEEN YOU BEFORE
TICKETS
NO, SIR. CHECK MY CARD.

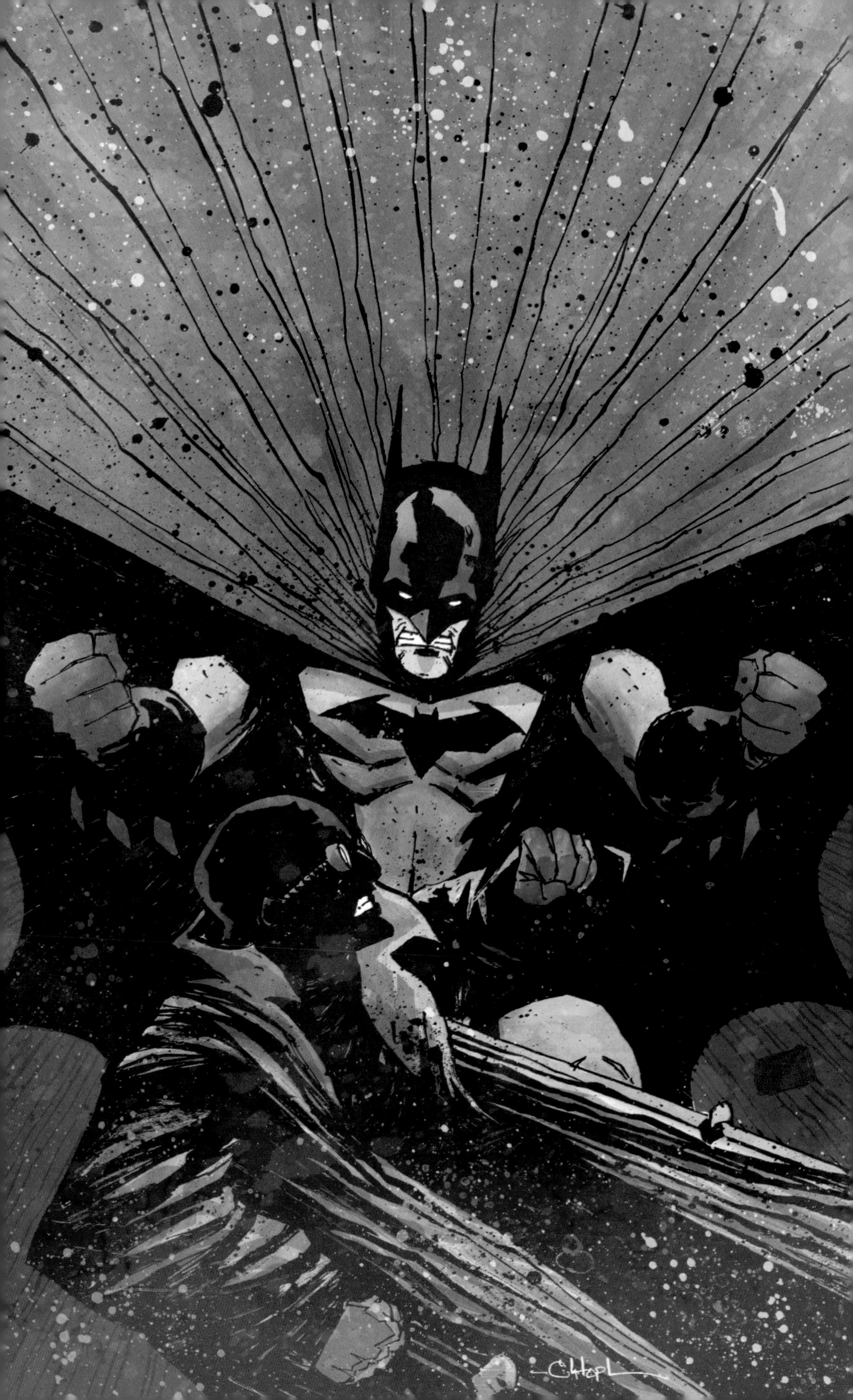

WELCOME
TO THE SLOUGH OF DESPOND
PART FIVE

WRITTEN BY: KAREN TRAVISS
ART BY: CHRISTIAN DUCE (PAGES 1-20)
& BEN LOBEL (PAGES 21-30)
COLORS BY: ALEJANDRO SANCHEZ
LETTERS BY: TRAVIS LANHAM
COVER BY: CHRIS MITTEN

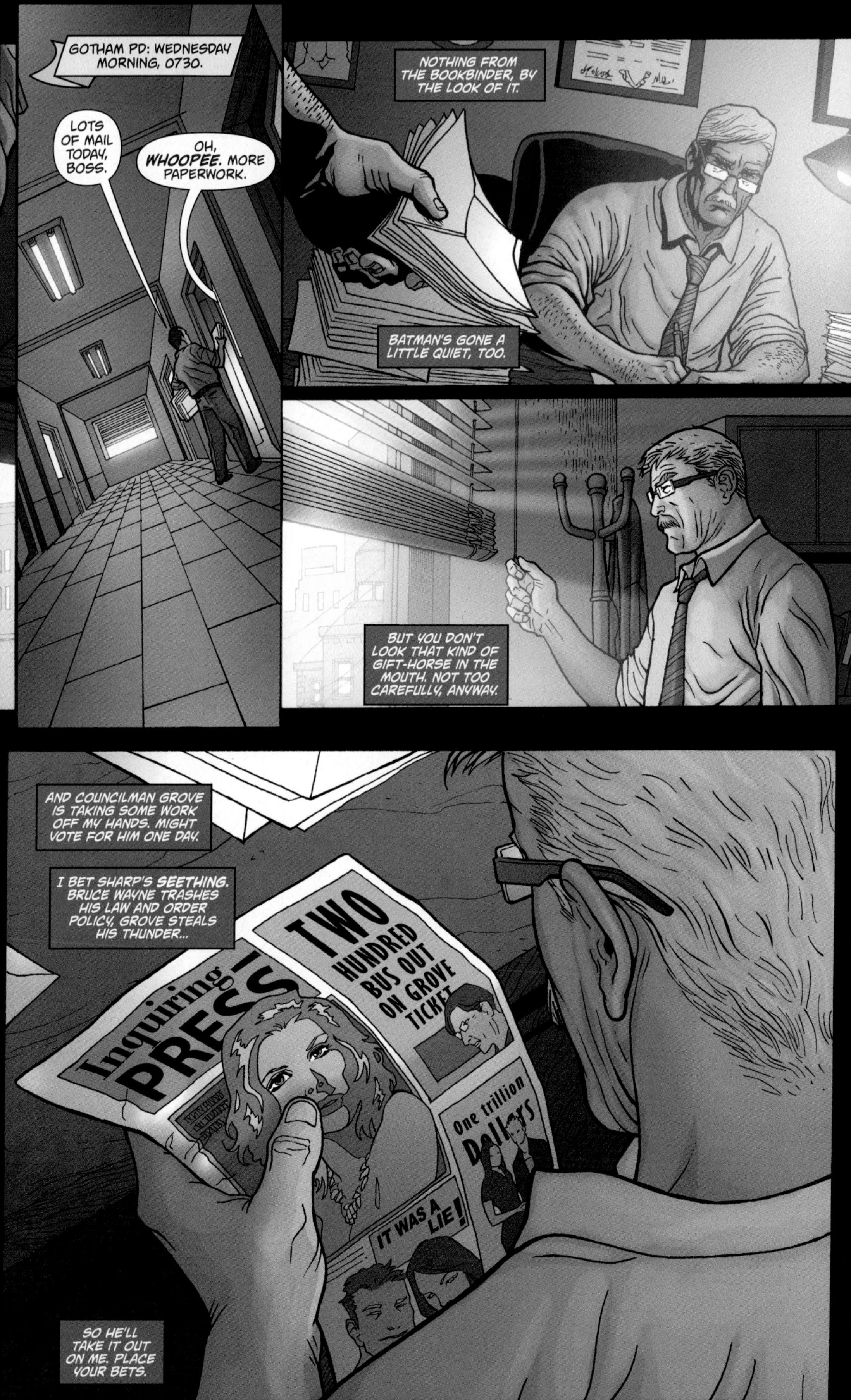

GOTHAM PD: WEDNESDAY MORNING, 0730.
LOTS OF MAIL TODAY, BOSS.
OH, WHOOPEE. MORE PAPERWORK.
NOTHING FROM THE BOOKBINDER, BY THE LOOK OF IT.
BATMAN'S GONE A LITTLE QUIET, TOO.
BUT YOU DON'T LOOK THAT KIND OF GIFT-HORSE IN THE MOUTH. NOT TOO CAREFULLY, ANYWAY.
AND COUNCILMAN GROVE IS TAKING SOME WORK OFF MY HANDS. MIGHT VOTE FOR HIM ONE DAY.
I BET SHARP'S SEETHING. BRUCE WAYNE TRASHES HIS LAW AND ORDER POLICY, GROVE STEALS HIS THUNDER...
Inquiring PRESS
TWO HUNDRED BUS OUT ON GROVE TICKET
One trillion Dollars
IT WAS A LIE!
SO HE'LL TAKE IT OUT ON ME. PLACE YOUR BETS.

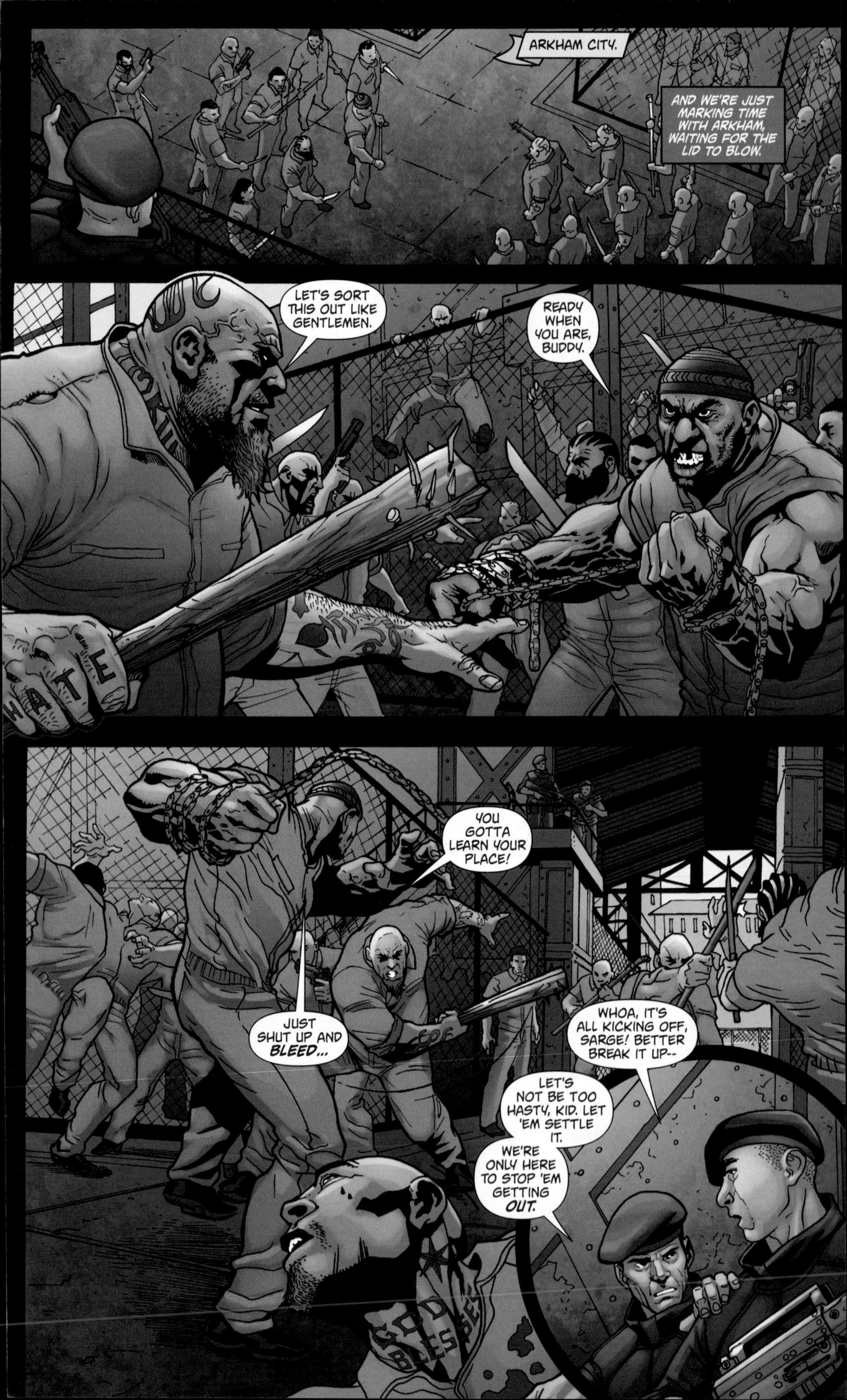
ARKHAM CITY.
AND WE'RE JUST MARKING TIME WITH ARKHAM, WAITING FOR THE LID TO BLOW.
LET'S SORT THIS OUT LIKE GENTLEMEN.
READY WHEN YOU ARE, BUDDY.
HATE
YOU GOTTA LEARN YOUR PLACE!
JUST SHUT UP AND BLEED...
WHOA, IT'S ALL KICKING OFF, SARGE! BETTER BREAK IT UP--
LET'S NOT BE TOO HASTY, KID. LET 'EM SETTLE IT.
WE'RE ONLY HERE TO STOP 'EM GETTING OUT.
GOD BLESS

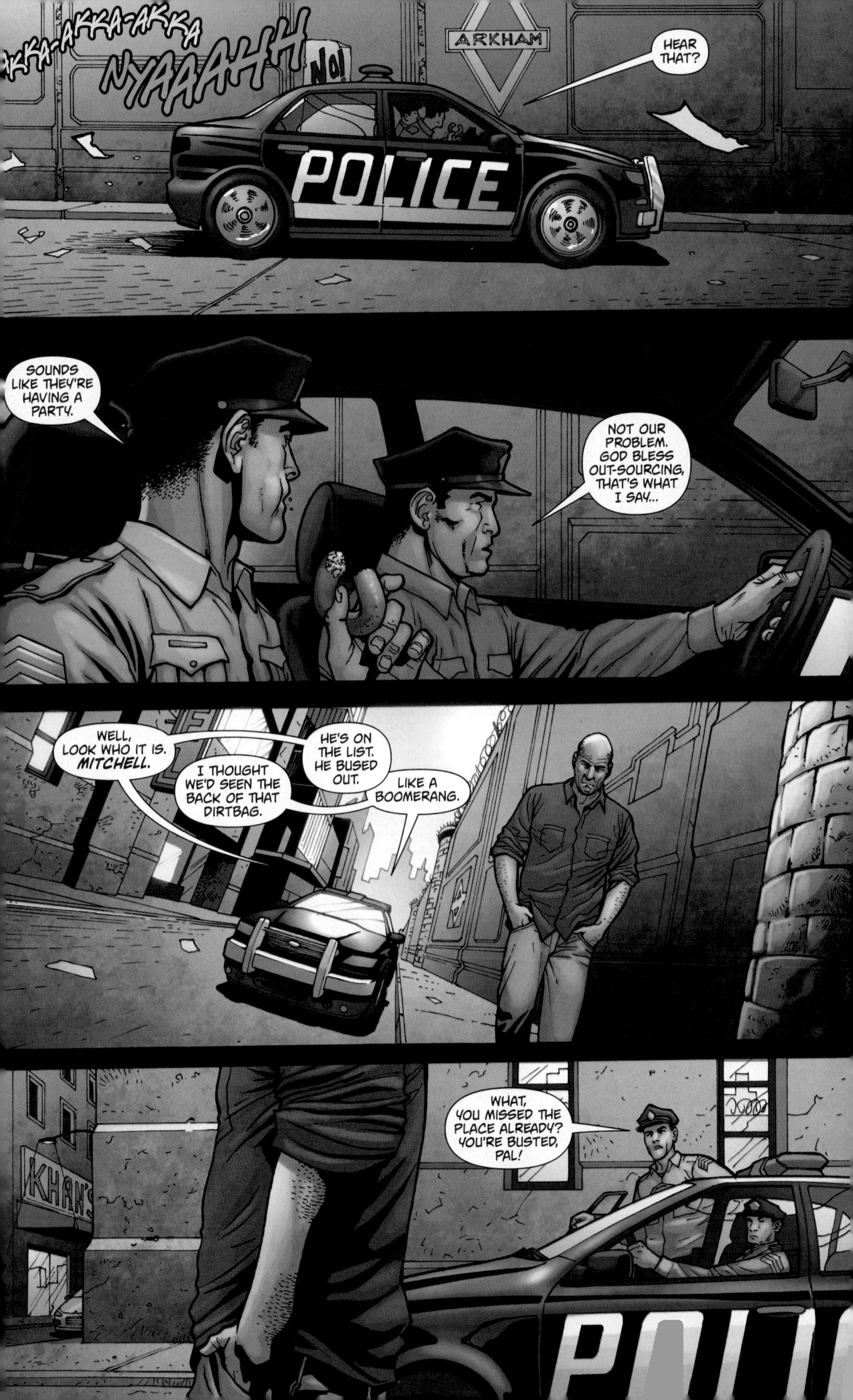
AKKA-AKKA-AKKA-AKKA
NYAAAHH
NO!
ARKHAM
HEAR THAT?
POLICE
SOUNDS LIKE THEY'RE HAVING A PARTY.
NOT OUR PROBLEM. GOD BLESS OUT-SOURCING, THAT'S WHAT I SAY...
WELL, LOOK WHO IT IS. MITCHELL.
I THOUGHT WE'D SEEN THE BACK OF THAT DIRTBAG.
HE'S ON THE LIST. HE BUSED OUT.
LIKE A BOOMERANG.
WHAT, YOU MISSED THE PLACE ALREADY? YOU'RE BUSTED, PAL!
KHAN'S

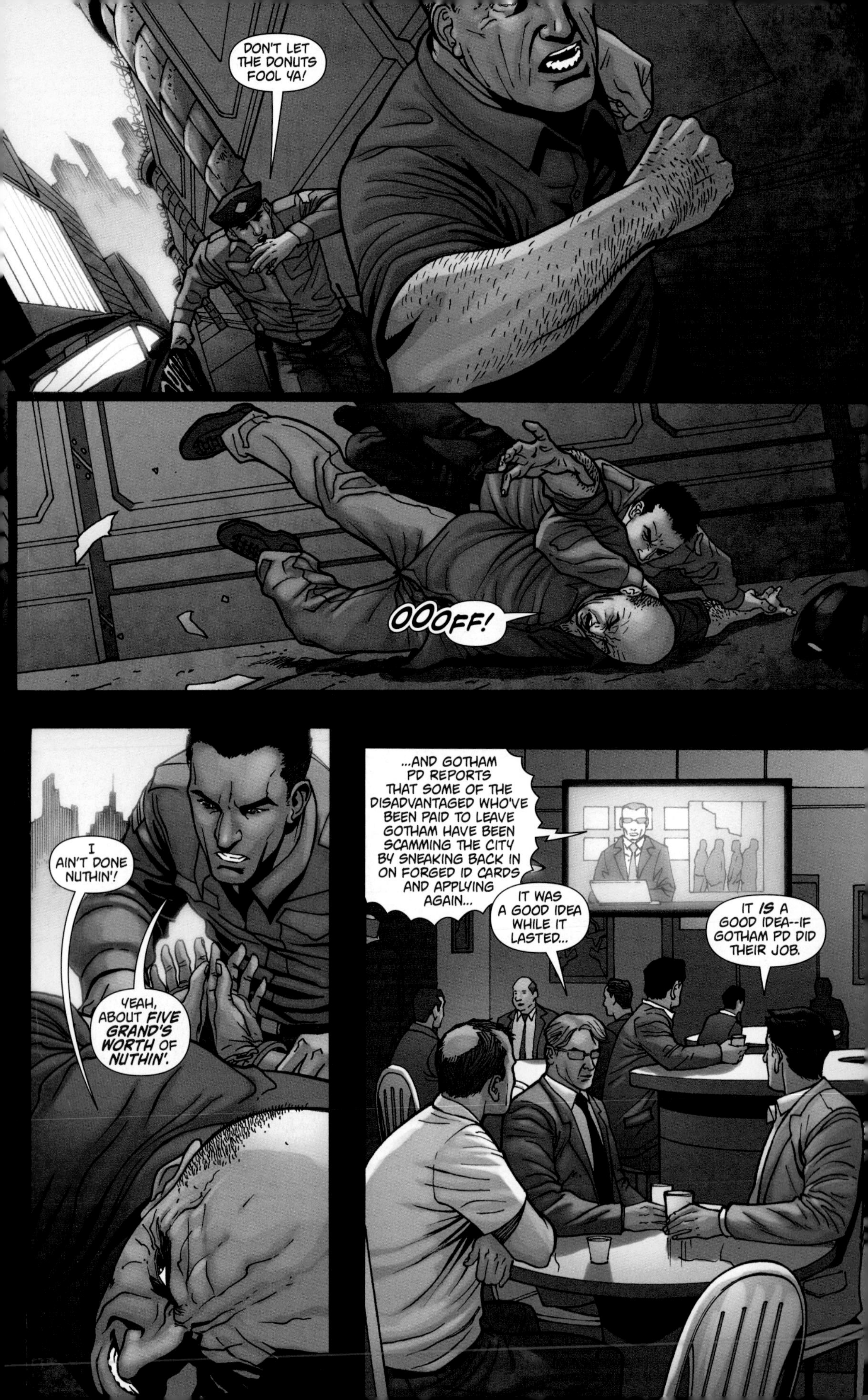
DON'T LET THE DONUTS FOOL YA!
OOOFF!
I AIN'T DONE NUTHIN'!
YEAH, ABOUT FIVE GRAND'S WORTH OF NUTHIN'.
...AND GOTHAM PD REPORTS THAT SOME OF THE DISADVANTAGED WHO'VE BEEN PAID TO LEAVE GOTHAM HAVE BEEN SCAMMING THE CITY BY SNEAKING BACK IN ON FORGED ID CARDS AND APPLYING AGAIN...
IT WAS A GOOD IDEA WHILE IT LASTED...
IT IS A GOOD IDEA--IF GOTHAM PD DID THEIR JOB.

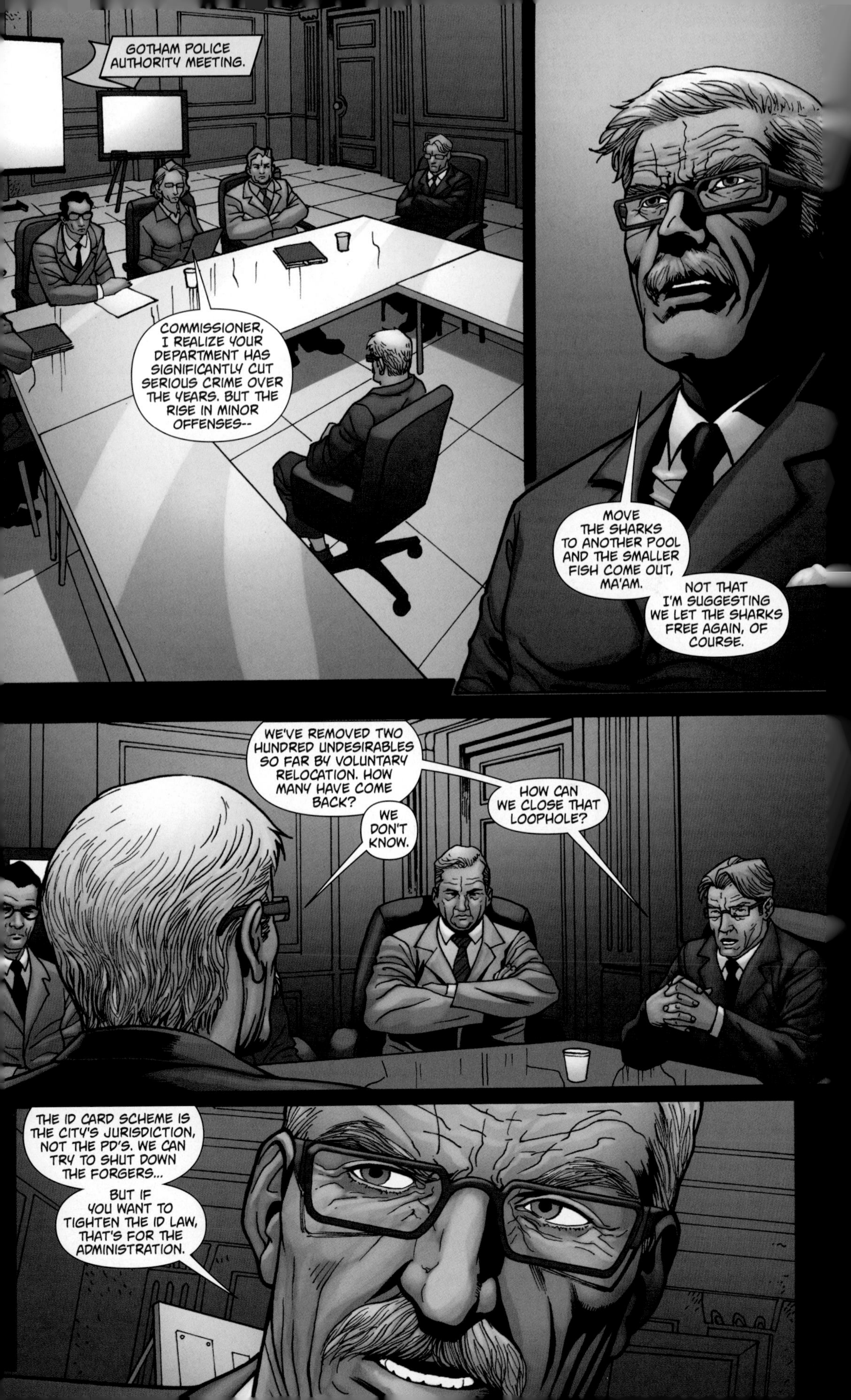
GOTHAM POLICE AUTHORITY MEETING.
COMMISSIONER, I REALIZE YOUR DEPARTMENT HAS SIGNIFICANTLY CUT SERIOUS CRIME OVER THE YEARS. BUT THE RISE IN MINOR OFFENSES--
MOVE THE SHARKS TO ANOTHER POOL AND THE SMALLER FISH COME OUT, MA'AM.
NOT THAT I'M SUGGESTING WE LET THE SHARKS FREE AGAIN, OF COURSE.
WE'VE REMOVED TWO HUNDRED UNDESIRABLES SO FAR BY VOLUNTARY RELOCATION. HOW MANY HAVE COME BACK?
WE DON'T KNOW.
HOW CAN WE CLOSE THAT LOOPHOLE?
THE ID CARD SCHEME IS THE CITY'S JURISDICTION, NOT THE PD'S. WE CAN TRY TO SHUT DOWN THE FORGERS...
BUT IF YOU WANT TO TIGHTEN THE ID LAW, THAT'S FOR THE ADMINISTRATION.

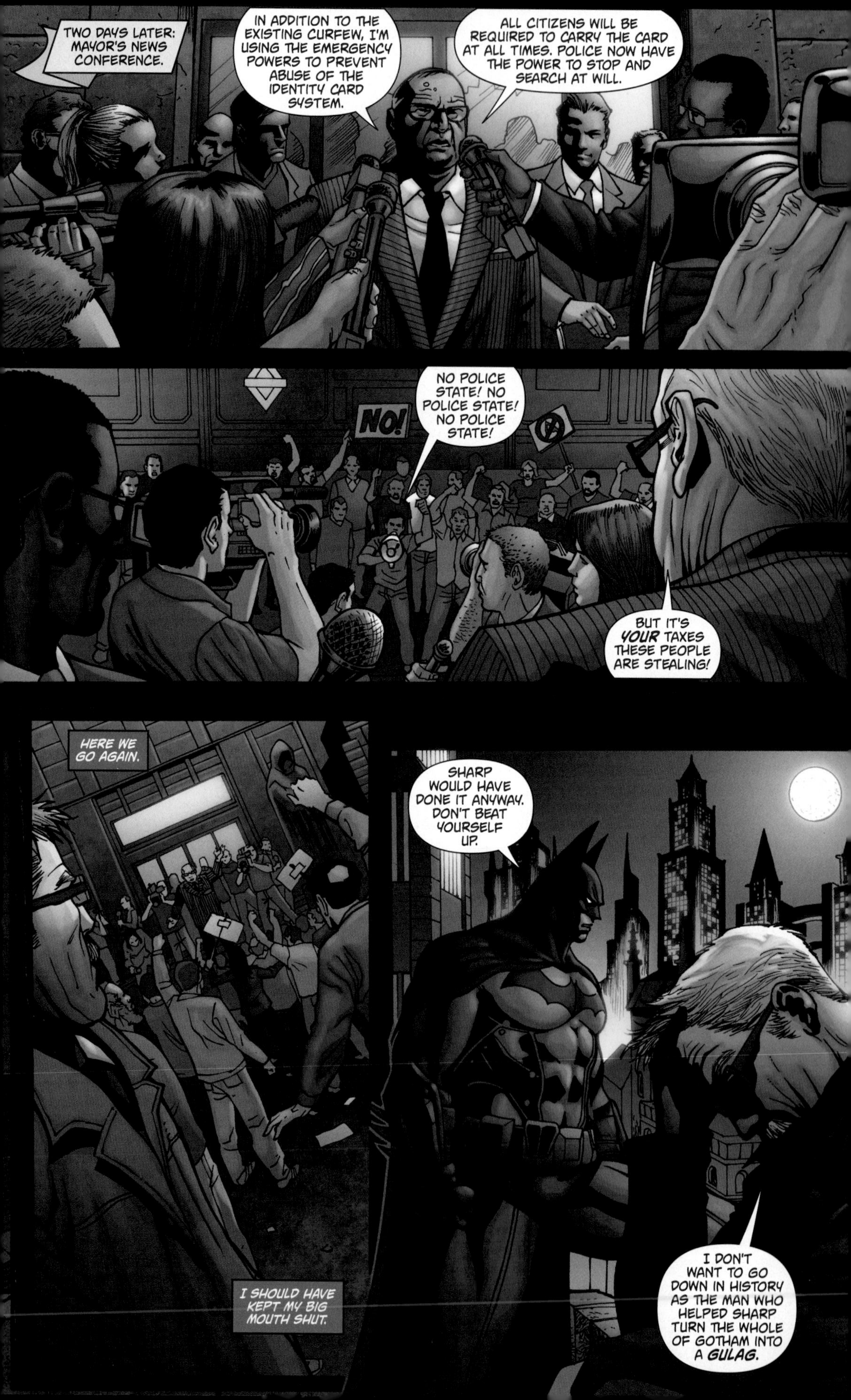
TWO DAYS LATER: MAYOR'S NEWS CONFERENCE.
IN ADDITION TO THE EXISTING CURFEW, I'M USING THE EMERGENCY POWERS TO PREVENT ABUSE OF THE IDENTITY CARD SYSTEM.
ALL CITIZENS WILL BE REQUIRED TO CARRY THE CARD AT ALL TIMES. POLICE NOW HAVE THE POWER TO STOP AND SEARCH AT WILL.
NO!
NO POLICE STATE! NO POLICE STATE! NO POLICE STATE!
BUT IT'S *YOUR* TAXES THESE PEOPLE ARE STEALING!
HERE WE GO AGAIN.
I SHOULD HAVE KEPT MY BIG MOUTH SHUT.
SHARP WOULD HAVE DONE IT ANYWAY. DON'T BEAT YOURSELF UP.
I DON'T WANT TO GO DOWN IN HISTORY AS THE MAN WHO HELPED SHARP TURN THE WHOLE OF GOTHAM INTO A *GULAG*.

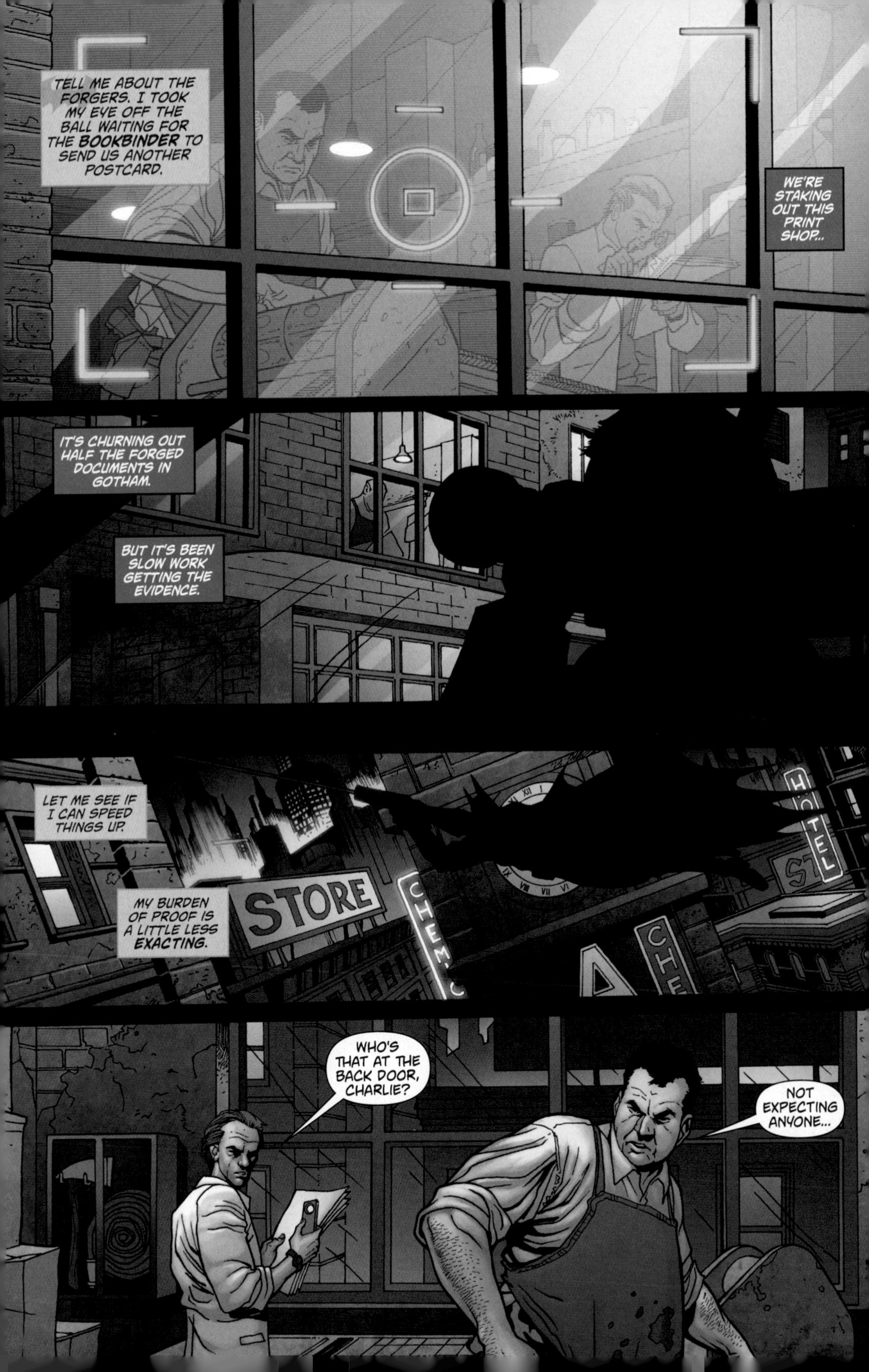
TELL ME ABOUT THE FORGERS. I TOOK MY EYE OFF THE BALL WAITING FOR THE BOOKBINDER TO SEND US ANOTHER POSTCARD.
WE'RE STAKING OUT THIS PRINT SHOP...
IT'S CHURNING OUT HALF THE FORGED DOCUMENTS IN GOTHAM.
BUT IT'S BEEN SLOW WORK GETTING THE EVIDENCE.
LET ME SEE IF I CAN SPEED THINGS UP.
MY BURDEN OF PROOF IS A LITTLE LESS EXACTING.
STORE
HOTEL
WHO'S THAT AT THE BACK DOOR, CHARLIE?
NOT EXPECTING ANYONE...

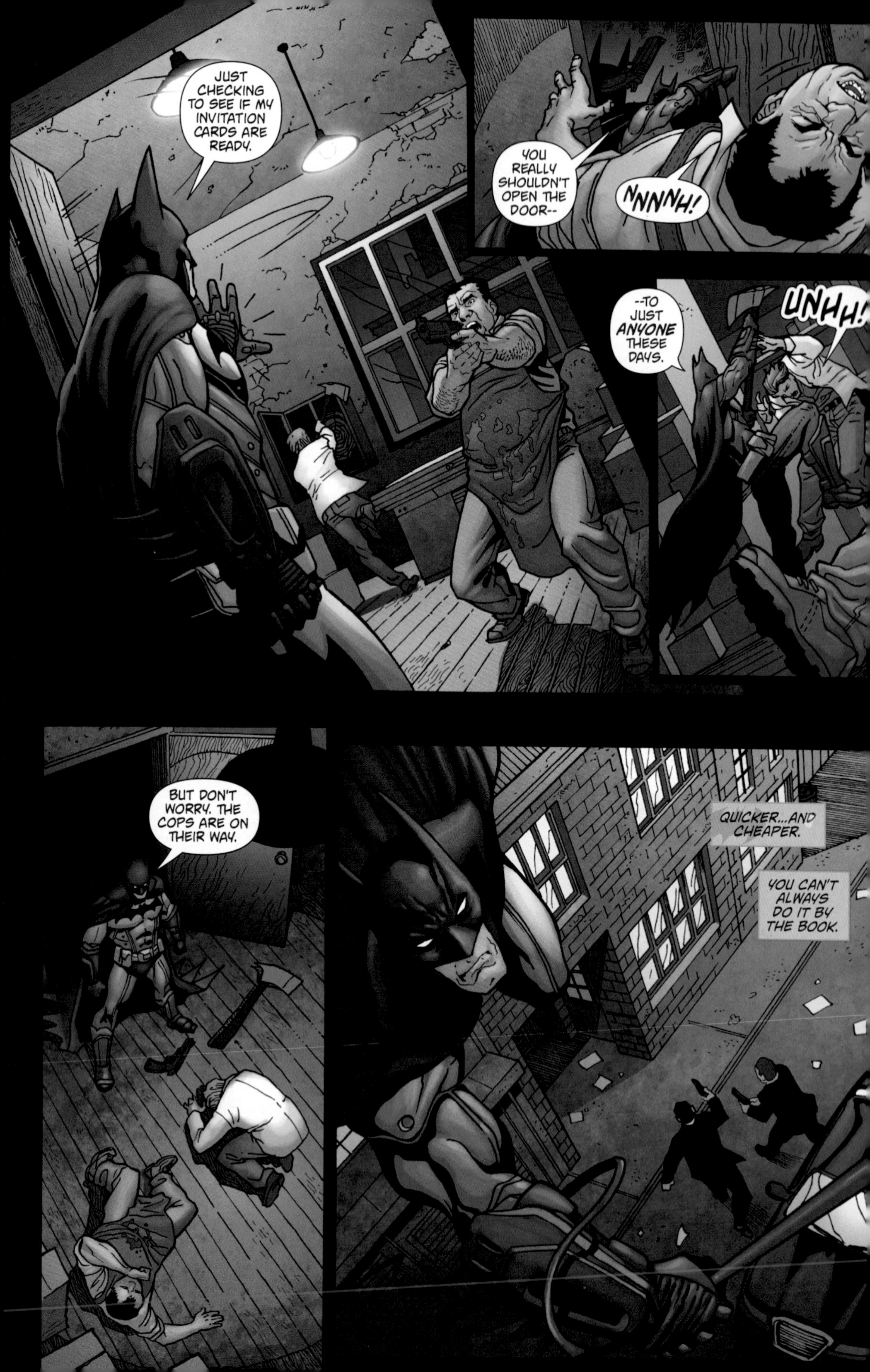

JUST CHECKING TO SEE IF MY INVITATION CARDS ARE READY.
YOU REALLY SHOULDN'T OPEN THE DOOR--
NNNNH!
--TO JUST ANYONE THESE DAYS.
UNHH!
BUT DON'T WORRY. THE COPS ARE ON THEIR WAY.
QUICKER...AND CHEAPER.
YOU CAN'T ALWAYS DO IT BY THE BOOK.

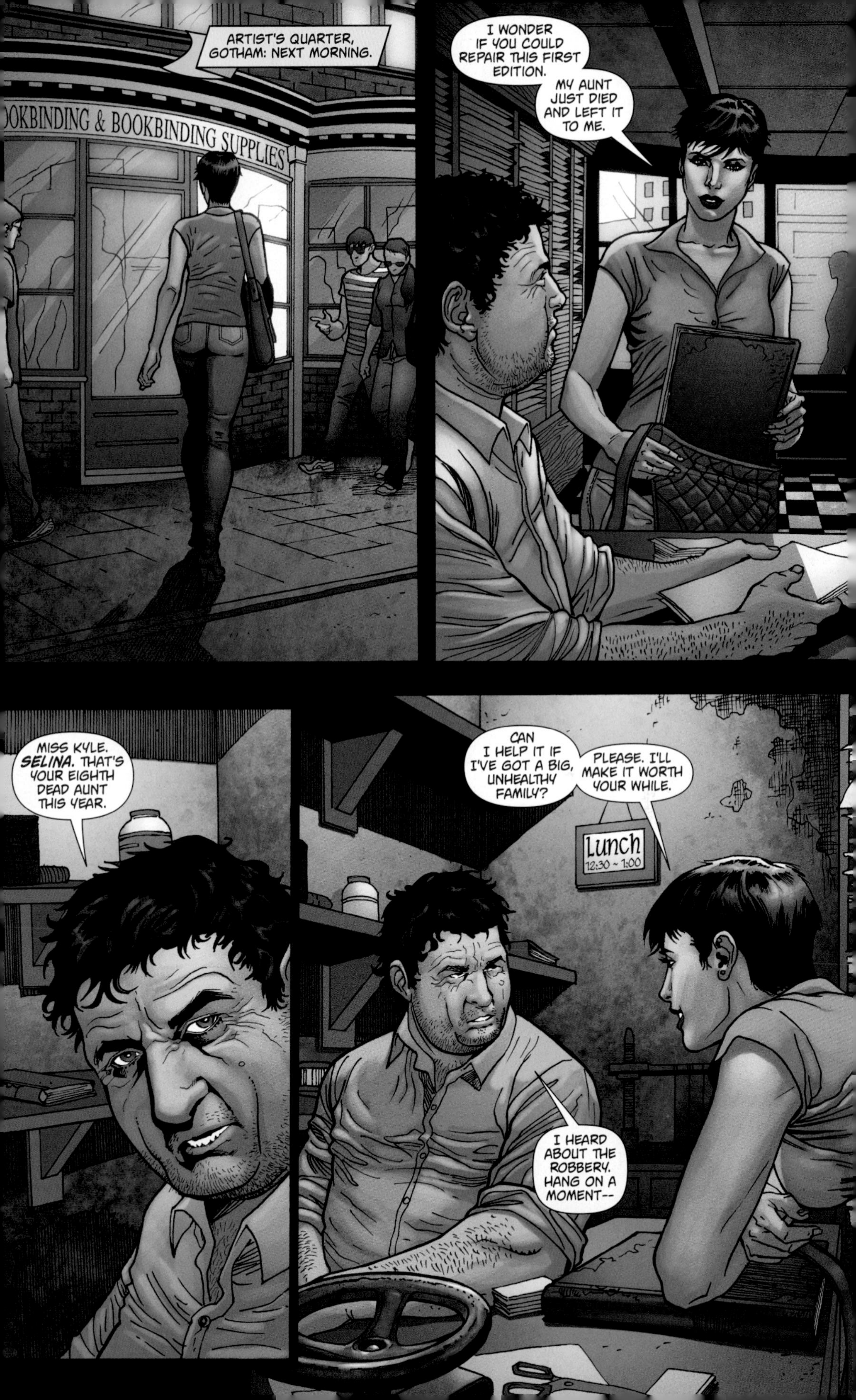
ARTIST'S QUARTER, GOTHAM: NEXT MORNING.
OOKBINDING & BOOKBINDING SUPPLIES
I WONDER IF YOU COULD REPAIR THIS FIRST EDITION.
MY AUNT JUST DIED AND LEFT IT TO ME.
MISS KYLE. SELINA. THAT'S YOUR EIGHTH DEAD AUNT THIS YEAR.
CAN I HELP IT IF I'VE GOT A BIG, UNHEALTHY FAMILY?
PLEASE. I'LL MAKE IT WORTH YOUR WHILE.
Lunch
12:30 ~ 1:00
I HEARD ABOUT THE ROBBERY. HANG ON A MOMENT--

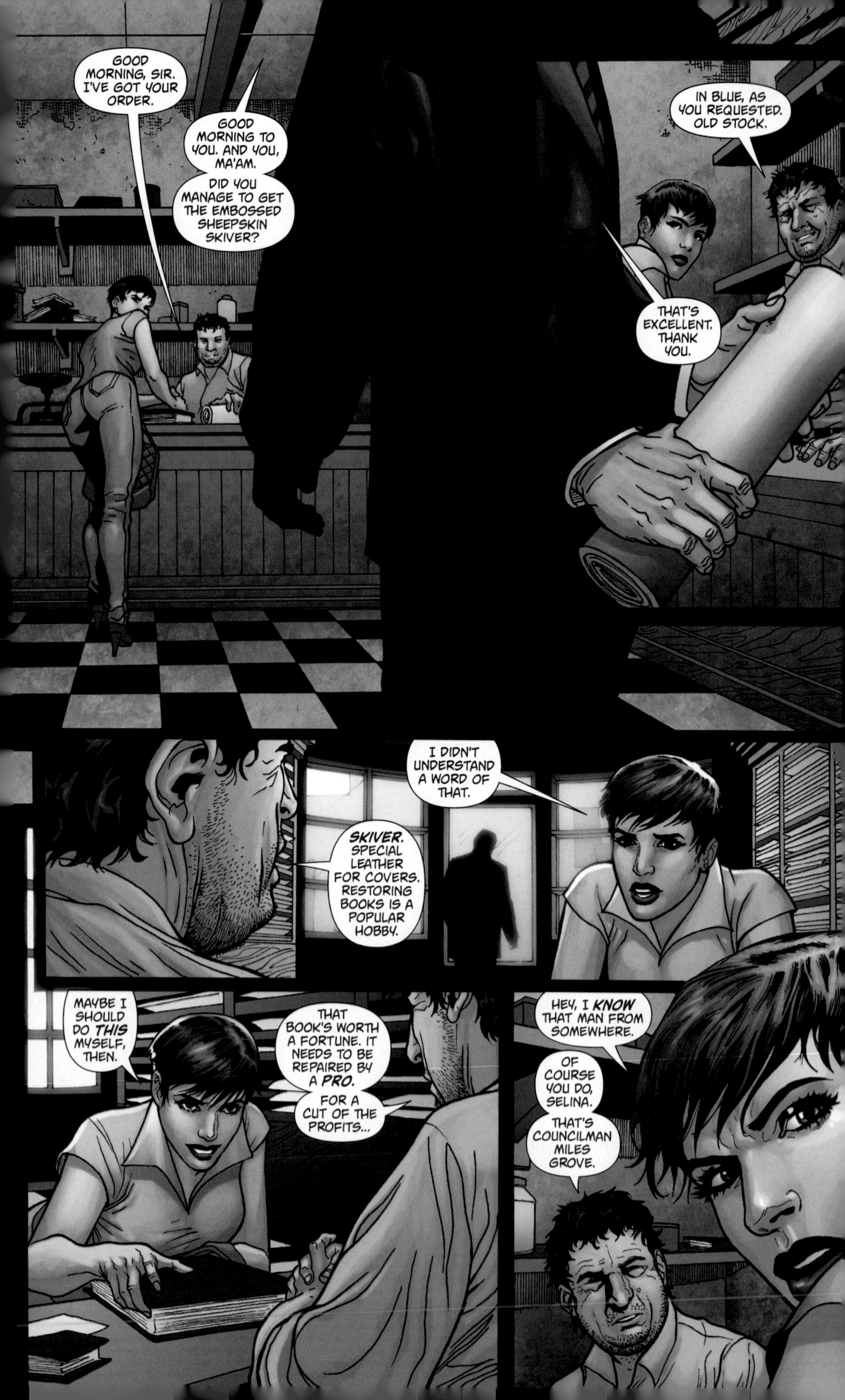
GOOD MORNING, SIR. I'VE GOT YOUR ORDER.
GOOD MORNING TO YOU. AND YOU, MA'AM.
DID YOU MANAGE TO GET THE EMBOSSED SHEEPSKIN SKIVER?
IN BLUE, AS YOU REQUESTED. OLD STOCK.
THAT'S EXCELLENT. THANK YOU.
I DIDN'T UNDERSTAND A WORD OF THAT.
SKIVER. SPECIAL LEATHER FOR COVERS. RESTORING BOOKS IS A POPULAR HOBBY.
MAYBE I SHOULD DO THIS MYSELF, THEN.
THAT BOOK'S WORTH A FORTUNE. IT NEEDS TO BE REPAIRED BY A PRO.
FOR A CUT OF THE PROFITS...
HEY, I KNOW THAT MAN FROM SOMEWHERE.
OF COURSE YOU DO, SELINA.
THAT'S COUNCILMAN MILES GROVE.

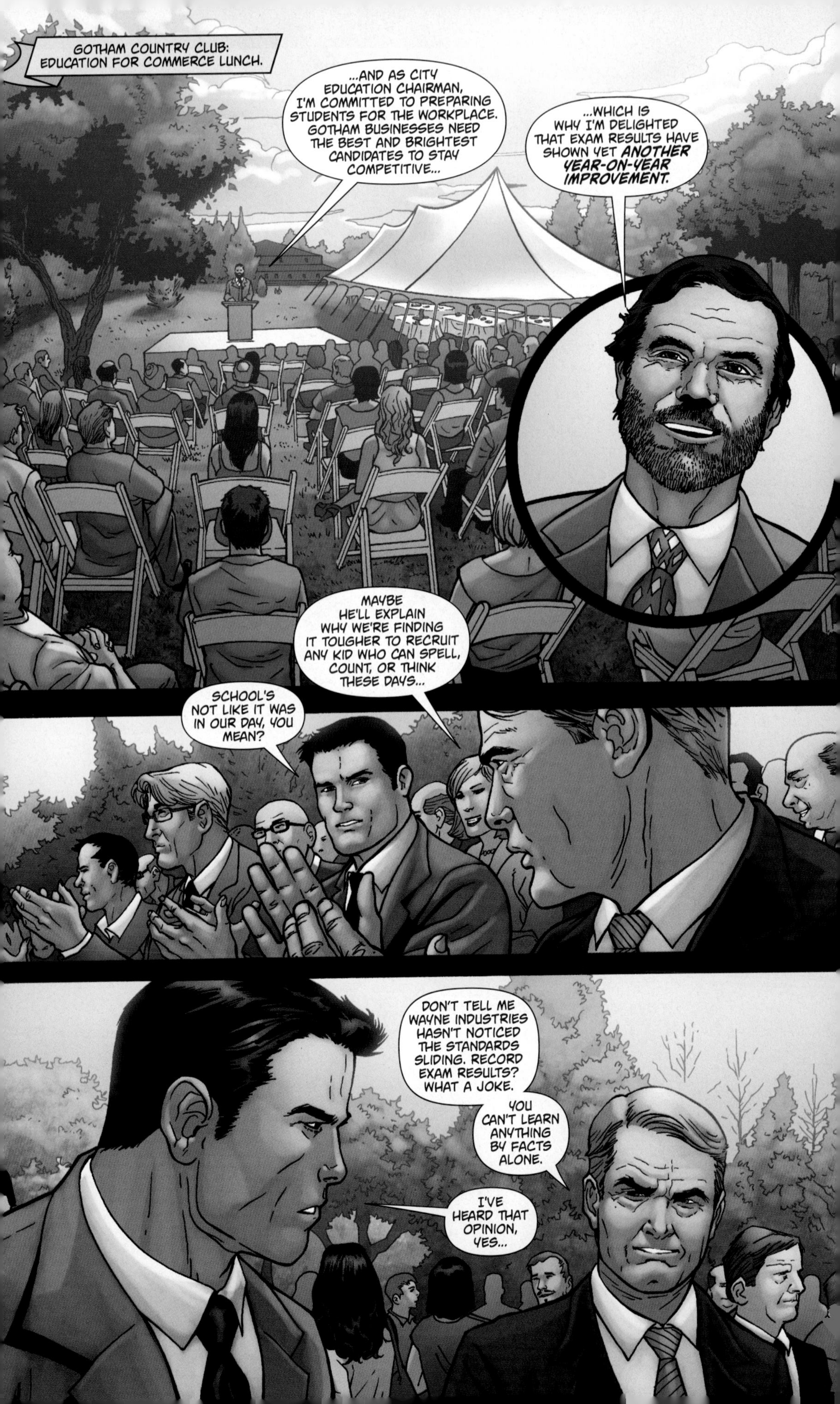
GOTHAM COUNTRY CLUB: EDUCATION FOR COMMERCE LUNCH.
...AND AS CITY EDUCATION CHAIRMAN, I'M COMMITTED TO PREPARING STUDENTS FOR THE WORKPLACE. GOTHAM BUSINESSES NEED THE BEST AND BRIGHTEST CANDIDATES TO STAY COMPETITIVE...
...WHICH IS WHY I'M DELIGHTED THAT EXAM RESULTS HAVE SHOWN YET ANOTHER YEAR-ON-YEAR IMPROVEMENT.
MAYBE HE'LL EXPLAIN WHY WE'RE FINDING IT TOUGHER TO RECRUIT ANY KID WHO CAN SPELL, COUNT, OR THINK THESE DAYS...
SCHOOL'S NOT LIKE IT WAS IN OUR DAY, YOU MEAN?
DON'T TELL ME WAYNE INDUSTRIES HASN'T NOTICED THE STANDARDS SLIDING. RECORD EXAM RESULTS? WHAT A JOKE.
YOU CAN'T LEARN ANYTHING BY FACTS ALONE.
I'VE HEARD THAT OPINION, YES...

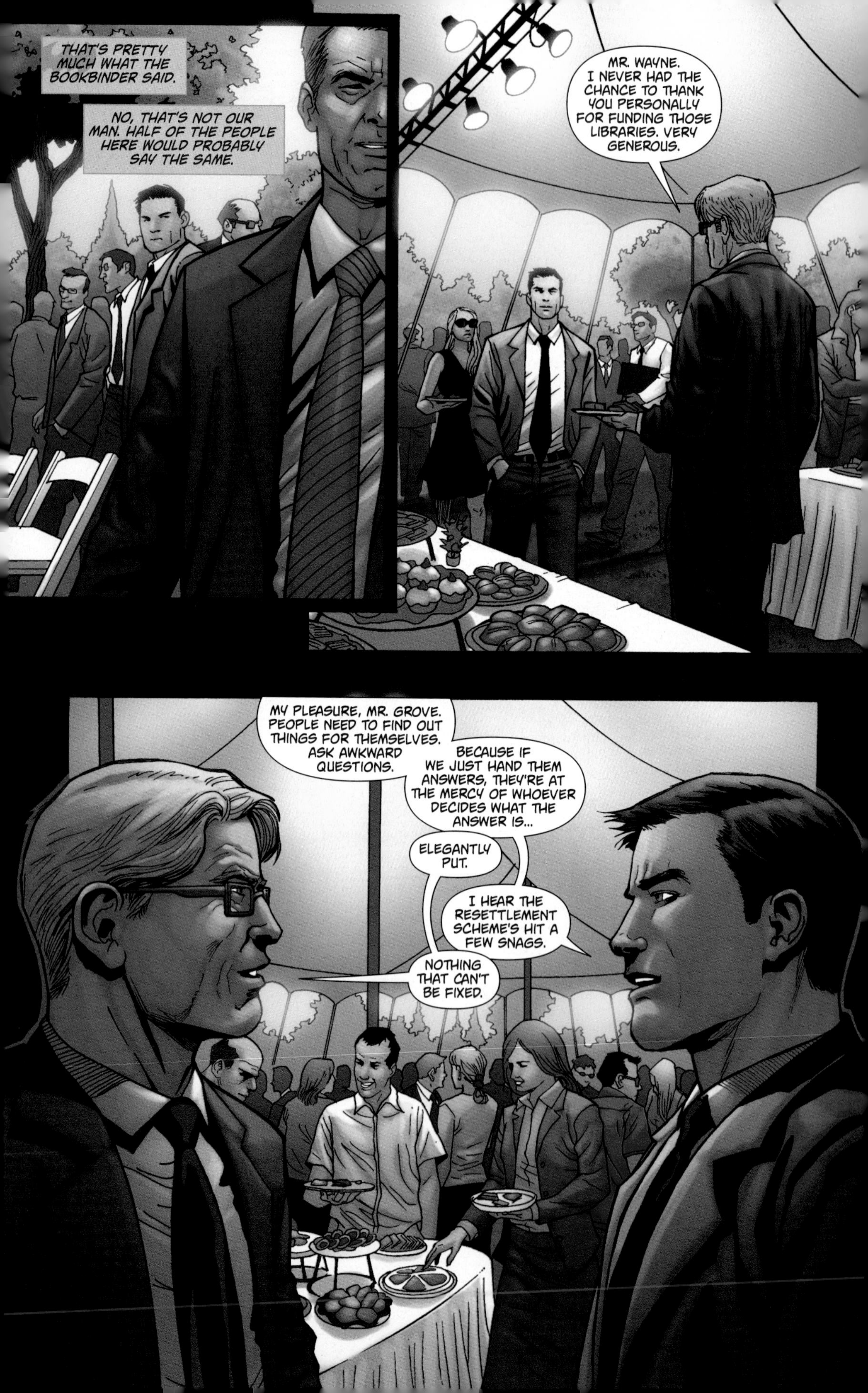
THAT'S PRETTY MUCH WHAT THE BOOKBINDER SAID.
NO, THAT'S NOT OUR MAN. HALF OF THE PEOPLE HERE WOULD PROBABLY SAY THE SAME.
MR. WAYNE. I NEVER HAD THE CHANCE TO THANK YOU PERSONALLY FOR FUNDING THOSE LIBRARIES. VERY GENEROUS.
MY PLEASURE, MR. GROVE. PEOPLE NEED TO FIND OUT THINGS FOR THEMSELVES. ASK AWKWARD QUESTIONS.
BECAUSE IF WE JUST HAND THEM ANSWERS, THEY'RE AT THE MERCY OF WHOEVER DECIDES WHAT THE ANSWER IS...
ELEGANTLY PUT.
I HEAR THE RESETTLEMENT SCHEME'S HIT A FEW SNAGS.
NOTHING THAT CAN'T BE FIXED.

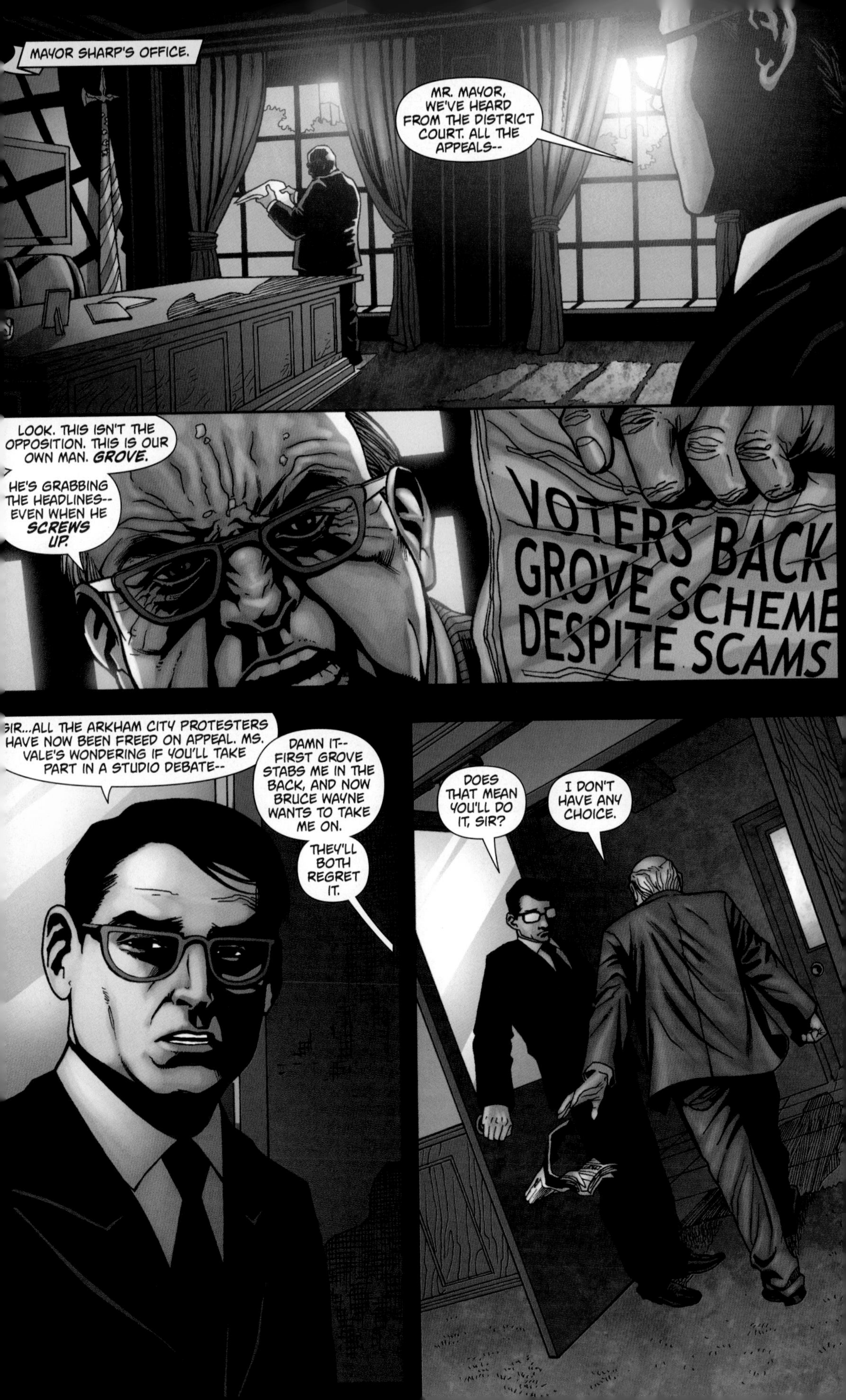
MAYOR SHARP'S OFFICE.
MR. MAYOR, WE'VE HEARD FROM THE DISTRICT COURT. ALL THE APPEALS--
LOOK. THIS ISN'T THE OPPOSITION. THIS IS OUR OWN MAN. GROVE.
HE'S GRABBING THE HEADLINES--EVEN WHEN HE SCREWS UP.
VOTERS BACK GROVE SCHEME DESPITE SCAMS
SIR...ALL THE ARKHAM CITY PROTESTERS HAVE NOW BEEN FREED ON APPEAL. MS. VALE'S WONDERING IF YOU'LL TAKE PART IN A STUDIO DEBATE--
DAMN IT--FIRST GROVE STABS ME IN THE BACK, AND NOW BRUCE WAYNE WANTS TO TAKE ME ON.
THEY'LL BOTH REGRET IT.
DOES THAT MEAN YOU'LL DO IT, SIR?
I DON'T HAVE ANY CHOICE.

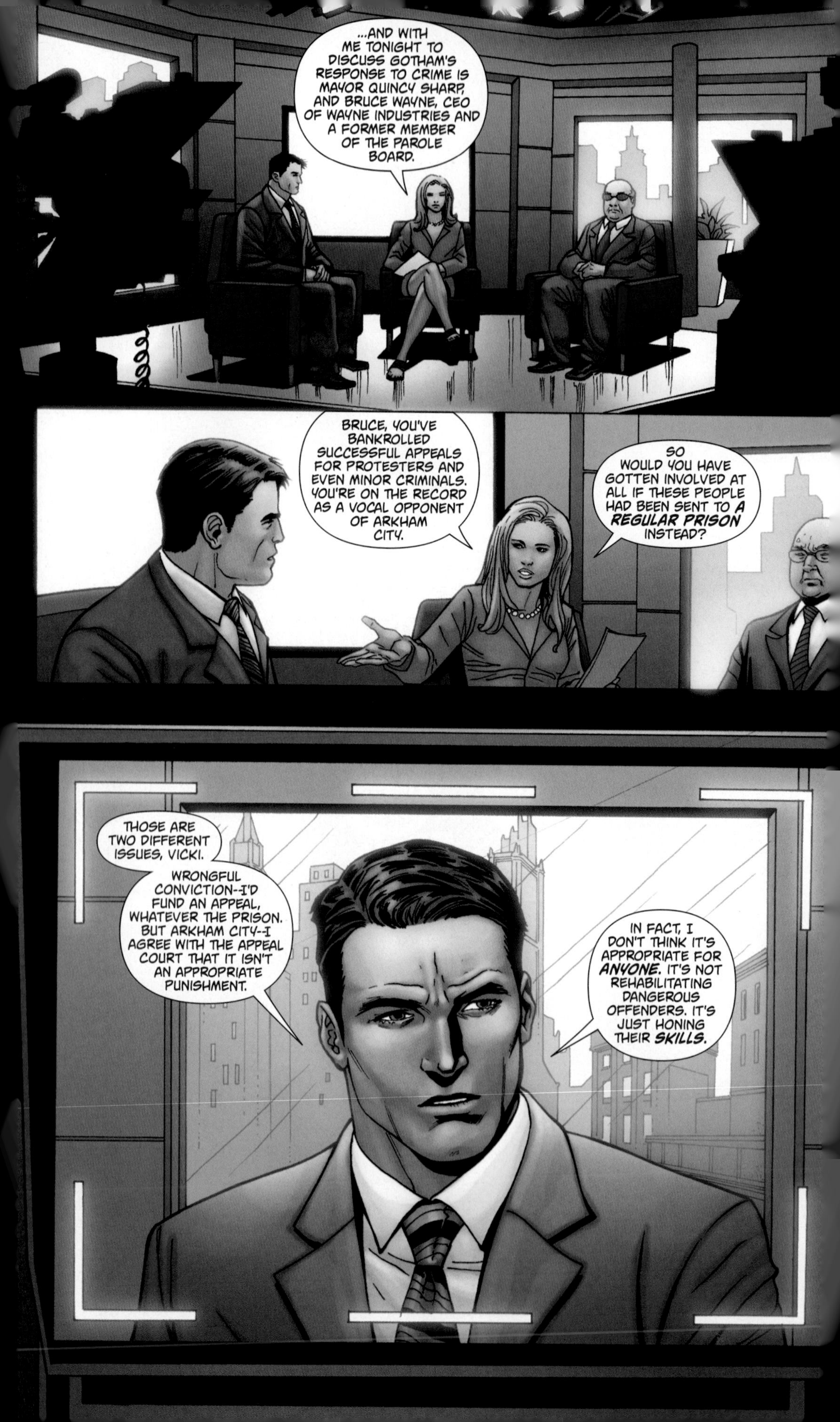
...AND WITH ME TONIGHT TO DISCUSS GOTHAM'S RESPONSE TO CRIME IS MAYOR QUINCY SHARP, AND BRUCE WAYNE, CEO OF WAYNE INDUSTRIES AND A FORMER MEMBER OF THE PAROLE BOARD.
BRUCE, YOU'VE BANKROLLED SUCCESSFUL APPEALS FOR PROTESTERS AND EVEN MINOR CRIMINALS. YOU'RE ON THE RECORD AS A VOCAL OPPONENT OF ARKHAM CITY.
SO WOULD YOU HAVE GOTTEN INVOLVED AT ALL IF THESE PEOPLE HAD BEEN SENT TO *A REGULAR PRISON* INSTEAD?
THOSE ARE TWO DIFFERENT ISSUES, VICKI.
WRONGFUL CONVICTION--I'D FUND AN APPEAL, WHATEVER THE PRISON. BUT ARKHAM CITY--I AGREE WITH THE APPEAL COURT THAT IT ISN'T AN APPROPRIATE PUNISHMENT.
IN FACT, I DON'T THINK IT'S APPROPRIATE FOR *ANYONE.* IT'S NOT REHABILITATING DANGEROUS OFFENDERS. IT'S JUST HONING THEIR *SKILLS.*

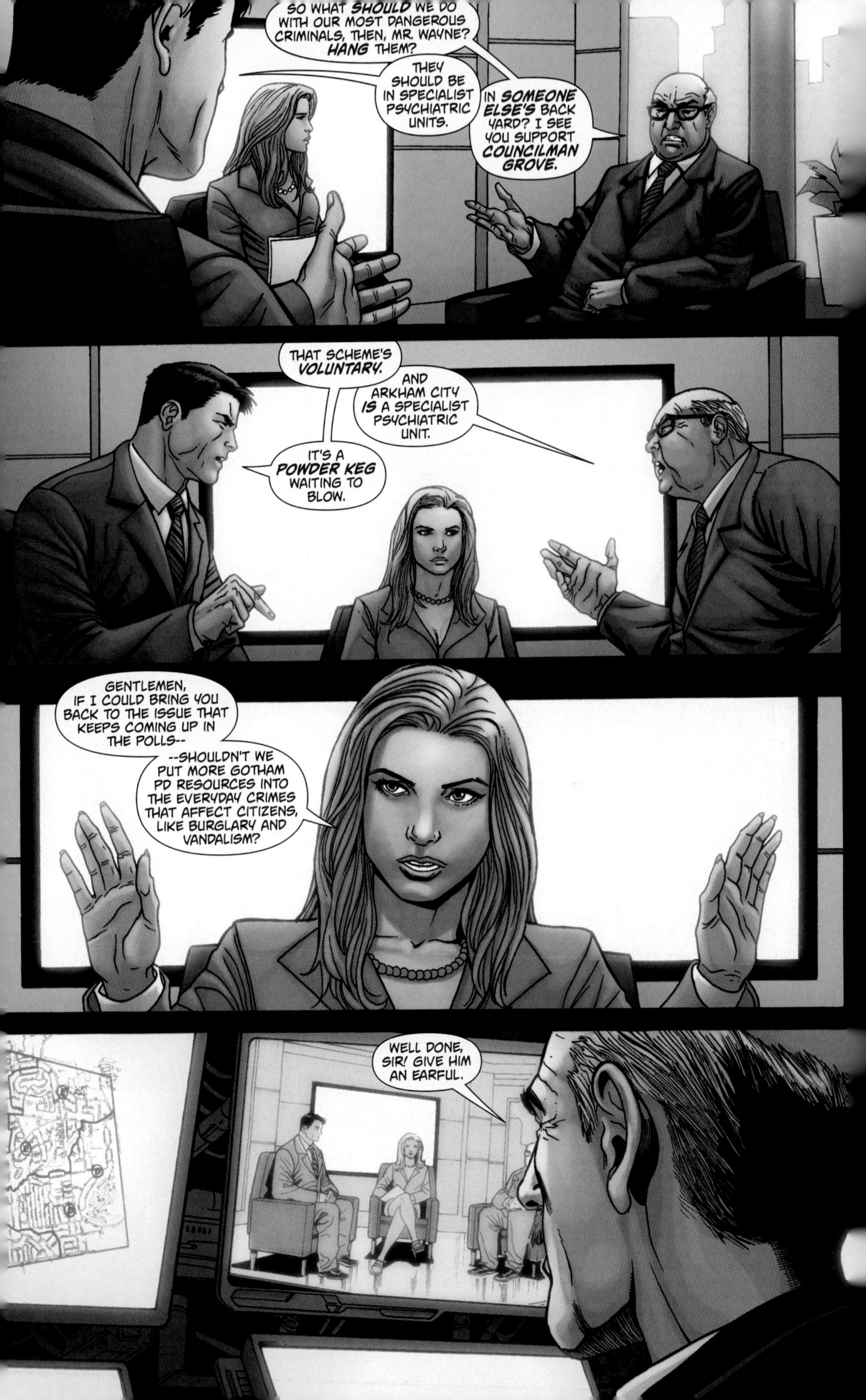
SO WHAT SHOULD WE DO WITH OUR MOST DANGEROUS CRIMINALS, THEN, MR. WAYNE? HANG THEM?
THEY SHOULD BE IN SPECIALIST PSYCHIATRIC UNITS.
IN SOMEONE ELSE'S BACK YARD? I SEE YOU SUPPORT COUNCILMAN GROVE.
THAT SCHEME'S VOLUNTARY.
IT'S A POWDER KEG WAITING TO BLOW.
AND ARKHAM CITY IS A SPECIALIST PSYCHIATRIC UNIT.
GENTLEMEN, IF I COULD BRING YOU BACK TO THE ISSUE THAT KEEPS COMING UP IN THE POLLS--
--SHOULDN'T WE PUT MORE GOTHAM PD RESOURCES INTO THE EVERYDAY CRIMES THAT AFFECT CITIZENS, LIKE BURGLARY AND VANDALISM?
WELL DONE, SIR! GIVE HIM AN EARFUL.

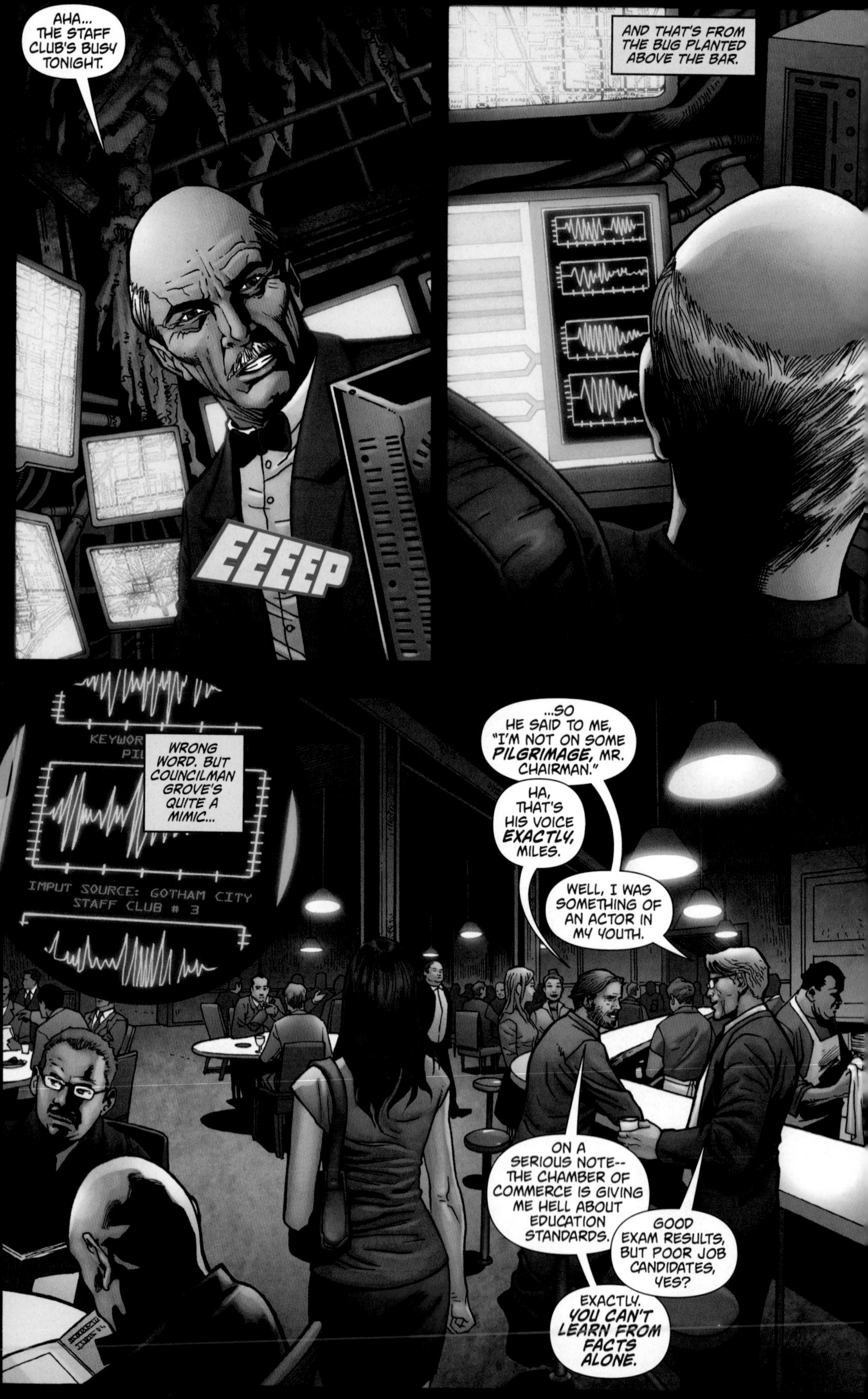

AHA... THE STAFF CLUB'S BUSY TONIGHT.
EEEEP
AND THAT'S FROM THE BUG PLANTED ABOVE THE BAR.
WRONG WORD. BUT COUNCILMAN GROVE'S QUITE A MIMIC...
IMPUT SOURCE: GOTHAM CITY STAFF CLUB # 3
...SO HE SAID TO ME, "I'M NOT ON SOME PILGRIMAGE, MR. CHAIRMAN."
HA, THAT'S HIS VOICE EXACTLY, MILES.
WELL, I WAS SOMETHING OF AN ACTOR IN MY YOUTH.
ON A SERIOUS NOTE-- THE CHAMBER OF COMMERCE IS GIVING ME HELL ABOUT EDUCATION STANDARDS.
GOOD EXAM RESULTS, BUT POOR JOB CANDIDATES, YES?
EXACTLY. YOU CAN'T LEARN FROM FACTS ALONE.

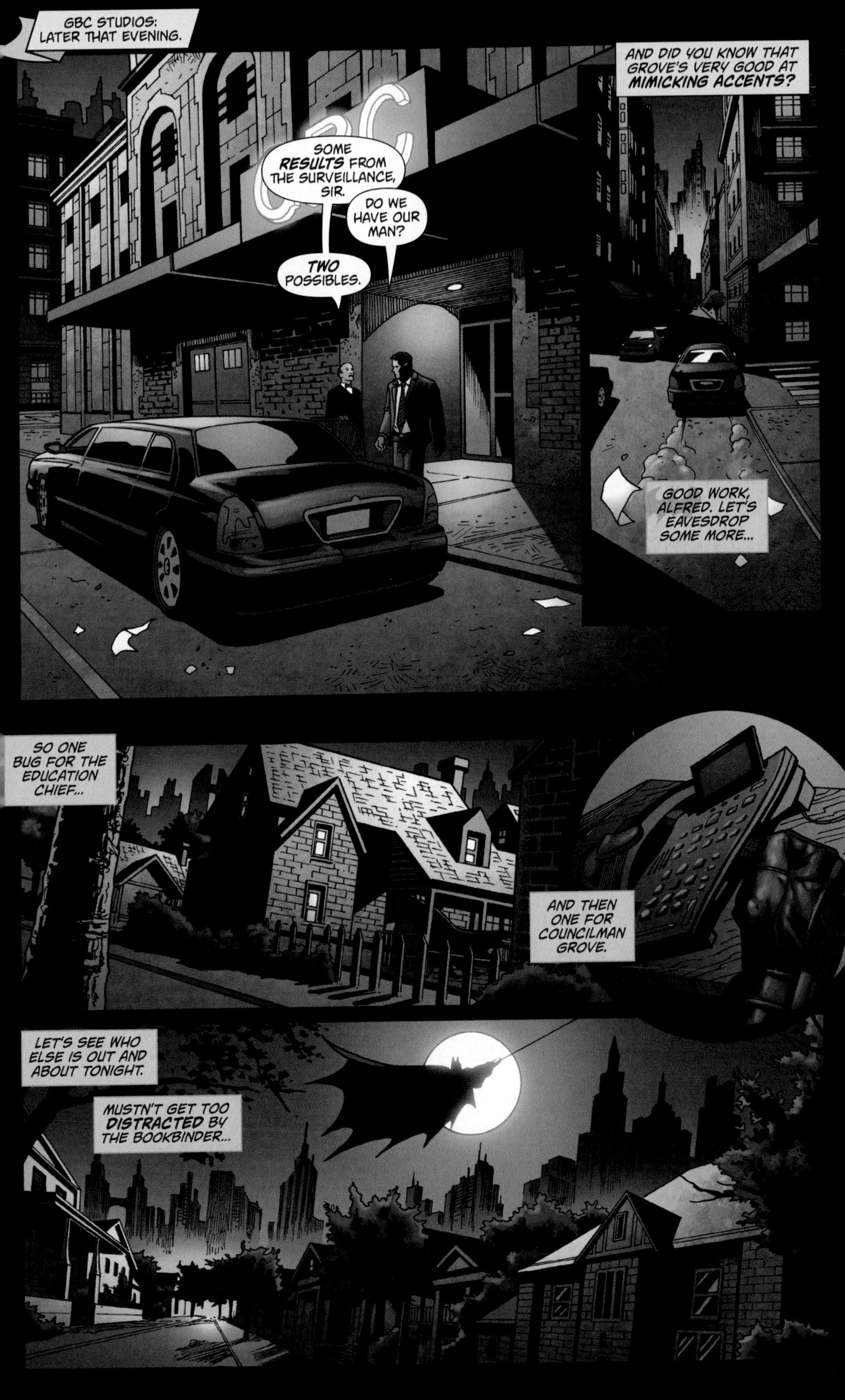
GBC STUDIOS: LATER THAT EVENING.
SOME RESULTS FROM THE SURVEILLANCE, SIR.
DO WE HAVE OUR MAN?
TWO POSSIBLES.
AND DID YOU KNOW THAT GROVE'S VERY GOOD AT MIMICKING ACCENTS?
GOOD WORK, ALFRED. LET'S EAVESDROP SOME MORE...
SO ONE BUG FOR THE EDUCATION CHIEF...
AND THEN ONE FOR COUNCILMAN GROVE.
LET'S SEE WHO ELSE IS OUT AND ABOUT TONIGHT.
MUSTN'T GET TOO DISTRACTED BY THE BOOKBINDER...

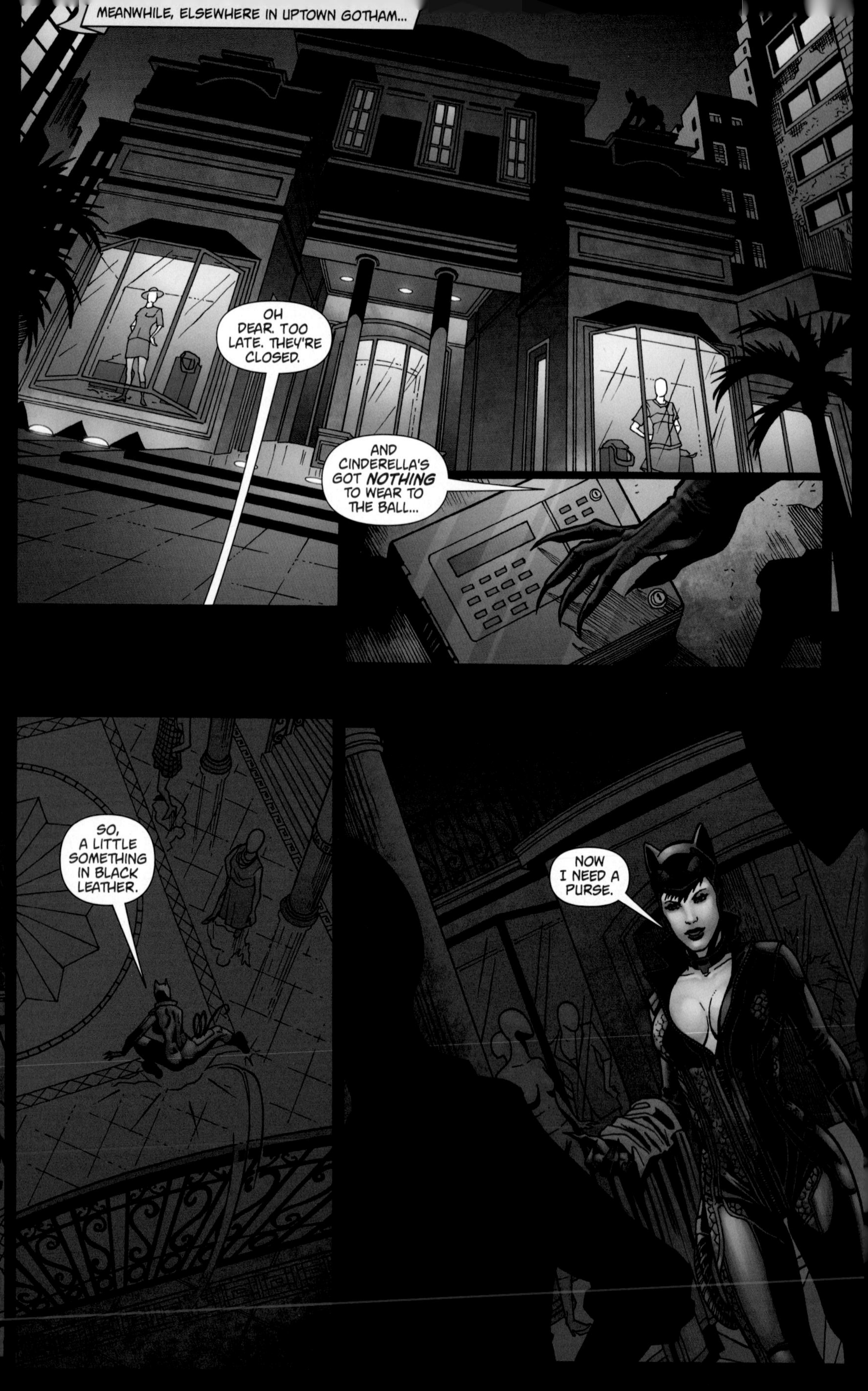
MEANWHILE, ELSEWHERE IN UPTOWN GOTHAM...
OH DEAR. TOO LATE. THEY'RE CLOSED.
AND CINDERELLA'S GOT NOTHING TO WEAR TO THE BALL...
SO, A LITTLE SOMETHING IN BLACK LEATHER.
NOW I NEED A PURSE.

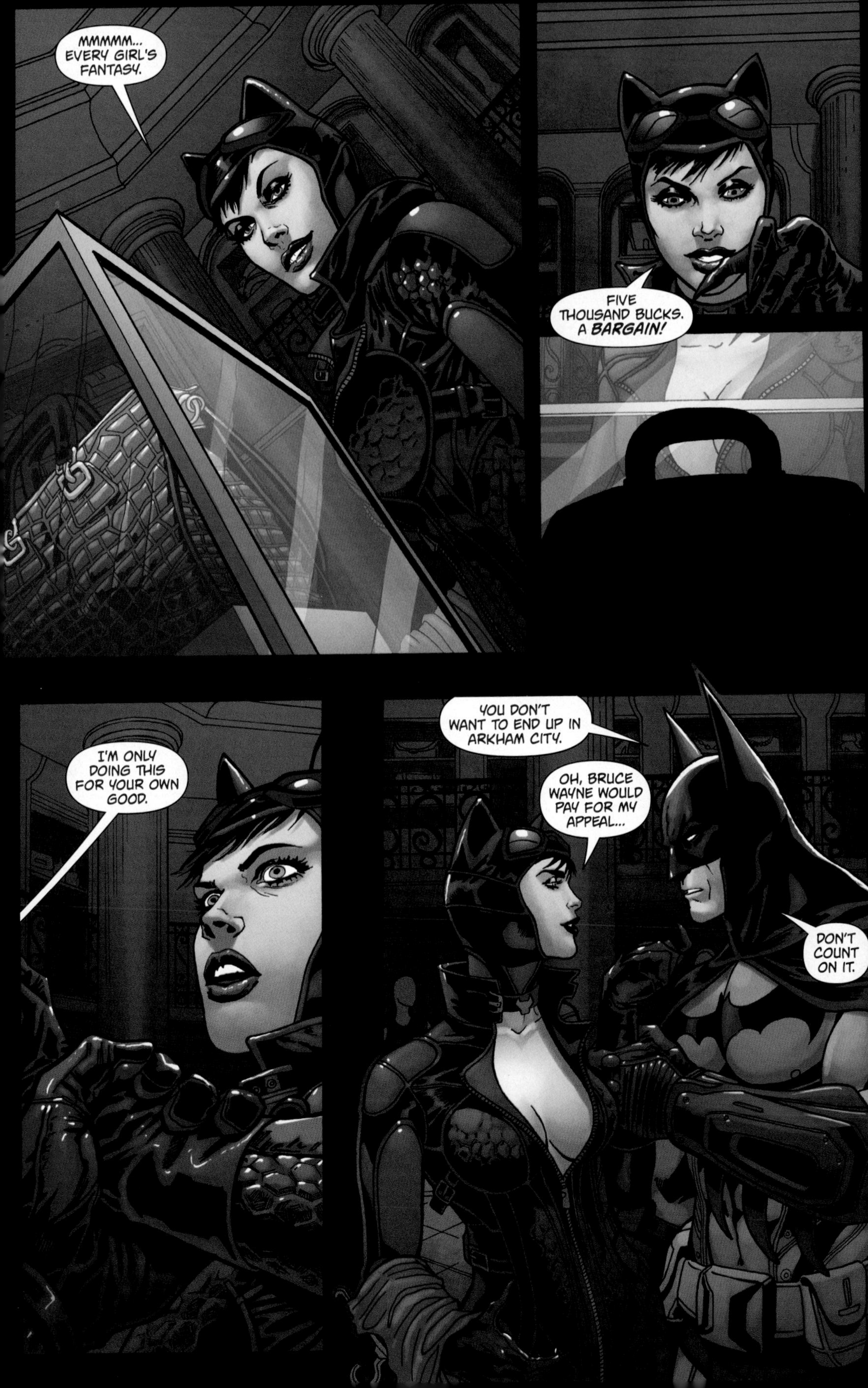
MMMMM... EVERY GIRL'S FANTASY.
FIVE THOUSAND BUCKS. A *BARGAIN!*
I'M ONLY DOING THIS FOR YOUR OWN GOOD.
YOU DON'T WANT TO END UP IN ARKHAM CITY.
OH, BRUCE WAYNE WOULD PAY FOR MY APPEAL...
DON'T COUNT ON IT.

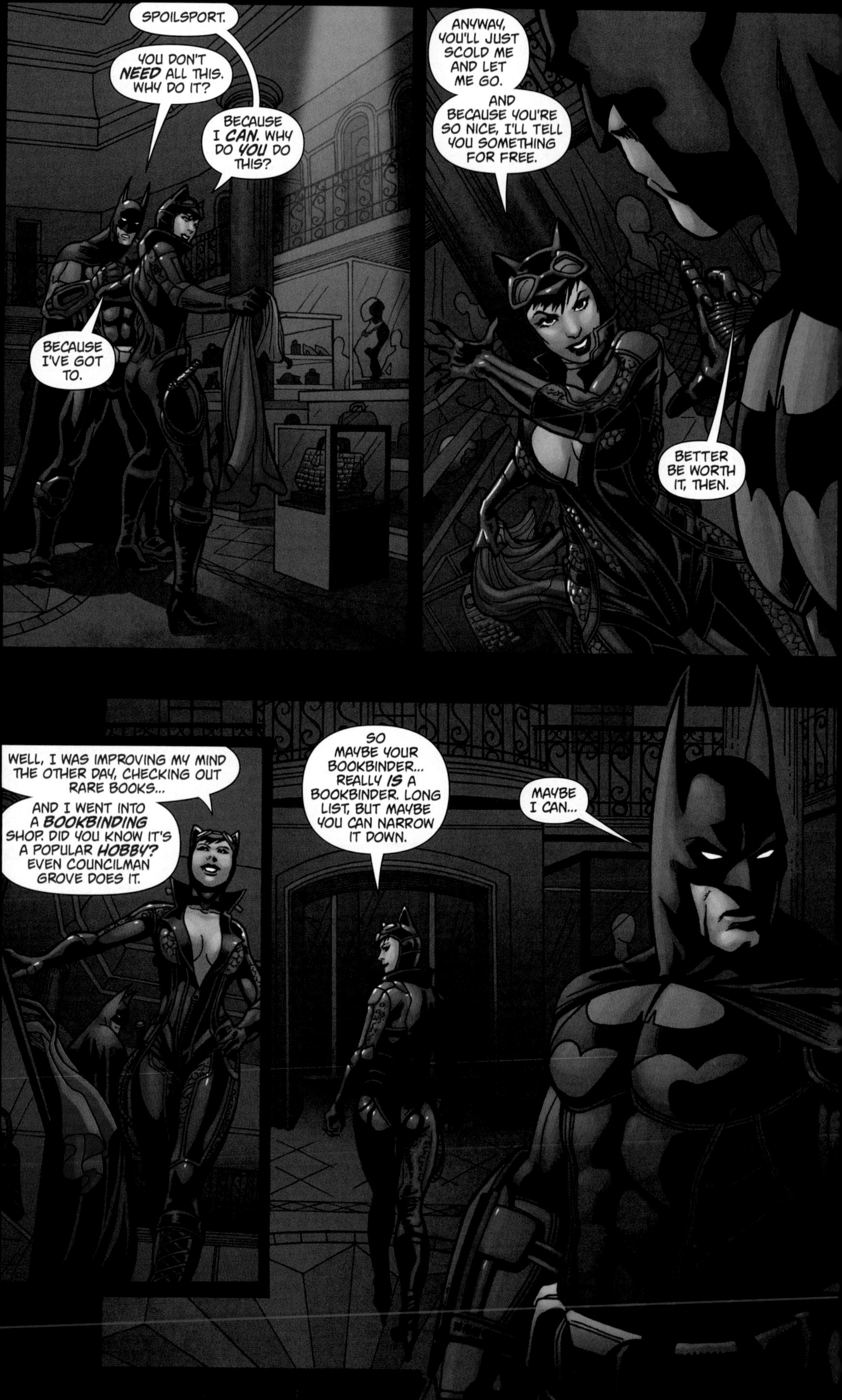
SPOILSPORT.
YOU DON'T NEED ALL THIS. WHY DO IT?
BECAUSE I CAN. WHY DO YOU DO THIS?
BECAUSE I'VE GOT TO.
ANYWAY, YOU'LL JUST SCOLD ME AND LET ME GO.
AND BECAUSE YOU'RE SO NICE, I'LL TELL YOU SOMETHING FOR FREE.
BETTER BE WORTH IT, THEN.
WELL, I WAS IMPROVING MY MIND THE OTHER DAY, CHECKING OUT RARE BOOKS...
AND I WENT INTO A BOOKBINDING SHOP. DID YOU KNOW IT'S A POPULAR HOBBY? EVEN COUNCILMAN GROVE DOES IT.
SO MAYBE YOUR BOOKBINDER... REALLY IS A BOOKBINDER. LONG LIST, BUT MAYBE YOU CAN NARROW IT DOWN.
MAYBE I CAN...

MAYOR SHARP'S OFFICE.

WHO'S THE MAYOR OF THIS CITY, GROVE? ARE YOU AFTER **THIS OFFICE?**

GROVE BUS PLAN - BUSINESS LEADERS BACK COUNCILMAN

I CAN'T AFFORD DISTRACTIONS LIKE YOU.

SO WHAT HAVE YOU GOT ON GROVE? YOU'VE HAD WEEKS TO TURN UP SOMETHING.

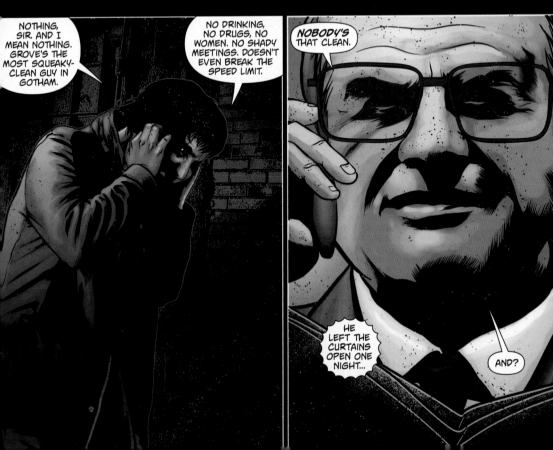

NOTHING, SIR. AND I MEAN NOTHING. GROVE'S THE MOST SQUEAKY-CLEAN GUY IN GOTHAM.

NO DRINKING, NO DRUGS, NO WOMEN. NO SHADY MEETINGS. DOESN'T EVEN BREAK THE SPEED LIMIT.

NOBODY'S THAT CLEAN.

HE LEFT THE CURTAINS OPEN ONE NIGHT...

AND?

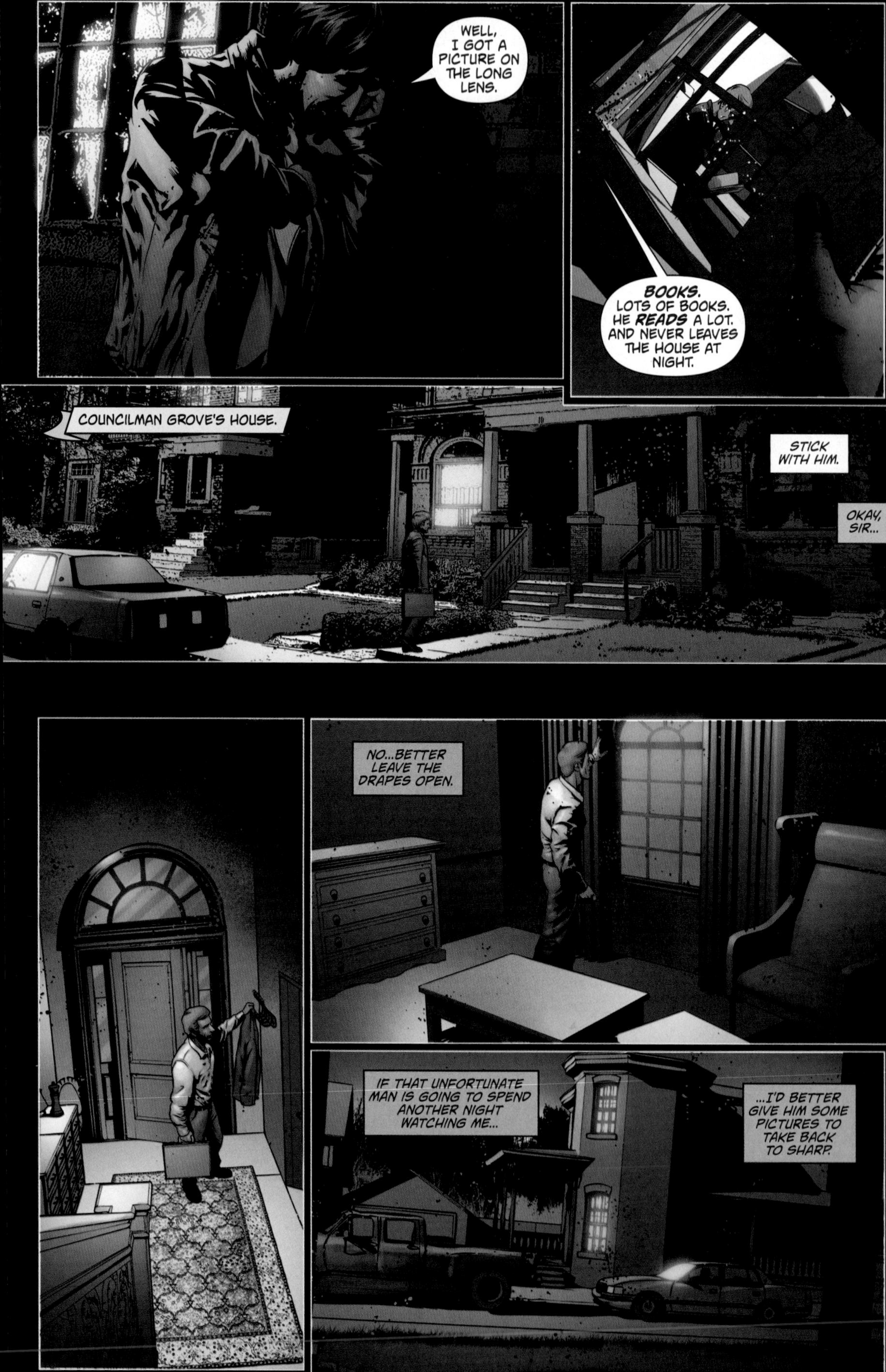

WELL, I GOT A PICTURE ON THE LONG LENS.
BOOKS. LOTS OF BOOKS. HE READS A LOT. AND NEVER LEAVES THE HOUSE AT NIGHT.
COUNCILMAN GROVE'S HOUSE.
STICK WITH HIM.
OKAY, SIR...
NO...BETTER LEAVE THE DRAPES OPEN.
IF THAT UNFORTUNATE MAN IS GOING TO SPEND ANOTHER NIGHT WATCHING ME...
...I'D BETTER GIVE HIM SOME PICTURES TO TAKE BACK TO SHARP.

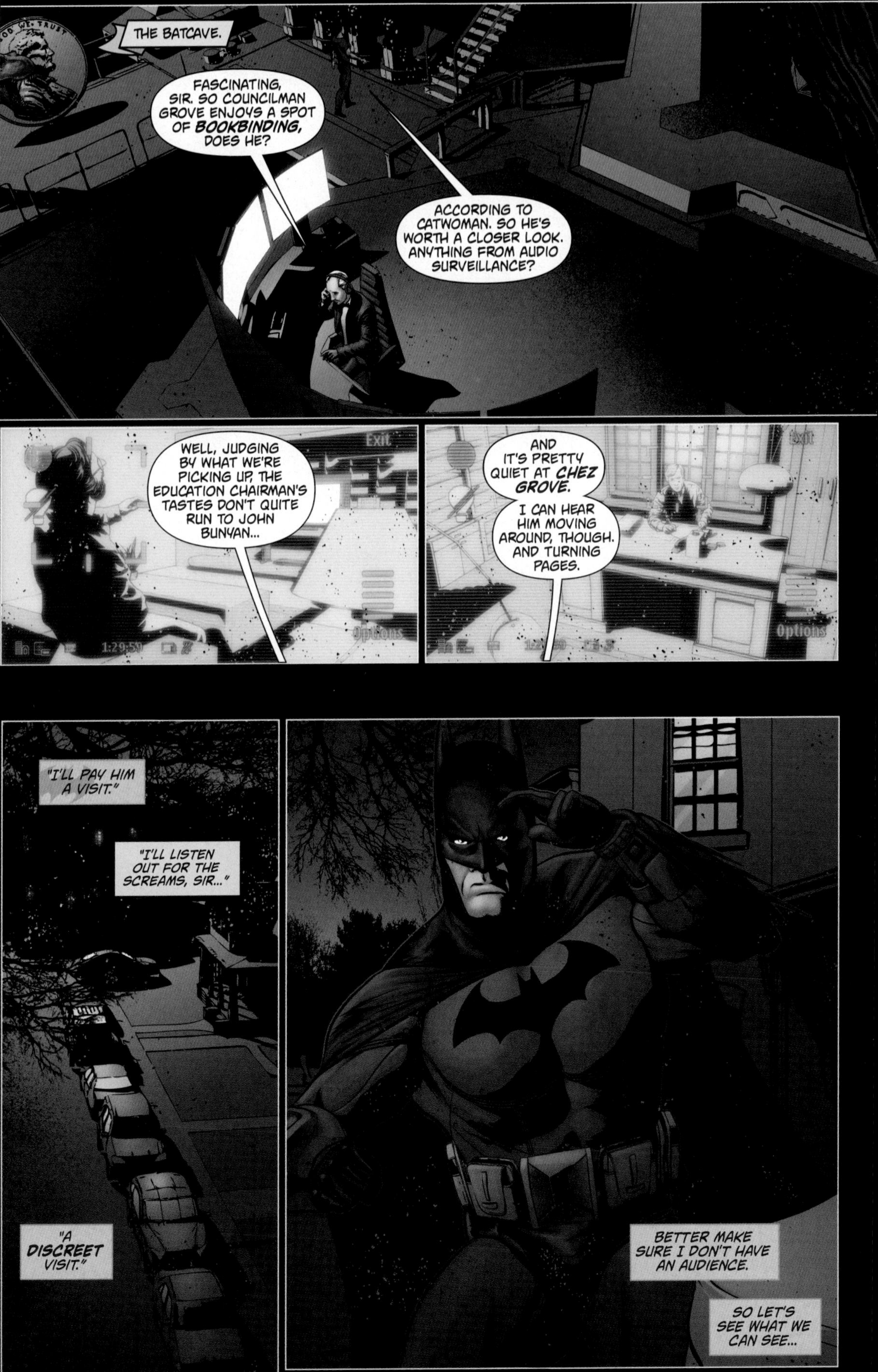
THE BATCAVE.
FASCINATING, SIR. SO COUNCILMAN GROVE ENJOYS A SPOT OF BOOKBINDING, DOES HE?
ACCORDING TO CATWOMAN. SO HE'S WORTH A CLOSER LOOK. ANYTHING FROM AUDIO SURVEILLANCE?
WELL, JUDGING BY WHAT WE'RE PICKING UP, THE EDUCATION CHAIRMAN'S TASTES DON'T QUITE RUN TO JOHN BUNYAN...
AND IT'S PRETTY QUIET AT CHEZ GROVE.
I CAN HEAR HIM MOVING AROUND, THOUGH. AND TURNING PAGES.
"I'LL PAY HIM A VISIT."
"I'LL LISTEN OUT FOR THE SCREAMS, SIR..."
"A DISCREET VISIT."
BETTER MAKE SURE I DON'T HAVE AN AUDIENCE.
SO LET'S SEE WHAT WE CAN SEE...

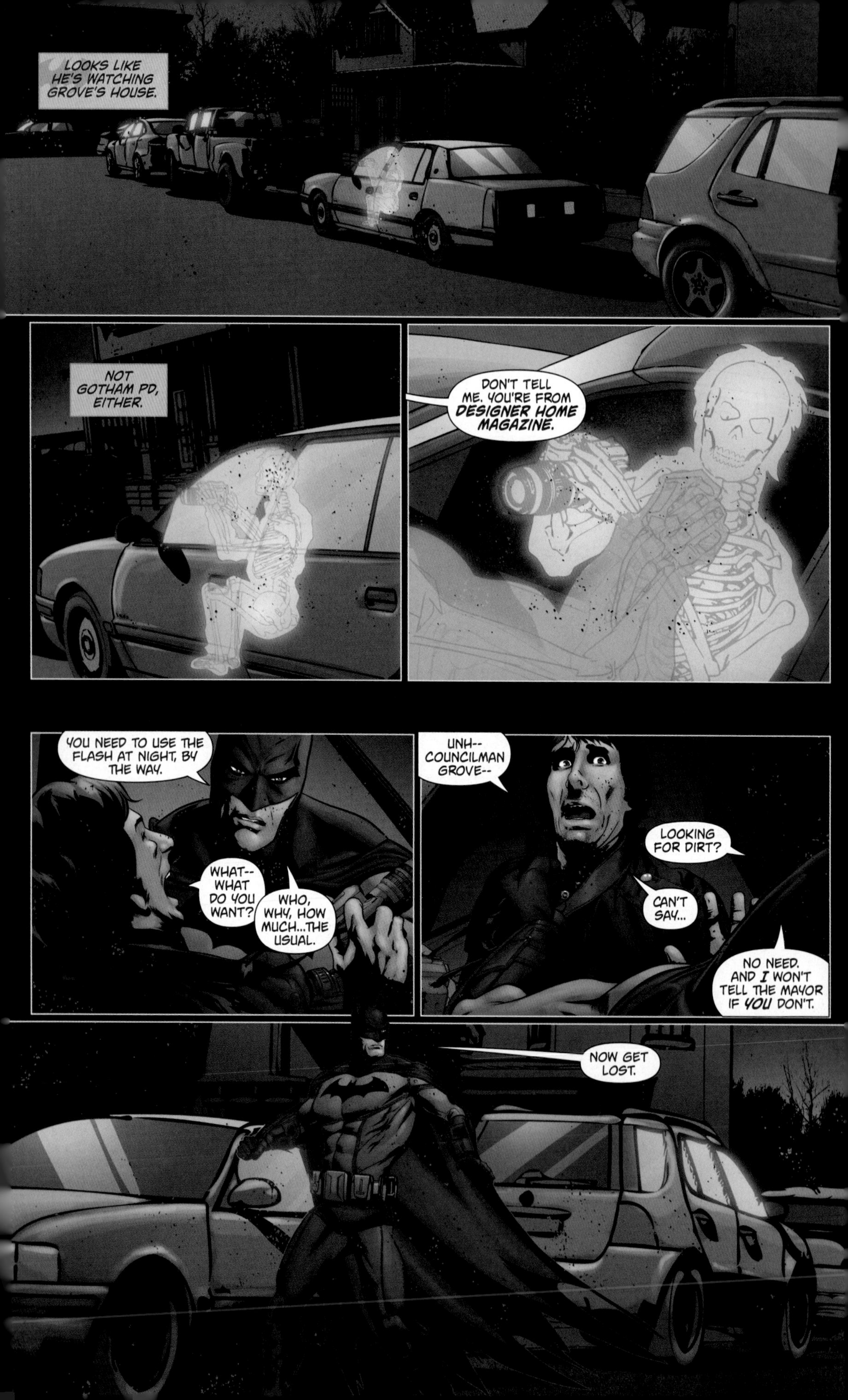
LOOKS LIKE HE'S WATCHING GROVE'S HOUSE.
NOT GOTHAM PD, EITHER.
DON'T TELL ME. YOU'RE FROM DESIGNER HOME MAGAZINE.
YOU NEED TO USE THE FLASH AT NIGHT, BY THE WAY.
WHAT-- WHAT DO YOU WANT?
WHO, WHY, HOW MUCH...THE USUAL.
UNH-- COUNCILMAN GROVE--
LOOKING FOR DIRT?
CAN'T SAY...
NO NEED. AND I WON'T TELL THE MAYOR IF YOU DON'T.
NOW GET LOST.

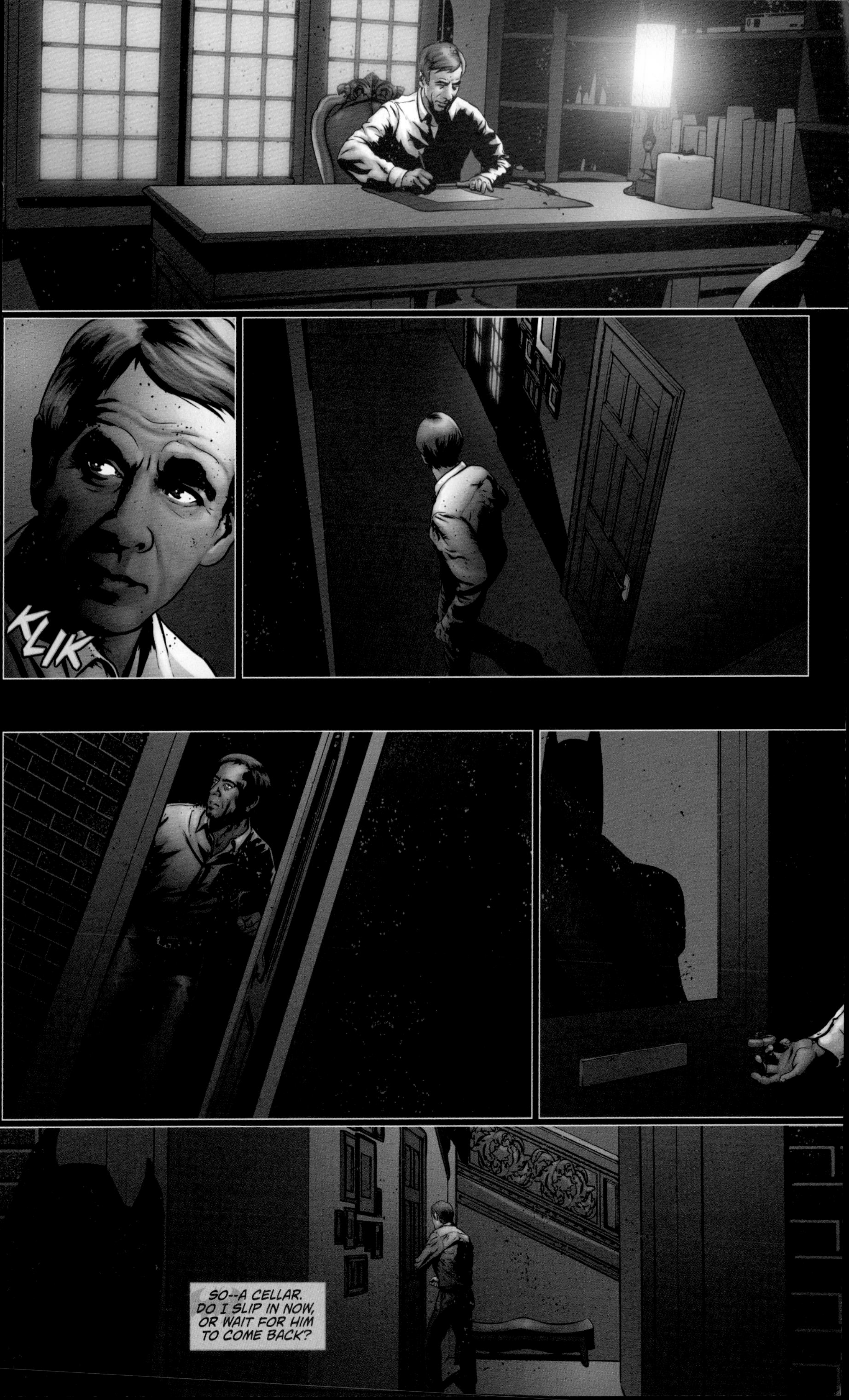
KLIK
SO--A CELLAR. DO I SLIP IN NOW, OR WAIT FOR HIM TO COME BACK?

30 MINUTES LATER.

MUST BE A VERY BIG CELLAR...

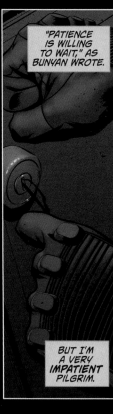

"PATIENCE IS WILLING TO WAIT," AS BUNYAN WROTE.

BUT I'M A VERY IMPATIENT PILGRIM.

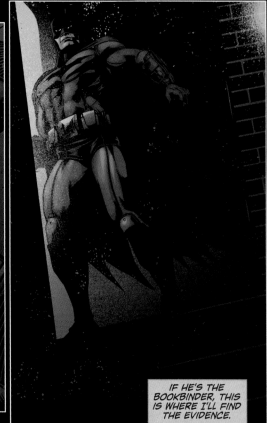

IF HE'S THE BOOKBINDER, THIS IS WHERE I'LL FIND THE EVIDENCE.

WHERE DID HE GO?

CAN'T WAIT TO FIND OUT WHERE THIS LEADS.

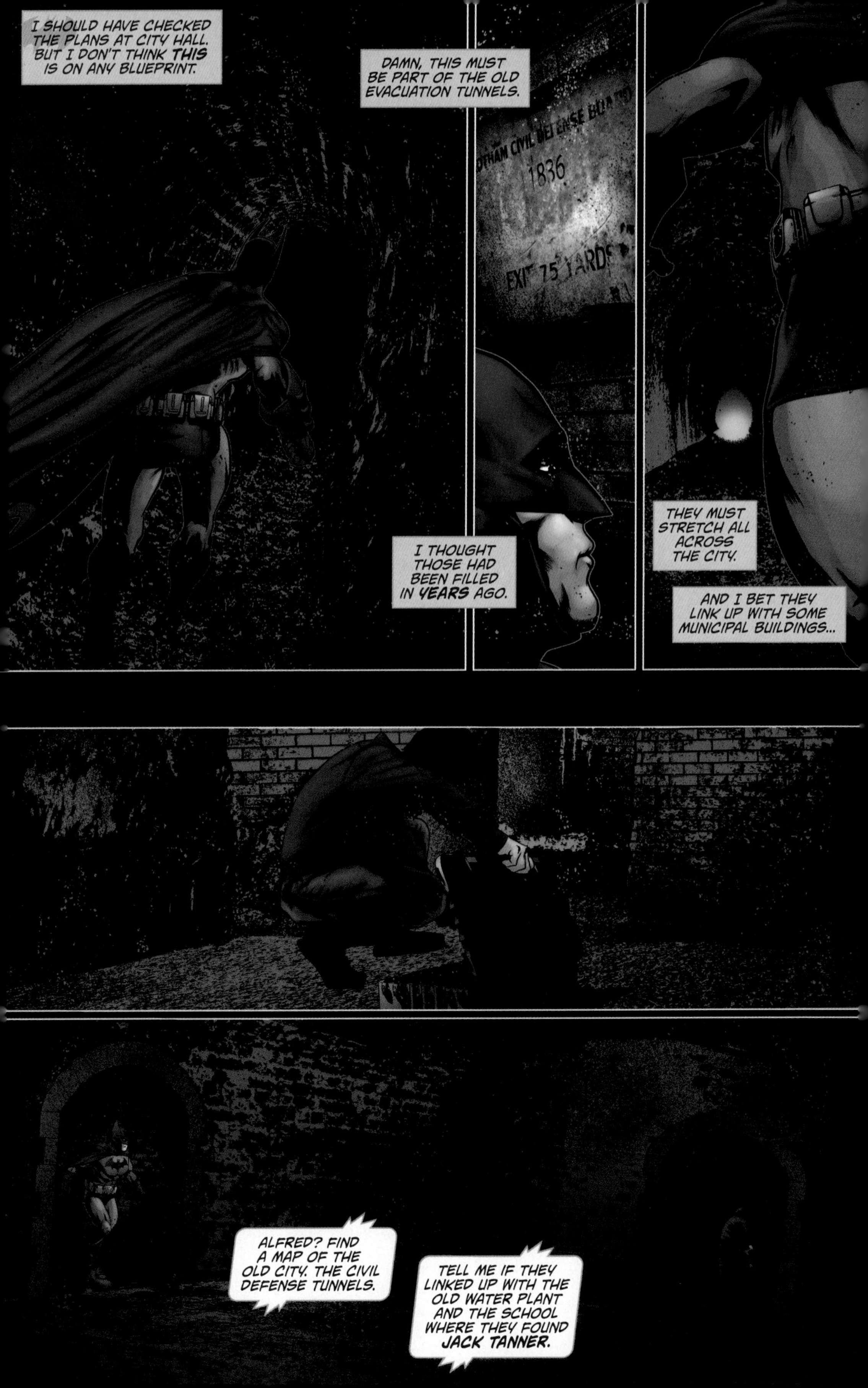

I SHOULD HAVE CHECKED THE PLANS AT CITY HALL. BUT I DON'T THINK **THIS** IS ON ANY BLUEPRINT.
DAMN, THIS MUST BE PART OF THE OLD EVACUATION TUNNELS.
GOTHAM CIVIL DEFENSE BOARD
1836
EXIT 75 YARDS
I THOUGHT THOSE HAD BEEN FILLED IN **YEARS** AGO.
THEY MUST STRETCH ALL ACROSS THE CITY.
AND I BET THEY LINK UP WITH SOME MUNICIPAL BUILDINGS...
ALFRED? FIND A MAP OF THE OLD CITY. THE CIVIL DEFENSE TUNNELS.
TELL ME IF THEY LINKED UP WITH THE OLD WATER PLANT AND THE SCHOOL WHERE THEY FOUND **JACK TANNER.**

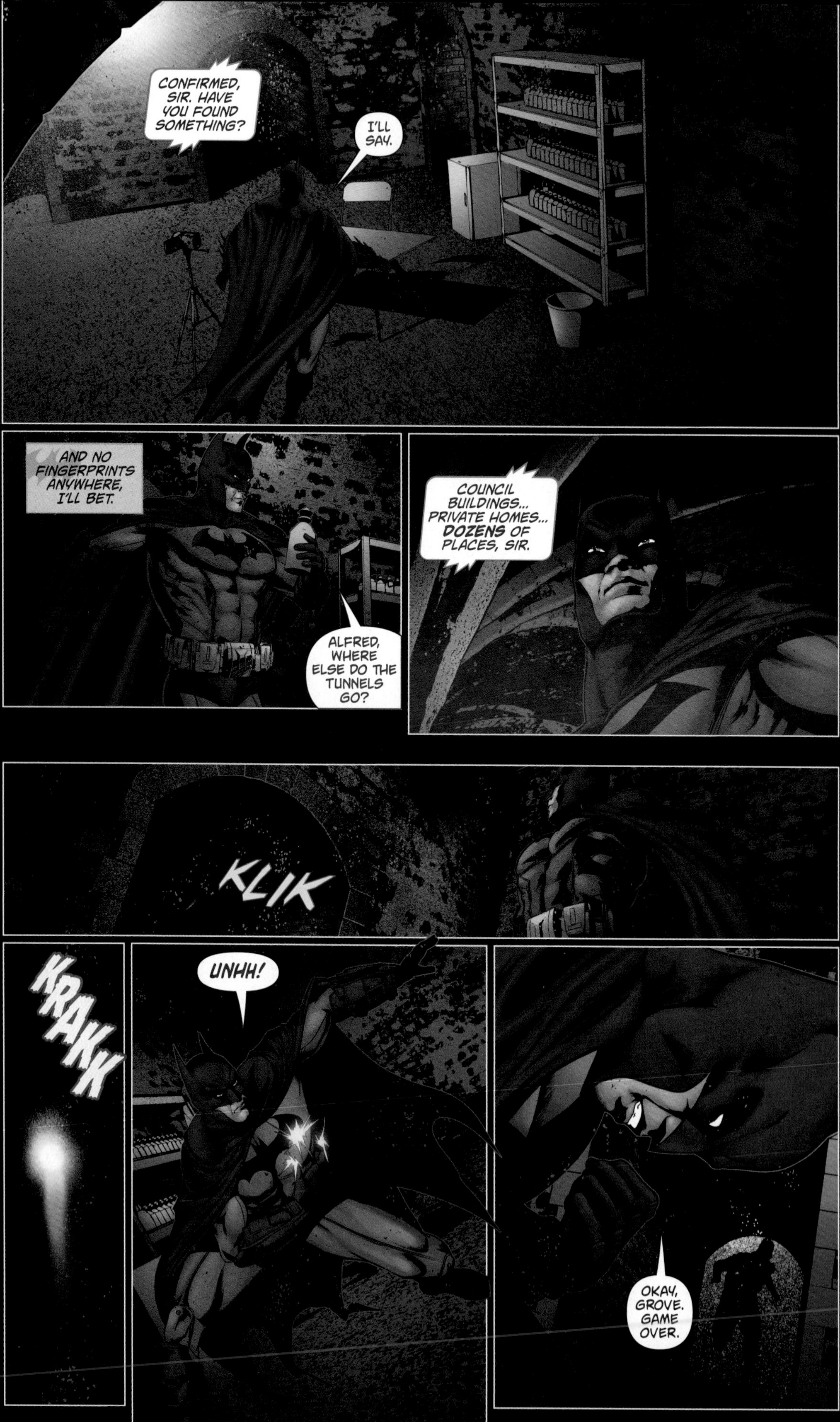

CONFIRMED, SIR. HAVE YOU FOUND SOMETHING?
I'LL SAY.
AND NO FINGERPRINTS ANYWHERE, I'LL BET.
ALFRED, WHERE ELSE DO THE TUNNELS GO?
COUNCIL BUILDINGS... PRIVATE HOMES... **DOZENS** OF PLACES, SIR.
KLIK
KRAKK
UNHH!
OKAY, GROVE. GAME OVER.

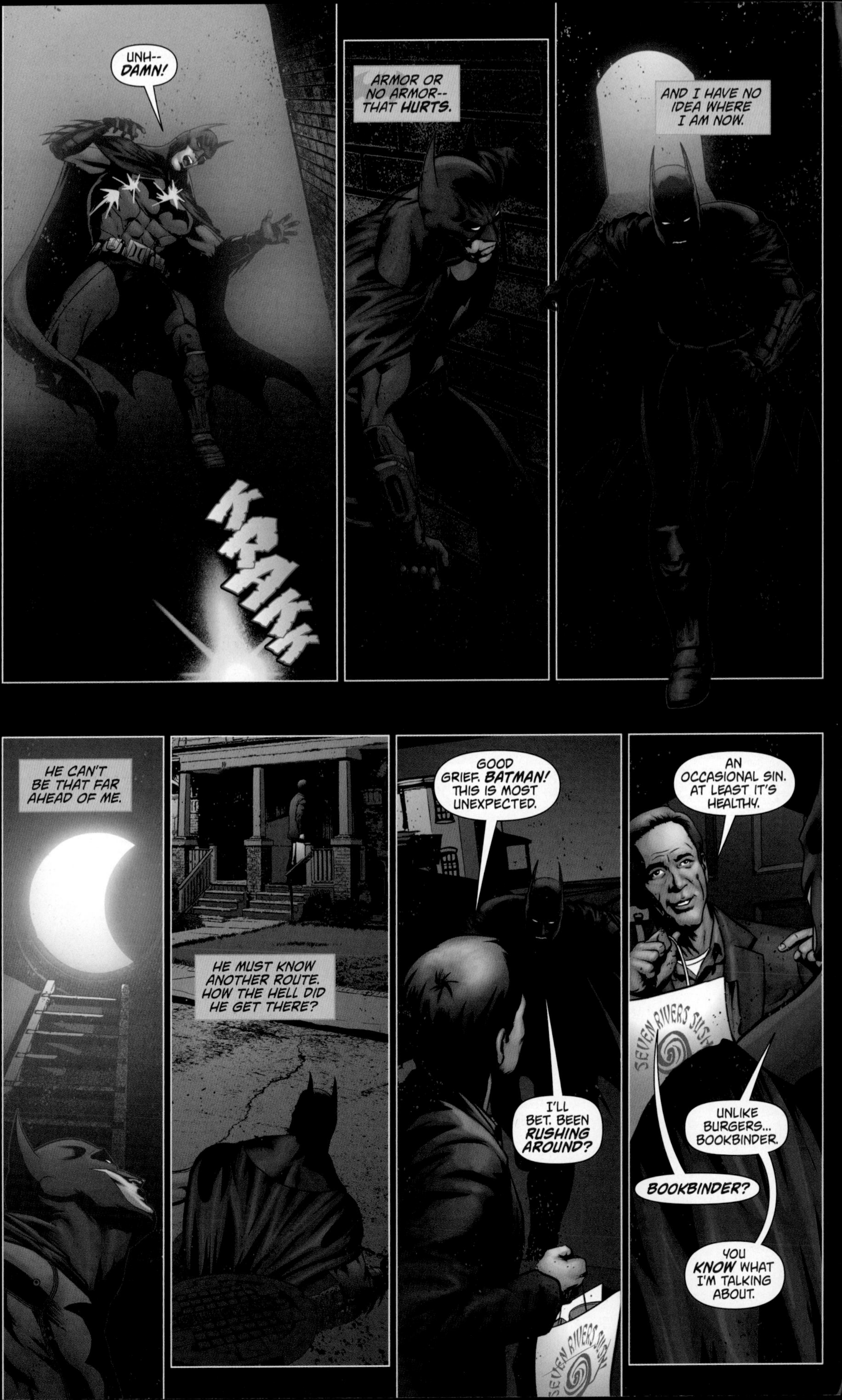
UNH-- DAMN!
KRAKK
ARMOR OR NO ARMOR-- THAT HURTS.
AND I HAVE NO IDEA WHERE I AM NOW.
HE CAN'T BE THAT FAR AHEAD OF ME.
HE MUST KNOW ANOTHER ROUTE. HOW THE HELL DID HE GET THERE?
GOOD GRIEF. BATMAN! THIS IS MOST UNEXPECTED.
I'LL BET. BEEN RUSHING AROUND?
SEVEN RIVERS SUSHI
AN OCCASIONAL SIN. AT LEAST IT'S HEALTHY.
SEVEN RIVERS SUSHI
UNLIKE BURGERS... BOOKBINDER.
BOOKBINDER?
YOU KNOW WHAT I'M TALKING ABOUT.

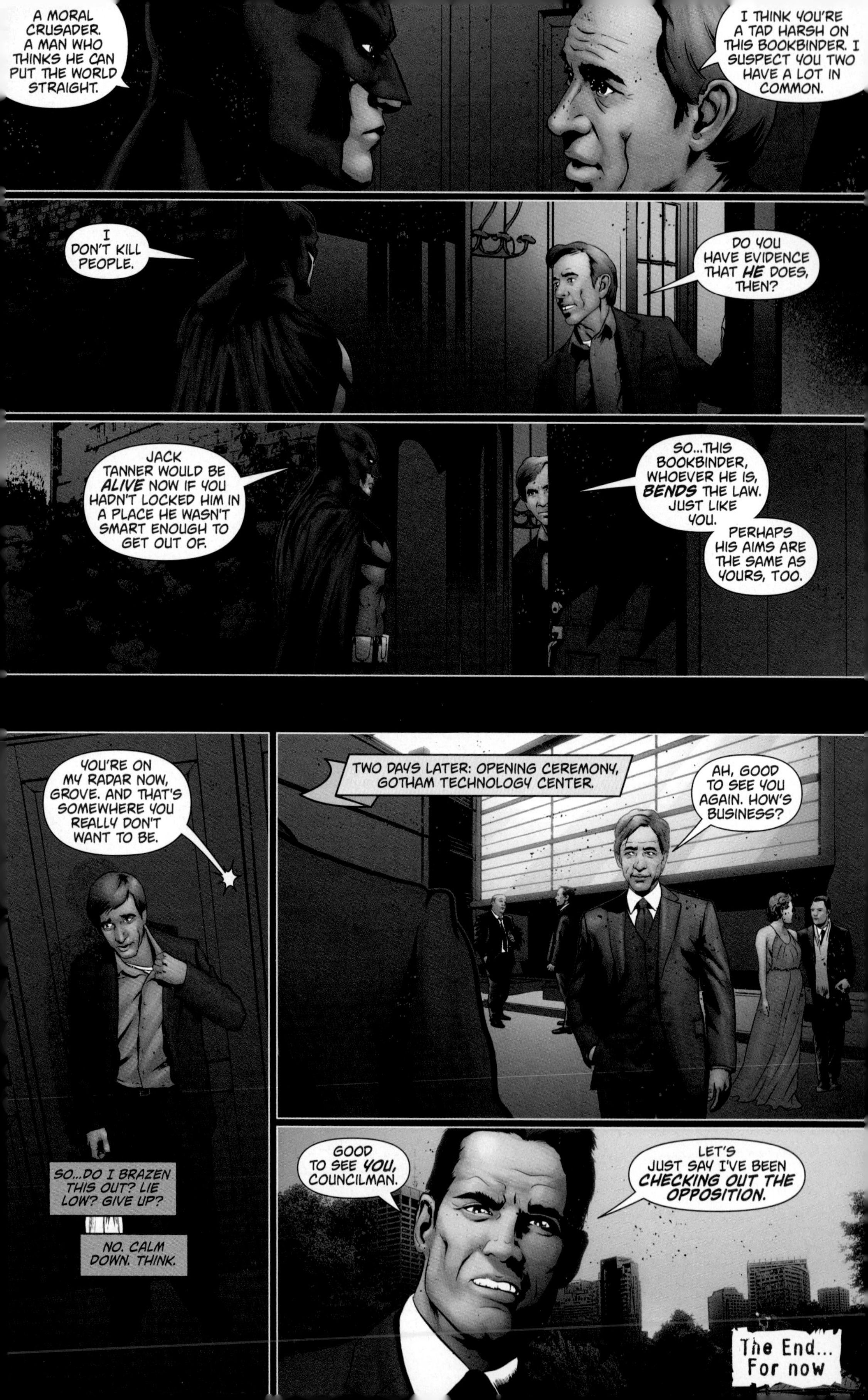
A MORAL CRUSADER. A MAN WHO THINKS HE CAN PUT THE WORLD STRAIGHT.
I THINK YOU'RE A TAD HARSH ON THIS BOOKBINDER. I SUSPECT YOU TWO HAVE A LOT IN COMMON.
I DON'T KILL PEOPLE.
DO YOU HAVE EVIDENCE THAT *HE* DOES, THEN?
JACK TANNER WOULD BE *ALIVE* NOW IF YOU HADN'T LOCKED HIM IN A PLACE HE WASN'T SMART ENOUGH TO GET OUT OF.
SO...THIS BOOKBINDER, WHOEVER HE IS, *BENDS* THE LAW. JUST LIKE YOU.
PERHAPS HIS AIMS ARE THE SAME AS YOURS, TOO.
YOU'RE ON MY RADAR NOW, GROVE. AND THAT'S SOMEWHERE YOU REALLY DON'T WANT TO BE.
SO...DO I BRAZEN THIS OUT? LIE LOW? GIVE UP?
NO. CALM DOWN. THINK.
TWO DAYS LATER: OPENING CEREMONY, GOTHAM TECHNOLOGY CENTER.
AH, GOOD TO SEE YOU AGAIN. HOW'S BUSINESS?
GOOD TO SEE *YOU*, COUNCILMAN.
LET'S JUST SAY I'VE BEEN *CHECKING OUT THE OPPOSITION*.
The End... For now